NEW YORK

NEW YORK

AN ANTHOLOGY

COMPILED BY MIKE MARQUSEE & BILL HARRIS

INTRODUCTION BY CLIVE BARNES

BARNES
&NOBLE
BOOKS
NEW YORK

This edition published by Barnes & Noble, Inc.,
by arrangement with Cadogan Publications Ltd.

1995 Barnes & Noble Books

ISBN 1-56619-763-5

Printed and bound in the United States of America

M 9 8 7 6 5 4 3 2 1

CONTENTS

Introduction

Chapter 1: THE ASPECT OF THE CITY

Chapter 2: NEW YORKERS

Chapter 3: MAMMON

Chapter 4: CITY OF ORGIES

Chapter 5: STREETLIFE

Chapter 6: ON THE MOVE

Chapter 7: LEISURE

Chapter 8: NEIGHBORHOODS

Chapter 9:   THE FIRE KING

Chapter 10:   CHANGE

Chapter 11:   BUT WHO'D WANT TO LIVE THERE

Chapter 12:   DEMOCRACY

Chapter 13:   RIOTS AND REBELLIONS

INTRODUCTION

by CLIVE BARNES

New York, New York,
It's a Wonderful Town!
The Bronx is Up,
And the Battery Down.

Yes, precisely. And, for that matter, the people ride in a hole in the ground, but you will have not come to this anthology for such information. At least I hope not, for it is not here. This is not a tourist guide, it is not even a collection of New York vignettes rather it is a thought book about New York, what the 18th-century would have dubbed a 'commonplace book,' or the early 20th-century termed a 'bedside companion.' It is a literary celebration and cerebration of the city – my city as it happens. It is a reference point, not a reference book, for resident, visitor and simple curiosity seeker alike. Only trippers need look no further. This book is not for them.

I see I wrote earlier 'my city as it happens.' Is it my city, and if it is, how did that happen? For I was born in London, and for all my later love of New York, I have never seen fit to question Dr. Johnson on the tireless charms of my birthplace. But now, I suppose New York must be considered my particular turf. I live there, I work there, my life has been based there – albeit still in that curious condition known legally, but not quite inaccurately, as 'resident alien' – for 20 years, and, most significant of all in these fiscal days, I pay American taxes.

So when did I become a New Yorker. I forget the date, but it was that first day in London when I first felt homesick . . . for New York. The transition had been made, the switch effected. From then on I was to be a stranger in my homeland, looking aghast at monopoly-numbered money, and shrinking at the habits of the natives. New York, once my glamorous mistress had become my wife, and London, once my mother, had become a flighty, and rather dangerous, girl-friend. And so, here I am with some kind of odd transatlantic credentials, an unplaced creature, a strange bird of passage, who seems faintly American to the English, and peculiarly English to the Americans. In the latter respect one is immeasurably helped by having the one accent universally recognized as 'foreign' in the United States – an English accent.

One of the many happy results of this Mid-Atlantic status is that one occasionally gets asked to contribute introductions to books such as these.

Appropriately, I suppose, if only because America is a land of immigrants, and New York a city of strangers, a city of born-again native New Yorkers. You get a strong flavour of that in this anthology. To be a New Yorker is as much an attitude as an accident. You hear it from the start of this collection, when E.B. White defines for us his 'roughly three New Yorks.' He discerns the New York of 'the man or woman who was born here', the New York of 'the commuter – the city that is devoured by locusts each day and spat out each night;' and then, finally, the last New York, the one belonging to 'the person who was born somewhere else and came to New York in quest of something.' He calls this third one the greatest of his overlapping cities, 'the city of final destination, the city that is a goal.' I started with one popular song – New York is, apart from anything else, a city of anthems – now let's have another, when the hero of 'New York, New York,' chants, with overweening confidence: 'If I can make it there, I can make it anywhere!' New York the final destination, but destination in what direction? Where is New York going, and why does it seem to be going there sooner and faster than anywhere else in the world?

Europeans have traditionally regarded New York with a mixture of fear, awe and uncomprehending, often grudging but sometimes totally comprehensive admiration. You can see that here, even, to an extent, from the oldest passage in the book, an excerpt from John Miller's New York, first published in 1695, and giving his account of the inhabitants, and a pretty drunken, licentious and ribald mob they seem to have been. But the European view – whether it comes from the shocked Maxim Gorki, the fascinated Federico Garcia Lorca, or the entranced Brendan Behan – always manages to convey an undertow of disbelief in its assessment. The suspension and exploitation of disbelief is very much part of the New York mystique. New Yorkers never cease to be amazed at their city, even if they studiously are amazed at nothing else. Also, for in New York even undertows can have undertows, there is often an element of masochistic joy in that amazement. In most cities, the citizens will regale one with what goes right. In New York we delight in what goes wrong, we love our hair shirts, and our machismo sense of survival against the impossible odds of urban disaster. So we tell tales of subway delays and traffic jams – we have even invented a word for these, which we call, most poetically, 'gridlocks' – and, of course, violence.

Violence, we were once told, is as American as apple pie, and in no other American city is that apple pie so carefully marketed. In sobering fact as urban areas go in the United States, statistically New York City, particularly Manhattan, is almost sissily safe. But we don't like people to know that – we prefer to tell the world, as we gulp down our very dry martini straight-up with a twist, or, nowadays more likely our very chic Perrier, that: 'it's a jungle out there, and the people are animals, just animals.'

I exaggerate – one way or another every New Yorker does, it comes with the territory – for there always has been violence or the threat of violence in New York; it is an ugly thread that has always disturbed the city's fabric. You see it very clearly reflected in this book, whether it be in a poem by Allen Ginsberg describing with heart-pulsing detail a mugging or in an anonymous 1874 account of Water Street – now redeveloped as part of the South Street Seaport tourist area – where we are warned of this neighborhood that is 'about the most notorious in the metropolis for deeds of violence, flagrant vice and scenes of debauchery.' The warning continues, as such warnings are apt to do, in almost titillatingly explicit fashion. But even Walt Whitman, one of this collection's most quoted and treasured contributors, along with that European exile, Henry James, felt impelled in 1856 to issue stern advice to tourists, starting: 'Don't go wandering about the streets or parks unnecessarily in the evening. The degrading confession and warning is necessary, that New York is one of the most crime-haunted and dangerous cities in Christendom.' No doubt. However, in 1856, I think I would have taken goodly care of myself on the streets of London or Paris, yet I doubt whether their avowed advocates would have numbered them among 'the most crime-haunted and dangerous cities in Christendom.' You see, we New Yorkers were masochists in our metropolitan pride and love even then.

Violence is luckily not the only continuing theme of the book. Look here for the description of our concept of 'neighborhoods,' a little different, I think, from most other cities, and our fervent love of and pride in Central Park. Central Park, and its lesser known kid brother, Riverside Park, are the two most wonderful city parks in the entire world, and I will twist the neck off any weakling or invalid who dares gainsay me. Also in these pages you will meet a number of New York characters, such as the strange, sad poet Frank O'Hara killed in a freak accident, who became part of New York's literary and art world during the late 'fifties and early 'sixties. Such characters remind us that New York is people in the streets, as well as the streets themselves, buildings, institutions and tribal habits.

I like this book. I like its tone, midway between the schoolmasterish-historical and affectionate-hysterical, and I like its feel for the place. Not only for its old buildings, but its strange sense of transience. (Why are there so few old buildings in New York, when the City, for all its protestations of flaming youth, is virtually, or at least in effect, as old as most European cities?)

A city is a many-headed monster with strange tentacles. And New York – despite the superior architectural claims of Chicago, and the odd sociological advances of Tokyo – is the 20th-century metropolis of our dreams and nightmares. That surely accounts for the repelled attraction that people register for it.

Personally I have discovered that it's a great place to live, although I don't think I'd ever want to visit there. Not now. Quite the reverse of the way I feel about London. Now. But you know how people grow to look like their pets – or is it their pets growing to look like them – well, by something of a similar token or necromancy, perhaps we become part of the city we belong to, part of its fabric, its look, its feel, its ethos.

Thumbing through this collection, wandering here, pondering there, toying with a little Scott Fitzgerald, considering Lewis Mumford,admiring Artie Shaw, I found myself asking what New York was all about. The glory of Greece, the grandeur of Rome, the whelks of Southend, the surprise of Paris, the canals of Venice and the waters of Bath, these we know. But New York? For one thing is it really Manhattan, and only Manhattan? Cole Porter could sing: 'I'll take Staten Island too,' but I doubt whether in fact and life he even took the Staten Island ferry! For another thing, is Manhattan really American? It speaks about as much Spanish/American as it speaks English, but in many respects it is a tiny European island moored precariously – like Hong Kong clinging to China – to the American continent. Once, Freudian-fashion, I literally found myself unconsciously taking a passport with me to go to Los Angeles, and in almost every vital respect (apart from the Spanish language issue) New York is more like London than it is like Chicago. But then London is more like New York than it is like Manchester.

So please don't expect to find out everything about New York from this pleasantly variegated anthology. Take it all with a dose of salt, and you will doubtless enjoy having your prejudices confirmed and your biases massaged. But finally – why New York? What is this fascination? Let me leave you with my favorite quotation from the book. It comes from my friend Joseph Papp, theatrical entrepreneur and guru, onlie beggeter of the New York Shakespeare Festival. Joe writes: 'Creative people get inspiration from their immediate environment, and New York has the most immediate environment in the world.' And, apart from all that, Joe, the people ride in a hole in the ground. New York, New York! My newfoundland – as John Donne once suggested.

CLIVE BARNES, C.B.E., is a London/New Yorker, and the dance and drama critic of THE NEW YORK POST.

CHAPTER 1

THE ASPECT OF THE CITY

You will have heard of our taking of New Amsterdam. . . . 'Tis a place of great importance to trade. It did belong to England heretofor, but the Dutch by degrees did drive our people out and built a very good town, but we have got the better of it and now 'tis called New York.

King Charles II

More and more, too, the *old name* absorbs into me – MANAHATTA, 'the place encircled by many swift tides and sparkling waters.' How fit a name for America's great democratic island city! The word itself, how beautiful! how aboriginal! how it seems to rise with tall spires, glistening in sunshine, with such New World atmosphere, vista and action!

Walt Whitman

MANAHATTA

I was asking for something specific and perfect for my city,
Whereupon lo! upsprang the aboriginal name.
Now I see what there is in a name, a word, liquid, sane, unruly,
    musical, self-sufficient,
I see that the word of my city is that word from of old,
Because I see that word nested in nests of water-bays, superb,
Rich, hemm'd thick all around with sailships and steamships, an
    island sixteen miles long, solid-founded,
Numberless crowded streets, high growths of iron, slender,
    strong, light, splendidly uprising toward clear skies,
Tides swift and ample, well-loved by me, toward sundown,
The flowing sea-currents, the little islands, larger adjoining
    islands, the heights, the villas,
The countless masts, the white shore-steamers, the lighters, the
    ferry-boats, the black sea-steamers well-model'd,
The down-town streets, the jobbers' houses of business, the
    houses of business of the ship-merchants and money-brokers,
    the river-streets,
Immigrants arriving, fifteen or twenty thousand in a week,

The carts hauling goods, the manly race of drivers of horses, the brown-faced sailors,
The summer air, the bright sun shining, and the sailing clouds aloft,
The winter snows, the sleigh-bells, the broken ice in the river, passing along up or down with the flood-tide or ebb-tide,
The mechanics of the city, the masters, well-form'd, beautiful-faced, looking you straight in the eyes,
Trottoirs throng'd, vehicles, Broadway, the women, the shops and shows,
A million people – manners free and superb – open voices – hospitality – the most courageous and friendly young men,
City of hurried and sparkling waters! city of spires and masts!
City nested in bays! my city!

Walt Whitman

New York is a different country. Maybe it ought to have a separate government. Everybody thinks differently, acts differently. They just don't know what the hell the rest of the United States is.

Henry Ford

Here I was in New York, city of prose and fantasy, of capitalist automatism, its streets a triumph of cubism; its moral philosophy that of the dollar. New York impressed me tremendously because, more than any other city in the world, it is the fullest expression of our modern age.

Leon Trotsky

It is the icing on the pie called Christian Civilization.

H.L. Mencken

When its 9:30 in New York, it's 1937 in Los Angeles.

Groucho Marx

3

New York City isn't a melting pot, it's a boiling pot.

Thomas E. Dewey

A hundred times I have thought, New York is a catastrophe, and fifty times: It is a beautiful catastrophe.

Le Corbusier

When an American stays away from New York too long, something happens to him. Perhaps he becomes a little provincial, a little dead, a little afraid.

Sherwood Anderson

New York is an arrogant city; it has always wanted to be all things to all people, and in a surprising amount of time it has succeeded.

Paul Goldberger

New York, the nation's thyroid gland.

Christopher Morley

When it is good, New York is very, very good. Which is why New Yorkers put up with so much that is bad.

Ada Louise Huxtable

What is barely hinted in other American cities is condensed and enlarged in New York.

Saul Bellow

> Vulgar of manner, overfed,
> Overdressed and underbred;
> Heartless, Godless, hell's delight,
> Rude by day and lewd by night.

4

Purple-robed and pauper-clad,
Raving, rotting, money-mad;
A squirming herd in Mammon's mesh,
A wilderness of human flesh;
Crazed with avarice, lust and rum,
New York, thy name's delirium.

Byron Rufus Newton

There are roughly three New Yorks. There is, first, the New York of the man or woman who was born here, who takes the city for granted and accepts its size and its turbulence as natural and inevitable. Second, there is the New York of the commuter – the city that is devoured by locusts each day and spat out each night. Third, there is the New York of the person who was born somewhere else and came to New York in quest of something. Of these three trembling cities the greatest is the last – *the city of final destination, the city that is a goal*. It is this third city that accounts for New York's high-strung disposition, its poetical deportment, its dedication to the arts, and its incomparable achievements. Commuters give the city its tidal restlessness; natives give it solidity and continuity; but the settlers give it passion. And whether it is a farmer arriving from Italy to set up a small grocery store in a slum, or a young girl arriving from a small town in Mississippi to escape the indignity of being observed by her neighbors, or a boy arriving from the Corn Belt with a manuscript in his suitcase and a pain in his heart, it makes no difference: each embraces New York with the intense excitement of first love, each absorbs New York with the fresh eyes of an adventurer, each generates heat and light to dwarf the Consolidated Edison Company.

E.B. White

The ambiguity is the element in which the whole thing swims for me – so nocturnal, so bacchanal, so hugely hatted and feathered and flounced, yet apparently so innocent, almost so patriarchal again, and matching, in its mixture, with nothing one had elsewhere known. It breathed its simple 'New York! New York!' at every impulse of inquiry; so that I can only echo contentedly, with analysis for once quite agreeably baffled, 'Remarkable, unspeakable New York!'

Henry James

5

After 20 annual visits, I am still surprised each time I return to see this giant asparagus bed of alabaster and rose and green skyscrapers.

Cecil Beaton

New York is a skyline, the most stupendous, unbelievable man-made spectacle since the hanging gardens of Babylon. Significantly, you have to be outside the city – on a bridge or the New Jersey Turnpike – to enjoy it.

Jacques Barzun

There were Babylon and Nineveh: they were built of brick. Athens was gold marble colums. Rome was held up on broad arches of rubble. In Constantinople the minarets flame like great candles round the Golden Horn . . . Steel, glass, tile, concrete will be the materials of the skyscrapers. Crammed on the narrow island the millionwindowed buildings will jut glittering, pyramid on pyramid like the white cloudhead above a thunderstorm.

John Dos Passos

Frances Trollope (1780-1863), mother of the novelist Anthony Trollope, left Britain with her husband in 1827 to live for four years in the United States, mostly in Ohio. Financially, their trip would have been a disaster were it not for the international success of her book, Domestic Manners of the Americans, *published on her return to Britain in 1832. It was her first book, and established a solid literary reputation which provided her with a substantial income for her remaining years.*

I have never seen the bay of Naples, I can therefore make no comparison, but my imagination is incapable of conceiving any thing of the kind more beautiful than the harbour of New York. Various and lovely are the objects which meet the eye on every

6

side, but the naming them would only be to give a list of words, without conveying the faintest idea of the scene. I doubt if ever the pencil of Turner could do it justice, bright and glorious as it rose upon us. We seemed to enter the harbour of New York upon waves of liquid gold, and as we darted past the green isles which rise from its bosom, like guardian sentinels of the fair city, the setting sun stretched his horizontal beams farther and farther at each moment, as if to point out to us some new glory in the landscape.

New York, indeed, appeared to us, even when we saw it by a soberer light, a lovely and a noble city. To us who had been so long travelling through half-cleared forests, and sojourning among an 'I'm-as-good-as-you' population, it seemed, perhaps, more beautiful, more splendid, and more refined than it might have done, had we arrived there directly from London; but making every allowance for this, I must still declare that I think New York one of the finest cities I ever saw, and as much superior to every other in the Union (Philadelphia not excepted), as London to Liverpool, or Paris to Rouen. Its advantages of position are, perhaps, unequalled any where. Situated on an island, which I think it will one day cover, it rises like Venice, from the sea, and like that fairest of cities in the days of her glory, receives into its lap tribute of all the riches of the earth.

Walt Whitman (1819-1892) was born on Long Island and spent his child-hood in Brooklyn, then a small rural village. As a young man he edited the Aurora *in New York and the* Brooklyn Eagle *and was sacked from both jobs for his radical views. Later he edited the* Brooklyn Times *and worked as a nurse in the civil war, besides establishing himself as the premier American poet of the nineteenth century. This extract is from* Specimen Days, *a book of prose jottings, published in 1882, which Whitman called the 'most wayward, spontaneous, fragmentary book ever printed.'*

June 25. – Returned to New York last night. Out to-day on the waters for a sail in the wide bay, southeast of Staten island – a rough, tossing ride, and a free sight – the long stretch of Sandy Hook, the highlands of Navesink, and the many vessels outward and inward bound. We came up through the midst of all, in the full sun. I especially enjoy'd the last hour or two. A moderate sea-breeze had set in; yet over the city, and the waters adjacent, was a thin haze, concealing nothing, only adding to the beauty. From my point of view, as I write amid the soft breeze, with a sea-temperature, surely nothing on earth of its kind can go beyond this show. To the left the North river with its far vista – nearer, three or four war-ships, anchor'd peacefully – the Jersey side, the banks of Weehawken, the Palisades, and the gradually receding blue, lost in the distance – to the right the East river – the mast-hemm'd shores – the grand obelisk-like towers of the bridge, one on either side, in haze, yet plainly defin'd, giant brothers twain, throwing free graceful interlinking loops high across the tumbled tumultuous current below – (the tide is just changing to its ebb) – the broad water-spread everywhere crowded – no, not crowded, but thick as stars in the sky – with all sorts and sizes of sail and steam vessels, plying ferry-boats, arriving and departing coasters, great ocean Dons, iron-black, modern, magnificent in size and power, fill'd with their incalculable value of human life and precious merchandise – with here and there, above all, those daring, careening things of grace and wonder, those white and shaded swift-darting fish-birds, (I wonder if shore or sea elsewhere can outvie them,) ever with their slanting spars, and fierce, pure, hawk-like beauty and motion – first-class New York sloop or schooner yachts, sailing, this fine day, the free sea in a good wind. And rising out of the midst, tall-topt, ship-hemm'd, modern, American, yet strangely oriental, V-shaped Manhattan, with its compact mass, its spires, its cloud-touching edifices group'd at the centre – the green of the trees, and all the white brown and gray of the architecture well blended, as I see it, under a miracle of limpid sky, delicious light of heaven above, and June haze on the surface below.

The great American novelist Henry James (1843-1916) was born in New York City and though educated largely in Europe and resident for many years in London his return to the city in 1904, after a twenty year absence, was very much a homecoming. In 1907 he published an account of what he had seen and felt in the United States, called The American Scene, *from which this excerpt, describing the view of New York from a boat in the Bay, is taken.*

The Bay had always, on other opportunities, seemed to blow its immense character straight into one's face – coming 'at' you, so to speak, bearing down on you, with the full force of a thousand prows of steamers seen exactly on the line of their longitudinal axis; but I had never before been so conscious of its boundless cool assurance or seemed to see its genius so grandly at play. This was presumably indeed because I had never before enjoyed the remarkable adventure of taking in so much of the vast bristling promontory from the water, of ascending the East River, in especial, to its upper diminishing expanses.

Something of the air of the occasion and of the mood of the moment caused the whole picture to speak with its largest suggestion; which suggestion is irresistible when once it is sounded clear. It is all, absolutely, an expression of things lately and currently *done,* done on a large impersonal stage and on the basis of inordinate gain – it is not an expression of any other matters whatever; and yet the sense of the scene (which had at several previous junctures, as well, put forth to my imagination its power) was commanding and thrilling, was in certain lights almost charming. So it befell, exactly, that an element of mystery and wonder entered into the impression – the interest of trying to make out, in the absence of features of the sort usually supposed indispensable, the reason of the beauty and the joy. It is indubitably a 'great' bay, a great harbour, but no one item of the romantic, or even of the picturesque, as commonly understood, contributes to its effect. The shores are low and for the most part depressingly furnished and prosaically peopled; the islands, though numerous, have not a grace to exhibit, and one thinks of the other, the real flowers of geography in this order, of Naples, of Capetown, of Sydney, of Seattle, of San Francisco, of Rio, asking how if *they* justify a reputation, New York should seem to justify one. Then, after all, we remember that there are reputations and reputations; we remember above all that the imaginative response to the conditions here presented may just happen to proceed from the intellectual extravagance of the given observer. When this personage is open to corruption by almost any large view of an intensity of life, his vibrations tend to become a matter difficult even for *him* to explain. . . There is the beauty of light and air, the great scale of space, and, seen far away to the west, the open gates of the Hudson, majestic in their degree, even at a distance, and announcing still nobler things. But the real appeal, unmistakably, is in that note of vehemence in the local life of which I have spoken, for it is the appeal of a particular type of dauntless power.

The aspect the power wears then is indescribable; it is the power of the most extravagant of cities, rejoicing, as with the voice of the morning, in its might, its fortune, its unsurpassable conditions, and imparting to every object and element, to the motion and expression of every floating, hurrying, panting thing, to the throb of ferries and tugs, to the plash of waves and the play of winds and the glint of lights and the shrill of whistles and the quality and authority of breeze-borne cries – all, practically, a diffused, wasted clamour of *detonations* – something of its sharp free accent; in the bigness and bravery and insolence, especially, of everything that rushed and shrieked; in the air as of a great intricate frenzied dance, half merry, half desperate, or at least half defiant, performed on the huge watery floor. This appearance of the bold lacing-together, across the waters, of the scattered members of the monstrous organism – lacing as by the ceaseless play of an enormous system of steam-shuttles or electric bobbins (I scarce know what to call them), commensurate in form with their infinite work – does perhaps more than anything else to give the pitch of the vision of energy. One has the sense that the monster grows and grows, flinging abroad its loose limbs even as some unmannered young giant at his 'larks,' and that the binding stitches must for ever fly further and faster and draw harder; the future complexity of the web, all under the sky and over the sea, becoming thus that of some colossal set of clockworks, some steel-souled machine-room of brandished arms and hammering fists and opening and closing jaws. The immeasurable bridges are but as the horizontal sheaths of pistons working at high pressure, day and night, and subject, one apprehends with perhaps inconsistent gloom, to certain, to fantastic, to merciless multiplication. . .

But memory and the actual impression keep investing New York with the tone, predominantly, of summer dawns and winter frosts, of sea-foam, of bleached sails and stretched awnings, of blanched hulls, of scoured decks, of new ropes, of polished brasses, of streamers clear in the blue air; and it is by this harmony, doubtless, that the projection of the individual character of the place, of the candour of its avidity and the freshness of its audacity, is most conveyed. The 'tall buildings,' which have so promptly usurped a glory that affects you as

10

rather surprised, as yet, at itself, the multitudinous sky-scrapers standing up to the view, from the water, like extravagant pins in a cushion already overplanted, and stuck in as in the dark, anywhere and anyhow, have at least the felicity of carrying out the fairness of tone, of taking the sun and the shade in the manner of towers of marble. They are not all of marble, I believe, by any means, even if some may be, but they are impudently new and still more impudently 'novel' – this in common with so many other terrible things in America – and they are triumphant payers of dividends; all of which uncontested and unabashed pride, with flash of innumerable windows and flicker of subordinate gilt attributions, is like the flare, up and down their long, narrow faces, of the lamps of some general permanent 'celebration.'

You see the pin-cushion in profile, so to speak, on passing between Jersey City and Twenty-third Street, but you get it broadside on, this loose nosegay of architectural flowers, if you skirt the Battery, well out, and embrace the whole plantation. Then the 'American beauty,' the rose of interminable stem, becomes the token of the cluster at large – to that degree that, positively, this is all that is wanted for emphasis of your final impression. Such growths, you feel, have confessedly arisen but to be 'picked,' in time, with a shears; nipped short off, by waiting fate, as soon as 'science,' applied to gain, has put upon the table, from far up its sleeve, some more winning card. Crowned not only with no history, but with no credible possibility of time for history, and consecrated by no uses save the commercial at any cost, they are simply the most piercing notes in that concert of the expensively provisional into which your supreme sense of New York resolves itself. They never begin to speak to you, in the manner of the builded majesties of the world as we have heretofore known such – towers or temples or fortresses or palaces – with the authority of things of permanence or even of things of long duration. One story is good only till another is told, and sky-scrapers are the last word of economic ingenuity only till another word be written. This shall be possibly a word of still uglier meaning, but the vocabulary of thrift at any price shows boundless resources, and the consciousness of that truth, the consciousness of the finite, the menaced, the essentially *invented* state, twinkles ever, to my perception, in the thousand glassy eyes of these giants of the mere market.

The Russian social critic, novelist and playwrite Maxim Gorki (1868-1936) arrived in New York after he was exiled from Czarist Russia for his participation in the failed Revolution of 1905. Socialists in New York prepared a gala reception but the newspapers lambasted him, dwelling particularly on the fact that he was not then married to the woman he was living with. He was evicted from his hotel, spurned by the literary notables of the day, and subsequently wrote a damning account of New York in The City of the Yellow Devil *(1906).*

. . . Over earth and ocean hangs a fog well mixed with smoke, and a fine slow rain is falling over the dark buildings of the city and the muddy waters of the roadstead.

The immigrants gather at the ship's side and gaze silently about them with the curious eyes of hope and apprehension, fear and joy.

'Who's that?' a Polish girl asks softly, staring in wonder at the Statue of Liberty.

'The American god,' someone replies.

The massive figure of the bronze woman is covered from head to foot with verdigris. The cold face stares blindly through the fog, out to the wastes of ocean, as though the bronze is waiting for the sun to bring sight to its sightless eyes. There is very little ground under Liberty's feet, she appears to rise from the ocean on a pedestal of petrified waves. Her arm, raised aloft over the ocean and the masts of the ships, gives a proud majesty and beauty to her pose. The torch so tightly gripped in her hand seems about to burst into a bright flame, driving away the grey smoke and bathing all around in fierce and joyous light.

And around that insignificant strip of land on which she stands, huge iron vessels glide over the waters like prehistoric monsters, and tiny launches dart about like hungry beasts of prey. Sirens wail, angry whistles shrill, anchor chains clang, and the ocean waves grimly slap against the shore.

Everything is running, hurrying, vibrating tensely. The screws and paddles of the steamers rapidly thresh the water which is covered with a yellow foam and seamed with wrinkles.

And everything – iron, stone, water and wood – seems to be protesting against a life without sunlight, without songs and happiness, in captivity to exhausting toil. Everything is groaning, howling, grating, in reluctant obedience to some mysterious force inimical to man. All over the bosom of the waters, ploughed and rent by iron, dirtied by greasy spots of oil, littered with chips and shavings, straw and remains of food, a cold and evil force labours unseen. Grimly and monotonously it operates this stupendous machine, in which ships and docks are only small parts, and man an insignificant screw, an invisible dot amid the unsightly, dirty tangle of iron and wood, the chaos of steamers, boats and barges loaded with cars.

Dazed, deafened by the noise, unnerved by this mad dance of inanimate matter, a two-legged creature, all sooty and oily, with his hands thrust deep in his pockets, stares curiously at me. There is a layer of greasy dirt on the face, relieved not by the gleam of human eyes but by the ivory of white teeth.

Slowly the steamer makes her way through the throng of vessels. The faces of the immigrants look strangely grey and dull, with something of a sheeplike sameness about the eyes. Gathered at the ship's side, they stare in silence at the fog.

In this fog something incomprehensibly vast, emitting a hollow murmur, is born; it grows, its heavy odorous breath is carried to the people and its voice has a threatening and avid note.

This is a city. This is New York. Twenty-storeyed houses, dark soundless skyscrapers, stand on the shore. Square, lacking in any desire to be beautiful, the bulky, ponderous buildings tower gloomily and drearily. A haughty pride in its height, and its ugliness is felt in each house. There are no flowers at the windows and no children to be seen. . .

From this distance the city seems like a vast jaw, with uneven black teeth. It breathes clouds of black smoke into the sky and puffs like a glutton suffering from his obesity.

Entering the city is like getting into a stomach of stone and iron, a stomach that has swallowed several million people and is grinding and digesting them.

The street is a slippery, greedy throat, in the depths of which float dark bits of the city's food – living people. Everywhere – overhead, underfoot, alongside, there is a clang of iron, exulting in its victory. Awakened to life and animated by the power of Gold, it casts its web about man, strangles him, sucks his blood and brain, devours his muscles and nerves, and grows and grows, resting upon voiceless stone, and spreading the links of its chain ever more widely.

Locomotives like enormous worms wriggle along, dragging cars behind them; the horns of the automobiles quack like fat ducks, electric wires hum drearily, the stifling air throbs with the thousands of strident sounds it has absorbed as a sponge absorbs moisture. Pressing down upon this grimy city, soiled with the smoke of factories, it hangs motionless among the high, soot-covered walls.

Federico García Lorca (1896-1936), the Spanish poet and dramatist, visited New York in the late twenties and came back with the poems collected in Poet in New York. *Here, in an excerpt from a lecture he gave while reading some of the poems, he describes his impressions of the city.*

I will not tell you what New York is like *from the outside,* because New York, like Moscow, those two antagonistic cities, is already the subject of countless descriptive books. Nor will I narrate a trip, but will give my lyrical reaction with all sincerity and simplicity, two qualities that come with difficulty to intellectuals, but easily to the poet. So much for modesty!

The two elements the traveler first captures in the big city are extra-human architecture and furious rhythm. Geometry and anguish. At first glance, the rhythm can seem to be gaiety, but when you look more closely at the mechanism of social life and the painful slavery of both men and machines you understand it as a typical, empty anguish that makes even crime and banditry forgivable means of evasion.

Willing neither clouds nor glory, the edges of the buildings rise to the sky. While Gothic edges rise from the hearts of the dead and buried, these ones climb coldly skyward with beauty that has no roots and no yearning, stupidly sure of themselves and utterly unable to conquer or transcend, as does spiritual architecture, the always inferior intentions of the architect. There is nothing more poetic and terrible than the skyscrapers' battle with the heavens that cover them. Snow, rain, and mist set off, wet, and hide the vast towers, but those towers, hostile to mystery, blind to any sort of play, shear off the rain's tresses and shine their three thousand swords through the soft swan of the mist.

It only takes a few days before you get the impression that that immense world has no roots, and you understand why the seer Edgar Poe had to hug mystery so close to him and let friendly intoxication boil in his veins.

The Irish dramatist Brendan Behan (1923-1964) spent many of the last years of his brief, sensational life in New York. He celebrated his time there in Brendan Behan's New York.

I am not afraid to admit that New York is the greatest city on the face of God's earth. You only have to look at it, from the air, from the river, from Father Duffy's statue. New York is easily recognizable as the greatest city in the world, view it any way and every way – back, belly and sides.

London is a wide flat pie of redbrick suburbs with the West End stuck in the middle like a currant. New York is a huge rich raisin and is the biggest city I can imagine.

A city is a place where Man lives, walks about, talks and eats and drinks in the bright light of day or electricity for twenty-four hours a day. In New York, at three o'clock in the morning, you can walk about, see crowds, read the papers and have a drink – orange juice, coffee, whiskey or anything. It is the greatest show on earth, for everyone. Its fabulous beauty at night, even forty years ago, was the wonder of the world.

When I arrived home from Broadway, where my play *The Hostage* was running, my wife said to me, 'Oh isn't it great to be back. How do you feel coming home?'

'Listen Beatrice,' I said, 'It's very dark!'

And I think anybody returning home after going to New York will find their native spot pretty dark too.

We don't come to a city to be alone, and the test of a city is the ease with which you can see and talk to other people. A city is a place where you are least likely to get a bite from a wild sheep and I'd say that New York is the friendliest city I know. The young Russian poet, Yevtushenko, said that in all honesty he had to admit that New York was the most exciting place that he had ever been to in his entire life.

Brooks Atkinson was drama critic of the New York Times from 1925 to 1960. Here, in his article Savage Sunsets, *he calls attention to one of the glories of the city.*

If New York were not celebrated for materialistic wonders, people would travel here to admire the splendor of the sunsets over New

15

Jersey. They are regular events of transcendent splendor. A savage might be frightened by them, for they have the flaming grandeur of primordial catastrophe. They fill our western sky with tongues of fire. Since we understand the science of sunset colors we can admire them with equanimity. There is a commonplace practical reason for their barbaric magnificence. The industrial plants, railroad locomotives and steamships of New Jersey send up a thick cloud of sullen smoke that rolls across the Palisades, showers us with specks of grit and soot, and breaks up the light. The blue rays, which have a short wave length, are widely scattered. But the red rays, which have long wave lengths, pierce the barrier of smoke and come through to us. When the sun gets low in the western sky, the light of the sun comes to us at a long angle through the whole width of the New Jersey smoke bank, and all the color except red is diffused. Our sunsets are, therefore, abnormally red. Our days end violently – the great western arch of the sky incarnadined as if the day had taken fire.

This afternoon the sun is transmuted into an enormous orange sphere when it slips behind the smoke above the Jersey shore. I can look at it with unprotected eyes as it sinks out of sight through the smoke, gas and fumes of a huge industrial bastion. For another quarter of an hour the clouds in the west are banks of crimson. South and north of the sunset pit the clouds are washed with blue, and blue swims on the placid surface of the river. Between the celestial blue of the river and the crimson of the sky the long crag of the Palisades wall is like a deep blue band dividing the firmament from the waters. Presently the Weehawken Boulevard lights come on, the jewels on the crown of the imperial Palisades.

Tomorrow's sunset will be quite different, for the sunset pattern is infinitely varied. The western sky never repeats a design. From day to day it retains nothing but its immutable magnificence.

The Dutch architect Rem Koolhaas celebrates what many others consider some of the city's worst features in his book Delirious New York *(1978). In it he seeks the unexpressed ideology of the city, which he calls 'Manhattanism.'*

Manhattan is the twentieth century's Rosetta Stone.

Not only are large parts of its surface occupied by architectural mutations (Central Park, the Skyscraper), utopian fragments (Rockefeller Center, the UN Building) and irrational phenomena (Radio City Music Hall), but in addition each block is covered with several layers of phantom architecture in the form of past occupancies, aborted projects and popular fantasies that provide alternative images to the New York that exists.

Especially between 1890 and 1940 a new culture (the Machine Age?) selected Manhattan as laboratory: a mythical island where the invention and testing of a metropolitan lifestyle and its attendant architecture could be pursued as a collective experiment in which the entire city became a factory of man-made experience, where the real and the natural ceased to exist. . .

ECSTASY

If Manhattan is still in search of a theory, then this theory, once identified, should yield a formula for an architecture that is at once ambitious and popular.

Manhattan has generated a shameless architecture that has been loved in direct proportion to its defiant lack of self-hatred, has been respected exactly to the degree that it went too far.

Manhattan has consistently inspired in its beholders *ecstasy about architecture*.

In spite – or perhaps because – of this, its performance and implications have been consistently ignored and even suppressed by the architectural profession.

DENSITY

Manhattanism is the one urbanistic ideology that has fed, from its conception, on the splendors and miseries of the metropolitan condition – hyper-density – without once losing faith in it as the basis for a desirable modern culture. *Manhattan's architecture is a paradigm for the exploitation of congestion.*

17

Elizabeth Bishop (1911-1979), innovative American poet, issued this imaginary invitation to another American poet, Marianne Moore.

INVITATION TO MISS MARIANNE MOORE

From Brooklyn, over the Brooklyn Bridge, on this fine morning,
    please come flying.
In a cloud of fiery pale chemicals,
    please come flying,
to the rapid rolling of thousands of small blue drums
descending out of the mackerel sky
over the glittering grandstand of harbor-water,
    please come flying.

Whistles, pennants and smoke are blowing. The ships are
signaling cordially with multitudes of flags rising and falling like
birds all over the harbor.
Enter: two rivers, gracefully bearing
countless little pellucid jellies
in cut-glass epergnes dragging with silver chains.
The flight is safe; the weather is all arranged.
The waves are running in verses this fine morning.
    Please come flying.

Come with the pointed toe of each black shoe
trailing a sapphire highlight,
with a black capeful of butterfly wings and bon-mots,
with heaven knows how many angels all riding
on the broad black brim of your hat,
    please come flying.

Bearing a musical inaudible abacus,
a slight censorious frown, and blue ribbons,
    please come flying.
Facts and skyscrapers glint in the tide; Manhattan
is all awash with morals this fine morning,
    so please come flying.

Mounting the sky with natural heroism,
above the accidents, above the malignant movies,
the taxicabs and injustices at large,

while horns are resounding in your beautiful ears
that simultaneously listen to
a soft uninvented music, fit for the musk deer,
    please come flying.

For whom the grim museums will behave
like courteous male bower-birds,
for whom the agreeable lions lie in wait
on the steps of the Public Library,
eager to rise and follow through the doors
up into the reading rooms,
    please come flying.
We can sit down and weep; we can go shopping,
or play at a game of constantly being wrong
with a priceless set of vocabularies,
or we can bravely deplore, but please
    please come flying.

With dynasties of negative constructions
darkening and dying around you,
with grammar that suddenly turns and shines
like flocks of sandpipers flying,
    please come flying.

Come like a light in the white mackerel sky,
come like a daytime comet
with a long unnebulous train of words,
from Brooklyn, over the Brooklyn Bridge, on this fine morning,
    please come flying.

CHAPTER 2

NEW YORKERS

Richard F. Shepard, long-time staff member at the New York Times, *defended the New York accent in its columns.*

THE NEW YORK ACCENT

They've been trying to abolish it for years. Teachers attack it. Students resist it. Users regret it, but it's harder to give up than smoking. It and obscenity may often keep you off the air. It's altogether unforgivable.

It, of course, is the New York accent. It's probably the city's longest-lived landmark and it is the one that everyone is trying to stamp out.

A fine German accent may bolster a psychiatrist's fee. A crisp British accent simply cries for a lecture tour. Regional variations across the city line command affectionate toleration. To speak as they do in Dixie – as long as it's intelligible – is a sentimental plus. The New England twang conjures up visions of democracy in the raw, small townsmen going to meeting and debating about raising money by lottery. The pioneer spirit infests the Western drawl, even when it emanates from a mouth that never shouted at a cow. Modified Midwestern is to us what Florentine is to Italian, the standard, the stated norm that few from elsewhere can more than approximate.

But they abominate the New York accent. New Yorkers abominate it, too. In school, patient teachers, with frustrating results, try to extirpate local aberrations, such as *oi* for *er, er* for *oi,* the *dese, dems* and *doses,* the *whatcha* for *what are you* and the lamentable, mystifying disappearance of the *r* that makes *Noo Yawkers* rush to *fi-uhs* when the *alahm* bell rings.

Add to this, ethnic variants with rising intonations and brutally misemphasized consonants and the city emerges as a linguistic disaster area, a desperate zone of pear-shaped poverty, in which even sizable federal aid will show no pronounced results. There are many degrees of disability; many New Yorkers have contrived to color their diction with accepted resonances and inflections, along with such critical minima as clear expression of *th's* and careful avoidance of caricaturelike vocal extremes.

Now, is the New York accent really all that bad? The answer, doubtless, is a resounding yeah. But it need not be so; that is a culturally bred reaction and nothing that a little positive thinking can't cure.

Happily, we have become a great nation and our immigrants have turned into true-blue Yankees, looking for roots. There is a passion for antiques dating back to Colonial days and homes with Ol' Virginny columns. We are in a preservation mood. We want to preserve old buildings. Why not old accents?

It is not as if the New York accent doesn't suit the environment. It is a rough-cut affair, matching the jagged skyline. It is as noisily slurred as a subway rush. It is as guttural as a traffic jam. If New Yorkers speak loudly without opening their mouths, it's not only a physiological triumph, it also avoids inhalation of the polluted air.

It is the dialect that unifies the fastest town in the world. It wastes no time on colorful metaphors and drawled verities. It runs toward a deed, a deal or a dollar, anything that has a goal from the most concrete transaction to the most abstruse research. It is not a time waster. It is the hurry-up, short-order accent of America.

This doesn't make it the best. But it doesn't make it the worst, either. Granted, New Yorkers should vocalize so that they may be understood by other English-speaking peoples (who have their problems, too, as anyone who has looked in on the Midlands can attest).

But must our accent be rooted out? Under New York's landmark laws, certain ancient buildings may be built anew inside but not a brick on the outside may be touched. Is there no way to harness the accent and its vigor, to reach a happy medium that will allow for some internal refurbishing while preserving the rugged exterior? Something between Mayor Lindsay and Zero Mostel?

It's one of the few things left to us that is untaxed and that we may call our own.

John Miller (1666-1724) served as chaplain to His Majesty's Forces in New York, recently seized from the Dutch, from 1692 to 1695. On the return voyage to England in 1695 his ship was captured by French privateers and Miller was imprisoned at St. Malo, France, where he wrote his account of the people and the province of New York.

THE INHABITANTS, 1695

The number of the Inhabitants in this Province are about 3000 families whereof almost one halfe are naturally Dutch a great part

English and the rest French. . . As to their Religion they are very much divided. few of them intelligent & sincere but the most part ignorant & conceited, fickle & regardless. As to their wealth & disposition thereto ye Dutch are rich & sparing, the English neither very rich nor too great husbands, the French are poor and therefore forced to be penurious: As to their way of trade & dealing they are all generally cunning and crafty but many of them not so just to their words as they should be.

. . . the wickedness & irreligion of the inhabitants which abounds in all parts of the Province & appears in so many shapes constituting so many sorts of sin that I can scarce tell which to begin withall. But as a great reason of & inlet to the rest I shall 1st. mention the great negligence of divine things that is generally found in most people of what Sect or party soever they p^{r}tend to be. their eternall interests are their least concerne & as if Salvation were not a matter of moment when they have opportunitys of Serving God they care not for making use thereof or if they go to church 'tis but too often out of curiosity & to find out faults in him that preacheth rather than to hear their own or what is yet worse to slight & deride where they should be Serious if they have none of those opportunities they are well contented & regard it little if their be any who seem otherwise & discontented many of them when they have them make appear by their Actions 'twas but in show; for tho at first they will pretend to have a great regard for Gods ordinances & a high esteem for the Ministry whether reall or p^{r}tended a little time will plainly evidence that they were more pleased at the novelty than truly affected with the Benefit when they slight that which they before seemingly so much admired & Speake evill of him who before was the subject of their praise & commendation & that without any other reason than their own fickle temper & envious humour. In a soile so ranke as this no marvail if the Evill one find a ready entertainm^t. for the seed he is minded to cast in & from a people so inconsistent & regardless of Heaven & holy things no wonder if God withdraw his grace & give them up a prey to those temptations which they so industriously seek to imbrace hence is it therefore that their naturall corruption without check or hinderance is by frequent acts improved into habits most evill in the practice & Difficult in the correction.

One of which & the 1st. I am minded to speake of is drunkenness which tho of itself a great sin is yet aggravated in that it is an occasion of many others . . .

. . . many in the City of New Yorke whose daily practice is to frequent the taverns & to Carouse & game their night imployment. This course is the ruine & destruction of many merchants especially those of the Younger sort who carrying over with them a stock whether as Facto^{rs} or on their own Account Spend even to prodigality till they find themselves bankrupt e'er they are aware.

In a town where this course of life is led by many tis no wonder if there be other vices in vogue because they are the naturall product of it such are cursing & Swearing to both of which People are here much accustomed some doing it in that frequent horrible & dreadfull manner as if they prided themselves both as to the number and invention of them this joyned with their profane Atheisticall & scoffing method of discourse makes their Company extreamly uneasy to sober & religious men who sometimes by reason of their affairs cannot help being of their society & becoming ear-witnesses of their blasphemy & folly. 'tis strange that men should ingage themselves so foolishly & run into ye Commission of so great a sin unto which they have no sufficient, often not a p^rtended, provocation & from which they reap no advantage nor any reall pleasure: & yet we see them even delight in it & no discourse is thought witty or eloquent except larded with oaths & execrations. . .

Walt Whitman published this essay on obscure and prominent New Yorkers in Life Illustrated *in 1856, shortly after the first publication of* Leaves of Grass.

STREET YARN

Soldiers and militiamen are not the only people who wear uniforms. A uniform serves two purposes; first, to distinguish the wearers from others, and secondly, to assimilate them to each other. The universal uniform is more for the former of these than the latter; and is not only the style and substance of garments, but appearance and carriage. Come and walk in New York streets, or sit in a restaurant; we will detect some people for you by their uniforms.

Mild, foolish, dough-colored, simpering face; black cloth suit —

shad-bellied, single-breasted coat, with low standing collar all round, vest buttoned close to throat, knees a little bent, toes turned out, and chin down. Episcopalian deacon.

Wild cataract of hair; absurd, bunged-up felt hat, with peaked crown; velvet coat, all friggled over with gimp, but worn; eyes rather staring, look upward. Third-rate artist.

Dress strictly respectable; hat well down on forehead; face thin, dry, close-shaven; mouth with a gripe like a vice; eye sharp and quick; brows bent; forehead scowling; step jerky and bustling. Wall Street broker.

Hands crossed behind him; step slow; dress well enough, but careless all over; face bent downward, and full of thought. Leading lawyer.

Rusty black costume; white choker; look oddly compounded of severity, superiority, curiosity, apprehension, and suspicion; shoulders stooping, chest flat. Country clergyman.

Half-a-dozen ill-dressed fellows together (this in the evening); dirty, unshorn faces; debauched expression; the half-shut eyes, and loose, hanging lips of the tribe; hoarse voices, incredibly tuneless; oaths and curses; laughs made up of a yell and a cackle; a peculiar quick, eager step, as they flock along close together. Short-boys; damnable dangerous villains.

Dirty finery, excessively plentiful; paint, both red and white; draggle-tailed dress, ill-fitting; coarse features, unintelligent; bold glance, questioning, shameless, perceptibly anxious; hideous croak or dry, brazen ring in voice; affected, but awkward, mincing, waggling gait. Harlot.

Heavy moustache; obtrusively expensive dress; big breast pin; heavy gold chain; rings; hat down over brows; loafing attitude on corner; eye furtive, glassy, expressionless; oaths; tobacco-spit. Gambler.

There, somewhat in that manner, you may learn even to distinguish the trades from each other. But now let us sketch individuals. We are sitting, we will suppose, in the St. Nicholas front windows, or standing in front of Delmonico's, or anywhere in a thoroughfare. The crowd flows by; among it goes, now and then, one of these following:

A tall, slender man, round-shouldered, chin stuck out, deep-set eyes, sack-coat. His step is quick, and his arms swing awkwardly, as if he were trying to knock his elbows together behind him. Albert Brisbane the Socialist; the capitalist, too – an odd

26

circumstance for a radical in New York! Somehow or other he always looks as if he were attempting to think out some problem a little too hard for him.

Old gentleman in carriage. A well-built, portly old man, full, ruddy face, abundant wavy – almost frizzly – white hair, good forehead, kindly, intelligent look. Dr. Francis, the encyclopædia of historical information, especially in local history and genealogy.

Tall, large, rough-looking man, in a journeyman carpenter's uniform. Coarse, sanguine complexion; strong, bristly, grizzled beard; singular eyes, of a semi-transparent, indistinct light blue, and with that sleepy look that comes when the lid rests half way down over the pupil; careless, lounging gait. Walt Whitman, the sturdy, self-conscious microcosmic prose-poetical author of that incongruous hash of mud and gold – 'Leaves of Grass.'

Middle-sized person, upright and alert; dark, sallow, Spanish-looking phiz; jet black hair and beard, a wild and glittering eye, and a certain air of satisfaction, is if well content to be of importance. That is Stephen H. Branch, the Alligator; the burr in the skirts of Mr. Matsell; the 'indefigitable' searcher after Brandon records; the great worm-doctor, and the only writer of the Branch school known to exist.

Oldish, tall, large-framed, slouching man, in negligent costume of blue cloth; drags his feet along like 'flat irons hung on a string; seems much interested in the sidewalk; if he looks up, shows a face as blank as a brick wall, yet with a benign and pleasant look. The benign and pleasant look Professor Robinson can't get rid of; and if his learning and intelligence don't always appear on the outside of his capacious head, it is because they are 'urgently engaged' within. For that careless, lumbering old gentleman is Professor Edward Robinson, of Union Theological Seminary; the first scholar of the country, if not of his time, in Biblical Learning, and whose discoveries in Palestine, and other labors, have made him a name all over Protestant Christendom, and proved him fully equal to the greatest of the great Germans who have done so much in that department, and in whose own language and literature he is himself so thorough a scholar.

A short, 'chunked,' light-haired, fair-faced, big-headed, jolly roly-poly man, with a ready smile and a prompt step, like a bold little game-cock. Robert Bonner, the hero of unheard-of and tremendous advertising, who fires cannon, fills page upon page of

27

newspapers, and – if he could – would placard the very walls of Paradise with hifalutin handbills, to sell that gorgeous and unprecedented sheet, the New York *Ledger*.

Somebody in an open barouche, driving daintily. He looks like a doll; is it alive? We'll cross the street and so get close to him. Did you see? Fantastic hat, turned clear over in the rim above the ears; blue coat and shiny brass buttons; patent leathers; shirt-frill; gold specs; bright red cheeks, and singularly definite jetty black eyebrows, moustache, and imperial. You could see that from the sidewalk; but you saw, when you stood at his wheel, not only the twinkling diamond ring and breast-pin, but the heavy, slabby red paint; and even the substratum of grizzly gray under that jetty dye; and upon our word there's a hair of the same straggling out under the jaunty oiled wig! How straight he sits, and how he simpers, and how he fingers the reins with a delicate white little finger stuck out, as if a mere touch were all – as if his whole hand might govern a team of elephants! The Baron Spolasco, with no end of medical diplomas from all sorts of universities across the ocean, who cures everything immediately; you may consult him confidentially, or by letter, if you choose. It would be worth money to see that old gentleman – they say he is nearly eighty – undress himself! Clothes, wig, calves, stays, moustache, teeth, complexion – what a bald, bare, wizened, shriveled old granny he would be!

A lady – slender and elegant – in black from head to foot; pure white complexion, pale, striking chiseled features, perfect profile, abundant fair hair; abstracted look, and rather rapid, purposeful step. That his Miss Ada Clare, called by many a perfect beauty; questionless, of decided talent; one about whom many interesting stories might be told, and a persevering and energetic votary of the mimetic art. Possessed of some wealth, great personal attractions, no inconsiderable share of intellect and cultivation, she has already often appeared upon the stage, which she may possibly adopt as a profession.

A straight, trim-built, prompt, vigorous man, well dressed with strong brown hair, beard, and moustache, and a quick and watchful eye. He steps alertly by, watching everybody. Charles A. Dana, chief editor of the New York *Tribune*, a man of rough, strong intellect, tremendous prejudices firmly relied on, and excellent intentions.

Down the other side goes one with a dry, spare, hard visage, black eyes, and a huge white beard of somewhat ragged appearance. He strides along regardlessly and rapidly, a book in his hand, a thought – and more too – inside of his head, a most rustical straw hat outside of it, turned sharp up behind and down before, like a country boy's, and a summer coat streaming flag-like from his shoulders. He is senior partner of a book and job printing firm, down town. 'Pshaw! what is he worth describing for?' Wait a minute. That firm is also a firm of newspaper editors and publishers. It is the firm of William C. Bryant & Co.; and the senior partner, the white-bearded, scrawny, striding old gentle-man, is, if not our foremost and noblest poet, abreast with the foremost; and, moreover, a strong, valiant, and uncompromising – and more yet, and rarer – an absolutely fair and courteous political newspaper editor, on what side it is unnecessary to say.

A big, heavy, overgrown man, with a face like a raw beef-steak, little piggy eyes, queer, dry, straight, harsh, coarse hair, 'of a speckled color,' made up of brownish red and gray, rather dirty clothes, and quite dirty, yellow dog-skin gloves. He goes rolling along in an elephantine style, and for fear of being trod on, probably, people get out of the way. That is George Law, who never will be President. Those people, and many more, go about the streets of New York.

Dorothy Parker (1893-1967), drama and literary critic, poet and satirist, wrote for Vogue, Vanity Fair, *and the* New Yorker *and in her hey-day was acknowledged to be the quickest wit in the city. This account of a certain kind of New Yorker first appeared in 1919.*

FROM THE DIARY OF A NEW YORK LADY

During Days of Horror, Despair, and World Change

Monday. Breakfast tray about eleven; didn't want it. The champagne at the Amory's last night was *too* revolting, but what *can* you do? You can't stay until five o'clock on just *nothing*. They had those *divine* Hungarian musicians in the green coats, and Stewie Hunter took off one of his shoes and led them with it, and it *couldn't* have been funnier. He is *the* wittiest number in the *entire* world; he *couldn't* be more perfect. Ollie Martin brought me home and we both fell asleep in the car – *too* screaming. Miss Rose came about noon to do my nails, simply *covered* with *the* most divine gossip. The Morrises are going to separate *any minute,* and Freddie Warren *definitely* has ulcers, and Gertie Leonard simply *won't* let Bill Crawford out of her sight even with Jack Leonard *right there in the room,* and it's all *true* about Sheila Phillips and Babs Deering. It *couldn't* have been more thrilling. Miss Rose is *too* marvelous; I really think that a lot of times people like that are a lot more intelligent than a lot of people. Didn't notice until after she had gone that the damn fool had put that *revolting* tangerine-colored polish on my nails; *couldn't* have been more furious. Started to read a book, but too nervous. Called up and found I could get two tickets for the opening of "Run like a Rabbit" tonight for forty-eight dollars. Told them they had *the* nerve of the world, but what *can* you do? Think Joe said he was dining out, so telephoned some *divine* numbers to get someone to go to the theater with me, but they were all tied up. Finally got Ollie Martin. He *couldn't* have more poise, and what do *I* care if he *is* one? *Can't* decide whether to wear the green crepe or the red wool. Every time I look at my finger nails, I could *spit. Damn* Miss Rose.

Tuesday. Joe came barging in my room this morning at *practically nine o'clock. Couldn't* have been more furious. Started to fight, but *too* dead. Know he said he wouldn't be home to dinner. Absolutely *cold* all day; couldn't *move.* Last night *couldn't* have been more perfect. Ollie and I dined at Thirty-Eight East, absolutely *poisonous* food, and not one *living* soul that you'd be seen *dead* with, and "Run like a Rabbit" was *the* world's worst. Took Ollie up to the Barlows' party and it *couldn't* have been more attractive – *couldn't* have been more people absolutely *stinking.* They had those Hungarians in the green coats, and Stewie Hunter was leading them with a fork – everybody simply *died.* He had *yards* of green toilet paper hung around his neck like a lei; he *couldn't* have been in better form. Met a *really new number,* very tall, *too* marvelous, and one of those people that you can *really* talk to them. I told him sometimes I get so *nauseated* I could *yip,* and I felt I absolutely *had* to do something like write or paint. He said why didn't I write or paint. Came home alone; Ollie passed out *stiff.* Called up the new number three times today to get him to come to dinner and go with me to the opening of "Never Say Good Morning," but first he was out and then he was all tied up with his mother. Finally got Ollie Martin. Tried to read a book, but couldn't sit still. *Can't* decide whether to wear the red lace or the pink with the feathers. Feel *too* exhausted, but what *can* you do?

Wednesday. The most terrible thing happened *just this minute.* Broke one of my finger nails *right off short.* Absolutely *the* most horrible thing I ever had happen to me in my life. Called up Miss Rose to come over and shape it for me, but she was out for the day. I do have *the* worst luck in the *entire* world. Now I'll have to go around like this all day and all night, but what *can* you do? *Damn* Miss Rose. Last night *too* hectic. "Never Say Good Morning" *too* foul, *never* saw more poisonous clothes on the stage. Took Ollie up to the Ballards' party; *couldn't* have been better. They had those Hungarians in the green coats and Stewie Hunter was leading them with a freesia – *too* perfect. He had on Peggy Cooper's ermine coat and Phyllis Minton's silver turban; *simply* unbelievable. Asked simply *sheaves* of *divine* people to come here Friday night; got the address of those Hungarians in the green coats from Betty Ballard. She says just engage them until four, and then whoever gives them another three hundred dollars, they'll stay till five. *Couldn't* be cheaper. Started home with Ollie, but had to drop him at his house; he *couldn't* have been sicker. Called up the new number today to get him to come to dinner and go to the opening of "Everybody Up" with me tonight, but he was tied up. Joe's going to be out; he didn't *condescend* to say *where, of course.* Started to read the papers, but nothing in them except that Mona Wheatley is in Reno charging *intolerable cruelty.* Called up Jim Wheatley to see if he had anything to do tonight, but he was tied up. Finally got Ollie Martin. *Can't* decide whether to wear the white satin or the black chiffon or the yellow pebble crepe. Simply *wrecked* to the *core* about my finger nail. Can't *bear* it. *Never* knew *anybody* to have such *unbelievable* things to happen to them.

Thursday. Simply *collapsing* on my *feet.* Last night *too* marvelous "Everybody Up" *too* divine, *couldn't* be filthier, and the new number was there, *too* celestial, only he didn't see me. He was with Florence Keeler in that *loathsome* gold Schiaparelli model of hers that every *shopgirl* has had since *God* knows. He must be out of his *mind;* she wouldn't *look* at a man. Took Ollie to the Watsons' party; *couldn't* have been more thrilling. Everybody simply *blind.* They had those Hungarians in the green coats and

Stewie Hunter was leading them with a lamp, and, after the lamp got broken, he and Tommy Thomas did adagio dances – *too* wonderful. Somebody told me Tommy's doctor told him he had to absolutely get *right out of town,* he has *the* world's worst stomach, but you'd *never* know it. Came home alone, couldn't find Ollie *anywhere.* Miss Rose came at noon to shape my nail, *couldn't* have been more fascinating. Sylvia Eaton can't go *out the door* unless she's had a hypodermic, and Doris Mason *knows every single word* about Douggie Mason and that girl up in Harlem, and Evelyn North won't be *induced* to keep away from those three acrobats, and they don't *dare* tell Stuyvie Raymond *what* he's got the matter with him. *Never* knew anyone that had a more simply *fascinating* life than Miss Rose. Made her take that *vile* tangerine polish off my nails and put on dark red. Didn't notice until after she had one that it's practically *black* in electric light; *couldn't* be in a worse state. *Damn* Miss Rose. Joe left a note saying he was going to dine out, so telephoned the new number to get him to come to dinner and go with me to that new movie tonight, but he didn't answer. Sent him three telegrams to *absolutely surely* come tomorrow night. Finally got Ollie Martin for tonight. Looked at the papers, but nothing in them except that the Harry Motts are throwing a tea with Hungarian music on Sunday. Think will ask the new number to go to it with me; they must have meant to invite me. Began to read a book, but too exhausted. *Can't* decide whether to wear the new blue with the white jacket or save it till tomorrow night and wear the ivory moire. Simply *heartsick* every time I think of my nails. *Couldn't* be wilder. Could *kill* Miss Rose, but what *can* you do?

Friday. Absolutely *sunk; couldn't* be worse. Last night *too* divine, movie *simply* deadly. Took Ollie to the Kingslands' party, *too* unbelievable, everybody absolutely *rolling.* They had those Hungarians in the green coats, but Stewie Hunter wasn't there. He's got a *complete* nervous breakdown. Worried *sick* for fear he won't be well by tonight; will absolutely *never* forgive him if he doesn't come. Started home with Ollie, but dropped him at his house because he *couldn't* stop crying. Joe left word with the butler he's going to the country this afternoon for the week-end; *of course* he wouldn't *stoop* to say *what* country. Called up *streams* of marvelous numbers to get someone to come dine and go with me to the opening of "White Man's Folly," and then go somewhere

32

after to dance for a while; can't *bear* to be the first one there at your own party. Everybody was tied up. Finally got Ollie Martin. *Couldn't* feel more depressed; never should have gone *anywhere near* champagne and Scotch together. Started to read a book, but too restless. Called up Anne Lyman to ask about the new baby and *couldn't* remember if it was a boy or girl – *must* get a secretary *next week*. Anne *couldn't* have been more of a help; she said she didn't know whether to name it Patricia or Gloria, so then of course I knew it was a girl *right away*. Suggested calling Barbara; forgot she already had one. Absolutely *walking the floor* like a *panther* all day. Could *spit* about Stewie Hunter. Can't *face* deciding whether to wear the blue with the white jacket or the purple with the beige roses. Every time I look at those *revolting* black nails, I want to absolutely *yip*. I really have *the* most horrible things happen to me of anybody in the *entire* world. *Damn* Miss Rose.

Joseph Mitchell was born in the south but made his name in New York as a reporter with The Herald Tribune, The World Telegram, *and especially the* New Yorker, *for whom he was a staff writer for several decades. He first published this account of the American Indians who had moved to New York to work on the skyscrapers in 1949.*

THE MOHAWKS IN HIGH STEEL

Sometime in 1915 or 1916, a Caughnawaga bridgeman named John Diabo came down to New York City and got a job on Hell Gate Bridge. He was a curiosity and was called Indian Joe; two old foremen still remember him. After he had worked for some months as bucker-up in an Irish gang, three other Caughnawagas joined him and they formed a gang of their own. They had worked together only a few weeks when Diabo stepped off a scaffold and dropped into the river and was drowned. He was highly skilled and his misstep was freakish; recently, in trying to explain it, a Caughnawaga said, 'It must've been one of those cases, he got in the way of himself.' The other Caughnawagas went back to the reservation with his body and did not return. As well as the old men in the band can recollect, no other Caughnawagas worked here until the twenties. In 1926, attracted by the building boom three or four Caughnawaga gangs came down.

33

The old men say that these gangs worked first on the Fred F. French Building, the Graybar Building, and One Fifth Avenue. In 1928, three more gangs came down. They worked first on the George Washington Bridge. In the thirties, when Rockefeller Center was the biggest steel job in the country, at least seven additional Caughnawaga gangs came down. Upon arriving here, the men in all these gangs enrolled in the Brooklyn local of the high-steel union, the International Association of Bridge, Structural, and Ornamental Iron Workers, American Federation of Labor. Why they enrolled in the Brooklyn instead of the Manhattan local, no one now seems able to remember. The hall of the Brooklyn local is on Atlantic Avenue, in the block between Times Plaza and Third Avenue, and the Caughnawagas got lodgings in furnished-room houses and cheap hotels in the North Gowanus neighborhood, a couple of blocks up Atlantic from the hall. In the early thirties, they began sending for their families and moving into tenements and apartment houses in the same neighborhood. During the war, Caughnawagas continued to come down. Many of these enrolled in the Manhattan local, but all of them settled in North Gowanus.

At present, there are eighty-three Caughnawagas in the Brooklyn local and forty-two in the Manhattan local. Less than a third of them work steadily in the city. The others keep their families in North Gowanus and work here intermittently but spend much of their time in other cities. They roam from coast to coast, usually by automobile, seeking rush jobs that offer unlimited overtime work at double pay; in New York City, the steel-erecting companies use as little overtime as possible. A gang may work in half a dozen widely separated cities in a single year. Occasionally, between jobs, they return to Brooklyn to see their families. Now and then, after long jobs, they pick up their families and go up to the reservation for a vacation; some go up every summer. A few men sometimes take their families along on trips to jobs and send them back to Brooklyn by bus or train. Several foremen who have had years of experience with Caughnawagas believe that they roam because they can't help doing so, it is a passion, and that their search for overtime is only an excuse. A veteran foreman for the American Bridge Company says he has seen Caughnawagas leave jobs that offered all the overtime they could handle. When they are making up their minds to move on, he says, they become erratic. 'Everything will be going along fine

on a job,' he says. 'Good working conditions. Plenty of overtime.
A nice city. Then the news will come over the grapevine about
some big new job opening up somewhere; it might be a thousand
miles away. That kind of news always causes a lot of talk, what
we call water-bucket talk, but the Indians don't talk; they know
what's in each other's mind. For a couple of days, they're tensed
up and edgy. They look a little wild in the eyes. They've heard the
call. Then, all of a sudden, they turn in their tools, and they're
gone. Can't wait another minute. They'll quit at lunchtime, in the
middle of the week. They won't even wait for their pay. Some
other gang will collect their money and hold it until a postcard
comes back telling where to send it.' George C. Lane, manager of
erections in the New York district for the Bethlehem Steel
Company, once said that the movements of a Caughnawaga gang
are as impossible to foresee as the movements of a flock of
sparrows. 'In the summer of 1936,' Mr. Lane said, 'we finished
a job here in the city and the very next day we were starting in on
a job exactly three blocks away. I heard one of our foremen trying
his best to persuade an Indian gang to go on the new job. They
had got word about a job in Hartford and wanted to go up there.
The foreman told them the rate of pay was the same; there
wouldn't be any more overtime up there than here; their families
were here; they'd have travelling expenses; they'd have to root
around Hartford for lodgings. Oh, no; it was Hartford or nothing.
A year or so later I ran into this gang on a job in Newark, and I
asked the heater how they made out in Hartford that time. He
said they didn't go to Hartford. 'We went to San Francisco,
California,' he said. 'We went out and worked on the Golden
Gate Bridge.' '

In New York City, the Caughnawagas work mostly for the big
companies – Bethlehem, American Bridge, the Lehigh Structural
Steel Company, and the Harris Structural Steel Company.
Among the structures in and around the city on which they
worked in numbers are the R.C.A. Building, the Cities Service
Building, the Empire State Building, the Daily News Building,
the Chanin Building, the Bank of the Manhattan Company
Building, the City Bank Farmers Trust Building, the George
Washington Bridge, the Bayonne Bridge, the Passaic River
Bridge, the Triborough Bridge, the Henry Hudson Bridge, the
Little Hell Gate Bridge, the Bronx-Whitestone Bridge, the
Marine Parkway Bridge, the Pulaski Skyway, the West Side

Highway, the Waldorf-Astoria, London Terrace, and Knickerbocker Village.

North Gowanus is an old, sleepy, shabby neighborhood that
lies between the head of the Gowanus Canal and the Borough
Hall shopping district. There are factories in it, and coal tipples
and junk yards, but it is primarily residential, and red-brick
tenements and brownstone apartment houses are most numerous.
The Caughnawagas all live within ten blocks of each other, in an
area bounded by Court Street on the west, Schermerhorn Street
on the north, Fourth Avenue on the east, and Warren Street on
the south. They live in the best houses on the best blocks. As a
rule, Caughnawaga women are good housekeepers and keep their
apartments Dutch-clean. Most of them decorate a mantel or a
wall with heirlooms brought down from the reservation – a drum,
a set of rattles, a mask, a cradleboard. Otherwise, their
apartments look much the same as those of their white neighbors.
A typical family group consists of husband and wife and a couple
of children and a female relative or two. After they get through
school on the reservation, many Caughnawaga girls come down
to North Gowanus and work in factories. Some work for the Fred
Goat Company, a metal-stamping factory in the neighborhood,
and some work for the Gem Safety Razor Corporation, whose
factory is within walking distance. Quite a few of these girls have
married whites; several have broken all ties with the band and the
reservation. In the last ten years, Caughnawaga girls have
married Filipinos, Germans, Italians, Jews, Norwegians, and
Puerto Ricans. Many North Gowanus families often have
relatives visiting them for long periods; when there is a new baby
in a family, a grandmother or an aunt almost always comes down
from the reservation and helps out. Caughnawagas are allowed to
cross the border freely. However, each is required to carry a card,
to which a photograph is attached, certifying that he or she is a
member of the band. These cards are issued by the Indian Affairs
Branch; the Caughnawagas refer to them as "passports." More
than half of the North Gowanus housewives spend their spare
time making souvenirs. They make a lot of them. They specialize
in dolls, handbags, and belts, which they ornament with colored
beads, using variations of ancient Iroquois designs such as the sky
dome, the night sun, the day sun, the fern head, the evergrowing
tree, the world turtle, and the council fire. Every fall, a few of the

most Indian-looking of the men take vacations from structural steel for a month or so and go out with automobile loads of these souvenirs and sell them on the midways of state, county, and community fairs in New York, Connecticut, New Jersey, and Pennsylvania. The men wear buckskins and feathers on these trips and sleep in canvas tepees pitched on fairgrounds. Occasionally, on midways, to attract attention, they let out self-conscious wahoos and do fragments of the Duel Dance, the Dove Dance, the Falseface Dance, and other old half-forgotten Mohawk dances. The women obtain the raw materials for souvenirs from the Plume Trading & Sales Company, at 155 Lexington Avenue, in Manhattan, a concern that sells beads, deerskin, imitation eagle feathers, and similar merchandise to Indian handicraftsmen all over the United States and Canada. There are approximately fifty children of school age in the colony. Two-thirds go to Public School 47, on Pacific Street, and the others go to parochial schools – St. Paul's, St. Agnes's, and St. Charles Borromeo's. Caughnawaga children read comic books, listen to the radio while doing their homework, sit twice through double features, and play stick ball in vacant lots the same as the other children in the neighborhood; teachers say that they differ from the others mainly in that they are more reserved and polite. They have unusual manual dexterity; by the age of three, most of them are able to tie their shoelaces. The adult Caughnawagas are multilingual; all speak Mohawk, all speak English, and all speak or understand at least a little French. In homes where both parents are Caughnawagas, Mohawk is spoken almost exclusively, and the children pick it up. In homes where the mother is non-Indian and the father is away a good deal, a situation that is becoming more and more frequent, the children sometimes fail to learn the language, and this causes much sadness. . .

Occasionally, in a saloon or at a wedding or a wake, Caughnawagas become vivacious and talkative. Ordinarily, however, they are rather dour and don't talk much. There is only one person in the North Gowanus colony who has a reputation for garrulity. He is a man of fifty-four whose white name is Orvis Diabo and whose Indian name is O-ron-ia-ke-te, or He Carries the Sky. Mr. Diabo is squat and barrel-chested. He has small, sharp eyes and a round, swarthy, double-chinned, piratical face.

Unlike most other Caughnawagas, he does not deny or even minimize his white blood. 'My mother was half Scotch and half Indian,' he says. 'My grandmother on my father's side was Scotch-Irish. Somewhere along the line, I forget just where, some French immigrant and some full Irish crept in. If you were to take my blood and strain it, God only knows what you'd find.' He was born a Catholic; in young manhood, he became a Presbyterian; he now thinks of himself as 'a kind of a freethinker.' Mr. Diabo started working in riveting gangs when he was nineteen and quit a year and a half ago. He had to quit because of crippling attacks of arthritis. He was a heater and worked on bridges and buildings in seventeen states. 'I heated a million rivets,' he says. 'When they talk about the men that built this country, one of the men they mean is me.' Mr. Diabo owns a house and thirty-three acres of farmland on the reservation. He inherited the farmland and rents it to a French Canadian. Soon after he quit work, his wife, who had lived in North Gowanus off and on for almost twenty years but had never liked it, went back to the reservation. She tried to get him to go along, but he decided to stay on awhile and rented a room in the apartment of a cousin. 'I enjoy New York,' he says. 'The people are as high-strung as rats and the air is too gritty, but I enjoy it.'

Jack Kerouac (1922-1969), author of On the Road, The Dharma Bums, The Subterraneans, *and premier novelist of the Beat Generation, came down from his home town in Massachusetts to attend Horace Mann High School in the Bronx in 1939. In his last book,* The Vanity of Duluoz, *published in 1967, Kerouac looked back on that time and tried to recreate his first brush with New York and New Yorkers. Here he describes life following a successful autumn with the school football team.*

AN ACADEMY OF WITS

After that it was the usual resting on laurels, waiting to go to Columbia the following autumn, casual movies, casual love affairs (?) (no such thing), casualties not crass, in any case, in other words, since I didnt play basketball (too short) and didn't want to run outdoor track I had nothing to do all winter but enjoy my new friends, the classes too, a whole mess of idle stuff that can be summed up in a few succinct cameo sentences in a paragraph: as wit:

Weekends at Ray Olmsted's apartment with his parents and kid brother, in Yonkers, the affair with Betty there, skating on the Yonkers pond and a few kisses here and there. Sharpy Gimbel yelling 'Hi' from his convertible at the dance. Excited talks over scores with Izzy Carson in his West End Avenue apartment. A cigar given to me by a cigar manufacturer. New York Giants football games at Polo Grounds with Gene and his father. Central Park at dawn. Chuck Derounian the Armenian kid playing me old Bix records in Washington Heights. Hors d'oeuvres at Jake Kraft's on Fifth Avenue, incredibly thick rugs and huge marble statuettes and fragrance of coats in the hall. Walks in the blizzard across the Brooklyn Bridge, alone. Running down Fifth Avenue downtown pellmell with a small paralysed man in my arms, with . . . wait a minute, pushing a small paralysed man down lower Fifth Avenue in his wheelchair, taking him in my arms, putting him in the cab, folding in his wheelchair, he saying 'Thanks, that was a great run! I'm a music publisher, my name is Porter.'

(True.) (Cole Porter on a secret spree?)

Everybody sighing to kiss Babsy Schler who must be the ugliest bat on earth today by now. Interviewing Glen Miller backstage at the Paramount Theater for the school paper, Glen Miller saying 'Shit' Interviewing Count Basie in the Savoy Ballroom in Harlem, for the school paper, Count saying: 'I want quiet brass.' Hanging around lunchcarts hoping to meet Hemingway heroes. Lounging around with the Irish gang of Horace Mann, Hennessey, Gully Swift, O'Grady, with feet slightly stuck out and a certain accent. Same gang on street corner on Columbia campus when I visit Hennessey for weekends there, now with Jacky Cabot and others including one silent slender lad: William F. Buckley, Jr! Sunday mornings on Park Avenue looking out the Venetian blinds of David Knowles' bedroom, his parents away, his maid coming in with breakfast. Every one of them I went to their house. Dean John Goldthwaite introducing his son to me in front of the rose-covered granite cottage on HM campus, son turns out to be president of a giant airline today. Everybody in the school wants the two pretty girls in the office staff down in the lockers. Class photo Duluoz fails to show up, too busy somewhere. At a school play the Gerson twins come out of both ends of a box: both look alike: one of them later saw 'insects in the snow' in Red

China. Jimmy Winchel, pimply, playing the violin and chasing after girls all the way to the Riviera, it turned out, after which he had to charge to Brazil with two million. Jonathan Miller looking at me thru slitted eyes because of what his father said. Gully Swift playing pingpong. Reginald W. Klein putting on an English accent, saying he's going to be a poet. Mike Hennessey looking at me and saying 'Flazm.' Marty Churchill making extra money, tho rich, by walking an old invalid down upper Broadway every night at eight. Ray Olmsted combing his hair with Tyrone Power eyebrows. Jacob U. Gelsenheimer serious on the viola. S. Martin Gerber looking thru a microscope. Ern Salter patting his belly like comedian Jack E. Leonard. Biff Quinlan shaking his head at me. Irv Berg on the microphone. Joe A. Gold, later to be killed in the war, having me for weekend at his apartment on Riverside Drive, his two small older brothers discussing silk stocks. Bill Keresky looking at me and saying 'Schlazm.' Gene Mackstoll jerking down Broadway as tho being yanked at by the Invisible Man. Also looking at me and saying, 'Frazm.' Lionel Smart, eyes shining bright, making me listen to Lester Young on clarinet playing 'Way Down Yonder in New Orleans' and the other side, 'I Want a Little Girl.' Cy Zukove swimming in the pool with great athletic forward drive.

Not such a hot cameo. How about this? (I want to give you an exact but short picture of what it was like at that really remarkable school.) Because they were a bunch of wits. Now wits abound in Lowell too, wifey, like you know, but these are bigtown New York wits and to explain it:

Say, I do, that among the fantastic wits of this school Jimmy Winchel ranked practically number one. I was just an innocent New England athlete (well not so innocent, but of wit in the witty sense, yes) but I was suddenly thrown into what amounted to an academy of incunabular Milton Berles hundreds of them wise-cracking and ad libbing on all sides, in the classroom when possible, on the field, at recess, in the subway going home into downtown Manhattan, proper, over the phone at night, even years later in letters exchanged from college to college. We were all in stitches all the time. The chief claque of official huge wits was led by Bill Keresky, Gene Mackstoll, Marty Churchill (né Bernstein), Mike Hennessey, Gully Swift, Paul O'Grady and Ern Salter but when mention of Jimmy Winchel was made there fell a kind of stricken convulsion just at the thought of him. He was insanely witty. So much so that now, today, as I read about his recent escapade with the two million dollars I mentioned, I laugh, not because I think it's funny (and anyway Jimmy's paid it all back honestly, or tried) but because Jimmy is so funny, it's almost as tho he'd pulled this last fantastic joke to tear the funny-guys of HM apart for once and for all (in some dim way at the back of his mind when he absconded to Brazil I do seriously believe this to be true, God bless child even when he get old).

Prep school humor is always a little bit insular. At HM in that year there were three elements mainly involved: (1) A kind of Al Kelly doubletalk, 'Flazm,' 'Schmazm,' etc. (as I showed) used when you couldnt find the right word, the humour coming mainly from the particular adolescence of lip delivery (kid humor), and (2) saying 'mine' instead of 'me,' 'yours' instead of 'you,' 'his' instead of 'he,' 'His is going to write mine a letter' etc. in a completely madcap extension of phallic reference common among kids, and (3) using the names of classmates who were not 'wits' and were not 'athletes' but were rather obscure serious scholars behind their spectacles studying about Hérault de Séchelles and the Hortus Siccus and the Hindu Kush and the Manoeuvres Military and Louise de Quéroualles and the neuropathological *Spirochae pallidum* with Professor Lionel Greeting at dusk, and whose names, altho almost invariably hilarious in themselves (Bruno Golemus, Melvin Mandel, Otis Zimmerman, Randall Garstein, Matthew Gdansk), were infinitely more hilarious when you thought of their shabby pitiful demeanors and ridiculous obscurities about the campus and so amenably given to goof-off putdowns (sometimes little tiny weird fourth-formers with undeveloped masculinities, naturally, say, but already *strange*). So later I get letters at Columbia from Jimmy at Cornell in 1940 that go like this: Dear F———face, after all my flasimode talking to you etc. you must call her tonight and ask her when Dick's is coming into the city again and leap up to mine. So I'll see yours Saturday's. I'm coming into its this week's load . . . or in other words Dear Wang Load, how do you like this paper, I got so much of the Wang Load stuff that I will probably have to give it to my grandchildren to use for toilet paper. I'm really terribly sorry that I didnt write to yours sooner but mine was a little tired from overwork and I knew that yours wasnt so tired as mine so that if mine overexerted while writing to yours, yours might have

41

to also overexert and write to mine. Does yours get it? Mine does. How're Gussie Resbin, Minnie Donoff, Kittie Kolpitz, Mordecai Letterhandler, Ishmael Communevisch, Downey Coucle the Irish Tenor, and all the boys getting along? I heard that Gabe Irrgang, Andrew Lawrence Goldstein, Ted Dressman, Ray Flamm and you were really tearing your spheroids off playing football for Coach Lu Libble at Columbia, and that you and Mel Mandel and the Gerson brothers were really going to town' (these all scholars I'd never talked to, even, sort of expertise secret technicians studying in lower labs). 'Did you hear about the fellow who went to the doctor and said 'Doctor please look at my kidley' and the doctor said 'You mean your kidney dont you?' then the man said 'That's what I said diddle I?' . . . P.S. By the way, S. Martin Gerber sends his regards to all the boys back at HM including Joe Rappaport and Axel Finnkin.' And the letter's signed: 'J. Winchel, Alias Christian Goldberg.'

But just to show yours further, wifey, what it's like to be in that school, Bill Keresky was a classmate of Jimmy's at Cornell at the time (this is a year later but relevant to explaining the school in 1939) and tried to outdo Jimmy with the following letter: 'Dear Jack, how's everything at Columbia's? Have Hennessey and Mandel made the basketball team yet? Jerkit Winchel trades his '31 Chevy in for a '32 Windslammer so we've been riding ours around It's'hacas in style of late. It's been snowing up here and is as cold as a date in midwinter in Flushing. The seniors of the house had us shoveling snow and I almost froze it, I think next week might be initiation and mine is already begging for mercy's. We had our ends pounded off last week for excessive dubbing during the meal, without our frosh things on. It's so cold here I thought we could get out of wearing our frosh caps but I found out they have special winter fresh pulloffers that you must wear in winter. They probably even make you wear frosh things underneath when you have an affair with a coed's. Give my best to Flavius Fondle, Otis Outhouse, Duke Douche, Ann Enema, Schuyler Scrotum, Venus Venereal, Wanda Wantit, Schuyler Scuttle, Stephen Straddle, Scrag Scrotum, Terrence Tinkleman, Rod Railspitter, Flogg Itt, Vera Vajj, Pauline Parturient, Nessie Nightsoil, Messy Mingle, Olga Orgy and Phyllis Straddler. Write! Dont miss The Importance of Being Ernest's starring Reggie Klein and Irvie Sklar. P.S. Livia Lips, Tina Tip, Chad Chaff, Marmaduke Modess, Manny Monthly, Monty Mound,

Bea Between, Pierpont Pussnblood, Staunton Sterile, Charlotte Shriveled, Hank Hang, Eunice Underslung, Forrest Fieldcookie, Meadow Waffle, Terrence Tonguebath, Ray Roundtheworld and Flavious Fecal were all asking for you. P.P. S.S. Dont forget to drop a note to Apollo Goldfarb and Arapahoe Rappaport.' It was all moonlight on the lawn, J. D. Salinger middleclass Jewish livingrooms with the lights out and the futile teenage doubledate blind smooching in the park, all these kids who became financial wizards, restaurateurs of great renown, realtors, department store tycoons, scientists, here they are stalking around the halls of the school with incredible leers waiting like tigers to pounce on someone with a sleering joke, the latest, an academy of wits finally as I say.

CHAPTER 3

MAMMON

Mammon, n. The god of the world's leading religion. His chief temple is in the holy city of New York.

Ambrose Bierce

In Boston they ask, How much does he know?
In New York, How much is he worth?

Mark Twain

New York is the posthumous revenge of the Merchant of Venice.

Elbert Hubbard

Philip Hone (1780-1851) was a New York businessman, Whig leader, member of social and literary societies, and Mayor of the City between 1820 and 1824. After he finished his term of office he kept a diary for the remainder of his life which is an invaluable record of social and political developments in the city in the period leading up to the Civil War.

WALL STREET, 1835

October 14. – The gambling in stocks in Wall street has arrived at such a pitch, and the sudden reverses of fortune are so frequent, that it is a matter of every-day intelligence that some unlucky rascal has lost other people's money to a large amount, and run away, or been caught and consigned to the hands of justice. It is one taken from the mass; there is some swearing among the losers, some regret on the part of the immediate friends of the defaulter, but the chasm on the face of society which his detection and removal occasions is filled up in a day or two. They go to work again to cheat each other, and the catastrophe of Monday is forgotten by Saturday night.

The prolific writer of short stories who called himself O. Henry (actually W. S. Porter, 1862-1910) first came to New York in 1902. The city provided the settings and characters for many of his popular stories and indeed the title of one of his best collections, The Four Million, *who are, of course, the inhabitants of his adopted home.*

MAMMON AND THE ARCHER

Old Anthony Rockwall, retired manufacturer and proprietor of Rockwall's Eureka Soap, looked out of the library window of his Fifth Avenue mansion and grinned. His neighbor to the right – the aristocratic clubman, G. Van Schuylight Suffolk-Jones – came out to his waiting motor-car, wrinkling a contumelious nostril, as usual, at the Italian renaissance sculpture of the soap palace's front elevation.

'Stuck-up old statuette of nothing doing!' commented the ex-Soap King. 'The Eden Musee'll get that old frozen Nesselrode yet if he don't watch out. I'll have this house painted red, white, and blue next summer and see if that'll make his Dutch nose turn up any higher.'

And then Anthony Rockwall, who never cared for bells, went to the door of his library and shouted 'Mike!' in the same voice that had once chipped off pieces of the welkin on the Kansas prairies.

'Tell my son,' said Anthony to the answering menial, 'to come in here before he leaves the house.'

When young Rockwall entered the library the old man laid aside his newspaper, looked at him with a kindly grimness on his big, smooth, ruddy countenance, rumpled his mop of white hair with one hand, and rattled the keys in his pocket with the other.

'Richard,' said Anthony Rockwall, 'what do you pay for the soap that you use?'

Richard, only six months home from college, was startled a little. He had not yet taken the measure of this sire of his, who was as full of unexpectednesses as a girl at her first party.

'Six dollars a dozen, I think, dad.'

'And your clothes?'

'I suppose about sixty dollars, as a rule.'

'You're a gentleman,' said Anthony, decidedly. 'I've heard of these young bloods spending $24 a dozen for soap, and going over the hundred mark for clothes. You've got as much money to waste as any of 'em, and yet you stick to what's decent and moderate. Now I use the old Eureka – not only for sentiment, but it's the purest soap made. Whenever you pay more than ten cents a cake for soap you buy bad perfumes and labels. But fifty cents is doing very well for a young man in your generation, position, and condition. As I said, you're a gentleman. They say it takes three generations to make one. They're off. Money'll do it as slick as soap grease. It's made you one. By hokey – it's almost made one of me. I'm nearly as impolite and disagreeable and ill-mannered as these two old Knickerbocker gents on each side of me that can't sleep of nights because I bought in between 'em.'

'There are some things that money can't accomplish,' remarked young Rockwall, rather gloomily.

'Now, don't say that,' said old Anthony, shocked. 'I bet my money on money every time. I've been through the encyclopædia down to Y looking for something you can't buy with it; and I expect to have to take up the appendix next week. I'm for money against the field. Tell me something money won't buy.'

'For one thing,' answered Richard, rankling a little, 'it won't buy one into the exclusive circles of society.'

'Oho! won't it?' thundered the champion of the root of evil. 'You tell me where your exclusive circles would be if the first Astor hadn't had the money to pay for his steerage passage over?'

Richard sighed.

'And that's what I was coming to,' said the old man, less boisterously. 'That's why I asked you to come in. There's something going wrong with you, boy. I've been noticing it for two weeks. Out with it. I guess I could lay my hands on eleven millions within twenty-four hours, besides the real estate. If it's your liver, there's the *Rambler* down in the bay, coaled, and ready to steam down to the Bahamas in two days.'

'Not a bad guess, dad; you haven't missed it far.'

'Ah,' said Anthony, keenly; 'what's her name?'

Richard began to walk up and down the library floor. There was enough comradeship and sympathy in this crude old father of his to draw confidence.

'Why don't you ask her?' demanded old Anthony. 'She'll jump at you. You've got the money and the looks and you're a decent boy. Your hands are clean. You've got no Eureka soap on 'em. You've been to college, but she'll overlook that.'

'I haven't had a chance,' said Richard.

'Make one,' said Anthony. 'Take her for a walk in the park, or

48

a straw ride, or walk home with her from church. Chance! Pshaw!'

'You don't know the social mill, dad. She's part of the stream that turns it. Every hour and minute of her time is arranged for days in advance. I must have that girl, dad, or this town is a blackjack swamp forevermore. And I can't write it – I can't do that.'

'Tut!' said the old man. 'Do you mean to tell me that with all the money I've got you can't get an hour or two of a girl's time for yourself?'

'I've put it off too late. She's going to sail for Europe at noon day after to-morrow for a two years' stay. I'm to see her alone to-morrow evening for a few minutes. She's at Larchmont now at her aunt's. I can't go there. But I'm allowed to meet her with a cab at the Grand Central Station to-morrow evening at the 8.30 train. We drive down Broadway to Wallack's at a gallop, where her mother and a box party will be waiting for us in the lobby. Do you think she would listen to a declaration from me during that six or eight minutes under those circumstances? No. And what chance would I have in the theatre or afterward? None. No, dad, this is one tangle that your money can't unravel. We can't buy one minute of time with cash; if we could, rich people would live longer. There's no hope of getting a talk with Miss Lantry before she sails.'

'All right, Richard, my boy,' said old Anthony, cheerfully. 'You may run along down to your club now. I'm glad it ain't your liver. But don't forget to burn a few punk sticks in the joss house to the great god Mazuma from time to time. You say money won't buy time? Well, of course, you can't order eternity wrapped up and delivered at your residence for a price, but I've seen Father Time get pretty bad stone bruises on his heels when he walked through the gold diggings.'

That night came Aunt Ellen, gentle, sentimental, wrinkled, sighing, oppressed by wealth, in to brother Anthony at his evening paper, and began discourse on the subject of lovers' woes.

'He told me all about it,' said brother Anthony, yawning. 'I told him my bank account was at his service. And then he began to knock money. Said money couldn't help. Said the rules of society couldn't be bucked for a yard by a team of ten-millionaires.'

'Oh, Anthony,' sighed Aunt Ellen, 'I wish you would not think so much of money. Wealth is nothing where a true affection is concerned. Love is all-powerful. If he only had spoken earlier! She could not have refused our Richard. But now I fear it is too late. He will have no opportunity to address her. All your gold cannot bring happiness to your son.'

At eight o'clock the next evening Aunt Ellen took a quaint old gold ring from a moth-eaten case and gave it to Richard.

'Wear it to-night, nephew,' she begged. 'Your mother gave it to me. Good luck in love she said it brought. She asked me to give it to you when you had found the one you loved.'

Young Rockwall took the ring reverently and tried it on his smallest finger. It slipped as far as the second joint and stopped. He took it off and stuffed it into his vest pocket, after the manner of man. And then he 'phoned for his cab.

At the station he captured Miss Lantry out of the gadding mob at eight thirty-two.

'We mustn't keep mamma and the other waiting,' said she.

'To Wallack's Theatre as fast as you can drive!' said Richard loyally.

They whirled up Forty-second to Broadway, and then down the white-starred lane that leads from the soft meadows of sunset to the rocky hills of morning.

At Thirty-fourth Street young Richard quickly thrust up the trap and ordered the cabman to stop.

'I've dropped a ring,' he apologized, as he climbed out. 'It was my mother's, and I'd hate to lose it. I won't detain you a minute — I saw where it fell.'

In less than a minute he was back in the cab with the ring.

But within that minute a crosstown car had stopped directly in front of the cab. The cabman tried to pass to the left, but a heavy express wagon cut him off. He tried the right, and had to back away from a furniture van that had no business to be there. He tried to back out, but dropped his reins and swore dutifully. He was blockaded in a tangled mess of vehicles and horses.

One of those street blockades had occurred that sometimes tie up commerce and movement quite suddenly in the big city.

'Why don't you drive on?' said Miss Lantry, impatiently. 'We'll be late.'

Richard stood up in the cab and looked around. He saw a congested flood of wagons, trucks, cabs, vans, and street cars filling the vast space where Broadway, Sixth Avenue, and Thirty-fourth Street cross one another as a twenty-six inch maiden fills her twenty-two inch girdle. And still from all the cross streets they were hurrying and rattling toward the converging point at full speed, and hurling themselves into the struggling mass, locking wheels and adding their drivers' imprecations to the clamour. The entire traffic of Manhattan seemed to have jammed itself around them. The oldest New Yorker among the thousands of spectators that lined the sidewalks had not witnessed a street blockade of the proportions of this one.

'I'm very sorry,' said Richard, as he resumed his seat, 'but it looks as if we are stuck. They won't get this jumble loosened up in an hour. It was my fault. If I hadn't dropped the ring we——'

'Let me see the ring,' said Miss Lantry. 'Now that it can't be helped, I don't care. I think theatres are stupid, anyway.'

At 11 o'clock that night somebody tapped lightly on Anthony Rockwall's door.

'Come in,' shouted Anthony, who was in a red dressing-gown, reading a book of piratical adventures.

Somebody was Aunt Ellen, looking like a gray-haired angel that had been left on earth by mistake.

'They're engaged, Anthony,' she said, softly. 'She has promised to marry our Richard. On their way to the theatre there was a street blockade, and it was two hours before their cab could get out of it.

'And oh, brother Anthony, don't ever boast of the power of money again. A little emblem of true love – a little ring that symbolized unending and unmercenary affection – was the cause of our Richard finding his happiness. He dropped it in the street, and got out to recover it. And before they could continue the blockade occurred. He spoke to his love and won her there while the cab was hemmed in. Money is dross compared with true love, Anthony.'

'All right,' said old Anthony. 'I'm glad the boy has got what he wanted. I told him I wouldn't spare any expense in the matter if——'

'But, brother Anthony, what good could your money have done?'

'Sister,' said Anthony Rockwall, 'I've got my pirate in a devil of a scrape. His ship has just been scuttled, and he's too good a judge of the value of money to let drown. I wish you would let me go on with this chapter.'

51

The story should end here. I wish it would as heartily as you who read it wish it did. But we must go to the bottom of the well for truth.

The next day a person with red hands and a blue polka-dot necktie, who called himself Kelly, called at Anthony Rockwall's house, and was at once received in the library.

'Well,' said Anthony, reaching for his checkbook, 'it was a good bilin' of soap. Let's see – you had $5,000 in cash.'

'I paid out $300 more of my own,' said Kelly. 'I had to go a little above the estimate. I got the express wagons and cabs mostly for $5; but the trucks and two-horse teams mostly raised me to $10. The motormen wanted $10, and some of the loaded teams $20. The cops struck me hardest – $50 I paid two, and the rest $20 and $25. But didn't it work beautiful, Mr. Rockwall? I'm glad William A. Brady wasn't onto that little outdoor vehicle mob scene. I wouldn't want William to break his heart with jealousy. And never a rehearsal, either! The boys was on time to the fraction of a second. It was two hours before a snake could get below Greeley's statue.'

'Thirteen hundred – there you are, Kelly,' said Anthony, tearing off a check. 'Your thousand, and the $300 you were out. You don't despise money, do you, Kelly?'

'Me?' said Kelly. 'I can't lick the man that invented poverty.'

Anthony called Kelly when he was at the door.

'You didn't notice,' said he, 'anywhere in the tie-up, a kind of a fat boy without any clothes on shooting arrows around with a bow, did you?'

'Why, no,' said Kelly, mystified. 'I didn't. If he was like you say, maybe the cops pinched him before I got there.'

'I thought the little rascal wouldn't be on hand,' chuckled Anthony. 'Good-bye, Kelly.'

For Maxim Gorki New York was The City of the Yellow Devil, *by which he meant gold.*

THE YELLOW DEVIL

People hurry to and fro on the pavements, in every direction the streets take. They are sucked up by the deep pores in the stone walls. The exultant rumble of iron, the loud piercing whine of electricity, the clatter of work on some new steel construction or on new walls of stone, drown out human voices as a storm at sea drowns the cries of the birds.

The people's faces wear an expression of immobile calm; not one of them, apparently, is aware of his misfortune in being the slave of life, nourishment for the city monster. In their pitiable arrogance they imagine themselves to be the masters of their fate; consciousness of their independence gleams occasionally in their eyes, but clearly they do not understand that this is only the independence of the axe in the carpenter's hand, the hammer in the smith's hand, the brick in the hand of that unseen bricklayer, who, with a sly chuckle, is building one vast but cramping prison for all. There are many virile faces among them, but in each face, one notices the teeth first of all. Inner freedom, the freedom of the spirit does not shine in these people's eyes. And their freedomless energy reminds one of the cold gleam of a knife that has not yet been blunted. It is the freedom of blind tools in the hands of the Yellow Devil – Gold.

This is the first time I have seen so monstrous a city, and never before have people seemed to me so insignificant, so enslaved. At the same time nowhere have I met people so tragicomically satisfied with themselves as are these in this voracious and filthy stomach of the glutton, who has grown into an imbecile from greed and, with the wild bellowing of an animal, devours brains and nerves. . .

John Dos Passos (1896-1970), though born in Chicago, chose New York as the scene – and theme – of his first major work, Manhattan Transfer, *published in 1925. Composed of hundreds of separate episodes and characters, the book is a sprawling portrait of life in the city in the years before the First World War.*

FAILURE

Noon on Union Square. Selling out. Must vacate. WE HAVE MADE A TERRIBLE MISTAKE. Kneeling on the dusty asphalt little boys shine shoes lowshoes tans buttonshoes oxfords. The sun shines like a dandelion on the toe of each new-shined shoe. Right this way buddy, mister miss maam at the back of the store our new line of fancy tweeds highest value lowest price . . . Gents, misses, ladies, cutrate . . . WE HAVE MADE A TERRIBLE MISTAKE. Must vacate.

Noon sunlight spirals dimly into the chopsuey joint. Muted music spirals Hindustan. He eats fooyong, she eats chowmein. They dance with their mouths full, slim blue jumper squeezed to black slick suit, peroxide curls against black slick hair.

Down Fourteenth Street, Glory Glory comes the Army, striding lasses, Glory Glory four abreast, the rotund shining, navy blue, Salvation Army band.

Highest value, lowest price. Must vacate. WE HAVE MADE A TERRIBLE MISTAKE. Must vacate.

Federico García Lorca, in his lecture on Poet in New York, *described Wall Street in the aftermath of the Great Crash of 1929.*

THE CRASH

The terrible, cold, cruel part is Wall Street. Rivers of gold flow there from all over the earth, and death comes with it. There as nowhere else you feel a total absence of the spirit: herds of men who cannot count past three, herds more who cannot get past six, scorn for pure science, and demoniacal respect for the present. And the terrible thing is that the crowd who fills the street believes that the world will always be the same, and that it is their duty to move the huge machine day and night forever. The perfect result of a Protestant morality that I, as a (thank God) typical Spaniard, found unnerving. I was lucky enough to see with my own eyes the recent crash, where they lost various billions of dollars, a rabble of dead money that slid off into the sea, and never as then, amid suicides, hysteria, and groups of fainters, have I felt the sensation of real death, death without hope, death that is nothing but rottenness, for the spectacle was terrifying but devoid of greatness. And I, who come from a country where, as the great poet Unamuno said, 'at night the earth climbs to the sky,' I felt something like a divine urge to bombard that whole shadowy defile where ambulances collected suicides whose hands were full of rings.

That is why I included this dance of death. The typical African mask, death which is truly dead, without angels or 'resurrexit'; death as far removed from the spirit, as barbarous and primitive as the United States, which has never fought, and never will fight for heaven.

Mary McCarthy, born in 1912, arrived in New York after graduating from Vassar in 1933. She became a well-known critic and novelist and in 1963 published The Group, *a novel recreating the feelings and fortunes of a number of young women making their way in the city in the 1930's.*

TECHNOCRACY

Last night, he had explained technocracy to Dottie, to show her there was nothing to fear from the future, if it was managed with scientific intelligence. In an economy of plenty and leisure, which the machine had already made feasible, everybody would only have to work a few hours a day. It was through such an economy that his class, the class of artists and technicians, would come naturally to the top; the homage people paid to money today would be paid in the future to the engineers and contrivers of leisure-time activities. More leisure meant more time for art and culture. Dottie wanted to know what would happen to the capitalists (her father was in the import business), and Kay looked inquiringly at Harald. 'Capital will blend into government,' said Harald. 'After a brief struggle. That's what we're witnessing now. The administrator, who's just a big-scale technician, will replace the capitalist in industry. Individual ownership is becoming obsolete; the administrators are running the show.' 'Take Robert Moses,' put in Kay. 'He's transforming the whole face of New York with his wonderful new parkways and playgrounds.' And she urged Dottie to go to Jones Beach, which was an inspiring example, she really felt this herself, of planning on a large scale for leisure. 'Everybody from Oyster Bay,' she added, 'drives over there now to swim. It's quite the thing to do, instead of swimming at a club.' Private enterprise, suggested Harald, still had a part to play, if it had breadth of vision. Radio City, where he had worked for a while as a stage manager's assistant, was an example of civic planning, undertaken by enlightened capitalists, the Rockefellers. Kay brought in the

55

Modern Museum, which had Rockefeller backing too. New York, she honestly thought, was experiencing a new Renaissance, with the new Medicis competing with public ownership to create a modern Florence. You could see it even in Macy's, agreed Harald, where enlightened merchant-Jews, the Strauses, were training a corps of upper-middle-class technicians, like Kay, to make the store into something more than a business, something closer to a civic centre or permanent fairgrounds, with educational exhibits, like the old Crystal Palace. Then Kay talked about the smart new renovated tenements in the Fifties and Eighties, along the East River, black with white trim and white Venetian blinds; they were still another example of intelligent planning by capital! Vincent Astor had done them. Of course, the rents were rather high, but look at what you got: views of the river just as good as from Sutton Place mansions, sometimes a garden, the Venetian blinds, like the old jalousies but modernized, and completely up-to-date kitchens. When you thought that they had just been eyesores, probably full of vermin and unsanitary hall toilets, till the Astor interests fixed them up! And other landlords were following their example, turning old blocks of barracky tenements into compact apartment buildings four and five stories high, with central courts planted with grass and shrubs and two- and three-room apartments for young people — some with fireplaces and built-in bookcases and all with brand-new plumbing and stove and refrigerator.

CHAPTER 4

CITY OF ORGIES

Walt Whitman added this poem to Leaves of Grass *in 1867.*

CITY OF ORGIES

City of orgies, walks and joys,
City whom that I have lived and sung in your midst will one day
    make you illustrious,
Not the pageants of you, not your shifting tableaus, your
    spectacles, repay me,
Not the interminable rows of your houses, nor the ships at the
    wharves,
Nor the processions in the streets, nor the bright windows with
    goods in them,
Nor to converse with learn'd persons, or bear my share in the
    soiree or feast;
Not those, but as I pass O Manhattan, your frequent and swift
    flash of eyes offering me love,
Offering response to my own – these repay me,
Lovers, continual lovers, only repay me.

Moshe Leib Halpern (1886-1932), an immigrant from Eastern Europe,
became one of the major Yiddish poets of the century while earning his living
as a waiter, laborer, and jack-of-all-trades. He died penniless in the
Bronx but his poems were already widely known among the Jewish masses of
New York.

SONG: WEEKEND'S OVER

There in the shadowy, dank hall
Right alongside the ground-floor stair—
A weeping girl, attended by
A grimy hand in the mussed-up hair.
——A little love in big Manhattan.

The hair—a whiff of some cheap rinse
The hand—hard, stiff and leathery
Two equal lovers, for whom this is
As good as it'll ever be.
——A little love in big Manhattan.

It's strange to listen to two people
Standing there in the dark, unheard;
Why doesn't Sammy say a word?
Why doesn't Bessie say a word?
——A little love in big Manhattan.

They may be talking, but it's all
Blanketed by the howl, instead,
From a million iron fire escapes
And all the dark ceilings overhead.
——A little love in big Manhattan.

Ceilings on ceilings and beds over beds;
Steamy air, wrapped in smoking shrouds;
From the top floor down, a chasm falls;
From above, acres open to the clouds.
——A little love in big Manhattan.

O huge night city, such grim strangeness
Wraps you up in the darkness here!
Man and wife sleep by the million
Like drunks all bloated up with beer.
——A little love in big Manhattan.

Like monkeys in the trees, the children
Hang in their fire escapes, asleep;
Soot drifts down from above their heads,
Dropped by the moon, a chimney sweep.
——A little love in big Manhattan.

And the girl Bessie knows 'from nothing'
And Sammy, too, with his open mouth,
And Monday swims up before your eyes,
A desert of dead miles toward the south.
——A little love in big Manhattan.

And even Bessie's poor old mother
No longer asks, 'Where is that kid?'
It doesn't matter that black hair
Has all been bleached to blonde and red.
——A little love in big Manhattan.

59

It isn't that he's ill, the sad one
Who contemplates these things at night;
But sick of his own sadness only,
He lies and broods, his pipe alight.
——A little love in big Manhattan.

Translated by John Hollander

S. J. Perelman (1904-1979) was born in Brooklyn. A popular comic writer, satirist, screen writer, and stylist, he was a regular contributor to the New Yorker *for over forty-five years.*

GOODBYE BROADWAY, HELLO MR. SQUARE

When I was one-and-twenty, to paraphrase A. E. Housman a trifle, I heard a wise man say, 'Hey, how's about we nip down to New York for a week and live it up? I've got a scheme whereby it won't cost us a red cent!' The wise man, like myself a senior at Brown and an accomplished freeloader, was one Conrad Portnoy, business manager on the university's comic magazine of which I was editor, and the words were scarcely out of his mouth before the two of us were racing toward the Providence depot, our cheeks aflame with anticipation. New York! The Gay White Way! Visions of Dionysiac revels danced in our heads, bachelor suppers whereat naked actresses erupted from pies as we reeled around quaffing jeroboams of champagne. Reared in New England, Portnoy and I had only the foggiest conception of Gotham, as we persisted in calling it, but on two points we were unshakable: the plethora of chorus girls there and their inability to resist a couple of boulevardiers from Little Rhody. The gimmick the trip was predicated on was simplicity itself, and not at all larcenous. Several New York hotels had tendered our periodical due bills – vouchers, that is to say, in exchange for ads – entitling us to free lodging. Meals, regrettably, were excepted, but with a deluge of champagne impending, considerations of food seemed crass in the extreme. The prospect was dizzying, and it was with difficulty that I restrained Portnoy at New London from telegraphing Flo Ziegfeld that a pair of big butter-and-egg men were hell-bent for the Main Stem.

Within two days of our arrival, the rosy dreams had evaporated, leaving two haggard, anxiety-ridden tinhorns with shrunken wallets. Not a single dimpled darling had tossed us her garter; despite all our nudging and leering, no bellboy could direct us to a midnight orgy, however paltry. Between tips, subway fares and Spartan meals at a cafeteria run by a Spartan who watched us vigilantly, the pitiful store of cash we shared was fast dwindling, and the smallest indulgence – a milk shake or an extra pack of Fatimas – would have pauperized us. The one thing we could afford to be prodigal with was hotel linen. In a frantic effort to use up our due bills, we switched daily from the Astor to the Vanderbilt to the Martinique, lolling in bridal chambers and suites of Roman magnificence, and such was the superfluity of towels that we had to stay up half the night taking showers, wiping our shoes, and wantonly crumpling the remainder. Ultimately, an unrelieved five-day diet of crullers and coffee exacted its toll: both of us broke down with scurvy. Ingloriously we slunk back to Rhode Island, hitching rides in whatever vehicles we could. The last lap, in a truck laden with poultry, was especially humiliating, since the driver, another Spartan named Steve Magnanimos, insisted on delivering us, plastered with chicken feathers, directly to the campus.

It was small wonder, hence, that Portnoy and I reacted with bitterness the rest of the academic year whenever anybody extolled metropolitan life, but as graduation neared, our memories took on a roseate glow and we became increasingly sentimental about it. New York was the center of the universe, we declared flatly; we grew lyrical enumerating its advantages social, financial, and cultural, its profusion of concerts, theatres, and museums. (We carefully omitted any reference to chorus girls and orgies, feeling that only an adolescent cared about such trivialities.) The upshot of these dithyrambs was that on a sweltering morning in mid-July Portnoy and I once more emerged from Grand Central, this time freighted with all our wordly possessions, and drawing a deep breath, we plunged into the maelstrom.

Our first bivouac was the front parlour of a rooming house on West Twelfth Street operated by a Southern gentlewoman in reduced circumstances. Mrs. Sutphin, who sweetly importuned us to call her Jasmine, derived from Natchez and had an accent clotted with moonlight and magnolias. She wore heavy *maquillage*

61

around her eyes, a thick protective coat of Djer-Kiss face powder, and twin spots of rouge on her cheekbones; and the clash of bracelets as she moved sounded like Mosby's cavalry unsheathing their sabres for a charge. The room was equally dramatic, a dim cavern filled by three walnut armoires, massive twin bedsteads, and a Brobdingnagian pier glass. Between the velvet-draped windows stood a stuffed baby giraffe eleven feet in height, the base of whose neck had been weighted so that it swung freely at the slightest touch. Portnoy, by now a salesman of direct-mail advertising, was anesthetic to the pad, being absent all day, but I was an aspiring cartoonist, and my attempts to be waggish in the dark, faced with a giraffe shaking its head in constant negation, inevitably brought on melancholia. Luckily for me, Mrs. Sutphin saved my equilibrium by marrying a chiropodist who had rejuvenated her feet and who needed the premises for an office.

Over the next few months, my roommate and I tenanted a series of cheerless dovecotes around Greenwich Village made doubly desolate by his inability to cling to a job. Successively clerk in a brokerage house, cashier in a bankrupt tearoom, night watchman for an embalmer, and pool hustler, he finally forsook the hurly-burly of Manhattan for a Cleveland insurance firm. With his departure, my long-smoldering passion for a proper studio burst into flame. After a widespread search, I settled on a cozy *pied-à-terre*, five flights up and boasting its own skylight, a stone's throw from Jefferson Market Court. Having shrouded everything I could reach in monk's cloth, including the gas meter, I painted the bathroom walls black and the woodwork Chinese red, stuck half a dozen wax tapers in candle drippings, and impregnated the whole place with incense. The female callers I hoped to ensnare with this erotic décor reacted in unexpected fashion. Most of them dissolved into shrieks of helpless laughter; the rest assumed an air of arctic dignity and when, flushed with muscatel, I made romantic overtures, savagely fended me off with their parasols. The lacerations to my ego were such that it was months before I again dared essay the role of Don Juan.

New York baked under a blanket of heat that August, and reporters in quest of feature material were frying eggs on the sidewalks as I jubilantly packed my bags for a six-week vacation on Fire Island. I had sublet the studio to two decorous young chaps of good family – I.B.M. statisticians, they glibly assured me – who just wanted a quiet haven where they could listen to Mozart and study the Analects of Confucius. To demand references or surety from such paragons was unthinkable; we exchanged warm handclasps and vowed to attend Carnegie Hall concerts, lectures on flower arrangement, and classes in Dalcroze eurythmics together on my return. Three weeks later, a hysterical telegram from my landlord summoned me back to the mainland. The lessees had flown, and with them my bedding, utensils, curtains and Capehart. Some forerunner of Jackson Pollock had stippled the walls with ketchup and scrawled in lipstick a doggerel verse hymning the charms of Lya de Putti. In the center of the floor, a cherry-nosed vagrant the image of Popeye crouched over a bed of glowing coals, heating a can of Sterno and plucking somberly at a ukulele.

It was a crucial moment, the sort that exercises a profound effect on one's entire future. I felt an overwhelming need to cushion my head on somebody's shoulder and sob aloud, but since my landlord showed no disposition to cuddle, I fell back on the next-best person – a bold-eyed, willowy brunette who had been scanning me as a matrimonial prospect for some time. Scarcely had she sponged away my tears than the silvery peal of wedding bells assailed my ears, and I discovered I was a benedict. Other than her sterling self, my wife's sole contribution to the union was a piece of hard-nosed advice – viz., that I break my lease and skip. It took two years to pay off the landlord, during which time we honeymooned in a basement flat where I contracted a lifelong case of sciatica.

On the northwest corner of Washington Square, hard by the former Russian Embassy, there stood in those days a gracious five-storied mansion of rose-colored brick. Every once in a while a silver-haired doorman would totter forth supporting some old dragon in caracul or a palsied industrialist, and obsequiously hand them into a 1910 Panhard cabriolet. The only qualifications for residence in this landmark were a six-generation listing in the Social Register, a diploma from Groton or Miss Hewitt's classes, and eleven million dollars. How two parvenus like us ever wheedled a foothold there escapes me, but by strict adherence to a diet of fatback, corn pone and collards, we managed to scrape together the rent each month, if not to achieve social equality with the inmates. Among my fondest memories of the house was a midnight encounter in the Square with e.e. cummings, that most gifted of poets. I was schlepping a half-grown beagle around the park of a subzero evening and getting pretty well teed off with dogdom when I saw cummings headed toward me, plainly immersed in thought. Thinking to safeguard his privacy, I had just started to carom off when he hailed me.

'Look at that!' he said, gesturing theatrically toward three windows aglow in our building. 'Isn't it fantastic?'

'What do you mean?' I asked.

'Why, the drama being enacted up there,' he exclaimed. 'Can't you visualize it – the drunken brute of a husband, the wife spewing out her venom, the ferocity that only George Grosz can portray? I see the man suddenly overcome by homicidal mania – he snatches up a carving knife, the two of them grapple, the knife draws nearer and nearer to her breast, and then, with a convulsive, twisting stab—'

'Hold on there, bub,' I interrupted. 'If you're really so concerned, I can tell you what's cooking up there. A woman in her stocking feet is about to eat a bagel with cream cheese.'

'And how would you know that, pray?' he inquired with Olympian scorn.

'Because it's my apartment, wise guy,' I retorted.

'That's what I meant,' said cummings triumphantly. 'Isn't it fantastic?' He turned on his heel and, head cocked at a noble angle, strode off into the shadows.

We might have dwelt on forever in this Henry Jamesian milieu, a pair of musty patricians subsisting on bagels, but for a casual real-estate ad in the Sunday *Times*. Thirty-six hours after I read it, the czarevna and I were standing transfixed on a Pennsylvania hilltop, listening to a foxy-nosed agent rhapsodize about the countryside around us. So abundant was wildlife in the district, he told us emotionally, that rabbits, pheasants, squirrels and even deer leaped straight into the cook pot sprinkling themselves with salt and pepper. In these lush pastures one could grow his own tobacco, cobble his shoes with tough, fragrant birchbark. He painted a pastoral of my wife bottling raspberry jam and humming contentedly while I snoozed in a hammock amid barns bursting with alfalfa. My glasses misted over at the colored lantern slides flashing before me – the sleigh rides, Halloween parties, sugaring off, sugaring on, bringing in the Yule log. A fortnight later, in a simple ceremony at the county courthouse, two blushing innocents were united for all time, irretrievably and indissolubly, to fourscore and seven acres of the Keystone State.

And so ended my love affair with New York, intoxicating chameleon enchantress I worshipped this side of idolatry from youth. I knew her every mood, every foible; with the merest effort, I can recapture her unique, indefinable bouquet of monoxide, roast chestnuts and old landladies. Sometimes, in moments of nostalgia, I long to be trampled on again in the subway crush, to be spurned by headwaiters, fleeced by tradesmen and iced by theatre brokers. Ah, well, someday I suppose I will – but not as long as *I* can help it, Charlie.

Grace Paley, born in New York City in 1922, has continued to live in and write about the city all her life. This story is from The Little Disturbances of Man, *published in 1959.*

THE CONTEST

Up early or late, it never matters, the day gets away from me. Summer or winter, the shade of trees or their hard shadow, I never get into my Rice Krispies till noon.

I am ambitious, but it's a long-range thing with me. I have my confidential sights on a star, but there's half a lifetime to get to it. Meanwhile I keep my eyes open and am well dressed.

I told the examining psychiatrist for the Army: yes, I like girls. And I do. Not my sister – a pimp's dream. But girls, slim and tender or really stacked, dark brown at their centers, smeared by time. Not my mother, who should've stayed in Freud. I *have* got a sense of humor.

My last girl was Jewish, which is often a warm kind of girl, concerned about food intake and employability. They don't like you to work too hard, I understand, until you're hooked and then, you bastard, sweat!

A medium girl, size twelve, a clay pot with handles – she could be grasped. I met her in the rain outside some cultural activity at Cooper Union or Washington Irving High School. She had no umbrella and I did, so I walked her home to my house. There she remained for several hours, a yawning cavity, half asleep. The rain rained on the ailanthus tree outside my window, the wind rattled the shutters of my old-fashioned window, and I took my

65

time making coffee and carving an ounce of pound cake. I don't believe in force and I would have waited, but her loneliness was very great.

We had quite a nice time for a few weeks. She brought rolls and bagels from wherever the stuff can still be requisitioned. On Sundays she'd come out of Brooklyn with a chicken to roast. She thought I was too skinny. I am, but girls like it. If you're fat, they can see immediately that you'll never need their unique talent for warmth.

Spring came. She said: 'Where are we going?' In just those words! Now I have met this attitude before. Apparently, for most women good food and fun for all are too much of a good thing.

The sun absorbed July and she said it again. 'Freddy, if we're not going anywhere, I'm not going along any more.' We were beach-driven those windy Sundays: her mother must have told her what to say. She said it with such imprisoned conviction.

One Friday night in September I came home from an unlucky party. All the faces had been strange. There were no extra girls, and after some muted conversation with the glorious properties of other men, I felt terrible and went home.

In an armchair, looking at an *Art News* full of Dutchmen who had lived eighty years in forty, was Dorothy. And by her side an overnight case. I could hardly see her face when she stood to greet me, but she made tea first and steamed some of my ardor into the damp night.

'Listen, Freddy,' she said. 'I told my mother I was visiting Leona in Washington for two days and I fixed it with Leona. Everyone'll cover me' – pouring tea and producing seeded tarts from some secret Flatbush Avenue bakery – all this to change the course of a man's appetite and enable conversation to go forward.

'No, listen, Freddy, you don't take yourself seriously, and that's the reason you can't take anything else – a job, or a – a relationship – seriously. . . Freddy, you don't listen. You'll laugh, but you're very barbaric. You live at your nerve ends. If you're near a radio, you listen to music; if you're near an open icebox, you stuff yourself; if a girl is within ten feet of you, you have her stripped and on the spit.'

'Now, Dotty, don't be so graphic,' I said. 'Every man is his own rotisserie.'

What a nice girl! Say something vulgar and she'd suddenly be all over me, blushing bitterly, glad that the East River separated her from her mother. Poor girl, she was avid.

And she was giving. By Sunday night I had ended half a dozen conversations and nipped their moral judgments at the homiletic root. By Sunday night I had said I love you Dotty, twice. By Monday morning I realized the extent of my commitment and I don't mind saying it prevented my going to a job I had swung on Friday.

My impression of women is that they mean well but are driven to an obsessive end by greedy tradition. When Dot found out that I'd decided against that job (what job? a job, that's all) she took action. She returned my copy of *Nineteen Eighty-four* and said in a note that I could keep the six wineglasses her mother had lent me.

Well, I did miss her; you don't meet such wide-open kindness every day. She was no fool either. I'd say peasant wisdom is what she had. Not too much education. Her hair was long and dark. I had always seen it in neat little coiffures or reparably disarrayed, until that weekend.

It was staggering.

I missed her. And then I didn't have too much luck after that. Very little money to spend, and girls are primordial with intuition. There was one nice little married girl whose husband was puttering around in another postal zone, but her heart wasn't in it. I got some windy copy to do through my brother-in-law, a clean-cut croupier who is always crackling bank notes at family parties. Things picked up.

Out of my gasbag profits one weekend I was propelled into the Craggy-moor, a high-pressure resort, a star-studded haven with eleven hundred acres of golf course. When I returned, exhausted but modest, there she was, right in my parlor-floor front. With a few gasping, kind words and a modern gimmick, she hoped to breathe eternity into a mortal matter, love.

'Ah, Dotty,' I said, holding out my accepting arms. 'I'm always glad to see you.'

Of course she explained. 'I didn't come for that really, Freddy, I came to talk to you. We have a terrific chance to make some real money, if you'll only be serious a half hour. You're so clever, and you ought to direct yourself to something. God, you could live in the country. I mean, even if you kept living alone, you could have a decent place on a decent street instead of this dump.'

I kissed the tip of her nose. 'If you want to be very serious, Dot, let's get out and walk. Come on, get your coat on and tell me all about how to make money.'

She did. We walked out to the park and scattered autumn leaves for an hour. 'Now don't laugh, Freddy,' she told me. 'There's a Yiddish paper called *Morgenlicht*. It's running a contest: JEWS IN THE NEWS. Every day they put in a picture and two descriptions. You have to say who the three people are, add one more fact about them, and then send it in by midnight that night. It runs three months at least.'

'A hundred Jews in the news?' I said. 'What a tolerant country! So, Dot, what do you get for this useful information?'

'First prize, five thousand dollars and a trip to Israel. Also on return two days each in the three largest European capitals in the Free West.'

'Very nice,' I said. 'What's the idea, though? To uncover the ones that've been passing?'

'Freddy, why do you look at everything inside out? They're just proud of themselves, and they want to make Jews everywhere proud of their contribution to this country. Aren't you proud?'

'Woe to the crown of pride!'

'I don't care what you think. The point is, we know somebody who knows somebody on the paper – he writes a special article once a week – we don't know him really, but our family name is familiar to him. So we have a very good chance if we really do it. Look how smart you are, Freddy. I can't do it myself, Freddy, you have to help me. It's a thing I made up my mind to do anyway. If Dotty Wasserman really makes up her mind, it's practically done.'

I hadn't noticed this obstinacy in her character before. I had none in my own. Every weekday night after work she leaned thoughtfully on my desk, wearing for warmth a Harris-tweed jacket that ruined the nap of my arm. Somewhere out of doors a strand of copper in constant agitation carried information from her mother's Brooklyn phone to her ear.

Peering over her shoulder, I would sometimes discover a three-quarter view of a newsworthy Jew or a full view of a half Jew. The fraction did not interfere with the rules. They were glad to extract him and be proud.

The longer we worked the prouder Dotty became. Her face flushed, she'd raise her head from the hieroglyphics and read her own translation: 'A gray-headed gentleman very much respected; an intimate of Cabinet members; a true friend to a couple of

Presidents; often seen in the park, sitting on a bench.'

'Bernard Baruch!' I snapped.

And then a hard one: 'Has contributed to the easiness of interstate commerce; his creation is worth millions and was completed last year. Still he has time for Deborah, Susan, Judith, and Nancy, his four daughters.'

For this I smoked and guzzled a hot eggnog Dot had whipped up to give me strength and girth. I stared at the stove, the ceiling, my irritable shutters – then I said calmly: 'Chaim Pazzi – he's a bridge architect.' I never forget a name, no matter what type-face it appears in.

'Imagine it, Freddy. I didn't even know there was a Jew who had such accomplishment in that field.'

Actually, it sometimes took as much as an hour to attach a real name to a list of exaggerated attributes. When it took that long I couldn't help muttering, 'Well, we've uncovered another one. Put him on the list for Van 2.'

Dotty'd say sadly, 'I have to believe you're joking.'

Well, why do you think she liked me? All you little psychoanalyzed people, now say it at once, in a chorus: 'Because she is a masochist and you are a sadist.'

No. I was very good to her. And to all the love she gave me, I responded. And I kept all our appointments and called her on Fridays to remind her about Saturday, and when I had money I brought her flowers and once earrings and once a black brassière I saw advertised in the paper with some cleverly stitched windows for ventilation. I still have it. She never dared take it home.

But I will not be eaten by any woman.

My poor old mother died with a sizable chunk of me stuck in her gullet. I was in the Army at the time, but I understand her last words were: 'Introduce Freddy to Eleanor Farbstein.' Consider the nerve of that woman. Including me in a codicil. She left my sister to that ad man and culinary expert with a crew cut. She left my father to the commiseration of aunts, while me, her prize possession and the best piece of meat in the freezer of her heart, she left to Ellen Farbstein.

As a matter of fact, Dotty said it herself. 'I never went with a fellow who paid as much attention as you, Freddy. You're always there. I know if I'm lonesome or depressed all I have to do is call you and you'll meet me downtown and drop whatever you're doing. Don't think I don't appreciate it.'

The established truth is, I wasn't doing much. My brother-in-law could have kept me in clover, but he pretended I was a specialist in certain ornate copy infrequently called for by his concern. Therefore I was able to give my wit, energy, and attention to JEWS IN THE NEWS – *Morgenlicht*, the Morning Paper That Comes Out the Night Before.

And so we reached the end. Dot really believed we'd win. I was almost persuaded. Drinking hot chocolate and screwdrivers, we fantasied six weeks away.

We won.

I received a 9 a.m. phone call one midweek morning. 'Rise and shine, Frederick P. Sims. We did it. You see, whatever you really try to do, you can do.'

She quit work at noon and met me for lunch at an outdoor café in the Village, full of smiles and corrupt with pride. We ate very well and I had to hear the following information – part of it I'd suspected.

It was all in her name. Of course her mother had to get some. She had helped with the translation because Dotty had very little Yiddish actually (not to mention her worry about the security of her old age); and it was necessary, they had decided in midnight conference, to send some money to their old Aunt Lise, who had gotten out of Europe only ninety minutes before it was sealed forever and was now in Toronto among strangers, having lost most of her mind.

The trip abroad to Israel and three other European capitals was for two (2). They had to be married. If our papers could not include one that proved our conjunction by law, she would sail alone. Before I could make my accumulating statement, she shrieked oh! her mother was waiting in front of Lord and Taylor's. And she was off.

I smoked my miserable encrusted pipe and considered my position.

Meanwhile in another part of the city, wheels were moving, presses humming, and the next day the facts were composed from right to left across the masthead of *Morgenlicht:*

! SNIW NAMRESSAW YTTOD

SREWSNA EHT LLA SWONK LRIG NYLKOORB

Neatly boxed below, a picture of Dot and me eating lunch recalled a bright flash that had illuminated the rice pudding the day before, as I sat drenched in the fizzle of my modest hopes.

I sent Dotty a post card. It said: 'No can do.'

The final arrangements were complicated due to the reluctance of the Israeli Government to permit egress to dollar bills which were making the grandest tour of all. Once inside that province of cosmopolitans, the dollar was expected to resign its hedonistic role as an American toy and begin the presbyterian life of a tool.

Within two weeks letters came from abroad bearing this information and containing photographs of Dotty smiling at a kibbutz, leaning sympathetically on a wailing wall, unctuous in an orange grove.

I decided to take a permanent job for a couple of months in an agency, attaching the following copy to photographs of upright men!

THIS IS BILL FEARY. HE IS THE MAN WHO WILL TAKE YOUR ORDER FOR —— TONS OF RED LABEL FERTI-LIZER. HE KNOWS THE MIDWEST. HE KNOWS YOUR NEEDS. CALL HIM BILL AND CALL HIM NOW.

I was neat and brown-eyed, innocent and alert, offended by the chicanery of my fellows, powered by decency, going straight up.

The lean-shanked girls had been brought to New York by tractor and they were going straight up too, through the purgatory of man's avarice to Whore's Heaven, the Palace of Possessions.

While I labored at my dreams, Dotty spent some money to see the leaning tower of Pisa and ride in a gondola. She decided to stay in London at least two weeks because she felt at home there. And so all this profit was at last being left in the hands of foreigners who would invest it to their own advantage.

One misty day the boom of foghorns rolling round Manhattan Island reminded me of a cablegram I had determined to ignore. ARRIVING QUEEN ELIZABETH WEDNESDAY 4 P.M. I ignored it successfully all day and was casual with a couple of cool blondes. And went home and was lonely. I was lonely all evening. I tried writing a letter to an athletic girl I'd met in a ski lodge a few weeks before. . . . I thought of calling some friends, but the pure unmentionable fact is that women isolate you. There was no

71

one to call.

I went out for an evening paper. Read it. Listened to the radio. Went out for a morning paper. Had a beer. Read the paper and waited for the calculation of the morning.

I never went to work the next day or the day after. No word came from Dot. She must have been crawling with guilt. Poor girl. . .

I finally wrote her a letter. It was very strong.

My dear Dorothy:

When I consider our relationship and recall its seasons, the summer sun that shone on it and the winter snows it plowed through, I can still find no reason for your unconscionable behavior. I realize that you were motivated by the hideous examples of your mother and all the mothers before her. You were, in a word, a prostitute. The love and friendship I gave were apparently not enough. What did you want? You gave me the swamp waters of your affection to drown in, and because I refused you planned this desperate revenge.

In all earnestness, I helped you, combing my memory for those of our faith who have touched the press-happy nerves of this nation.

What did you want?

Marriage?

Ah, that's it! A happy daddy-and-mommy home. The home-happy day you could put your hair up in curlers, swab cream in the corner of your eyes. . . I'm not sure all this is for Fred.

I am twenty-nine years old and not getting any younger. All around me boy-graduates have attached their bow legs to the Ladder of Success. Dotty Wasserman, Dotty Wasserman, what can I say to you? If you think I have been harsh, face the fact that you haven't dared face me.

We had some wonderful times together. We could have them again. This is a great opportunity to start on a more human basis. You cannot impose your narrow view of life on me. Make up your mind, Dotty Wasserman.

Sincerely with recollected affection,
F.

P.S. This is your *last* chance.

Two weeks later I received a one-hundred-dollar bill.

A week after that at my door I found a carefully packed leather portfolio, hand-sewn in Italy, and a projector with a box of slides showing interesting views of Europe and North Africa.

And after that, nothing at all.

Don Marquis (1878-1937) worked as a journalist in New York between 1909 and 1922. He is best remembered for his free verse accounts of the lives of archy, a cockroach, and mehitabel, a cat.

IMMORALITY

i was up to central
park yesterday watching some
kids build a snow man when
they were done and had
gone away i looked it
over they had used two
little chunks of wood for
the eyes i sat on one
of these and stared at
the bystanders along came a
prudish looking
lady from flatbush she
stopped and regarded the
snow man i stood
up on my hind legs in
the eye socket and
waved myself at her
horrors she cried even the
snow men in manhattan
are immoral officer arrest
that statue it winked
at me madam said the cop
accept the tribute
as a christmas present
and be happy my own
belief is that some
people have immorality
on the brain

                    archy

Edmund White, author of A Boy's Own Story, *teaches literature in New York. This essay first appeared in his* States of Desire: Travels in Gay America.

FANTASIA ON THE SEVENTIES

For me New York gay life in the seventies came as a completely new beginning. In January 1970 I moved to Rome after having lived in the Village for eight years. When I returned ten months later to the United States, an old friend met me at the airport, popped an 'up' in my mouth, and took me on a tour of the back-room bars. In Rome there had been only one, the St. James, where hustlers stood around in fitted velvet jackets; the only sex scenes had been two movie theaters, where a businessman with a raincoat in his lap might tolerate a handjob, and the Colosseum, where in winter a few vacationing foreigners would cluster in nervous, shadowy groups. For real sex in bed I had to rely on other Americans and upper-class Italians, the only ones who didn't regard love between men as ludicrous. (I had an affair with an impoverished Florentine baron who was writing his dissertation on William Blake.) On the streets, even when shopping or going to lunch, I dressed in a fitted velvet jacket and kept my eyes neutral, uninquisitive. Today, of course, Italy has an active gay-liberation party, large annual gay congresses that choke on Marxist rhetoric, and articles in *Uomo* about gay fashions that purport to be without *any* historical precedent (actually they're just overalls or unironed shirts). But when I lived there Rome was still a bastion of the *piccolo borghese* and miniskirts were considered scandalous.

I have a disturbing knack for doing what used to be called 'conforming,' and by the end of my Roman holiday I was hiding my laundry in a suitcase (to avoid the disgrace of being seen – a man! – carrying dirty shirts through the streets), and I was even drifting into the national sport of cruising women. My assimilation of heterosexuality and respectability made the new New York all the more shocking to me. My friend took me to Christopher's End, where a go-go boy with a pretty body and bad skin stripped down to his jockey shorts and then peeled those off and tossed them at us. A burly man in the audience clambered up onto the dais and tried to fuck the performer but was, apparently, too drunk to get an erection. After a while we drifted into the back

74

room, which was so dark I never received a sense of its dimensions, although I do remember standing on a platform and staring through the slowly revolving blades of a fan at one naked man fucking another in a cubbyhole. A flickering candle illuminated them. It was never clear whether they were customers or hired entertainment; the fan did give them the look of actors in a silent movie. All this was new.

At another bar, called the Zoo or the Zodiac (both existed, I've just confused them), a go-go boy did so well with a white towel under black light that I waited around till he got off – at 8 a.m. In the daylight he turned out to be a bleached blond with chipped teeth who lived in remotest Brooklyn with the bouncer, a three-hundred-pound man who had just lost fifty pounds. I was too polite to back out and was driven all the way to their apartment, which was decorated with a huge blackamoor lamp from Castro Convertible.

For the longest time everyone kept saying the seventies hadn't started yet. There was no distinctive style for the decade, no flair, no slogans. The mistake we made was that we were all looking for something as startling as the Beatles, acid, Pop Art, hippies and radical politics. What actually set in was a painful and unexpected working-out of the terms the sixties had so blithely tossed off. Sexual permissiveness became a form of numbness, as rigidly codified as the old morality. Street cruising gave way to half-clothed quickies; recently I overheard someone say, 'It's been months since I've had sex in bed.' Drugs, once billed as an aid to self-discovery through heightened perception, became a way of injecting lust into anonymous encounters at the baths. At the baths everyone seemed to be lying face down on a cot beside a can of Crisco; fistfucking, as one French savant has pointed out, is our century's only brand-new contribution to the sexual armamentarium. Fantasy costumes (gauze robes, beaded headache bands, mirrored vests) were replaced by the new brutalism: work boots, denim, beards and mustaches, the only concession to the old androgyny being a discreet gold earbob or ivory figa. Today nothing looks more forlorn than the faded sign in a suburban barber shop that reads 'Unisex.'

Indeed, the unisex of the sixties has been supplanted by heavy sex in the seventies, and the urge toward fantasy has come out of the clothes closet and entered the bedroom or back room. The end to role-playing that feminism and gay liberation promised

75

has not occurred. Quite the reverse. Gay pride has come to mean the worship of machismo. No longer is sex confused with sentiment. Although many gay people in New York may be happily living in other, less rigorous decades, the gay male couple inhabiting the seventies is composed of two men who love each other, share the same friends and interests, and fuck each other almost inadvertently once every six months during a particularly stoned, impromptu three-way. The rest of the time they get laid with strangers in a context that bears all the stylistic marks and some of the reality of S and M. Inflicting and receiving excruciating physical pain may still be something of a rarity, but the sex rap whispered in a stranger's ear conjures up nothing but violence. The other day someone said to me, 'Are you into fantasies? I *do* five.' 'Oh?' 'Yes, five: rookie-coach; older brother-younger brother; sailor-slut; slave-master; and father-son.' I picked older brother-younger brother, although it kept lapsing into a pastoral fantasy of identical twins.

The temptation, of course, is to lament our lost innocence, but my Christian Science training as a child has made me into a permanent Pollyanna. What *good* is coming out of the seventies? I keep wondering.

Well, perhaps sex and sentiment *should* be separated. Isn't sex, shadowed as it always is by jealousy and ruled by caprice, a rather risky basis for a sustained, important relationship? Perhaps our marriages should be sexless, or 'white,' as the French used to say. And then, perhaps violence, or at least domination, is the true subtext of all sex, straight or gay; just recently I was reading an article in *Time* about a psychiatrist who has taped the erotic fantasies of lots of people and discovered to his dismay that most of them depend on a sadomasochistic scenario. Even Rosemary Rogers, the author of such gothic potboilers as *The Wildest Heart* and *Sweet Savage Love*, is getting rich feeding her women readers tales of unrelenting S and M. The gay leather scene may simply be more honest – and because it is explicit, less nasty – than more conventional sex, straight or gay.

As for the jeans, cowboy shirts and work boots, they at least have the virtue of being cheap. The uniform conceals the rise of what strikes me as a whole new class of gay indigents. Sometimes I have the impression every fourth man on Christopher Street is out of work, but the poverty is hidden by the costume. Whether this appalling situation should be disguised is another question altogether; is it somehow egalitarian to have both the rich and the poor dressed up as Paul Bunyan?

Finally, the adoration of machismo is intermittent, interchangeable, between parentheses. Tonight's top is tomorrow's bottom. We're all like characters in a Genet play and more interested that the ritual be enacted than concerned about which particular role we assume. The sadist barking commands at his slave in bed is, ten minutes after climax, thoughtfully drawing him a bubble bath or giving him hints about how to keep those ankle restraints brightly polished.

The characteristic face in New York these days is seasoned, wry, weathered by drama and farce. Drugs, heavy sex, and the ironic, highly concentrated experience (so like that of actors everywhere) of leading uneventful, homebodyish lives when not on stage for those two searing hours each night – this reality, or release from it, has humbled us all. It has even broken the former tyranny youth and beauty held over us. Suddenly it's okay to be thirty, forty, even fifty, to have a streak of white crazing your beard, to have a deviated septum or eyes set too close together. All the looks anyone needs can be bought – at the army-navy store, at the gym, and from the local pusher; the lisped shriek of 'Miss Thing!' has faded into the passing, over-the-shoulder offer of 'loose joints.' And we do in fact seem looser, easier in the joints, and if we must lace ourselves nightly into chaps and rough up more men than seems quite coherent with our softspoken, gentle personalities, at least we need no longer be relentlessly witty or elegant, nor need we stand around gilded pianos bawling out choruses from *Hello, Dolly*, our slender bodies embalmed in youth, bedecked with signature scarves, and soaked in eau de cologne.

My enthusiasm for the seventies, as might be guessed, is not uninflected. Politically, the war will not take place. Although Anita Bryant has given us the temporary illusion of solidarity, gay liberation as a militant program has turned out to be ineffectual, perhaps impossible; I suspect individual gays will remain more loyal to their different social classes than to their sexual colleagues. The rapport between gay men and lesbians, still strong in small communities, has collapsed in the city, and this rupture has also weakened militancy. A general American rejection of the high stakes of shared social goals for the small change of personal life (study of the self has turned out to be a form of escapism) has left the movement bankrupt.

But in the post-Stonewall decade there is a new quality to New York gay life. We don't hate ourselves so much (although I do wish everyone would stop picking on drag queens; I at least continue to see them as the Saints of Bleecker Street). In general, we're kinder to our friends. Discovering that a celebrity is gay does not automatically lower him now in our eyes; once it was enough to say such-and-such a conductor or pop singer was gay for him to seem to us a fake, as inauthentic as we perceived ourselves to be. The self-acceptance of the seventies might just give us the courage to experiment with new forms of love and camaraderie, including the *mariage blanc,* the three- or four-way marriage, bi- or trisexuality, a community of artists or craftsmen or citizens from which tiresome heterosexual competitiveness will be banished – a community of tested *seaworthy* New Yorkers.

Langston Hughes (1902-1967) was born in Missouri but became a major figure of the Harlem Renaissance. He wrote many poems, stories, plays, and political essays. This is from Montage of a Dream Deferred.

JUKE BOX LOVE SONG

I could take the Harlem night
and wrap around you
Take the neon lights and make a crown,
Take the Lenox Avenue busses,

Taxis, subways,
And for your love song tone their rumble down.
Take Harlem's heartbeat,
Make a drumbeat,
Put it on a record, let it whirl,
And while we listen to it play,
Dance with you till day—
Dance with you, my sweet brown Harlem girl.

Lorraine Hansberry (1930-1965) became the first black woman to have a play produced on Broadway when A Raisin in the Sun *opened in 1959. Her husband collected many of her writings in a book appropriately titled* To Be Young, Gifted, and Black.

CATCALLS

Light up on first black woman, a young domestic worker.
YOUNG WOMAN

All right. So now you know something 'bout me you didn't know! In these streets out there, any little white boy from Long Island or Westchester sees me and leans out of his car and yells – 'Hey there, *hot chocolate!* Say there, Jezebel! Hey you – 'Hundred Dollar Misunderstanding'! YOU! Bet you know where there's a good time tonight. . . .'

Follow me sometimes and see if I lie. I can be coming from eight hours on an assembly line or fourteen hours in Mrs. Halsey's kitchen. I can be all filled up that day with three hundred years of rage so that my eyes are flashing and my flesh is trembling – and the white boys in the streets, they look at me and think of sex. They look at me and that's *all* they think. . . . Baby, you could be Jesus in drag – but if you're brown they're sure you're selling!

CHAPTER 5

STREET LIFE

The Russian-born anarchist, Emma Goldman (1869-1940), arrived in the United States in 1886. In 1919 she and fellow anarchist Alexander "Sasha" Berkman were deported to the Soviet Union. She left, several years later, bitterly disillusioned, and spent the remainder of her life in France, where she wrote Living My Life. *In this excerpt she recalls an attempt to secure funding for Sasha's plan to assasinate the industrialist, Henry Clay Frick.*

TAKING TO THE STREETS

I woke up with a very clear idea of how I could raise the money for Sasha. I would go on the street. I lay wondering how such a notion could have come to me. I recollected Dostoyevsky's *Crime and Punishment*, which had made a profound impression on me, especially the character of Sonya, Marmeladov's daughter. She had become a prostitute in order to support her little brothers and sisters and to relieve her consumptive stepmother of worry. I visioned Sonya as she lay on her cot, face to the wall, her shoulders twitching. I could almost feel the same way. Sensitive Sonya could sell her body; why not I? My cause was greater than hers. It was Sasha – his great deed – the people. But should I be able to do it, to go with strange men – for money? The thought revolted me. I buried my face in the pillow to shut out the light. 'Weakling, coward,' an inner voice said. 'Sasha is giving his life, and you shrink from giving your body, miserable coward!' It took me several hours to gain control of myself. When I got out of bed my mind was made up.

My main concern now was whether I could make myself attractive enough to men who seek out girls on the street. I stepped over to the mirror to inspect my body. I looked tired, but my complexion was good. I should need no make-up. My curly blond hair showed off well with my blue eyes. Too large in the hips for my age, I thought; I was just twenty-three. Well, I came from Jewish stock. Besides, I would wear a corset and I should look taller in high heels (I had never worn either before).

Corsets, slippers with high heels, dainty underwear – where should I get money for it all? I had a white linen dress, trimmed with Caucasian embroidery. I could get some soft flesh-coloured material and sew the underwear myself. I knew the stores on Grand Street carried cheap goods.

I dressed hurriedly and went in search of the servant in the apartment who had shown a liking for me, and she lent me five dollars without any question. I started off to make my purchases. When I returned, I locked myself in my room. I would see no one. I was busy preparing my outfit and thinking of Sasha. What would he say? Would he approve? Yes, I was sure he would. He had always insisted that the end justified the means, that the true revolutionist will not shrink from anything to serve the Cause.

Saturday evening, July 16, 1892, I walked up and down Fourteenth Street, one of the long procession of girls I had so often seen plying their trade. I felt no nervousness at first, but when I looked at the passing men and saw their vulgar glances and their manner of approaching the women, my heart sank. I wanted to take flight, run back to my room, tear off my cheap finery, and scrub myself clean. But a voice kept on ringing in my ears: 'You must hold out; Sasha – his act – everything will be lost if you fail.'

I continued my tramp, but something stronger than my reason would compel me to increase my pace the moment a man came near me. One of them was rather insistent, and I fled. By eleven o'clock I was utterly exhausted. My feet hurt from the high heels, my head throbbed. I was close to tears from fatigue and disgust with my inability to carry out what I had come to do.

I made another effort. I stood on the corner of Fourteenth Street and Fourth Avenue, near the bank building. The first man that invited me – I would go with him, I had decided. A tall, distinguished-looking person, well dressed, came close. 'Let's have a drink, little girl,' he said. His hair was white, he appeared to be about sixty, but his face was ruddy. 'All right,' I replied. He took my arm and led me to a wine house on Union Square which Most had often frequented with me. 'Not here!' I almost screamed; 'please, not here.' I led him to the back entrance of a saloon on Thirteenth Street and Third Avenue. I had once been there in the afternoon for a glass of beer. It had been clean and quiet then.

That night it was crowded, and with difficulty we secured a table. The man ordered drinks. My throat felt parched and I asked for a large glass of beer. Neither of us spoke. I was conscious of the man's scrutiny of my face and body. I felt myself growing resentful. Presently he asked: 'You're a novice in the business, aren't you?' 'Yes, this is my first time – but how did you know?' 'I watched you as you passed me,' he replied. He told me that he had noticed my haunted expression and my increased pace the moment a man came near me. He understood then that I was inexperienced; whatever might have been the reason that brought me to the street, he knew it was not mere looseness or love of excitement. 'But thousands of girls are driven by economic necessity,' I blurted out. He looked at me in surprise. 'Where did you get that stuff?' I wanted to tell him all about the social question, about my ideas, who and what I was, but I checked myself. I must not disclose my identity: it would be too dreadful if he should learn that Emma Goldman, the anarchist, had been found soliciting on Fourteenth Street. What a juicy story it would make for the press!

He said he was not interested in economic problems and did not care what the reason was for my actions. He only wanted to tell me that there was nothing in prostitution unless one had the knack for it. 'You haven't got it, and that's all there is to it,' he assured me. He took out a ten-dollar bill and put it down before me. 'Take this and go home,' he said. 'But why should you give me money if you don't want me to go with you?' I asked. 'Well, just to cover the expenses you must have had to rig yourself out like that,' he replied; 'your dress is awfully nice, even if it does not go with those cheap shoes and stockings.' I was too astounded for speech.

I had met two categories of men: vulgarians and idealists. The former would never have let an opportunity pass to possess a woman and they would give her no other thought save sexual desire. The idealists stoutly defended the equality of the sexes, at least in theory, but the only men among them who practised what they preached were the Russian and Jewish radicals. This man, who had picked me up on the street and who was now with me in the back of a saloon, seemed an entirely new type. He interested me. He must be rich. But would a rich man give something for nothing? The manufacturer Garson came to my mind; he would not even give me a small raise in wages.

Perhaps this man was one of those soul-savers I had read about, people who were always cleansing New York City of vice. I asked him. He laughed and said he was not a professional busybody. If he had thought that I really wanted to be on the street, he would not have cared. 'Of course, I may be entirely mistaken,' he added, 'but I don't mind. Just now I am convinced that you are not intended to be a streetwalker, and that even if you do succeed, you will hate it afterwards.' If he were not convinced of it, he would take me for his mistress. 'For always?' I cried. 'There you are!' he replied; 'you are scared by the mere suggestion and yet you hope to succeed on the street. You're an awfully nice kid, but you're silly, inexperienced, childish.' 'I was twenty-three last month,' I protested, resentful of being treated like a child. 'You are an old lady,' he said with a grin, 'but even old folks can be babes in the woods. Look at me; I'm sixty-one and I often do foolish things.' 'Like believing in my innocence, for instance,' I retorted. The simplicity of his manner pleased me. I asked for his name and address so as to be able to return his ten dollars some day. But he refused to give them to me. He loved mysteries, he said. On the street he held my hand for a moment, and then we turned in opposite directions.

F. Scott Fitzgerald (1869-1940) was himself a midwesterner resettled in the East. In this excerpt from The Great Gatsby *(1925) the midwestern narrator describes his days and nights in the city.*

A MIDWESTERNER IN NEW YORK

Most of the time I worked. In the early morning the sun threw my shadow westward as I hurried down the white chasms of lower New York to the Probity Trust. I knew the other clerks and young bond-salesmen by their first names, and lunched with them in dark, crowded restaurants on little pig sausages and mashed potatoes and coffee. I even had a short affair with a girl who lived in Jersey City and worked in the accounting department, but her brother began throwing mean looks in my direction, so when she went on her vacation in July I let it blow quietly away.

I took dinner usually at the Yale Club – for some reason it was the gloomiest event of my day – and then I went upstairs to the library and studied investments and securities for a conscientious hour. There were generally a few rioters around, but they never came into the library, so it was a good place to work. After that, if the night was mellow, I strolled down Madison Avenue past the old Murray Hill Hotel, and over 33rd Street to the Pennsylvania Station.

I began to like New York, the racy, adventurous feel of it at night, and the satisfaction that the constant flicker of men and women and machines gives to the restless eye. I liked to walk up Fifth Avenue and pick out romantic women from the crowd and imagine that in a few minutes I was going to enter into their lives, and no one would ever know or disapprove. Sometimes, in my mind, I followed them to their apartments on the corners of hidden streets, and they turned and smiled back at me before they faded through a door into warm darkness. At the enchanted metropolitan twilight I felt a haunting loneliness sometimes, and felt it in others – poor young clerks in the dusk, wasting the most poignant moments of night and life.

Again at eight o'clock, when the dark lanes of the Forties were lined five deep with throbbing taxicabs, bound for the theatre district, I felt a sinking in my heart. Forms leaned together in the taxis as they waited, and voices sang, and there was laughter from unheard jokes, and lighted cigarettes made unintelligible circles inside. Imagining that I, too, was hurrying towards gaiety and sharing their intimate excitement, I wished them well.

Jane Jacobs's book, The Death and Life of Great American Cities, *causd a furore when it first appeared in 1961. As one of the first investigations into the nature of inner-city decay it lead many people to re-think old ideas about urban planning and what, exactly, we expect from life in a big city.*

HUDSON STREET BALLET

Under the seeming disorder of the old city, wherever the old city is working successfully, is a marvelous order for maintaining the safety of the streets and the freedom of the city. It is a complex order. Its essence is intricacy of sidewalk use, bringing with it a constant succession of eyes. This order is all composed of movement and change, and although it is life, not art, we may fancifully call it the art form of the city and liken it to the dance – not to a simple-minded precision dance with everyone kicking up at the same time, twirling in unison and bowing off en masse, but to an intricate ballet in which the individual dancers and ensembles all have distinctive parts which miraculously reinforce each other and compose an orderly whole. The ballet of the good city sidewalk never repeats itself from place to place, and in any

86

one place is always replete with new improvisations.

The stretch of Hudson Street where I live is each day the scene of an intricate sidewalk ballet. I make my own first entrance into it a little after eight when I put out the garbage can, surely a prosaic occupation, but I enjoy my part, my little clang, as the droves of junior high school students walk by the center of the stage dropping candy wrappers. (How do they eat so much candy so early in the morning?)

While I sweep up the wrappers I watch the other rituals of morning: Mr. Halpert unlocking the laundry's handcart from its mooring to a cellar door, Joe Cornacchia's son-in-law stacking out the empty crates from the delicatessen, the barber bringing out his sidewalk folding chair, Mr. Goldstein arranging the coils of wire which proclaim the hardware store is open, the wife of the tenement's superintendent depositing her chunky three-year-old with a toy mandolin on the stoop, the vantage point from which he is learning the English his mother cannot speak. Now the primary children, heading for St. Luke's, dribble through to the south; the children for St. Veronica's cross, heading to the west, and the children for P.S. 41, heading toward the east. Two new entrances are being made from the wings: well-dressed and even elegant women and men with brief cases emerge from doorways and side streets. Most of these are heading for the bus and subways, but some hover on the curbs, stopping taxis which have miraculously appeared at the right moment, for the taxis are part of a wider morning ritual: having dropped passengers from midtown in the downtown financial district, they are now bringing downtowners up to midtown. Simultaneously, a number of women in housedresses have emerged and as they crisscross with one another they pause for quick conversations that sound with either laughter or joint indignation, never, it seems, anything between. It is time for me to hurry to work too, and I exchange my ritual farewell with Mr. Lofaro, the short, thick-bodied, white-aproned fruit man who stands outside his doorway a little up the street, his arms folded, his feet planted, looking solid as earth itself. We nod; we each glance quickly up and down the street, then look back to each other and smile. We have done this many a morning for more than ten years, and we both know what it means: All is well.

The heart-of-the-day ballet I seldom see, because part of the nature of it is that working people who live there, like me, are mostly gone, filling the roles of strangers on other sidewalks. But from days off, I know enough of it to know that it becomes more and more intricate. Longshoremen who are not working that day gather at the White Horse or the Ideal or the International for beer and conversation. The executives and business lunchers from the industries just to the west throng the Dorgene restaurant and the Lion's Head coffee house; meat-market workers and communications scientists fill the bakery lunchroom. Character dancers come on, a strange old man with strings of old shoes over his shoulders, motor-scooter riders with big beards and girl friends who bounce on the back of the scooters and wear their hair long in front of their faces as well as behind, drunks who follow the advice of the Hat Council and are always turned out in hats, but no hats the Council would approve. Mr. Lacey, the locksmith, shuts up his shop for a while and goes to exchange the time of day with Mr. Slube at the cigar store. Mr. Koochagian, the tailor, waters the luxuriant jungle of plants in his window, gives them a critical look from the outside, accepts a compliment on them from two passers-by, fingers the leaves on the plane tree in front of our house with a thoughtful gardener's appraisal, and crosses the street for a bite at the Ideal where he can keep an eye on customers and wigwag across the message that he is coming. The baby carriages come out, and clusters of everyone from toddlers with dolls to teen-agers with homework gather at the stoops.

When I get home after work, the ballet is reaching its crescendo. This is the time of roller skates and stilts and tricycles, and games in the lee of the stoop with bottletops and plastic cowboys; this is the time of bundles and packages, zigzagging from the drug store to the fruit stand and back over to the butcher's, this is the time when teen-agers, all dressed up, are pausing to ask if their slips show or their collars look right; this is the time when beautiful girls get out of MG's; this is the time when the fire engines go through; this is the time when anybody you know around Hudson Street will go by.

As darkness thickens and Mr. Halpert moors the laundry cart to the cellar door again, the ballet goes on under lights, eddying back and forth but intensifying at the bright spotlight pools of Joe's sidewalk pizza dispensary, the bars, the delicatessen, the restaurant and the drug store. The night workers stop now at the delicatessen, to pick up salami and a container of milk. Things have settled down for the evening but the street and its ballet have not come to a stop.

I know the deep night ballet and its seasons best from waking long after midnight to tend a baby and, sitting in the dark, seeing the shadows and hearing the sounds of the sidewalk. Mostly it is a sound like infinitely pattering snatches of party conversation and, about three in the morning, singing, very good singing. Sometimes there is sharpness and anger or sad, sad weeping, or a flurry of search for a string of beads broken. One night a young man came roaring along, bellowing terrible language at two girls whom he had apparently picked up and who were disappointing him. Doors opened, a wary semicircle formed around him, not too close, until the police came. Out came the heads, too, along Hudson Street, offering opinion, 'Drunk . . . Crazy . . . A wild kid from the suburbs.'*

Deep in the night, I am almost unaware how many people are on the street unless something calls them together, like the bagpipe. Who the piper was and why he favored our street I have no idea. The bagpipe just skirled out in the February night, and as if it were a signal the random, dwindled movements of the sidewalk took on direction. Swiftly, quietly, almost magically a little crowd was there, a crowd that evolved into a circle with a Highland fling inside it. The crowd could be seen on the shadowy sidewalk, the dancers could be seen, but the bagpiper himself was almost invisible because his bravura was all in his music. He was a very little man in a plain brown overcoat. When he finished and vanished, the dancers and watchers applauded, and applause came from the galleries too, half a dozen of the hundred windows on Hudson Street. Then the windows closed, and the little crowd dissolved into the random movements of the night street.

The strangers on Hudson Street, the allies whose eyes help us natives keep the peace of the street, are so many that they always seem to be different people from one day to the next. That does not matter. Whether they are so many always-different people as they seem to be, I do not know. Likely they are. When Jimmy Rogan fell through a plate-glass window (he was separating some scuffling friends) and almost lost his arm, a stranger in an old T shirt emerged from the Ideal bar, swiftly applied an expert

* He turned out to be a wild kid from the suburbs. Sometimes, on Hudson Street, we are tempted to believe the suburbs must be a difficult place to bring up children.

tourniquet and, according to the hospital's emergency staff, saved Jimmy's life. Nobody remembered seeing the man before and no one has seen him since. The hospital was called in this way: a woman sitting on the steps next to the accident ran over to the bus stop, wordlessly snatched the dime from the hand of a stranger who was waiting with his fifteen-cent fare ready, and raced into the Ideal's phone booth. The stranger raced after her to offer the nickel too. Nobody remembered seeing him before, and no one has seen him since. When you see the same stranger three or four times on Hudson Street, you begin to nod. This is almost getting to be an acquaintance, a public acquaintance, of course.

I have made the daily ballet of Hudson Street sound more frenetic than it is, because writing it telescopes it. In real life, it is not that way. In real life, to be sure, something is always going on, the ballet is never at a halt, but the general effect is peaceful and the general tenor even leisurely. People who know well such animated city streets will know how it is. I am afraid people who do not will always have it a little wrong in their heads – like the old prints of rhinoceroses made from travelers' descriptions of rhinoceroses.

On Hudson Street, the same as in the North End of Boston or in any other animated neighborhoods of great cities, we are not innately more competent at keeping the sidewalks safe than are the people who try to live off the hostile truce of Turf in a blind-eyed city. We are the lucky possessors of a city order that makes it relatively simply to keep the peace because there are plenty of eyes on the street. But there is nothing simple about that order itself, or the bewildering number of components that go into it. Most of those components are specialized in one way or another. They unite in their joint effect upon the sidewalk, which is not specialized in the least. That is its strength.

Saul Bellow was born in Canada in 1915. Many of his novels, for which he was awarded the Nobel Prize in 1976, including Seize the Day, Herzog, *and* Humboldt's Gift, *are largely set in New York. In* Mr. Sammler's Planet *(1969) the protagonist, a survivor of Nazi Concentration Camps, observes the city with a jaundiced eye.*

Homeward

On Second Avenue the springtime scraping of roller skates was heard on hollow, brittle sidewalks, a soothing harshness. Turning from the new New York of massed apartments into the older New York of brownstone and wrought-iron, Sammler saw through large black circles in a fence daffodils and tulips, the mouths of these flowers open and glowing, but on the pure yellow the fallout of soot already was sprinkled. You might in this city become a flower-washer. There was an additional business opportunity for Wallace and Feffer.

He walked once around Stuyvesant Park, an ellipse within a square with the statue of the peg-legged Dutchman, corners bristling with bushes. Tapping the flagstones with his ferrule every fourth step, Sammler held Dr. Govinda Lal's manuscript under his arm. He had brought it to read on the subway, though he didn't like being conspicuous in public, passing pages back and forth before the eye, pressing back the hat brim and his face intensely concentrated. He seldom did that . . .

. . . Sammler had learned to be careful on public paths in New York, invariably dog-fouled. Within the iron-railed plots the green lights of the grass were all but put out, burned by animal excrements. The sycamores, blemished bark, but very nice, brown and white, getting ready to cough up leaves. Red brick, the Friends Seminary, and ruddy coarse warm stone, broad, clumsy, solid, the Episcopal church, St. George's. Sammler had heard that the original J. Pierpont Morgan had been an usher there. In Austro-Hungarian-Polish-Cracovian antiquity old fellows who had read of Morgan in the papers spoke of him with high regard as Piepernotter-Morgan. At St. George's, Sundays, the god of stockbrokers could breathe easy awhile in the riotous city. In thought, Mr. Sammler was testy with White Protestant America for not keeping better order. Cowardly surrender. Not a strong ruling class. Eager in a secret humiliating way to come down and mingle with all the minority mobs, and scream against themselves. And the clergy? Beating swords into plowshares? No, rather converting dog collars into G strings. But this was neither here nor there.

Watching his steps (the dogs), looking for a bench for ten minutes, to think or avoid thinking of Gruner. Perhaps despite great sadness to read a few paragraphs of this fascinating moon manuscript. He noted a female bum drunkenly sleeping like a dugong, a sea cow's belly rising, legs swollen purple; a short dress, a mini-rag. At a corner of the fence, a wino was sullenly pissing on newspapers and old leaves. Cops seldom bothered about these old-fashioned derelicts. Younger people, autochthonous-looking, were also here. Bare feet, the boys like Bombay beggars, beards clotted, breathing rich hair from their nostrils, heads coming through woolen ponchos, somewhat Peruvian. Natives of somewhere. Innocent, devoid of aggression, opting out, much like Ferdinand the Bull. No *corrida* for them; only smelling flowers under the lovely cork tree. How similar also to the Eloi of H. G. Wells' fantasy *The Time Machine*. Lovely young human cattle herded by the cannibalistic Morlocks who lived a subterranean life and feared light and fire. Yes, that tough brave little old fellow Wells had had prophetic visions after all. . .

In The Avenue Bearing the Initial of Christ into the New World, *poet Galway Kinnell, born in Rhode Island in 1927, evoked the sights, sounds, and people of Avenue C on New York's Lower East Side.*

(from) THE AVENUE BEARING THE INITIAL OF
CHRIST INTO THE NEW WORLD
Was diese kleine Gasse doch für ein Reich an sich war . . .

verse 14

Behind the Power Station on 14th, the held breath
Of light, as God is a held breath, withheld,
Spreads the East River, into which fishes leak:
The brown sink or dissolve,
The white float out in shoals and armadas,
Even the gulls pass them up, pale
Bloated socks of riverwater and rotted seed,
That swirl on the tide, punched back
To the Hell Gate narrows, and on the ebb
Steam seaward, seeding the sea.

On the Avenue, through air tinted crimson
By neon over the bars, the rain is falling.
You stood once on Houston, among panhandlers and winos
Who weave the eastern ranges, learning to be free,
To not care, to be knocked flat and to get up clear-headed
Spitting the curses out. 'Now be nice,'
The proprietor threatens; 'Be nice,' he cajoles.
'Fuck you,' the bum shouts as he is hoisted again,
'God fuck your mother.' (In the empty doorway,
Hunched on the empty crate, the crone gives no sign.)

That night a wildcat cab whined crosstown on 7th.
You knew even the traffic lights were made by God,
The red splashes growing dimmer the farther away
You looked, and away up at 14th, a few green stars;
And without sequence, and nearly all at once,
The red lights blinked into green,
And just before there was one complete Avenue of green,
The little green stars in the distance blinked.

It is night, and raining. You look down
Towards Houston in the rain, the living streets,
Where instants of transcendence
Drift in oceans of loathing and fear, like lanternfishes,
Or phosphorus flashings in the sea, or the feverish light
Skin is said to give off when the swimmer drowns at night.

From the blind gut Pitt to the East River of Fishes
The Avenue cobbles a swath through the discolored air,
A roadway of refuse from the teeming shores and ghettos
And the Caribbean Paradise, into the new ghetto and new
      paradise,
This God-forsaken Avenue bearing the initial of Christ
Through the haste and carelessness of the ages,
The sea standing in heaps, which keeps on collapsing,
Where the drowned suffer a C-change,
And remain the common poor.

Since Providence, for the realization of some unknown purpose,
has seen fit to leave this dangerous people on the face of the
earth, and did not destroy it . . .

Listen! the swish of the blood,
The sirens down the bloodpaths of the night,
Bone tapping on the bone, nerve-nets
Singing under the breath of sleep —

We scattered over the lonely seaways,
Over the lonely deserts did we run,
In dark lanes and alleys we did hide ourselves . . .

The heart beats without windows in its night,
The lungs put out the light of the world as they
Heave and collapse, the brain turns and rattles
In its own black axlegrease —

        In the nighttime
Of the blood they are laughing and saying,
Our little lane, what a kingdom it was!

        oi weih, oi weih

Noel Rico is a contemporary Nuyorican (New Yorker of Puerto Rican descent) poet.

THE FIRST PLACE

Conga beats pouring out a window
makes the curtains tremble
A man is laughing
A woman leans out
a window her fingers running
through her hair over her blouse
down to her thighs
I hear Ismael Miranda
singing
A mulata with cheeks
red as two drops of blood
walks past me
pushing a baby carriage

A little girl is cutting open the face
of the sidewalk with a piece of red chalk . . .
The jewish store owner
turns keys in hundreds of locks,
he dreams that thieves
grow out of the sidewalk
like plants
when no one is around

on the corner by the police phone
two boys are stealing a drunk's money
as he sleeps
on an old piece of newspaper
garbage dancing
at his feet
to a rhythm
played by the cold

it is a mambo
lined with ice.

CHAPTER 6

ON THE MOVE

Walt Whitman wrote Crossing Brooklyn Ferry *in 1856, when he regularly took the ferry to travel between his home in Brooklyn and his newspaper job in Manhattan.*

CROSSING BROOKLYN FERRY

verse 1

Flood-tide below me! I see you face to face!
Clouds of the west – sun there half an hour high – I see you also
    face to face.

Crowds of men and women attired in the usual costumes, how
    curious you are to me!
On the ferry-boats the hundreds and hundreds that cross,
    returning home, are more curious to me than you suppose,
And you that shall cross from shore to shore years hence are more
    to me, and more in my meditations, than you might suppose.

verse 8

Ah, what can ever be more stately and admirable to me than
    mast-hemm'd Manhattan?
River and sunset and scallop-edg'd waves of flood-tide?
The sea-gulls oscillating their bodies, the hay-boat in the twilight,
    and the belated lighter?
What gods can exceed these that clasp me by the hand, and with
    voices I love call me promptly and loudly by my nighest
    name as I approach?
What is more subtle than this which ties me to the woman or man
    that looks in my face?
Which fuses me into you now, and pours my meaning into you?

We understand then do we not?
What I promis'd without mentioning it, have you not accepted?
What the study could not teach – what the preaching could not
    accomplish is accomplish'd, is it not?

One of the great chroniclers of daily life in New York was Stephen Crane (1871-1900), who came to the city as a young man and learned first hand of its squalor and glory while working as a reporter for the New York Herald *and* The Tribune. *His first novel,* Maggie: A Girl of the Streets, *was a realistic study of slum life in the 1890s and was considered too provocative for publication. His next book,* The Red Badge of Courage, *was a huge success and is now revered as an American classic.*

IN THE BROADWAY CARS

The cable cars come down Broadway as the waters come down at Lodore. Years ago Father Knickerbocker had convulsions when it was proposed to lay impious rails on his sacred thoroughfare. At the present day the cars, by force of column and numbers, almost dominate the great street, and the eye of even an old New Yorker is held by these long yellow monsters which prowl intently up and down, up and down, in a mystic search.

In the grey of the morning they come out of the up-town, bearing janitors, porters, all that class which carries the keys to set alive the great downtown. Later, they shower clerks. Later still, they shower more clerks. And the thermometer which is attached to a conductor's temper is steadily rising, rising, and the blissful time arrives when everybody hangs to a strap and stands on his neighbour's toes. Ten o'clock comes, and the Broadway cars, as well as elevated cars, horse cars, and ferryboats innumerable, heave sighs of relief. They have filled lower New York with a vast army of men who will chase to and fro and amuse themselves until almost nightfall.

The cable car's pulse drops to normal. But the conductor's pulse begins now to beat in split seconds. He has come to the crisis in his day's agony. He is now to be overwhelmed with feminine shoppers. They all are going to give him two-dollar bills to change. They all are going to threaten to report him. He passes his hand across his brow and curses his beard from black to grey and from grey to black.

Men and women have different ways of hailing a car. A man – if he is not an old choleric gentleman, who owns not this road but some other road – throws up a timid finger, and appears to be believe that the King of Abyssinia is careering past on his war-chariot, and only his opinion of other people's Americanism keeps him from deep salaams. The gripman usually jerks his thumb

99

over his shoulder and indicates the next car, which is three miles away. Then the man catches the last platform, goes into the car, climbs upon some one's toes, opens his morning paper, and is happy.

When a woman hails a car there is no question of its being the King of Abyssinia's war-chariot. She has bought the car for three dollars and ninety-eight cents. The conductor owes his position to her, and the gripman's mother does her laundry. No captain in the Royal Horse Artillery ever stops his battery from going through a stone house in a way to equal her manner of bringing that car back on its haunches. Then she walks leisurely forward, and after scanning the step to see if there is any mud upon it, and opening her pocket-book to make sure of a two-dollar bill, she says: 'Do you give transfers down Twenty-eighth Street?'

Some time the conductor breaks the bell strap when he pulls it under these conditions. Then, as the car goes on, he goes and bullies some person who had nothing to do with the affair.

The car sweeps on its diagonal path through the Tenderloin with its hotels, its theatres, its flower shops, its 10,000,000 actors who played with Booth and Barret. It passes Madison Square and enters the gorge made by the towering walls of great shops. It sweeps around the double curve at Union Square and Fourteenth Street, and a life insurance agent falls in a fit as the car dashes over the crossing, narrowly missing three old ladies, two old gentlemen, a newly-married couple, a sandwich man, a newsboy, and a dog. At Grace Church the conductor has an altercation with a brave and reckless passenger who beards him in his own car, and at Canal Street he takes dire vengeance by tumbling a drunken man on to the pavement. Meanwhile, the gripman has become involved with countless truck drivers, and inch by inch, foot by foot, he fights his way to City Hall Park. On past the Post Office the car goes, with the gripman getting advice, admonition, personal comment, an invitation to fight from the drivers, until Battery Park appears at the foot of the slope, and as the car goes sedately around the curve the burnished shield of the bay shines through the trees.

It is a great ride, full of exciting actions. Those inexperienced persons who have been merely chased by Indians know little of the dramatic quality which life may hold for them. These jungles of men and vehicles, these cañons of streets, these lofty mountains of iron and cut stone – a ride through them affords plenty of excitement. And no lone panther's howl is more serious in intention than the howl of the truck driver when the cable car bumps one of his rear wheels.

Owing to a strange humour of the gods that make our comfort, sailor hats with wide brims come into vogue whenever we are all engaged in hanging to cable-car straps. There is only one more serious combination known to science, but a trial of it is at this day impossible. If a troup of Elizabethan courtiers in large ruffs should board a cable car, the complication would be a very awesome one, and the profanity would be in old English, but very inspiring. However, the combination of wide-brimmed hats and crowded cable cars is tremendous in its power to cause misery to the patient New York public.

Suppose you are in a cable car, clutching for life and family a creaking strap from overhead. At your shoulder is a little dude in a very wide-brimmed straw hat with a red band. If you were in your senses you would recognise this flaming band as an omen of blood. But you are not in your senses; you are in a Broadway cable car. You are not supposed to have any senses. From the forward end you hear the gripman uttering shrill whoops and running over citizens. Suddenly the car comes to a curve. Making a swift running start, it turns three hand-springs, throws a cart wheel for luck, bounds into the air, hurls six passengers over the nearest building, and comes down a-straddle of the track. That is the way in which we turn curves in New York.

Meanwhile, during the car's gamboling, the corrugated rim of the dude's hat has swept naturally across your neck, and has left nothing for your head to do but to quit your shoulders. As the car roars your head falls into the waiting arms of the proper authorities. The dude is dead; everything is dead. The interior of the car resembles the scene of the battle of Wounded Knee, but this gives you small satisfaction.

There was once a person possessing a fund of uncanny humour who greatly desired to import from past ages a corps of knights in full armour. He then purposed to pack the warriors into a cable car and send them around a curve. He thought that he could gain much pleasure by standing near and listening to the wild clash of steel upon steel – the tumult of mailed heads striking together, the bitter grind of armoured legs bending the wrong way. He thought that this would teach them that war is grim.

Towards evening, when the tides of travel set northward, it is

101

curious to see how the gripman and conductor reverse their tempers. Their dispositions flop over like patent signals. During the down-trip they had in mind always the advantages of being at Battery Park. A perpetual picture of the blessings of Battery Park was before them, and every delay made them fume – made this picture all the more alluring. Now the delights of up-town appear to them. They have reversed the signs on the cars; they have reversed their aspiration. Battery Park has been gained and forgotten. There is a new goal. Here is a perpetual illustration which the philosophers of New York may use.

In the Tenderloin, the place of theatres, and of the restaurant where gayer New York does her dining, the cable cars in the evening carry a stratum of society which looks like a new one, but it is of the familiar strata in other clothes. It is just as good as a new stratum, however, for in evening dress the average man feels that he has gone up three pegs in the social scale, and there is considerable evening dress about a Broadway car in the evening. A car with its electric lamp resembles a brilliantly-lighted salon, and the atmosphere grows just a trifle strained. People sit more rigidly, and glance sidewise, perhaps, as if each was positive of possessing social value, but was doubtful of all others. The conductor says: 'Ah, gwan. Git off th' earth.' But this is to a man at Canal Street. That shows his versatility. He stands on the platform and beams in a modest and polite manner into the car. He notes a lifted finger and grabs swiftly for the bell strap. He reaches down to help a woman aboard. Perhaps his demeanour is a reflection of the manner of the people in the car. No one is in a mad New York hurry; no one is fretting and muttering; no one is perched upon his neighbour's toes. Moreover, the Tenderloin is a glory at night. Broadway of late years has fallen heir to countless signs illuminated with red, blue, green, and gold electric lamps, and the people certainly fly to these as the moths go to a candle. And perhaps the gods have allowed this opportunity to observe and study the best-dressed crowds in the world to operate upon the conductor until his mood is to treat us with care and mildness.

Late at night, after the diners and theatre-goers have been lost in Harlem, various inebriate persons may perchance emerge from the darker regions of Sixth Avenue and swing their arms solemnly at the gripman. If the Broadway cars run for the next 7000 years this will be the only time when one New Yorker will address another in public without an excuse sent direct from heaven. In these cars late at night it is not impossible that some fearless drunkard will attempt to inaugurate a general conversation. He is quite willing to devote his ability to the affair. He tells of the fun he thinks he has had; describes his feelings; recounts stories of his dim past. None reply, although all listen with every ear. The rake probably ends by borrowing a match, lighting a cigar, and entering into a wrangle with the conductor with an *abandon,* a ferocity, and a courage that do not come to us when we are sober.

In the meantime the figures on the street grow fewer and fewer. Strolling policemen test the locks of the great dark-fronted stores. Nighthawk cabs whirl by the cars on their mysterious errands. Finally the cars themselves depart in the way of the citizen, and for the few hours before dawn a new sound comes into the still thoroughfare – the cable whirring in its channel underground.

Hart Crane (1899-1932) was born in Ohio and came to live in Brooklyn in 1924. He worked at many casual jobs in New York and struggled with increasing alcoholism and poverty. His poem, The Bridge, *published in 1930, is, among other things, an attempt to create a new vision of American experience which would reunite and redeem its diverse, fragmentary, inhuman character in the industrial age. In this section of the poem many of its themes are gathered in the image of a subway ride from Columbus Circle to Brooklyn.*

THE TUNNEL

Performances, assortments, résumés—
Up Times Square to Columbus Circle lights
Channel the congresses, nightly sessions,
Refractions of the thousand theatres, faces—
Mysterious kitchens. . . . You shall search them all.
Someday by heart you'll learn each famous sight
And watch the curtain lift in hell's despite;
You'll find the garden in the third act dead,
Finger your knees – and wish yourself in bed
With tabloid crime-sheets perched in easy sight.

    Then let you reach your hat
    and go.
    As usual, let you – also

walking down – exclaim
to twelve upward leaving
a subscription praise
for what time slays.

Or can't you quite make up your mind to ride;
A walk is better underneath the L a brisk
Ten blocks or so before? But you find yourself
Preparing penguin flexions of the arms,—
As usual you will meet the scuttle yawn:
The subway yawns the quickest promise home.

Be minimum, then, to swim the hiving swarms
Out of the Square, the Circle burning bright—
Avoid the glass doors gyring at your right,
Where boxed alone a second, eyes take fright
—Quite unprepared rush naked back to light:
And down beside the turnstile press the coin
Into the slot. The gongs already rattle.

And so
of cities you bespeak
subways, rivered under streets
and rivers. . . . In the car
the overtone of motion
underground, the monotone
of motion is the sound
of other faces, also underground—

'Let's have a pencil Jimmy – living now
at Floral Park
Flatbush – on the fourth of July—
like a pigeon's muddy dream – potatoes
to dig in the field – travlin the town – too—
night after night – the Culver line – the
girls all shaping up – it used to be –'

Our tongues recant like beaten weather vanes.
This answer lives like verdigris, like hair
Beyond extinction, surcease of the bone;
And repetition freezes – 'What

'what do you want? getting weak on the links?
fandaddle daddy don't ask for change — IS THIS
FOURTEENTH? it's half past six she said — if
you don't like my gate why did you
swing on it, why *didja*
swing on it
anyhow —'

    And somehow anyhow swing—

The phonographs of hades in the brain
Are tunnels that re-wind themselves, and love
A burnt match skating in a urinal—
Somewhere above Fourteenth TAKE THE EXPRESS
To brush some new presentiment of pain—

'But I want service in this office SERVICE
I said — after
the show she cried a little afterwards but —'

Whose head is swinging from the swollen strap?
Whose body smokes along the bitten rails,
Bursts from a smoldering bundle far behind
In back forks of the chasms of the brain,—
Puffs from a riven stump far out behind
In interborough fissures of the mind. . . ?

And why do I often meet your visage here,
Your eyes like agate lanterns — on and on

Below the toothpaste and the dandruff ads?
— And did their riding eyes right through your side,
And did their eyes like unwashed platters ride?
And Death, aloft, — gigantically down
Probing through you — toward me, O evermore!
And when they dragged your retching flesh,
Your trembling hands that night through Baltimore—
That last night on the ballot rounds, did you
Shaking, did you deny the ticket, Poe?

For Gravesend Manor change at Chambers Street.
The platform hurries along to a dead stop.

The intent escalator lifts a serenade
Stilly
Of shoes, umbrellas, each eye attending its shoe, then
Bolting outright somewhere above where streets
Burst suddenly in rain. . . . The gongs recur:
Elbows and levers, guard and hissing door.

Thunder is galvothermic here below. . . . The car
Wheels off. The train rounds, bending to a scream,
Taking the final level for the dive
Under the river—
And somewhat emptier than before,
Demented, for a hitching second, humps; then
Lets go. . . . Toward corners of the floor
Newspapers wing, revolve and wing.
Blank windows gargle signals through the roar.

And does the Dæmon take you home, also,
Wop washerwoman, with the bandaged hair?
After the corridors are swept, the cuspidors—
The gaunt sky-barracks cleanly now, and bare,
O Genoese, do you bring mother eyes and hands
Back home to children and to golden hair?

Dæmon, demurring and eventful yawn!
Whose hideous laughter is a bellows mirth
– Or the muffled slaughter of a day in birth—
O cruelly to inoculate the brinking dawn
With antennæ toward worlds that glow and sink;—
To spoon us out more liquid than the dim
Locution of the eldest star, and pack
The conscience navelled in the plunging wind,
Umbilical to call – and straightway die!

O caught like pennies beneath soot and steam,
Kiss of our agony thou gatherest;
Condensed, thou takest all – shrill ganglia
Impassioned with some song we fail to keep.
And yet, like Lazarus, to feel the slope,
The sod and billow breaking, – lifting ground,

– A sound of waters bending astride the sky
Unceasing with some Word that will not die. . . !

     . . . . .

A tugboat, wheezing wreaths of steam,
Lunged past, with one galvanic blare stove up the River.
I counted the echoes assembling, one after one,
Searching, thumbing the midnight on the piers.
Lights, coasting, left the oily tympanum of waters;
The blackness somewhere gouged glass on a sky.

And this thy harbor, O my City, I have driven under,
Tossed from the coil of ticking towers. . . . Tomorrow,
And to be. . . . Here by the River that is East—
Here at the waters' edge the hands drop memory;
Shadowless in that abyss they unaccounting lie.
How far away the star has pooled the sea—
Or shall the hands be drawn away, to die?

Kiss of our agony Thou gatherest,
          O Hand of Fire
             gatherest—

E. B. White was born in 1899 in Mt. Vernon, a suburb of New York City. As a writer for the New Yorker, *and in particular as a long-standing contributor of its Talk of the Town column, White wrote with style and wit on many subjects dear to the hearts of New Yorkers. His book,* Here is New York, *was published in 1949.*

COMMUTERS

The commuter is the queerest bird of all. The suburb he inhabits has no essential vitality of its own and is a mere roost where he comes at day's end to go to sleep. Except in rare cases, the man who lives in Mamaroneck or Little Neck or Teaneck, and works in New York, discovers nothing much about the city except the time of arrival and departure of trains and buses, and the path to a quick lunch. He is desk-bound, and has never, idly roaming in the gloaming, stumbled suddenly on Belvedere Tower in the

Park, seen the ramparts rise sheer from the water of the pond, and the boys along the shore fishing for minnows, girls stretched out negligently on the shelves of the rocks; he has never come suddenly on anything at all in New York as a loiterer, because he has had no time between trains. He has fished in Manhattan's wallet and dug out coins, but has never listened to Manhattan's breathing, never awakened to its morning, never dropped off to sleep in its night. About 400,000 men and women come charging onto the Island each week-day morning, out of the mouths of tubes and tunnels. Not many among them have ever spent a drowsy afternoon in the great rustling oaken silence of the reading room of the Public Library, with the book elevator (like an old water wheel) spewing out books onto the trays. They tend their furnaces in Westchester and in Jersey, but have never seen the furnaces of the Bowery, the fires that burn in oil drums on zero winter nights. They may work in the financial district downtown and never see the extravagant plantings of Rockefeller Center — the daffodils and grape hyacinths and birches and the flags trimmed to the wind on a fine morning in spring. Or they may work in a midtown office and may let a whole year swing round without sighting Governors Island from the sea wall. The commuter dies with tremendous mileage to his credit, but he is no rover. His entrances and exits are more devious than those in a prairie-dog village; and he calmly plays bridge while buried in the mud at the bottom of the East River. The Long Island Rail Road alone carried forty million commuters last year; but many of them were the same fellow retracing his steps.

John Dos Passos, from Manhattan Transfer.

Ebb and Flood

The sun's moved to Jersey, the sun's behind Hoboken.

Covers are clicking on typewriters, rolltop desks are closing; elevators go up empty, come down jammed. It's ebbtide in the downtown district, flood in Flatbush, Woodlawn, Dyckman Street, Sheepshead Bay, New Lots Avenue, Canarsie.

Pink sheets, green sheets, gray sheets, FULL MARKET REPORTS, FINALS ON HAVRE DE GRACE. Print squirms among the shopworn officeworn, sagging faces, sore fingertips, aching insteps, strongarm men cram into subway expresses. SENATORS 8, GIANTS 2, DIVA RECOVERS PEARLS, $800,000 ROBBERY.

It's ebbtide on Wall Street, floodtide in the Bronx.

The sun's gone down in Jersey.

Edmund G. Love wrote his study of a vagrant living in the New York City subways in 1956.

SUBWAYS ARE FOR SLEEPING

On March 4, 1953, at approximately 11:30 p.m., Henry Shelby walked into the New York City hotel where he had maintained an apartment for five months. Upon asking for his key at the desk, he was informed by the clerk that he had been locked out until such time as his bill was settled. The bill amounted to about one hundred and thirteen dollars. At the moment, Shelby had about fourteen dollars, no job, and no friends upon whom he felt free to call for help. Without any argument, he turned and walked back out the door.

In the time that has passed since that night, he has returned to the hotel only once, and then merely to see if he had any mail. He has not attempted to retrieve any of his belongings held by the management. With the exception of approximately three and one-half months, in the summer of 1953, he has been one of the thousands of men in various stages of vagrancy who wander the streets of New York City at all hours of the day and night.

Henry Shelby, today, is forty-one years old, but looks at least five years younger. He is five feet, eleven and one-half inches tall, weighs 162 pounds. His hair is black but thinning, and his eyes are a deep blue. He has no disfigurements, and his bearing is good. The key to his personality lies in his eyes which express the depth of his feeling, or a quiet humor, depending upon his mood. When he is deep in thought, or troubled, he is apt to trace patterns on the floor, or in the dirt, with the toe of his shoe. At other times he moves briskly, and with some of the grace and sureness of an athlete. . .

The city of New York has long been noted for the number and

109

variety of its vagrants. Estimates as to the number of homeless and penniless men and women run from a conservative ten thousand to somewhere around half a million. Vagrants in other parts of the United States are a migratory lot, usually moving with the weather, but the New York variety stay put, occupying park benches, flophouses, gutters, and doorways in all seasons. There are many who possess qualifications as rich as Henry Shelby's. There are many who are literally human derelicts living out their days in a drunken stupor, waiting for an obscure death in the river or a ward at Bellevue. In between there are as many gradations as there are strata in normal society. Almost the only things all vagrants have in common are a hard luck story and an air of bewilderment. Not all of them have lost hope.

Henry Shelby is not a hopeless man, but he is certainly bewildered. He himself describes his present life as treading water, waiting to see how things come out. 'In the meantime,' he says, 'I'm getting along all right. I'm perfectly happy.'

In his months as a vagrant he has become an expert at management and has learned to put first things first. In his case this means food, cleanliness, and shelter, in that order. He prides himself on the fact that he has never panhandled, never visited a soup kitchen, or taken a night's lodging in one of the various hostels maintained by charitable agencies in the city. He has accepted handouts, but he can recall only one instance where anyone ever stepped up to him and gave him money: One night in the middle of winter he noticed advertisements for the première of a motion picture at a Broadway theater. He arrived early and took up a prominent position against the ropes under the marquee. As he stood there, watching the celebrities arrive in their limousines, a man came over to him and placed an unfolded ten-dollar bill in his hand.

Shelby has never been completely penniless except for one very brief period when he left New York. He has set fifteen cents, which represents subway fare, as the absolute minimum below which he will not allow his finances to sink. He has no maximum, but rarely possesses more than thirty dollars, which represents about one week's salary at present minimum levels. He acquires his money in a variety of ways. He is able to pick up a day's work here and there, carrying sandwich boards, working as a roustabout on the waterfront, washing dishes in cheap restaurants, shoveling snow for the city.

When he gets money, he nurses it carefully. He can tell, one minute after he gets it, exactly how long it will last, because he knows what he's going to eat, how many cigarettes he is going to smoke and the amount it will cost him for lodging, or incidentals. There are no extras in his life.

Virtually all of Shelby's cash goes for food and cigarettes. His breakfasts, invariably, consist of a glass of fruit or vegetable juice; his lunches, of a sandwich, usually a frankfurter, and a glass of milk. His one substantial meal is supper, and into it he piles all the dietary necessities he has missed since he last ate such a meal. His plate is apt to be loaded with green vegetables, cooked vegetables, and meat. He will haggle back and forth with the counterman in order to get these items, usually trading off potatoes and dessert for them. He never looks at the contents of a meal until he looks at the prices and he always chooses the cheapest meal on the menu, unless it contains sea food, which he detests. He knows where all the best food bargains in town are to be found. A bargain means quantity, but once or twice a week he will seek out a place which serves something of which he is especially fond.

Between meals he drinks coffee, usually two cups during the morning and three cups during the afternoon and evening. When he is especially broke he cuts out regular meals and subsists entirely on coffee, loading all the sugar and cream he can into his cup. He explains that these are free calories, and that calories, no matter what form they take, will keep him going until he is able to eat regularly again.

Shelby says that the truest statement he has ever heard is that no one will ever starve to death in the United States, and his technique for getting food when he is low on money is a simple one. He walks the streets until he finds a restaurant with a sign in the window that reads 'dishwasher wanted,' or 'counterman wanted.' He goes in and works long enough to pay for a meal and earn a little extra money. Usually he completes whatever constitutes a full day's work, but if the restaurant is a pleasant place, if he is treated well and the food is good, he may stay a week, or even longer. He is a good worker, and is well liked by his bosses and fellow employees. Many of the latter are men like himself.

He has learned a lot of odd jobs around kitchens and has filled in as a chef at two cafeterias, and as a short-order cook at a counter restaurant. At one place where he worked for five weeks, the manager recommended him for the managership of another unit in the chain which had fallen vacant. In this particular restaurant Shelby can always be sure of a job of some kind when he is broke; the manager will put him to work washing windows if there is nothing else available. The same condition holds true at five or six other places in town, but Shelby never uses them unless he is really desperate. He refers to them humorously as his social security.

Shelby usually allots no more than fifteen cents a day for shelter. Occasionally he pays more than this, but only when he has gotten by for two or three days without spending anything extra. Shelter means a place to sleep to Shelby, nothing else. His great preference, month in and month out, is for the Sixth and Eighth Avenue subways. He very rarely sleeps on the IRT or BMT. The IRT, with its ramshackle, noisy cars and its seating arrangement, is uncomfortable. The BMT has suitable accommodations, but, as Shelby describes it, 'an undesirable clientele.'

Shelby usually boards the Eighth Avenue Subway at Pennsylvania Station between midnight and one in the morning and takes the first express that comes along. At that hour there is usually a seat, especially in the front car, and he immediately settles down and drops off to sleep. He has developed the happy faculty of being able to drop off, or awaken, almost at will. He sleeps lightly, not because he is afraid of being robbed – he never has enough money to worry about that – but because he is very cautious about oversleeping. The vagrant who is still sleeping soundly when the train reaches the end of the line is more than likely to be picked up and lodged in jail by the transportation police.

Upon reaching the end of the line, Shelby walks up the stairs from the train platform to the next level. The turnstiles are at this level, and rest rooms have been placed inside the turnstiles. He retires to one of these rest rooms, finds a booth, fastens the door, and smokes a leisurely cigarette. It is supposedly a misdemeanor to carry lighted tobacco within the turnstile area, but Shelby says he discovered quite early in his career that even the police use the privacy of the rest rooms to have a quiet cigarette. Of course, he takes no chances. If there is a policeman anywhere on the turnstile level he will forgo his smoke.

After his cigarette, he goes back to the train platform and

boards the next train going in the opposite direction from the one he has just come. He quickly settles into a seat and goes to sleep again. He remains asleep until he reaches the other end of the line, then, as before, has his smoke and reboards a train. This time his nap is much shorter because he debarks at the Jay Street-Borough Hall station in Brooklyn and transfers to the Sixth Avenue Subway. On this he makes a full round trip, going all the way out to Queens, back to the Brooklyn end of the line, and then back to Jay Street. There he reboards the Eighth Avenue, which he rides back to Penn Station.

The whole trip consumes from four and a half to five and a half hours, during the course of which he has probably netted four hours of sleep. Over the months he has learned many of the habits and assignments of the transportation police, and he tries to keep himself from being too familiar a figure. For this reason he does not depend entirely upon the subway and does not dare ride it oftener than every other night.

On his off nights, in good weather, he sometimes uses the two great parks, Central and Prospect. By varying his hours of repose, carefully selecting secluded spots, and transferring his resting places often, he can spend one night a week in either one or the other of them. Also, in warm weather, there are fire escapes. Because he knows the city as well as he does, Shelby has been able to locate several covered, and therefore secluded, ones. Most of them are attached to theaters or warehouses and offer ideal accommodations. For some reason, the police never seem to bother vagrants who occupy these emergency exits. And on three or four occasions during the summer Shelby manages to get out to one of the beaches near the city. He can sleep unmolested there, especially on a hot night. There are always legitimate sleepers, as he calls them, who are trying to escape the heat.

Naturally, in the fall, winter, and early spring, Shelby has to find other places. The benches in the waiting room at Grand Central, Penn Station, and the Port Authority Bus Terminal are his favorite outside of the subway. As in every other place, however, there are strict rules of conduct which must be observed. Shelby learned early that the station police in each of the three establishments have set habits. They make two routine checks during the course of a night. At Grand Central, for example, these checks come at one-thirty and five-thirty. Between the checks there are both policemen and plain-clothes men on

113

duty in the waiting room throughout the night, and they wander up and down, carefully checking trouble spots. Ordinarily, however, these roving guardians will not disturb people who are stretched out on the benches asleep. Between the checks, therefore, it is possible to get almost four hours of uninterrupted sleep in a prone position. Conditions at Penn Station are about the same, and at the bus terminal the checks are farther apart, but the lights are brighter and the crowds larger, giving less room to stretch out.

Shelby keeps, as part of his equipment for sleeping in one of the three terminals, three tickets: to Poughkeepsie, New York; Princeton, New Jersey; and Elizabeth, New Jersey, one for each of the three lines. Inspection of timetables has revealed that there are no busses or trains leaving New York for these points between one and six in the morning. In emergencies, should the station police question him too closely, Shelby flashes the appropriate ticket and claims that he missed the last train and is waiting for the first one in the morning. This has always worked, but on one occasion a station policeman escorted him to a six-thirty train and made certain he got on it. Shelby got off at 125th Street and walked back to Grand Central. . .

CHAPTER 7

LEISURE

'William M. Bobo' was the pseudonym of a Southern gentleman who travelled in the North in the 1850s.

TAYLOR'S SALOON

Now we will go to the largest bowling-saloon in the world; it *must be so,* as the *sign* on the house *says so.* This whole building is appropriated to ten-pins; what an idea! a house which could not have cost less than seventy-five thousand dollars, may be more, devoted exclusively to ten-pins! We are a great people, and this is a great country when it gets to be fenced in, as the Western man would express it.

New York, with its great wealth, has always possessed many of those establishments, the sole design of which is to minister to the tastes of the opulent, refined, and fashionable classes of society. With each succeeding year it has steadily increased in wealth, and consequently in the number and splendor of all those matters of elegance and luxury, which, gratifying and delighting only the senses, are found only amid abundance of wealth.

This is especially true of those far-famed refreshment saloons, *Taylor's* and *Thompson's,* and most truly of *Taylor's.* Ten years ago an establishment like *Taylor's* would have been considered an extravagant folly, and it first would have been visited chiefly to gratify curiosity in seeing it, and not the palate to partake of its delicacies. Mr. Taylor led off in this great reform, by introducing many new luxuries into his ice-cream saloon, and it was soon evident from the success attending this movement, that the fashionable world was delighted with the inauguration of this regime of epicurean administration.

Lately Mr. Taylor has erected an establishment which is, or will be, worthy of its name – TAYLOR'S EPICUREAN PALACE – which is now approaching completion, and which will surpass every thing in the world in the way of refreshment saloons. Think for a moment of an expense of $350,000 for a refreshment saloon! Mr. Taylor's plan embraces all the luxuries and the rôle of a modern first-class hotel upon the European plan, where magnificent suits of rooms are to be furnished to those who are willing to pay a liberal price, in order to secure an absolute exemption from the confusion and bustle of a common stopping-place for the herd, like the Irving House.

But let us go in and take a seat near the back part of the room,

116

so that we can see all who come in and go out, without looking or appearing as if we were paying any attention to what is going on.

See that tall chap coming in, he is one of the fancies who *amble* up and down Broadway, at particular periods in the day. She, who is under his protection, is a cousin of his, from the country, supposed to be very rich. His name is Van Antwerp – hers Edwards. They seat themselves, and call for a bottle of the coldest champagne.

That elderly gentleman and lady are strangers, here on a visit; been here often before, and take things deliberately. What a difference it makes. Over to the left, near the wall, under the lamp, sit a bevy of ladies – these are 'up town folks,' who happened to meet, while out shopping, and just stepped into Taylor's, to exchange a dish of scandal or gossip, as well as sweetmeats.

Beyond them is a pair of Avenuedle daisies, I guess – but we can tell when they call the waiter again. Ah, I told you so – *'ices for two.'*

Opposite sit a lady and a gentleman in close conversation, a little sighing and playing with the corners of pocket handkerchiefs; that is a pair of doves, billing and cooing a little.

That fellow coming towards us, hat off, quizzing-glass stuck over his left eye, exquisitely curled moustache, whiskers a-la-Scott, flashing cravat, in the broad-band tie, white vest and fancy blue-striped pants, elegant patent-leather boots, with his hat and stick in one hand, and the other sticking in the arm-hole of his vest, with the odd glove in it – is young Brown, whose father belongs to the firm of Brown Brothers & Co., of Wall-street, rich bankers. He will make some of their hard earnings go like chaff before the wind.

I think that Taylor, or whoever is managing the house, must be clearing at least several hundred dollars clear of all expenses daily. It is a very pretty business. Here you can get all the tropical fruits as soon as they appear in the markets where they are grown. I have seen watermelons in at Taylor's before they appeared in Charleston, S.C., or Augusta, Ga., two of the greatest melon markets in the world.

New-York could do no more without Taylor's than without her tailors and milliners; and the fashionable portion of japonicadom, were these saloons closed, would heave as many sighs, and make as many complaints over the event as if a famine had visited the nation.

117

The actress Tallulah Bankhead was a great fan of one of New York's vanished institutions – the New York Giants baseball team. She recounted her life as a supporter in her Autobiography.

THE GIANTS AND ME

Attending a Giant game with me, say my cronies, is an experience comparable to shooting the Snake River rapids in a canoe. When they lose I taste wormwood. When they win I want to do a tarantella on top of the dugout. A Giant rally brings out the Roman candle in me. The garments of adjoining box-holders start to smolder.

I once lured the young Viennese actor, Helmut Dantine, to a set-to between the Giants and the Pirates. Mr. Dantine had never seen a game before. My airy explanations confused the *émigré*. Rapt in his attention to my free translation of the sacrifice hit, Helmut was almost decapitated by a foul ball. Mr. Dantine looked upon the *faux pas* as a hostile act. He felt I had tricked him into a false sense of security that the hitter might have an unsuspecting target. He left before the ninth, a grayer if not a wiser man.

It's true I run a temperature when watching the Giants trying to come from behind in the late innings, either at the Polo Grounds or on my TV screen. I was hysterical for hours after Bobby Thomson belted Ralph Branca for that ninth inning homer in the final game of the Dodger-Giant playoff in '51. The Giants had to score four runs in the ninth to win. Remember? There was blood on the moon that night in Bedford Village. But I don't know nearly as much about baseball as Ethel Barrymore. Ethel is a real fan, can give you batting averages, the text of the infield fly rule, and comment on an umpire's vision.

Someone has said that Ethel Barrymore has the reticence born of assurance whereas my monologues indicate my insecurity. The point is moot. It's unlikely I'll ever submit to a psychiatrist's couch. I don't want some stranger prowling around through my psyche, monkeying with my id. I don't need an analyst to tell me that I have never had any sense of security. Who has?

My devotion to the Giants, dating back to 1939, has drawn the fire of renegades, eager to deflate me. One of these wrote that on my first visit to Ebbets Field in Brooklyn, I rooted all afternoon for Dolph Camilli, the Dodger first baseman. I had been tricked into this treason, swore my enemy, because I wasn't aware that the Giants wore gray uniforms when traveling, the residents white. Though I invaded Flatbush to cheer Mel Ott, Giant right fielder, I wound up in hysterics over Camilli because both had the numeral '4' on the back of their uniform. Stuff, balderdash and rot, not to use a few other words too hot to handle in a memoir.

A daughter of the deep South, I have little time for the 'Yankees.' They're bleak perfectionists, insolent in their confidence, the snobs of the diamond. The Yankees are all technique, no color or juice. But they keep on winning pennants year after year. Not the Giants! They've won one flag in the last fourteen years.

I blew my first fuse over the Giants in the summer of '39, when introduced to Harry Danning and Mel Ott. Ott was so good-looking, so shy, so gentlemanly – and from Louisiana. For two weeks I got up in the middle of the night – around noon by the actor's clock – to charge up to the Polo Grounds.

I worked myself up into such a fever that I invited the team to see a performance of *The Little Foxes*. After the play I served them a buffet supper, and drinks compatible with their training rules, on the promenade which fringed the rear of the balcony. The Giants, following this soiree, dropped eight games in a row. Had I hexed them? The suspicion chilled me. I denied myself the Polo Grounds and they started to win again.

Calvin Trillin was born in Kansas City in 1935. He is a staff-writer for the New Yorker.

DINNER AT THE DE LA RENTAS'

January 17, 1981

Another week has passed without my being invited to the de la Rentas'. Even that overstates my standing. Until I read in *The New York Times Magazine* a couple of weeks ago about the de la Rentas having become 'barometers of what constitutes fashionable society' ('Françoise and Oscar de la Renta have created a latter-day salon for *le nouveau grand monde* – the very rich, very powerful and very gifted'), I wasn't even aware of what I wasn't being invited to week after week. Once I knew, of course, it hurt.

Every time the phone rang, I thought it must be Mrs. de la Renta with an invitation ('Mr. Trillin? Françoise de la Renta here. We're having a few very rich, very powerful and/or very gifted people over Sunday evening to celebrate Tisha B'av, and we thought you and the missus might like to join us'). The phone rang. It was my mother calling from Kansas City to ask if I'm sure I sent a thank-you note to my Cousin Edna for the place setting of stainless Edna and six other cousins went in on for our wedding gift in 1965. The phone rang. An invitation! Fats Goldberg, the pizza baron, asked if we'd like to bring the kids to his uptown branch Sunday night to sample the sort of pizza he regularly describes as 'a gourmet tap-dance.'

'Thanks, Fat Person, but I'll have to phone you,' I said. 'We may have another engagement Sunday.'

The phone quit ringing.

'Why aren't I in *le nouveau grand monde?*' I asked my wife, Alice.

'Because you speak French with a Kansas City accent?' she asked in return.

'Not at all,' I said. 'Sam Spiegel, the Hollywood producer, is a regular at the de la Rentas', and I hear that the last time someone asked him to speak French he said 'Gucci.' '

'Why would you want to go there anyway?' Alice said. 'Didn't you read that the host is so phony he added his own 'de la' to what had been plain old Oscar Renta?'

'Who can blame a man for not wanting to go through life sounding like a taxi driver?' I said. 'Family background's not important in *le nouveau grand monde*. Diana Vreeland says Henry Kissinger is the star. The Vicomtesse de Ribes says 'Françoise worships intelligence.' You get invited by accomplishment – taking over a perfume company, maybe, or invading Cambodia.'

'Why don't we just call Fats and tell him we'll be there for a gourmet tap-dance?' Alice said.

'Maybe it would help if you started wearing dresses designed by Oscar de la Renta,' I said. 'Some of his guests say they would feel disloyal downing Mrs. d's chicken fricassee while wearing someone else's merchandise.'

Alice shook her head. 'Oscar de la Renta designs those ruffly dresses that look like what the fat girl made a bad mistake wearing to the prom,' she said.

'Things were a lot easier when fashionable society was limited to old-rich goyim, and all the rest of us didn't have to worry about being individually rejected,' I said.

'At least they knew better than to mingle socially with their dressmakers,' Alice said.

Would I be ready if the de la Rentas phoned? The novelist Jerzy Kosinski, after all, told the *Times* that evenings with them were 'intellectually demanding.' Henry Kissinger, the star himself, said that the de la Rentas set 'an interesting intellectual standard' – although, come to think of it, that phrase could also be applied to Fats Goldberg.

Alone at the kitchen table, I began to polish my dinner-table chitchat, looking first to the person I imagined being seated on my left (the Vicomtesse de Ribes, who finds it charming that her name reminds me of barbecue joints in Kansas City) and then to the person on my right (Barbara Walters, another regular, who has tried to put me at my ease by confessing that in French she doesn't do her r's terribly well). 'I was encouraged when it leaked that the Reagan Cabinet was going to be made up of successful managers from the world of business,' I say, 'but I expected them all to be Japanese.'

Barbara and the Vicomtesse smile. Alice, who had just walked into the kitchen, looked concerned.

'Listen,' Alice said. 'I read in the *Times* that Mrs. de la Renta is very strict about having only one of each sort of person at a dinner party. Maybe they already have someone from Kansas City.'

Possible. Jerzy Kosinski mentioned that Mrs. d is so careful about not including more than one stunning achiever from each walk of life ('she understands that every profession generates a few princes or kings') that he and Norman Mailer have never been at the de la Rentas' on the same evening ('when I arrive, I like to think that, as a novelist, I'm unique'). Only one fabulous beauty. Only one world-class clotheshorse.

Then I realized that the one-of-each rule could work to my advantage. As I envisioned it, Henry Kissinger phones Mrs. d only an hour before dinner guests are to arrive. He had been scheduled to pick up fifteen grand that night explaining SALT II to the Vinyl Manufacturers Association convention in Chicago, but the airports are snowed in. He and Nancy will be able to come to dinner after all. 'How marvelous, darling!' Mrs. d. says.

She hangs up and suddenly looks stricken. 'My God!' she says to Oscar. 'What are we going to do? We already have one war criminal coming!'

What to do except to phone the man who conflicts with the star and tell him the dinner had to be called off because Mr. d had come down with a painful skin disease known as the Seventh Avenue Shpilkes. What to do about the one male place at the table now empty – between Vicomtesse de Ribes and Barbara Walters?

The phone rings. 'This is Françoise de la Renta,' the voice says. 'This is Calvin of the Trillin,' I say. 'I'll be right over.'

Andy Warhol was born in Philadelphia in 1928 and came to New York in the fifties. He became famous in the next decade as an artist, film-maker and promoter of all manner of new and provocative things. In those days he frequented Max's Kansas City, a restaurant and bar and second-home for many of the era's famous and infamous.

MAX'S

In September we started going regularly to a two-story bar/ restaurant on Park Avenue South off Union Square that Mickey Ruskin had opened in late '65. It was called Max's Kansas City and it became the ultimate hangout. Max's was the farthest uptown of any of the restaurants Mickey had ever operated. He'd had a place on East 7th Street called Deux Mégots that later became the Paradox, and then he'd had the Ninth Circle, a Village bar with a format similar to what Max's would have, and then an Avenue B bar called the Annex. Mickey had always been attracted to the downtown art atmosphere – at Deux Mégots, he'd held poetry readings – and now painters and poets were starting to drift into Max's. The art heavies would group around the bar and the kids would be in the back room, basically.

Max's Kansas City was the exact place where Pop Art and pop life came together in New York in the sixties – teeny boppers and sculptors, rock stars and poets from St. Mark's Place, Hollywood actors checking out what the underground actors were all about, boutique owners and models, modern dancers and go-go dancers – everybody went to Max's and everything got homogenized there.

Larry Rivers once said to me, 'I've often asked myself, 'What is

122

a bar?' It's a space that has liquor that's usually fairly dark, where you go for a certain kind of social interaction. It's not a dinner party. It's not a dance. It's not an opening. You move in a certain way through this space, over a period of time, and you begin to recognize faces that begin to recognize you. And you may have had experiences with some of these people before which you kind of pick up on in another way in this space.'

I started going to Max's a lot. Mickey was an art fan, so I'd give him a painting and he'd give us credit, and everybody in our group could just sign for their dinners until the credit was used up. It was a really pleasant arrangement.

The back room at Max's, lit by Dan Flavin's red light piece, was where everybody wound up every night. After all the parties were over and all the bars and all the discotheques closed up, you'd go on to Max's and meet up with everybody – and it was like going home, only better.

Max's became the showcase for all the fashion changes that had been taking place at the art openings and shows: now people weren't going to the art openings to show off their new looks – they just skipped all the preliminaries and went straight to Max's. Fashion wasn't what you wore someplace anymore; it was the whole reason for going. The event itself was optional – the way Max's functioned as a fashion gallery proved that. Kids would crowd around the security mirror over the night deposit slot in the bank next door ('Last mirror before Max's') to check themselves out for the long walk from the front door, past the bar, past all the fringe tables in the middle, and finally into the club room in the back.

Max's is where I started meeting the really young kids who had dropped out of school and been running around the streets for a couple of years – hard-looking, beautiful little girls with perfect makeup and fabulous clothes, and you'd find out later they were fifteen and already had a baby. These kids really knew how to dress, they had just the right fashion instincts, somehow. They were a type of kid I hadn't been around much before. Although they weren't educated like the Boston crowd or the San Remo crowd, they were very sharp in a comical sort of way – I mean, they certainly knew how to put each other down, standing on chairs and screaming insults. Like, if Gerard walked in with his fashion look really together and had that very serious Roman god-like expression on his face that people get when they think they're looking good, one of the little girls at Max's (the Twin-Twats, they were called) would jump up on the table and swoon, 'Oh my God, it's Apollo! Oh, Apollo, will you sit with us tonight?'

I couldn't decide if these kids were intelligent but crazy, or just plain pea-brained with a flair for comedy and clothes. It was impossible to tell whether their problem was lack of intelligence or lack of sanity.

Composer and writer Ned Rorem's New York Diaries (1966) *described many hitherto hidden facets of the lives of New York's gay community.*

THE BATHS

A Turkish bath, like the Quaker service, is a place of silent meeting. The silence is shared solely by men, men who come uniquely together not to speak but to act. More even than the army, the bath is by definition a male, if not a masculine, domain. (Though in Paris, whimsically, it's a lady who presents you your *billet d'entrée*, robe and towel.) There are as many varieties of bath as of motel, from the scorpion-ridden hammams of Marrakech, where like Rimbaud in a boxcar you'll be systematically violated by a regiment, to the carpeted saunas of Frisco, where like a corpse in a glossy morgue you'll be a slab of flab on marble with Musak. There is no variety, however, in the purpose served: anonymous carnality. As in a whorehouse, you check inter-personal responsibility at the door; but unlike the whorehouse, here a *ménage* might accidentally meet in mutual infidelity. The ethical value too is like prostitution's: the consolation that no one can prove you are not more fulfilled by a stranger (precisely because there's no responsibility to deflect your fantasies – fantasies which now are real) than by the mate you dearly love, and the realization that Good Sex is not in performing as the other person wants but as you want. You will reconfirm this as you retreat into time through every bath of history.

For decades there has existed in central Manhattan one such establishment, notorious throughout the planet but never written about. Certainly this one seeks no publicity: word of mouth seems sufficient to promote its million-dollar business. Located in the heart of a wholesale floral district, there's small chance that an unsuspecting salesman might happen in for a simple rundown, the nearest hotel being the Martha Washington – for women only. The customers do constitute as heterogeneous a cross section as you'll ever find. (There are only two uncategorizable phenomena: the care and feeding of so-called creative artists, and the nature of a Turkish bath's clientele.) Minors and majors, beatniks and bartenders, all ages and proclivities of the married and single, the famous and tough, so *many* from Jersey! but curiously few mad queens because it's hard to maintain a style stark naked. To run across your friends is less embarrassing than cumbersome: who wants gossip now?

You enter at any age, in any condition, any time of night or week, pay dearly for a fetid cubicle, and are given a torn gown and a pair of mismated slippers (insufficient against the grime that remains in your toes for days). You penetrate an obscure world, disrobe in private while reading graffiti, emerge rerobed into the public of gray wanderers so often compared to the lost souls of Dante, although this geography is not built of seven circles but of four square stories each capable of housing some eighty mortals. Once, you are told, this was a synagogue; today it's a brothel lit like *Guernica* by one nude bulb. The top floor is a suite of squalid rooms giving onto a corridor from *The Blood of a Poet* with background music of a constant pitty-pat, whips and whispers, slurps and groans. The second floor, more of same, plus massive dormitory. On the ground floor are cubicles, a television room, a monastic refectory. The basement contains fringe benefits: a dryer, a massage room, a large dirty pool, and the famous steam-room wherein *partouzes* are not discouraged.

The personnel, working in shifts, comprises at any given time some ten people, including two masseurs and a uniformed policeman. Each of these appears dull-witted due to years of inhaling the gloomy disinfectant of locker room and hamburger grease.

There are feast and fast days, rough Spanish mornings and sneaky afternoons, even Embryo Night at the Baths. Eternal motion, never action (meaning production): despite a daily ocean of orgasm the ceaseless efforts at cross-breeding could hardly make a mule. Not from want of trying: at any time you may witness couplings of white with black, beauty with horror, aardvark with dinosaur, panda with pachyderm, skinny-old-slate-gray-potbelly-bald with chubby-old-slate-gray-potbelly-

125

bald, heartbreakingly gentle with stimulatingly rugged – but always, paradoxically, like with like. Your pupils widen as a faun mounts that stevedore, or when a mountain descends on Mohammed. Some cluster forever together in a throbbing Medusa's head; others disentangle themselves to squat in foggy corners, immobile as carnivorous orchids, waiting to 'go up' on whatever passes. There's one! on his knees, praying with tongue more active than a windmill in a hurricane, neck thrown back like Mata Hari's and smeared with tears nobody notices mingling with steam. All are centered on the spasm that in a fraction switches from sublime to ridiculous, the sickening spasm sought by poets and peasants, and which, like great love, makes the great seem silly. . . Yet if at those suburban wife-swapping gangbangs there's risk of pregnancy, these mirthless matings stay sterile – not because the sexes aren't mixed but because the species *are*.

If you don't believe me, says Maldoror, go see for yourself. You won't believe it *of* yourself, the money and months you've passed, a cultured person lurking in shadows governed by groin! Did you *honestly* spend the night? Can you, with your splitting head, manage it down the hall to pee, through shafts of black sunlight and idiot eyes and churning mouths that never say die, and crunched on the floor those tropical roaches you hadn't noticed last evening? Don't slip in the sperm while retching at the fact that it's 8 a.m. and there's still a dull moan and a sound of belts (they've really no sense of proportion). So leave, descend while cackling still rends the ear, reclaim that responsibility checked with your wallet. Hate all those bad people; or, if you will, feel lightened and purged. Allow the sounds to dim – the anti-climactic puffing and shooting and slippery striving, the friendless hasty jerkings that could fertilize a universe in the dirty dark (*quel embarras de richesses!*). Quit the baths to go home and bathe, but make clear to yourself that such uncommitted hilarity doesn't necessarily preclude a throbbing heart. For three times there you found eternal love.

CHAPTER 8

NEIGHBORHOODS

From E. B. White's Here is New York.

THE NEIGHBORHOOD PATTERN

I have an idea that people from villages and small towns, people accustomed to the convenience and the friendliness of neighborhood over-the-fence living, are unaware that life in New York follows the neighborhood pattern. The city is literally a composite of tens of thousands of tiny neighborhood units. . .

So complete is each neighborhood, and so strong the sense of neighborhood, that many a New Yorker spends a lifetime within the confines of an area smaller than a country village. Let him walk two blocks from his corner and he is in a strange land and will feel uneasy till he gets back.

Storekeepers are particularly conscious of neighborhood boundary lines. A woman friend of mine moved recently from one apartment to another, a distance of three blocks. When she turned up, the day after the move, at the same grocer's that she had patronized for years, the proprietor was in ectasy – almost in tears – at seeing her. 'I was afraid,' he said, 'now that you've moved away I wouldn't be seeing you any more.' To him, *away* was three blocks, or about seven hundred and fifty feet.

Malcolm Cowley was born in Pennsylvania in 1898, served in the First World War, and lived in the Village in the twenties. In 1934 he published Exile's Return, *analysing the post-war 'lost' generation and recalling their lives and struggles.*

THE GREENWICH VILLAGE IDEA

In those days when division after division was landing in Hoboken and marching up Fifth Avenue in full battle equipment, when Americans were fighting the Bolshies in Siberia and guarding the Rhine – in those still belligerent days that followed the Armistice there was a private war between Greenwich Village and the *Saturday Evening Post*.

Other magazines fought in the same cause, but the *Post* was persistent and powerful enough to be regarded as chief of the aggressor nations. It published stories about the Villagers, editorials and articles against them, grave or flippant serials dealing with their customs in a mood of disparagement or alarm, humorous pieces done to order by its staff writers, cartoons in which the Villagers were depicted as long-haired men and short-haired women with ridiculous bone-rimmed spectacles – in all, a long campaign of invective beginning before the steel strike or the Palmer Raids and continuing through the jazz era, the boom and the depression. The burden of it was always the same: that the Village was the haunt of affectation; that it was inhabited by fools and fakers; that the fakers hid Moscow heresies under the disguise of cubism and free verse; that the fools would eventually be cured of their folly: they would forget this funny business about art and return to domesticity in South Bend, Indiana, and sell motorcars, and in the evenings sit with slippered feet while their children romped about them in paper caps made from the advertising pages of the *Saturday Evening Post*. The Village was dying, had died already, smelled to high heaven and Philadelphia. . .

The Villagers did not answer this attack directly: instead they carried on a campaign of their own against the culture of which the *Post* seemed to be the final expression. They performed autopsies, they wrote obituaries of civilization in the United States, they shook the standardized dust of the country from their feet. Here, apparently, was a symbolic struggle: on the one side, the great megaphone of middle-class America; on the other, the American disciples of art and artistic living. Here, in its latest incarnation, was the eternal warfare of bohemian against bourgeois, poet against propriety – Villon and the Bishop of Orléans, Keats and the quarterly reviewers, Rodolphe, Mimi and the landlord. . .

. . .But the Village, when we first came there to live, was undergoing a crisis. People were talking about the good old days of 1916. It seemed unlikely that they would ever return.

The Village, before America entered the war, contained two mingled currents: one of those had now disappeared. It contained two types of revolt, the individual and the social – or the aesthetic and the political, or the revolt against puritanism and the revolt against capitalism – we might tag the two of them briefly as *bohemianism* and *radicalism*. In those prewar days, however, the two currents were hard to distinguish. Bohemians read Marx and all the radicals had a touch of the bohemian: it seemed that both

129

types were fighting in the same cause. Socialism, free love, anarchism, syndicalism, free verse – all these creeds were lumped together by the public, and all were physically dangerous to practice. Bill Haywood, the one-eyed man-mountain, the Cyclops of the IWW, appeared regularly at Mabel Dodge's Wednesday nights, in a crowd of assorted poets and Cubist painters who, listening to his slow speech, might fancy themselves in the midst of the fight at Cœur d'Alene. During the bread riots of 1915 the Wobblies made their headquarters in Mary Vorse's studio on Tenth Street; and Villagers might get their heads broken in Union Square by the police before appearing at The Liberal Club to recite Swinburne in bloody bandages. The Liberal Club was the social center of the Village, just as the *Masses,* which also represented both tendencies, was its intellectual center.

But the war, and especially the Draft Law, separated the two currents. People were suddenly forced to decide what kind of rebels they were: if they were merely rebels against puritanism they could continue to exist safely in Mr. Wilson's world. The political rebels had no place in it. Some of them yielded, joined the crusade for democracy, fought the Bolsheviks at Archangel, or volunteered to help the Intelligence Service by spying on their former associates and submitting typewritten reports about them to the Adjutant General's office. Others evaded the draft by fleeing to Mexico, where they were joined by a number of the former aesthetes, who had suddenly discovered that they were political rebels too. Still others stood by their opinions and went to Leavenworth Prison. Whatever course they followed, almost all the radicals of 1917 were defeated by events. The bohemian tendency triumphed in the Village, and talk about revolution gave way to talk about psychoanalysis. The *Masses,* after being suppressed, and after temporarily reappearing as the *Liberator,* gave way to magazines like the *Playboy,* the *Pagan* (their names expressed them adequately) and the *Little Review.*

After the war the Village was full of former people. There were former anarchists who had made fortunes manufacturing munitions, former Wobblies about to open speakeasies, former noblewomen divorced or widowed, former suffragists who had been arrested after picketing the White House, former conscientious objectors paroled from Leavenworth, former aviators and soldiers of fortune, former settlement workers, German spies, strike leaders, poets, city editors of Socialist dailies. But the distinguished foreign artists who had worked in the Village from 1914 till 1917, and given it a new character, had disappeared along with the active labor leaders. Nobody seemed to be doing anything now, except lamenting the time's decay. For the moment the Village was empty of young men.

But the young men were arriving from week to week, as colleges held commencement exercises or troops were demobilized. One of the first results of their appearance was the final dissolution of the Liberal Club.

Its members had been resigning or leaving their dues unpaid. As a means of paying off its debts, the club voted to hold a dance – not an ordinary Webster Hall affair, but a big dance, uptown at the Hotel Commodore, with a pageant, and thousands of tickets sold, and none given away. But of course they were given away in the end. Everybody in the Village expected to be invited to every Village function, simply by right of residence, and the Liberal Club was forced to yield to a massed demand that was accompanied by threats of gate-crashings and riots.

On one of our free tickets we took with us a young lady who had just graduated from Radcliffe.

The dance at the Commodore was something new in Village history: there were so many youngsters, such high spirits, so many people not drinking quietly as in the old days, but with a frantic desire to get drunk and enjoy themselves. After midnight there were little commotions everywhere in the ballroom. Laurence Vail was deciding that people were disagreeable and telling them so in a most polite way, but some of them didn't like being called smug – it took four detectives to throw him out, and he left behind him a great handful of bloodstained yellow hair. I noticed people gathering about the Radcliffe young lady admiringly, and later I saw them avoiding her; she had developed the habit of biting them in the arm and shrieking. Once, having bitten a strange Pierrot, she jumped backward with a shriek into a great Chinese vase. It crashed to the floor.

We never saw her after that night. She had met a copy-desk man and later I heard that he was asking the address of an abortionist; still later she wrote that she was married and had a baby. There were many people like that; they appeared in the Village, made themselves the center of a dance or a crowd, everybody liked or hated them and told stories about them; then suddenly they were gone, living in Flatbush, Queens or Keokuk, holding down jobs or wheeling baby carriages. But the vase was the end of the Liberal Club, the broken vase that cost so much to replace and the free tickets. The dance at the Commodore had been a great success and had emptied the treasury. After that the social centers of the Village were two saloons: the Hell Hole, on Sixth Avenue at the corner of West Fourth Street, and the Working Girls' Home, at Greenwich Avenue and Christopher Street. The Hell Hole was tough and dirty; the proprietor kept a pig in the cellar and fed it scraps from the free-lunch counter. The boys in the back room were small-time gamblers and petty thieves, but the saloon was also patronized by actors and writers from the Provincetown Playhouse, which was just around the corner. Sometimes the two groups mingled. The gangsters admired Dorothy Day because she could drink them under the table; but they felt more at home with Eugene O'Neill, who listened to their troubles and never criticized. They pitied him, too, because he was thin and shabbily dressed. One of them said to him, 'You go to any department store, Gene, and pick yourself an overcoat and tell me what size it is and I steal it for you.' The Hell Hole stayed in business during the first two or three years of prohibition, but then it was closed and I don't know where the gangsters met after that. The actors and playwrights moved on to the Working Girls' Home, where the front door was locked, but where a side door on Christopher Street still led into a room where Luke O'Connor served Old Fashioneds and the best beer and stout he could buy from the wildcat breweries.

It was in the Working Girls' Home that I first became conscious of the difference between two generations. There were two sorts of people here: those who had lived in the Village before 1917 and those who had just arrived from France or college. For the first time I came to think of them as 'they' and 'we.'

'They' wore funny clothes: it was the first thing that struck you about them. The women had evolved a regional costume, then widely cartooned in the magazines: hair cut in a Dutch bob, hat carried in the hand, a smock of some bright fabric (often embroidered Russian linen), a skirt rather shorter than the fashion of the day, gray cotton stockings and sandals. With heels set firmly on the ground and abdomens protruding a little – since they wore no corsets and dieting hadn't become popular – they had a look of unexampled solidity; it was terrifying to be advanced upon by six of them in close formation. But this costume wasn't universal. Some women preferred tight-fitting tailored suits with Buster Brown collars; one had a five-gallon hat which she wore on all occasions, and there was a girl who always appeared in riding boots, swinging a crop, as if she had galloped down Sixth Avenue, watered her horse and tied him to a pillar of the Elevated; I called her Yoicks. The men, as a rule, were more conventional, but tweedy and unpressed. They did not let their hair grow over their collars, but they had a good deal more of it than was permitted by fashion. There were a few Russian blouses among them, a few of the authentic Windsor ties that marked the bohemians of the 1890s.

'They' tried to be individual, but there is a moment when individualism becomes a uniform in spite of itself. 'We' were accustomed to uniforms and content to wear that of the American middle classes. We dressed inconspicuously, as well as we were able.

'They' were older, and this simple fact continued to impress me long after I ceased to notice their clothes. Their ages ran from sixty down to twenty-three; at one end of the scale there was hardly any difference. But the Village had a pervading atmosphere of middle-agedness. To stay in New York during the war was a greater moral strain than to enter the army: there were more decisions to be made and uneasily justified; also there were defeats to be concealed. The Village in 1919 was like a conquered country. Its inhabitants were discouraged and drank joylessly. 'We' came among them with an unexpended store of energy: we had left our youth at home, and for two years it had been accumulating at compound interest; now we were eager to lavish it even on trivial objects.

And what did the older Villagers think of us? We had fresh faces and a fresh store of jokes and filthy songs collected in the army; we were nice to take on parties, to be amused by and to lecture. Sometimes they were cruel to us in a deliberately thoughtless way. Sometimes they gave us advice which was never taken because it was obviously a form of boasting. I don't believe they thought much about us at all.

Leroi Jones was born in Newark, New Jersey, in 1934. After being thrown out of the Air Force in 1957 he moved to the Village in search of the artist's life. He gained recognition as a poet and notoriety as a playwright for his

Dutchman (1964). In that year he moved to Harlem and later changed his name to Imamu Amiri Baraka. He continues to be a leading Black political activist and writer.

THE FIFTIES

Now I began to read the real estate section. Apartments to Let. I was not in a panic but I felt I should look. And it gave me something to do on the bus in the mornings or during the 45-minute lunches Mrs. Steloff gave us. Talking to Tim and Brad was occasionally encouraging. They wanted to move too. They were ready. But then one morning I saw an ad in the paper for an apartment on East 3rd Street. An ex-UN worker was leaving, he had sublet the apartment, down just off First Avenue, and now he was splitting to go somewhere! Lunchtime I found my way down there. I'd wanted the Village proper, but this was close and it cost only $28 a month for three rooms, a cold-water walk-up. But to me it was right. When I walked in the apartment a couple of people were there talking to an Indian-looking guy about this and that and various qualifications. I walked in saying, 'I'll take it! I'll take it.' It didn't matter to me. I'd take it! And in a few minutes the business was all but concluded.

An apartment in New York? What? How can you handle that? These kind of questions bounced subtly off the walls of my parents' house. (I didn't have much to take. Most of my civilian clothes had thinned out being in the Air Force. I had no great library to transport. It wouldn't be that bad.)

'But how can you deal with the rent? That job?' Fifty dollars a week was what Mrs. Steloff was paying me. I'd have money to spare. I had no other responsibilities and besides I'd have roommates. But Wilson and Davis squared up on me. They never left Jersey at all.

At the Gotham, I was constantly picking up on whatever in all directions. Authors' names I'd never heard of before, books I knew nothing about. Gotham has always been the home of 'We Moderns,' as it was listed in the catalogue: the post-WWI explosion of Western art and literature that brought these expressions into the 20th century, redefining the form and content of Euro-American life, still explosive as the French Revolution and Commune of 1871, but distorted by the cynicism and disillusion created by World War I and the abject crumbling of the Brotherhood of (white) Man on the battlefields of Belgium, France, and Germany. The maturation of Imperialism!

The New Directions books, the sacred texts of 20's modernity: Sartre, Cocteau, Djuna Barnes, Fitzgerald, D. H. Lawrence, Stein, and the contemporary bridge into our own day, existentialism. *The Little Review, Blast,* stream of consciousness, the mythology of Eliot, Pound, Joyce, Shakespeare & Co., Hemingway, the *Cantos,* all these things I was picking up on much deeper than before, buying books and carrying them back on the bus readying for my move.

Then one day I went over with my few things and few books. There was a little furniture, a bed, a couple chairs. My father drove me, my mother went with us, searching East 3rd Street and First Avenue for some sign she could understand or feel comfortable with. The joint looked even grimmer inside, going up the narrow dark halls, opening the door and into the tiny cold-water flat. I could see my mother's eyes misting over. She looked hurt. My father went on talking about how I had better get some furniture. (They'd given me some sheets and towels, a blanket.) He was trying to make a joke of it all. I guess he knew, at least, that I was determined to do that, that I was off on my own, like it or not! And that, in itself, was encouraging. But my mother could barely see or speak. She mostly grunted at the place and whatever she thought the future held. And suddenly I was alone!

There were no lights burning. Con Ed hadn't yet turned on the power. There was no gas. I couldn't even cook – not that I knew how. I was using candles and they shed their errie light, stuttering and crooked. I was where I wanted, I thought. Living by myself. (I'd wanted that, hadn't I?) Throughout the service I'd groaned under the weight of different roommates from the unobtrusive to the repulsive.

But now, I was alone. Yet I sat up in the candle glare and was almost feeling regret. I knew no one for miles. I was a stranger in New York. The few friends I still knew in Jersey had vanished. Wilson and Davis had copped out. I had no phone, I couldn't even call anybody. That's a lonely feeling. But I had an apartment and a job. I was in New York on my own, by my lonesome, and that was good enough for me!

I started walking around now after work, mostly on the West Side, Greenwich Village. Looking. Watching people. I walked around midtown where I worked. I had very little money. I'd gotten the gas and electric turned on. I made contact with Steve Korret and would go there once in a while. He seemed amused that I'd moved over. 'So many had said they were coming (like Tim and Brad) and they were never strong enough to do it,' he said. Like some ominous editorial. But I didn't want to hang around him too much. The stuff he was doing was on another level. Though I longed to be really included in his circle of friends. I'd seen a few people on the streets and spoken. 'Yes, I've moved to New York. I'm on East 3rd Street.' Not the Village, but close, they seemed to say. (This was before the Lower East Side became fashionable. It was then just *outside* of the Village, the romantic center.)

I began to stop by the few places I knew or heard Steve went to. Rienzi's, a coffeehouse on MacDougal Street. The San Remo, a bar at the end of the block. I found out about Romero's, on Minetta Lane, 'run' by a flashy mulatto, Johnny Romero (who later left for Puerto Rico, it was rumored, because of some run-in with the Mafia). It seemed to be the maximum hangout spot for many blacks in the Village then.

There was also a coffeehouse on West 4th near Sheridan Square called Pandora's Box, where Steve McQueen used to sit on the steps and watch the passing parade until he went off to Hollywood and became one of its drum majors. Coffeehouses, at that time, were very popular. The post-WWII decade of American visitors to Europe had brought back the coffeehouse as one evidence of a new reacquaintanceship with Continental cool. Certainly, for me, the coffeehouse was something totally new. Downtown New York coffee smells I associate with this period of my first permanent residence in the city. When you came up out of the subway or the PATH, the smell of coffee seemed to dominate everything.

I made the rounds of the coffeehouses, checking them and the people in them out. I'd heard certain names around Steve Korret. In fact we'd gone over to Rienzi's and had espresso, café au lait, hot cider, or cappuccino, which I really liked. That might even have been before I got out of the service. But coming in the old Rienzi, with its gestures in the direction of Continental sophistication, had turned me on. I thought everyone in those places was a writer or painter or something heavy.

Even when I got out of the service and was floating in and out of these places, I still thought for a while that all the customers were heavyweight intellectuals. Intellectual paperbacks were just coming out about that period as well. And people could be seen with the intriguingly packaged soft pocket books, folding and unfolding them out of bags and pockets. Sipping coffee and poking deeply, it seemed, into *Moses and Monotheism* or *Seven Types of Ambiguity* or Aristophanes' comedies, mostly reissues with the slick arty covers that made merchandising moguls attribute 'genius' to the young men who conceived and orchestrated this paperback explosion.

But I was struck by the ambience of the place. People in strange clothes. (One dude I saw on the streets then dressed up like a specter from the Middle Ages, like some *jongleur* wandering through the streets, complete with bells and all. In fact this dude still can be seen bouncing bowlegged through those streets, always alone. I wondered then, and still wonder, what wild shit lurks behind this creature's eyes?) The supposed freedom well advertised as the animating dream of that mixed-matched Village flock I believed as well. It was what I needed, just come out of the extreme opposite. Suddenly, I *was* free, I felt. I could do anything I could conceive of. Some days walking down the streets, with the roasted coffee bean aroma in my nose, I almost couldn't believe I had gotten out of the service and could walk down the street. And though I still had to get up work-early, to get uptown to the Gotham Book Mart and Mrs. Steloff's madness, I felt liberated.

The idea that the Village was where Art was being created, where there was a high level of intellectual seriousness, was what I thought. And the strange dress and mores that I perceived even from the distant jailhouse of Air Force blue I thought part of the equipment necessary to have such heavy things go on. The trips home, on leave, and before that, from school life, helped cement these notions in my mind. So that I did think that coffeehouse after coffeehouse and the other establishments down around West 4th and MacDougal, Bleecker or 8th Street, were filled with World Class intellectuals. And I felt a little uneasy just appearing on those streets or inside those places with no real qualifications save desire.

The streets themselves held a magic for my young self as well. Names like Minetta Lane and Jane Street and Waverly Place or Charles or Perry or Sheridan Square or Cornelia all carried with them, for me, notions of the strange, the exotic, and I dug it all, believed in it all.

137

There were deep assumptions these Village people lived by and I did too, but who knew what they were? I didn't, and I am clear that unconsciousness is a ubiquitous condition. The rule of confusion is terrifying. But I followed now, eagerly, happily, assured in myself that this, finally, was what I had been looking for. Not only as the place where my intellectual pursuit would take place, but the life there, as I knew it, as it seemed to me then, this was the life I wanted.

When Charlene, Steve's wife, served cheese omelet and black bread along with ale, for me it was the sheerest revelation. Korret's white apartment to me was the essence of hip bohemianism. I had known nothing about white apartments. Even the word 'bohemian' I thought of as intriguing, positive, something to be found out about and emulated. The conversations, both their form and content, one heard around Steve or in those coffeehouses, or around Washington Square and MacDougal or Bleecker. The long-haired mysterious women with their eyes painted, 'free-looking' in sandals. Dudes with berets or bookish pipe-smoking people. I was drawn to all of them and all of it. Who knew that all of this sat in a particular way in the world of meaning? Who knew the significance of all of it measured against a real world?

Like it was Tim who hipped me to the dangerous state of race relations in the Village. And other of my friends did too. I found out myself from a few bad incidents. But Tim would fall back in his chair chortling and spilling the wine on his pants or shirt. 'And watch out for the Italians, Leee-Roy, they'll bop you in the head. They don't like us black boys. They'll beat you up. Especially if you with a white woman. I always carry a blackjack with me or a knife.' And he'd show you this limp-ass blackjack didn't look like it could do anything. 'Watch out for the Italians, Leee-Roy.' It'd crack Tim up.

He was right, to a certain extent. The 'local people,' as folks were wont to call the largely Italian population that was intermingled with the more exotic Villagey part, apparently did not care for the wild antics and bohemian carryings-on of the permanent visitors to their neighborhood. It was like the 'townies' and the campus types. Like the 'DC boys' and those of us up on The Hill down at the Capstone. Except, with the blacks, it was, as usual, even worse. The general resentment the locals felt toward the white bohemians was quadrupled at the sight of the black species. And there were plenty people with grim stories to verify Tim's charges. Like a guy I came to know named Will Ribbon, who went with this one white woman for years and lived down below Houston Street, where it was really reputed to be dangerous for white-black liaisons. He got jumped on by a gang of the young locals and they pummeled him and called his woman names. Will goes home and gets his Beretta, and he walks up and down Thompson Street and Sullivan Street down by Broome and Prince and Spring, looking for these guys. He even goes into some of those private clubs (reputed Mafia relaxation stations) hunting for these guys. When I started working down around that area I used to carry a lead pipe in a manila envelope, the envelope under my arm like a good messenger, not intimidated but nevertheless ready.

Walt Whitman, from Leaves of Grass, *1888.*

BROADWAY

What hurrying human tides, or day or night!
What passions, winnings, losses, ardors, swim thy waters!
What whirls of evil, bliss and sorrow, stem thee!
What curious questioning glances – glints of love!
Leer, envy, scorn, contempt, hope, aspiration!
Thou portal – thou arena – thou of the myriad long-drawn lines and groups!
(Could but thy flagstones, curbs, façades, tell their inimitable tales;
Thy windows rich, and huge hotels – thy side-walks wide;)
Thou of the endless sliding, mincing, shuffling feet!
Thou, like the parti-colored world itself – like infinite, teeming, mocking life!
Thou visor'd, vast, unspeakable show and lesson!

G. K. Chesterton (1874-1936), English novelist, creator of Father Brown, poet, social critic, Catholic apologist, visited the United States in 1922. He recorded his thoughts in his book, What I Saw in America.

A MEDITATION IN BROADWAY

When I had looked at the lights of Broadway by night, I made to my American friends an innocent remark that seemed for some reason to amuse them. I had looked, not without joy, at that long kaleidoscope of coloured lights arranged in large letters and sprawling trade-marks, advertising everything, from pork to pianos, through the agency of the two most vivid and most mystical of the gifts of God; colour and fire. I said to them, in my simplicity, 'What a glorious garden of wonder this would be, to any one who was lucky enough to be unable to read.'

Here it is but a text for a further suggestion. But let us suppose that there does walk down this flaming avenue a peasant, of the sort called scornfully an illiterate peasant; by those who think that insisting on people reading and writing is the best way to keep out the spies who read in all languages and the forgers who write in all hands. On this principle indeed, a peasant merely acquainted with things of little practical use to mankind, such as ploughing, cutting wood, or growing vegetables, would very probably be excluded; and it is not for us to criticise from the outside the philosophy of those who would keep out the farmer and let in the forger. But let us suppose, if only for the sake of argument, that the peasant is walking under the artificial suns and stars of this tremendous thoroughfare; that he has escaped to the land of liberty upon some general rumour and romance of the story of its liberation, but without being yet able to understand the arbitrary signs of its alphabet. The soul of such a man would surely soar higher than the sky-scrapers, and embrace a brotherhood broader than Broadway. Realising that he had arrived on an evening of exceptional festivity, worthy to be blazoned with all this burning heraldry, he would please himself by guessing what great proclamation or principle of the Republic hung in the sky like a constellation or rippled across the street like a comet. He would be shrewd enough to guess that the three festoons fringed with fiery words of somewhat similar pattern stood for 'Government of the People, For the People, By the People'; for it must obviously be that, unless it were 'Liberty,

140

Equality, Fraternity.' His shrewdness would perhaps be a little shaken if he knew that the triad stood for 'Tang Tonic To-day; Tang Tonic To-morrow; Tang Tonic All the Time.' He will soon identify a restless ribbon of red lettering, red hot and rebellious, as the saying, 'Give me liberty or give me death.' He will fail to identify it as the equally famous saying, 'Skyoline Has Gout Beaten to a Frazzle.' Therefore it was that I desired the peasant to walk down that grove of fiery trees, under all that golden foliage and fruits like monstrous jewels, as innocent as Adam before the Fall. He would see sights almost as fine as the flaming sword or the purple and peacock plumage of the seraphim; so long as he did not go near the Tree of Knowledge.

In other words, if once he went to school it would be all up; and indeed I fear in any case he would soon discover his error. If he stood wildly waving his hat for liberty in the middle of the road as Chunk Chutney picked itself out in ruby stars upon the sky, he would impede the excellent but extremely rigid traffic system of New York. If he fell on his knees before a sapphire splendour, and began saying an Ave Maria under a mistaken association, he would be conducted kindly but firmly by an Irish policeman to a more authentic shrine. But though the foreign simplicity might not long survive in New York, it is quite a mistake to suppose that such foreign simplicity cannot enter New York. He may be excluded for being illiterate, but he cannot be excluded for being ignorant, nor for being innocent. Least of all can he be excluded for being wiser in his innocence than the world in its knowledge. There is here indeed more than one distinction to be made. New York is a cosmopolitan city; but it not a city of cosmopolitans. Most of the masses in New York have a nation, whether or no it be the nation to which New York belongs. Those who are Americanised are American, and very patriotically American. Those who are not thus nationalised are not in the least internationalised. They simply continue to be themselves; the Irish are Irish; the Jews are Jewish; and all sorts of other tribes carry on the traditions of remote European valleys almost untouched. In short, there is a sort of slender bridge between their old country and their new, which they either cross or do not cross, but which they seldom simply occupy. They are exiles or they are citizens; there is no moment when they are cosmopolitans. But very often the exiles bring with them not only rooted traditions, but rooted truths.

141

Indeed it is to a great extent the thought of these strange souls in crude American garb that gives a meaning to the masquerade of New York. In the hotel where I stayed the head waiter in one room was a Bohemian; and I am glad to say that he called himself a Bohemian. I have already protested sufficiently, before American audiences, against the pedantry of perpetually talking about Czecho-Slovakia. I suggested to my American friends that the abandonment of the word Bohemian in its historical sense might well extend to its literary and figurative sense. We might be expected to say, 'I'm afraid Henry has got into very Czecho-Slovakian habits lately,' or 'Don't bother to dress; it's quite a Czecho-Slovakian affair.' Anyhow my Bohemian would have nothing to do with such nonsense; he called himself a son of Bohemia, and spoke as such in his criticisms of America, which were both favourable and unfavourable. He was a squat man, with a sturdy figure and a steady smile; and his eyes were like dark pools in the depth of a darker forest; but I do not think he had ever been deceived by the lights of Broadway.

But I found something like my real innocent abroad, my real peasant among the sky-signs, in another part of the same establishment. He was a much leaner man, equally dark, with a hook nose, hungry face, and fierce black moustaches. He was also a waiter, and was in the costume of a waiter, which is a smarter edition of the costume of a lecturer. As he was serving me with clam chowder or some such thing, I fell into speech with him and he told me he was a Bulgar. I said something like, 'I'm afraid I don't know as much as I ought to about Bulgaria. I suppose most of your people are agricultural, aren't they?' He did not stir an inch from his regular attitude, but he slightly lowered his low voice and said, 'Yes. From the earth we come and to the earth we return; when people get away from that they are lost.'

To hear such a thing said by the waiter was alone an epoch in the life of an unfortunate writer of fantastic novels. To see him clear away the clam chowder like an automaton, and bring me more iced water like an automaton or like nothing on earth except an American waiter (for piling up ice is the cold passion of their lives), and all this after having uttered something so dark and deep, so starkly incongruous and so startlingly true, was an indescribable thing, but very like the picture of the peasant admiring Broadway. So he passed, with his artificial clothes and manners, lit up with all the ghastly artificial light of the hotel, and all the ghastly artificial life of the city; and his heart was like his own remote and rocky valley, where those unchanging words were carved as on a rock.

The Drifters had a hit with this song in 1963. It was written for them by Barry Mann, Cynthia Weill, Jerry Leiber, and Mike Stoller.

ON BROADWAY

They say the neon lights are bright
On Broadway
They say there's always magic in the air
On Broadway
But when you're walking down the street
And you ain't got enough to eat
The glitter all rubs off
And you're nowhere
On Broadway

James Weldon Johnson (1871-1938) was a leading figure of the Harlem Renaissance and active in Black politics and education. His book, Black Manhattan, *published in 1930, chronicles the struggles of the Black community in New York from the eighteenth century to the 1920s.*

THE CITY WITHIN A CITY

The fact that within New York, the greatest city of the New World, there is found the greatest single community anywhere of people descended from age-old Africa appears at a thoughtless glance to be the climax of the incongruous. Harlem is today the Negro metropolis and as such is everywhere known. In the history of New York the name Harlem has changed from Dutch to Irish to Jewish to Negro; but it is through this last change that it has gained its most widespread fame. Throughout coloured America Harlem is the recognized Negro capital. Indeed, it is Mecca for the sightseer, the pleasure-seeker, the curious, the adventurous, the enterprising, the ambitious, and the talented of the entire Negro world; for the lure of it has reached down to every island of the Carib Sea and penetrated even into Africa. It is almost as well known to the white world, for it has been much talked and written about.

So here we have Harlem – not merely a colony or a community or a settlement – not at all a 'quarter' or a slum or a fringe – but a black city, located in the heart of white Manhattan, and containing more Negroes to the square mile than any other spot on earth. It strikes the uninformed observer as a phenomenon, a miracle straight out of the skies. . .

. . . Within the past ten years Harlem has acquired a world-wide reputation. It has gained a place in the list of famous sections of great cities. It is known in Europe and the Orient, and it is talked about by natives in the interior of Africa. It is farthest known as being exotic, colourful, and sensuous; a place of laughing, singing, and dancing; a place where life wakes up at night. This phase of Harlem's fame is most widely known because, in addition to being spread by ordinary agencies, it has been proclaimed in story and song. And certainly this is Harlem's most striking and fascinating aspect. New Yorkers and people visiting New York from the world over go to the night-clubs of Harlem and dance to such jazz music as can be heard nowhere else; and they get an exhilaration impossible to duplicate. Some of these seekers after new sensations go beyond the gay night-clubs; they peep in under the more seamy side of things; they nose down into lower strata of life. A visit to Harlem at night – the principal streets never deserted, gay crowds skipping from one place of amusement to another, lines of taxicabs and limousines standing under the sparkling lights of the entrances to the famous night-clubs, the subway kiosks swallowing and disgorging crowds all night long – gives the impression that Harlem never sleeps and that the inhabitants thereof jazz through existence. But, of course, no one can seriously think that the two hundred thousand and more Negroes in Harlem spend their nights on any such pleasance. Of a necessity the vast majority of them are ordinary, hard-working people, who spend their time in just about the same way that other ordinary, hard-working people do. Most of them have never seen the inside of a night-club. The great bulk of them are confronted with the stern necessity of making a living, of making both ends meet, of finding money to pay the rent and keep the children fed and clothed neatly enough to attend school;

their waking hours are almost entirely consumed in this un-romantic task. And it is a task in which they cannot escape running up against a barrier erected especially for them, a barrier which pens them off on the morass – no, the quicksands – of economic insecurity. Fewer jobs are open to them than to any other group; and in such jobs as they get, they are subject to the old rule, which still obtains, 'the last to be hired and the first to be fired.'

Notwithstanding all that, gaiety is peculiarly characteristic of Harlem. The people who live there are by nature a pleasure-loving people; and though most of them must take their pleasures in a less expensive manner than in nightly visits to clubs, they nevertheless, as far as they can afford – and often much farther – do satisfy their hunger for enjoyment. And since they are constituted as they are, enjoyment being almost as essential to them as food, perhaps really a compensation which enables them to persist, it is well that they are able to extract pleasure easily and cheaply. An average group of Negroes can in dancing to a good jazz band achieve a delightful state of intoxication that for others would require nothing short of a certain per capita imbibition of synthetic gin. The masses of Harlem get a good deal of pleasure out of things far too simple for most other folks. In the evenings of summer and on Sundays they get lots of enjoyment out of strolling. Strolling is almost a lost art in New York; at least, in the manner in which it is generally practised in Harlem. Strolling in Harlem does not mean merely walking along Lenox or upper Seventh Avenue or One Hundred and Thirty-fifth Street; it means that those streets are places for socializing. One puts on one's best clothes and fares forth to pass the time pleasantly with the friends and acquaintances and, most impor-tant of all, the stranger he is sure of meeting. One saunters along, he hails this one, exchanges a word or two with that one, stops for a short chat with the other one. He comes up to a laughing, chattering group, in which he may have only one friend or acquaintance, but that gives him the privilege of joining in. He does join in and takes part in the joking, the small talk and gossip, and makes new acquaintances. He passes on and arrives in front of one of the theatres, studies the bill for a while, undecided about going in. He finally moves on a few steps farther and joins another group and is introduced to two or three pretty girls who have just come to Harlem, perhaps only for a visit; and finds a reason to be glad that he postponed going into the theatre. The hours of a summer evening run by rapidly. This is not simply going out for a walk; it is more like going out for adventure.

In almost as simple a fashion the masses of Harlem get enjoyment out of church-going. This enjoyment, however, is not quite so inexpensive as strolling can be made. Some critics of the Negro – especially Negro critics – say that religion costs him too much; that he has too many churches, and that many of them are magnificent beyond his means; that church mortgages and salaries and upkeep consume the greater part of the financial margin of the race and keep its economic nose to the grindstone. All of which is, in the main, true. There are something like one hundred and sixty coloured churches in Harlem. . .

. . . The multiplicity of churches in Harlem, and in every other Negro community, is commonly accounted for by the innate and deep religious emotion of the race. Conceding the strength and depth of this emotion, there is also the vital fact that coloured churches provide their members with a great deal of enjoyment, aside from the joys of religion. Indeed, a Negro church is for its members much more besides a place of worship. It is a social centre, it is a club, it is an arena for the exercise of one's capabilities and powers, a world in which one may achieve self-realization and preferment. Of course, a church means something of the same sort to all groups; but with the Negro all these attributes are magnified because of the fact that they are so curtailed for him in the world at large. Most of the large Harlem churches open early on Sunday morning and remain open until ten or eleven o'clock at night; and there is not an hour during that time when any one of them is empty. A good many people stay in church all day; there they take their dinner, cooked and served hot by a special committee. Aside from any spiritual benefits derived, going to church means being dressed in one's best clothes, forgetting for the time about work, having the chance to acquit oneself with credit before one's fellows, and having the opportunity of meeting, talking, and laughing with friends and of casting an appraising and approving eye upon the opposite sex. Going to church is an outlet for the Negro's religious emotions; but not the least reason why he is willing to support so many churches is that they furnish so many agreeable activities and so much real enjoyment. He is willing to support them because he has not yet, and will not have until there is far greater economic and intellectual development and social organization, any other agencies that can fill their place.

. . . In Harlem, as in all American Negro communities, the fraternal bodies also fill an important place. These fraternities, too, are in a very large degree social organizations, but they have also an economic feature. In addition to providing the enjoyment of lodge meetings, lodge balls and picnics, and the interest and excitement of lodge politics, there are provisions for taking care of the sick and burying the dead. Both of these latter provisions are highly commendable and are the means of attracting a good many members; however, the criticism can be made that very often the amount of money spent for burying the dead is out of proportion to that spent in caring for the living. Indeed, this is so general that it makes 'the high cost of dying' a live question among Negroes.

Harlem is also a parade ground. During the warmer months of the year no Sunday passes without several parades. There are brass bands, marchers in resplendent regalia, and high dignitaries with gorgeous insignia riding in automobiles. Almost any excuse for parading is sufficient – the funeral of a member of the lodge, the laying of a corner-stone, the annual sermon to the order, or just a general desire to 'turn out.' Parades are not limited to Sundays; for when the funeral of a lodge member falls on a weekday, it is quite the usual thing to hold the exercises at night, so that members of the order and friends who are at work during the day may attend. Frequently after nightfall a slow procession may be seen wending its way along and a band heard playing a dirge that takes on a deeply sepulchral tone. But generally these parades are lively and add greatly to the movement, colour, and gaiety of Harlem. A brilliant parade with very good bands is participated in not only by the marchers in line, but also by the marchers on the sidewalks. For it is not a universal custom of Harlem to stand idly and watch a parade go by; a good part of the crowd always marches along, keeping step to the music.

Now, it would be entirely misleading to create the impression that all Harlem indulges in none other than these Arcadian-like pleasures. There is a large element of educated, well-to-do metropolitans among the Negroes of Harlem who view with indulgence, often with something less, the responses of the masses to these artless amusements. There is the solid, respectable, bourgeois class, of the average proportion, whose counterpart is to be found in every Southern city. There are strictly social sets that go in for bridge parties, breakfast parties, cocktail parties, for high-powered cars, week-ends, and exclusive dances. Occasionally an exclusive dance is held in one of the ballrooms of a big downtown hotel. Harlem has its sophisticated, fast sets, initiates in all the wisdom of worldliness. And Harlem has, too, its underworld, its world of pimps and prostitutes, of gamblers and thieves, of illicit love and illicit liquor, of red sins and dark crimes. In a word, Harlem posesses in some degree all of the elements of a cosmopolitan centre. And by that same word, striking an average, we find that the overwhelming majority of its people are people whose counterparts may be found in any American community. Yet as a whole community it possesses a sense of humour and a love of gaiety that are distinctly characteristic.

Federico García Lorca, from his lecture on Poet in New York.

THE GREAT BLACK CITY

What I had before my eyes was neither an esthetic norm nor a blue paradise. What I looked at, strolled though, dreamed about, was the great black city of Harlem, the most important black city in the world, where lewdness has an innocent accent that makes it disturbing and religious. A neighborhood of rosy houses, full of pianolas and radios and cinemas, but with the *mistrust* that characterizes the race. Doors left ajar, jasper children afraid of the rich people from Park Avenue, phonographs that suddenly stop singing, the wait for the enemies who can arrive by the East River and show just where the idols are sleeping. I wanted to make the poem of the black race in North America and to emphasize the pain that the blacks feel to be black in a contrary world. They are slaves of all the white man's inventions and machines, perpetually afraid that some day they will forget how to light the gas stove or steer the automobile or fasten the starched collar, afraid of sticking a fork in their eyes. I mean that these inventions do not belong to them. The blacks live on credit, and the fathers have to maintain strict discipline at home lest their women and children adore the phonograph record or eat flat tires.

And yet, as any visitor can see, for all their ebullience, they yearn to be a nation, and even though they occasionally make theater out of themselves, their spiritual depths are unbribable. In one cabaret – Small's Paradise – whose dancing audience was as black, wet, and grumous as a tin of caviar, I saw a naked dancer shaking convulsively under an invisible rain of fire. But while everyone shouted as though believing her possessed by the rhythm, I was able, for a second, to catch remoteness in her eyes – remoteness, reserve, the conviction that she was far away from that admiring audience of foreigners and Americans. All Harlem was like her.

Another time I saw a little black girl riding a bicycle. Nothing could have been more touching: smokey legs, teeth frozen in the moribund rose of her lips, the balled-up sheep's hair of her head. I stared at her and she stared right back. But my look was saying, 'Child, why are you riding a bicycle? Can a little black girl really ride such an apparatus? Is it yours? Where did you steal it? Do you think you can steer it?' And sure enough, she did a somersault and fell – all legs and wheels – down a gentle slope.

But every day I protested. I protested to see little black children guillotined by hard collars, suits, and violent boots as they emptied the spittoons of cold men who talk like ducks.

I protested to see so much flesh robbed from paradise and managed by Jews with gelid noses and blotting-paper souls, and I protested the saddest thing of all, that the blacks do not want to be black, that they invent pomades to take away the delicious curl of their hair and powders that turn their faces gray and syrups that fill out their waists and wither the succulent persimmon of their lips.

I protested, and the proof of it is this 'Ode to the King of Harlem,' spirit of the black race, a cry of encouragement to those who tremble and doubt and sluggishly, shamefully search for the flesh of the white woman.

And yet, the truly savage, phrenetic part of New York is not Harlem. In Harlem there is human steam and the noise of children and hearths and weeds, and pain that finds comfort and the wound that finds its sweet bandage.

Langston Hughes remembered the passing of an era in his autobiography,
The Big Sea, *published in 1940.*

PARTIES AND FUNERALS

In those days of the late 1920's, there were a great many parties, in Harlem and out, to which various members of the New Negro group were invited. These parties, when given by important Harlemites (or Carl Van Vechten) were reported in full in the society pages of the Harlem press, but best in the sparkling Harlemese of Geraldyn Dismond who wrote for the *Interstate Tattler*. On one of Taylor Gordon's fiestas she reports as follows:

> What a crowd! All classes and colors met face to face, ultra aristocrats, Bourgeois, Communists, Park Avenuers galore, bookers, publishers, Broadway celebs, and Harlemites giving each other the once over. The social revolution was on. And yes, Lady Nancy Cunard was there all in black (she would) with 12 of her grand bracelets. . . And was the entertainment on the up and up! Into swell dance music was injected African drums that played havoc with blood pressure. Jimmy Daniels sang his gigolo hits. Gus Simons, the Harlem crooner, made the River Stay Away From His Door and Taylor himself brought out everything from 'Hot Dog' to 'Bravo' when he made high C.

A'Lelia Walker was the then great Harlem party giver, although Mrs. Bernia Austin fell but little behind. And at the Seventh Avenue apartment of Jessie Fauset, literary soirées with much poetry and but little to drink were the order of the day. The same was true of Lillian Alexander's, where the older intellectuals gathered.

A'Lelia Walker, however, big-hearted, night-dark, hair-straightening heiress, made no pretense at being intellectual or exclusive. At her 'at homes' Negro poets and Negro number bankers mingled with downtown poets and seat-on-the-stock-exchange racketeers. Countee Cullen would be there and Witter Bynner. Muriel Draper and Nora Holt, Andy Razaf and Taylor Gordon. And a good time was had by all.

A'Lelia Walker had an apartment that held perhaps a hundred people. She would usually issue several hundred invitations to each party. Unless you went early there was no possible way of getting in. Her parties were as crowded as the New York subway at the rush hour – entrance, lobby, steps, hallway, and apartment a milling crush of guests, with everybody seeming to enjoy the crowding. Once, some royal personage arrived, a Scandinavian prince, I believe, but his equerry saw no way of getting him through the crowded entrance hall and into the party, so word was sent in to A'Lelia Walker that His Highness, the Prince, was waiting without. A'Lelia sent word back that she saw no way of getting His Highness in, either, nor could she herself get out through the crowd to greet him. But she offered to send refreshments downstairs to the Prince's car.

A'Lelia Walker was a gorgeous dark Amazon, in a silver turban. She had a town house in New York (also an apartment where she preferred to live) and a country mansion at Irvington-on-the-Hudson, with pipe organ programs each morning to awaken her guests gently. Her mother made a great fortune from the Madame Walker Hair Straightening Process, which had worked wonders on unruly Negro hair in the early nineteen hundreds – and which continues to work wonders today. The daughter used much of that money for fun. A'Lelia Walker was the joy-goddess of Harlem's 1920's.

She had been very much in love with her first husband, from whom she was divorced. Once at one of her parties she began to cry about him. She retired to her boudoir and wept. Some of her friends went in to comfort her, and found her clutching a memento of their broken romance.

'The only thing I have left that he gave me,' she sobbed, 'it's all I have left of him!'

It was a gold shoehorn.

When A'Lelia Walker died in 1931, she had a grand funeral. It was by invitation only. But, just as for her parties, a great many more invitations had been issued than the small but exclusive Seventh Avenue funeral parlor could provide for. Hours before the funeral, the street in front of the undertaker's chapel was crowded. The doors were not opened until the cortège arrived – and the cortège was late. When it came, there were almost enough family mourners, attendants, and honorary pallbearers in the procession to fill the room; as well as the representatives of the various Walker beauty parlors throughout the country. And there were still hundreds of friends outside, waving their white, engraved invitations aloft in the vain hope of entering.

Once the last honorary pallbearers had marched in, there was a great crush at the doors. Muriel Draper, Rita Romilly, Mrs. Roy Sheldon, and I were among the fortunate few who achieved an entrance.

We were startled to find De Lawd standing over A'Lelia's casket. It was a truly amazing illusion. At that time *The Green Pastures* was at the height of its fame, and there stood De Lawd in the person of Rev. E. Clayton Powell, a Harlem minister, who looked exactly like Richard B. Harrison in the famous role in the play. He had the same white hair and kind face, and was later offered the part of De Lawd in the film version of the drama. Now, he stood there motionless in the dim light behind the silver casket of A'Lelia Walker.

Soft music played and it was very solemn. When we were seated and the chapel became dead silent, De Lawd said: 'The Four Bon Bons will now sing.'

A night club quartette that had often performed at A'Lelia's parties arose and sang for her. They sang Noel Coward's 'I'll See You Again,' and they swung it slightly, as she might have liked it. It was a grand funeral and very much like a party. Mrs. Mary McCleod Bethune spoke in that great deep voice of hers, as only she can speak. She recalled the poor mother of A'Lelia Walker in old clothes, who had labored to bring the gift of beauty to Negro womanhood, and had taught them the care of their skin and their hair; and had built up a great business and a great fortune to the pride and glory of the Negro race – and then had given it all to her daughter, A'Lelia.

Then a poem of mine was read by Edward Perry, 'To A'Lelia.' And after that the girls from the various Walker beauty shops throughout America brought their flowers and laid them on the bier.

That was really the end of the gay times of the New Negro era in Harlem, the period that had begun to reach its end when the crash came in 1929 and the white people had much less money to spend on themselves, and practically none to spend on Negroes, for the depression brought everybody down a peg or two. And the Negroes had but few pegs to fall.

Ben E. King was the first of many artists to record this song, written in 1960 by Phil Spector and Jerry Leiber.

SPANISH HARLEM

There is a rose in Spanish Harlem
A rare rose up in Spanish Harlem
It is a special one
It's never seen the sun
It only comes up when the moon is on the run
And all the stars are gleaming
It's growing in the street
Right up through the concrete
But soft and sweet and dreaming

H. Leivick (1888-1962) was born in Russia and served imprisonment and Siberian exile for his socialist activities before coming to the United States in 1913. He is a major poet of the suffering of the Jewish diaspora in New York.

HERE LIVES THE JEWISH PEOPLE

The imprisoned life of the prison city
burns with a white blaze.
In the streets of the Jewish East Side
white fires burn still whiter.

I love to wander in the fieriness of the Jewish East Side,
to shove in and out of the cramped stalls and pushcarts,
breathing the smell and saltiness
of a feverish stripped life.
And always when, gazing, I see creep up through the whiteness
Jews bearded and from head to toe hung with
Ladies' and girls' dresses dragging them down,
and Jewish men, or women, with sick little birds
that for a penny pick out a fortune card and turn yearning and
    pleading eyes on the buyer,

and Jews pushing themselves along on two-wheeled platforms,
    blind cripples, who sit sunk down deep
in their shoulders and can see with their shoulders
the color and size of every thrown coin –
then I am roused by a buried longing, a boyhood longing
to be transformed into the lame beggar
who used to hop from street to street of our town
(Luria was his name)
and clatter with his crutch over sidewalks and thresholds.

Who knows, if sometimes I see the same beggar sitting on that
    barrow,
the beggar my boyhood craved? His blindness sees my staring.
Once the world was not imprisoned as now,
though white as now,
fiery and white.

Hour by hour I walk the streets of the Jewish East Side,
and in the fiery whiteness my eyes paint fantastic turrets,
elongated columns soaring up over the ruined stalls,
up to the emptied sky of New York.
Turrets hung all over their parapets with signs flashing and
glowing:
Here Lives the Jewish People.

The imprisoned life of the prison city
slips into yellow-gray shadows
and in the streets of the Jewish East Side
the yellow-gray deepens.
Step by step the Jews dragging dresses for sale,
for ladies, for girls – they vanish around some corner;
the woman is carrying the cage with its sick little bird,
and the box still full of fortunes.
The blind cripple is trundling home
through streets cleared of pushcarts and stalls.
My longing grows. I let myself follow
the hard jutting shoulders of the cripple.
(Luria was his name.)
I am enticed by his progress, his nest-seeking.
Until suddenly I am knifed by a look,
the look of an eye sprung open in the middle of his back.

154

Stillness. Midnight.
Once the world was not as now,
dark and shadowed.

And in the darkness the turrets loom in earnest,
they that in the white flame of day were a dream;
they reveal themselves in all their vastness and roundness,
like the thick towers of fortresses.
Turrets hung all over their parapets with red warning signs:
Here Sleeps the Jewish People.

Stillness. Midnight.
The years of my childhood cry in me, the longing.

Translated by Cynthia Ozick

Michael Gold (1893-1967) was born and reared on the Lower East Side. He became a Communist, a writer for the Daily Worker *and the* New Masses, *and in the 1930s published his classic novel* Jews Without Money.

Jews Without Money

On the East Side people buy their groceries a pinch at a time; three cents' worth of sugar, five cents' worth of butter, everything in penny fractions. The good Jewish black bread that smells of harvest-time, is sliced into a dozen parts and sold for pennies. But that winter even pennies were scarce.

There was a panic on Wall Street. Multitudes were without work; there were strikes, suicides, and food riots. The prostitutes roamed our streets like wolves; never was there so much competition among them.

Life froze. The sun vanished from the deathly gray sky. The streets reeked with snow and slush. There were hundreds of evictions. I walked down a street between dripping tenement walls. The rotten slush ate through my shoes. The wind beat on my face. I saw a stack of furniture before a tenement: tables, chairs, a washtub packed with crockery and bed-clothes, a broom, a dresser, a lamp.

The snow covered them. The snow fell, too, on a little Jew and his wife and three children. They huddled in a mournful group by their possessions. They had placed a saucer on one of the tables. An old woman with a market bag mumbled a prayer in passing. She dropped a penny in the saucer. Other people did the same. Each time the evicted family lowered its eyes in shame. They were not beggars, but 'respectable' people. But if enough pennies fell in the saucer, they might have rent for a new home. This was the one hope left them.

Winter. Building a snow fort one morning, we boys dug out a litter of frozen kittens and their mother. The little ones were still blind. They had been born into it, but had never seen our world.

Other dogs and cats were frozen. Men and women, too, were found dead in hallways and on docks. Mary Sugar Bum met her end in an alley. She was found half-naked, clutching a whisky bottle in her blue claw. This was her last 'love' affair.

Horses slipped on the icy pavement, and quivered there for hours with broken legs, until a policeman arrived to shoot them.

The boys built a snow man. His eyes were two coals; his nose a potato. He wore a derby hat and smoked a corncob pipe. His arms were flung wide; in one of them he held a broom, in the other a newspaper. This Golem with his amazed eyes and idiotic grin amused us all for an afternoon.

The next morning we found him strangely altered. His eyes and nose had been torn out; his grin smashed, like a war victim's. Who had played this joke? The winter wind.

Mrs. Rosenbaum owned a grocery store on our street. She was a widow with four children, and lived in two rooms back of the store. She slaved from dawn until midnight; a big, clumsy woman with a chapped face and masses of untidy hair; always grumbling, groaning, gossiping about her ailments. Sometimes she was nervous and screamed at her children, and beat them. But she was a kind-hearted woman, and that winter suffered a great deal. Every one was very poor, and she was too good not to give them groceries on credit.

'I'm crazy to do it!' she grumbled in her icy store. 'I'm a fool! But when a child comes for a loaf of bread, and I have the bread, and I know her family is starving, how can I refuse her? Yet I have my own children to think of! I am being ruined! The store is being emptied! I can't meet my bills!'

She was kind. Kindness is a form of suicide in a world based on the law of competition.

One day we watched the rewards of kindness. The sheriff's men arrived to seize Mrs. Rosenbaum's grocery. They tore down the shelves and fixtures, they carted off tubs of butter, drums of kerosene, sacks of rice, flour, and potatoes.

Mrs. Rosenbaum stood by watching her own funeral. Her fat kind face was swollen with crying as with toothache. Her eyes blinked in bewilderment. Her children clung to her skirts and cried. Snow fell from the sky, a crowd muttered its sympathy, a policeman twirled his club.

What happened to her after that, I don't know. Maybe the Organized Charities helped her; or maybe she died. O golden dyspeptic God of America, you were in a bad mood that winter. We were poor, and you punished us harshly for this worst of sins.

My father lay in bed. His shattered feet ached in each bone. His painter's sickness came back on him; he suffered with lung and kidney pains.

He was always depressed. His only distraction was to read the Yiddish newspapers, and to make gloomy conversation at night over the suicides, the hungry families, the robberies, murders, and catastrophes that newspapers record.

'It will come to an end!' said my father. 'People are turning into wolves! They will soon eat each other! They will tear down the cities, and destroy the world in flames and blood!'

'Drink your tea,' said my mother cheerfully, 'God is still in the world. You will get better and work and laugh again. Let us not lose courage.'

My father was fretful and nervous with an invalid's fears.

'But what if we are evicted, Katie?'

'We won't be evicted, not while I have my two hands and can work,' said my mother.

'But I don't want you to work!' my father cried. 'It breaks our home!'

'It doesn't!' said my mother. 'I have time and strength for everything.'

At first my mother had feared going out to work in a cafeteria among Christians. But after a few days she settled easily into the life of the polyglot kitchen, and leaned to fight, scold, and mother the Poles, Germans, Italians, Irish, and Negroes who worked there. They liked her, and soon called her 'Momma,' which made her vain.

'You should hear how a big black dishwasher named Joe, how he comes to me today and says, 'Momma, I'm going to quit. Every one is against me here because I am black,' he says. 'The whole world is against us black people.'

'So I said to him, 'Joe, I am not against you. Don't be foolish, don't go out to be a bum again. The trouble with you here is you are lazy. If you would work harder the others would like you, too.' So he said, 'Momma, all right I'll stay.' So that's how it is in the restaurant. They call me Momma, even the black ones.'

It was a large, high-priced cafeteria for business-men on lower Broadway. My mother was a chef's helper, and peeled and scoured tons of vegetables for cooking. Her wages were seven dollars a week.

She woke at five, cooked our breakfast at home, then had to walk a mile to her job. She came home at five-thirty, and made supper, cleaned the house, was busy on her feet until bedtime. It hurt my father's masculine pride to see his wife working for wages. But my mother liked it all; she was proud of earning money, and she liked her fights in the restaurant.

My dear, tireless, little dark-faced mother! Why did she always have to fight? Why did she have to give my father a new variety of headache with accounts of her battles for 'justice' in the cafeteria? The manager there was a fat blond Swede with a *Kaiserliche* mustache, and the manners of a Mussolini. All the workers feared this bull-necked tyrant, except my mother. She told him 'what was what.' When the meat was rotten, when the drains were clogged and smelly, or the dishwashers overworked, she told him so. She scolded him as if he were her child, and he listened meekly. The other workers fell into the habit of telling their complaints to my mother, and she would relay them to the Swedish manager.

'It's because he needs me,' said my mother proudly. 'That's why he lets me scold him. I am one of his best workers; he can depend on me in the rush. And he knows I am not like the other kitchen help; they work a day or two; then quit, but I stay on. So he's afraid to fire me, and I tell him what is what.'

It was one of those super-cafeterias, with flowers on the tables,

158

a string orchestra during the lunch hour, and other trimmings. But my mother had no respect for it. She would never eat the lunch served there to the employees, but took along two cheese sandwiches from home.

'Your food is *Dreck*, it is fit only for pigs,' she told the manager bluntly. And once she begged me to promise never to eat hamburger steak in a restaurant when I grew up.

'Swear it to me, Mikey!' she said. 'Never, never eat hamburger!'

'I swear it, momma.'

'Poison!' she went on passionately. 'They don't care if they poison the people, so long as there's money in it. I've seen with my own eyes. If I could write English, I'd write a letter to all the newspapers.'

'Mind your own business!' my father growled. 'Such things are for Americans. It is their country and their hamburger steak.'

Miguel Piñero lives on the Lower East Side. His play Short Eyes *won wide critical acclaim when it was produced off-Broadway in 1973.*

A LOWER EAST SIDE POEM

Just once before I die
I want to climb up on a
tenement sky
to dream my lungs out till
I cry
then scatter my ashes thru
the Lower East Side

So let me sing my song tonight
let me feel out of sight
and let all eyes be dry
when they scatter my ashes thru
the Lower East Side

From Houston to 14th Street
from Second Avenue to the mighty D
here the hustlers & suckers meet

the faggots & freaks will all get high
on the ashes that have been scattered
thru the Lower East Side

There's no other place for me to be
there's no other place that I can see
there's no other town around that
brings you up or keeps you down
no food little heat sweeps by
fancy cars & pimp bars & juke saloons
& greasy spoons make my spirits fly
with my ashes scattered thru the
Lower East Side. . .

A thief a junkie I've been
committed every known sin
Jews & Gentiles. . . Bums and Men
of style. . . run away child
police shooting wild. . .
mother's futile wails. . . pushers
making sales. . . dope wheelers
& cocaine dealers. . . smoking pot
streets are hot & feed off those who
bleed to death. . .
all that's true
all that's true
all that is true
but this ain't no lie
when I ask that my ashes be scattered thru
the Lower East Side

So here I am look at me
I stand proud as you can see
pleased to be from the Lower East
a street fighting man
a problem of this land
I am the Philosopher of the Criminal Mind
a dweller of prison time
a cancer of rockerfeller's ghettocide
this concrete tomb is my home
to belong to survive you gotta be strong

you can't be shy less without request
someone will scatter your ashes thru
the Lower East Side

I don't wanna be buried in Puerto Rico
I don't wanna rest in long island cemetery
I wanna be near the stabbing shooting
gambling fighting & unnatural dying
& new birth crying
so please when I die. . .
don't take me far away
keep me near by
take my ashes and scatter them thru out
the Lower East Side. . .

Lorraine Hansberry, from To Be Young, Gifted, and Black.

COURAGE

I suppose that the most heroic expression that I have ever seen
was that on the face of a certain tough-looking, brutalized, slum-
slaughtered woman at Coney Island. She had her arm around a
girl child who looked hardly any less brutalized and slum-
slaughtered – *'We is going to have a good time tonight!'* the look said.

Marshal Berman grew up in the Bronx in the forties. His book, All That
is Solid Melts in the Air, *is – among other things – a study of the modern
city and the experience of those who live in it. Here he proposes a mural, to be
painted along the length of the Cross-Bronx Expressway, telling in images
the history and struggles of the community.*

THE BRONX MURAL

The Bronx Mural, as I imagine it, would be painted onto the
brick and concrete retaining walls that run alongside most of the
eight miles of the Cross-Bronx Expressway, so that every
automobile trip through and out of the Bronx would become a
trip into its buried depths. In the places where the road runs close

161

to or above ground level and the walls recede, the driver's view of the Bronx's past life would alternate with sweeping vistas of its present ruin. The mural might depict cross-sections of streets, of houses, even of rooms full of people just as they were before the Expressway cut through them all.

But it would go back before this, to our century's early years, at the height of the Jewish and Italian immigration, with the Bronx growing along the rapidly expanding subway lines, and (in the words of the *Communist Manifesto*) whole populations conjured out of the ground: to tens of thousands of garment workers, printers, butchers, house painters, furriers, union militants, socialists, anarchists, communists. Here is D. W. Griffith, whose old Biograph Studio building still stands, solid but battered and neglected, at the Expressway's edge; here is Sholem Aleichem, seeing the New World and saying that it was good, and dying on Kelly Street (the block where Bella Abzug was born); and there is Trotsky on East 164th Street, waiting for his revolution (did he really play a Russian in obscure silent films? we will never know). Now we see a modest but energetic and confident bourgeoisie, springing up in the 1920s near the new Yankee Stadium, promenading on the Grand Concourse for a brief moment in the sun, finding romance in the swan boats in Crotona Park; and not far away, 'the coops,' a great network of workers' housing settlements, cooperatively building a new world beside Bronx and Van Cortlandt parks. We move on to the bleak adversity of the 1930s, unemployment lines, home relief, the WPA (whose splendid monument, the Bronx County Courthouse, stands just above the Yankee Stadium), radical passions and energies exploding, street-corner fights betwen Trotskyites and Stalinists, candy stores and cafeterias ablaze with talk all through the night; then to the excitement and anxiety of the postwar years, new affluence, neighborhoods more vibrant than ever, even as new worlds beyond the neighborhoods begin to open up, people buy cars, start to move; to the Bronx's new immigrants from Puerto Rico, South Carolina, Trinidad, new shades of skin and clothes on the street, new music and rhythms, new tensions and intensities; and finally, to Robert Moses and his dread road, smashing through the Bronx's inner life, transforming evolution into devolution, entropy into catastrophe, and creating the ruin on which this work of art is built.

The mural would have to be executed in a number of radically different styles, so as to express the amazing variety of imaginative visions that sprang from these apparently uniform streets, apartment houses, schoolyards, kosher butcher shops, appetizing and candy stores. Barnett Newman, Stanley Kubrick, Clifford Odets, Larry Rivers, George Segal, Jerome Weidman, Rosalyn Drexler, E. L. Doctorow, Grace Paley, Irving Howe, would all be there; along with George Meany, Herman Badillo, Bella Abzug and Stokely Carmichael; John Garfield, Tony Curtis' Sidney Falco, Gertrude Berg's Molly Goldberg, Bess Myerson (an iconic monument to assimilation, the Bronx's Miss America, 1945), and Anne Bancroft; Hank Greenberg, Jake La Motta, Jack Molinas (was he the Bronx's greatest athlete, its most vicious crook, or both?); Nate Archibald; A. M. Rosenthal of the *New York Times* and his sister, the communist leader Ruth Witt; Phil Spector, Bill Graham, Dion and the Belmonts, the Rascals, Laura Nyro, Larry Harlow, the brothers Palmieri; Jules Feiffer and Lou Meyers; Paddy Chayevsky and Neil Simon; Ralph Lauren and Calvin Klein, Garry Winogrand, George and Mike Kuchar; Jonas Salk, George Wald, Seymour Melman, Herman Kahn – all these, and so many more.

Children of the Bronx would be encouraged to return and put themselves in the picture: the Expressway wall is big enough to hold them all; as it got increasingly crowded, it would approach the density of the Bronx at its peak. To drive past and through all this would be a rich and strange experience. Drivers might feel captivated by the figures, environments and fantasies on the mural, ghosts of their parents, their friends, even of themselves, like sirens enticing them to plunge into the abyss of the past. On the other hand, so many of these ghosts would be urging and driving them on, dying to leap into a future beyond the Bronx's walls and join the stream of traffic on the way out. The Bronx Mural would end at the end of the Expressway itself, where it interchanges on the way to Westchester and Long Island. The end, the boundary between the Bronx and the world, would be marked with a gigantic ceremonial arch, in the tradition of the colossal monuments that Claes Oldenburg conceived in the 1960s. This arch would be circular and inflatable, suggesting both an automobile tire and a bagel. When fully pumped up, it would look indigestibly hard as a bagel, but ideal as a tire for a fast getaway; when soft, it would appear leaky and dangerous as a tire but, as a bagel, inviting to settle down and eat.

In recent years the South Bronx has become an international byword for slum squalor and violence. Noel Rico's poem gives a contemporary image for the Borough.

THE BRONX, 1979
for Miguel Piñero

I think of you
as a woman
with no legs;
Your stumps
rest on a dead pigeon
while your eyes fill
slowly with pus.

Everytime one wants
to touch you with the love
they feel will save you

you cough up a dead Puertorican.

As New York City steadily expanded in the nineteenth century it became apparent that if nothing was done to stop it the whole of Manhattan Island would soon be built over. A section of wasteland occupied by squatters' shacks was set aside for a park and a competition was held in 1858 for a design. The winning proposal was submitted by Frederick Law Olmsted, a former Staten Island farmer, travel writer, and conservationist, and Calvert Vaux, an English architect. Reconstructing the natural landscape according to their ideas proved a mammoth task and the Park was only completed in 1876. Olmsted, in particular, was a genius of outdoor design. His other parks in New York include Riverside, Prospect, and Morningside.

THE PLAN FOR THE PARK

The Park throughout is a single work of art, and as such subject to the primary law of every work of art, namely, that it shall be framed upon a single, noble motive, to which the design of all its parts, in some more or less subtle way, shall be confluent and helpful.

To find such a general motive of design for the Central Park, it will be necessary to go back to the beginning and ask, for what worthy purpose could the city be required to take out and keep excluded from the field of ordinary urban improvements, a body of land in what was looked forward to as its very centre, so large as that assigned for the Park? For what such object of great prospective importance would a smaller body of land not have been adequate?

To these questions a sufficient answer can, we believe, be found in the expectation that the whole of the island of New York would, but for such a reservation, before many years be occupied by buildings and paved streets; that millions upon millions of men were to live their lives upon this island, millions more to go out from it, or its immediate densely populated suburbs, only occasionally and at long intervals, and that all its inhabitants would assuredly suffer, in greater or less degree, according to their occupations and the degree of their confinement to it, from influences engendered by these conditions.

Provisions for the improvement of the ground, however, pointed to something more than mere exemption from urban conditions, namely, to the formation of an opposite class of conditions; conditions remedial of the influences of urban conditions.

Two classes of improvements were to be planned for this purpose; one directed to secure pure and wholesome air, to act through the lungs; the other to secure an antithesis of objects of vision to those of the streets and houses, which should act remedially by impressions on the mind and suggestions to the imagination.

It is one great purpose of the Park to supply to the hundreds of thousands of tired workers, who have no opportunity to spend their summers in the country, a specimen of God's handiwork that shall be to them, inexpensively, what a month or two in the White Mountains or the Adirondacks is, at great cost, to those in easier circumstances. The time will come when New York will be built up, when all the grading and filling will be done, and when the picturesquely-varied, rocky formations of the Island will have been converted into formations for rows of monotonous straight streets, and piles of erect buildings. There will be no suggestion left of its present varied surface, with the single exception of the few acres contained in the Park. Then the priceless value of the present picturesque outlines of the ground will be more distinctly perceived, and its adaptability for its purpose more fully recognized. It therefore seems desirable to interfere with its easy, undulating outlines, and picturesque, rocky scenery as little as possible, and, on the other hand, to endeavor rapidly, and by every legitimate means, to increase and judiciously develop these particularly individual and characteristic sources of landscape effects.

Considering that large classes of rural objects and many types of natural scenery are not practicable to be introduced on the site of the Park, – mountain, ocean, desert and prairie scenery for example, – it will be found that the most valuable form that could have been prescribed is that which may be distinguished from all others as pastoral. But the site of the Park having had a very heterogeneous surface, which was largely formed of solid rock, it was not desirable that the attempt should be made to reduce it all to the simplicity of pastoral scenery. What would the central motive of design require of the rest? Clearly that it should be given such a character as, while affording contrast and variety of scene, would as much as possible be confluent to the same end, namely, the constant suggestion to the imagination of an unlimited range of rural conditions.

The question of localizing or adjusting these two classes of landscape elements to the various elements of the natural topography of the Park next occurs, the study of which must begin with the consideration that the Park is to be surrounded by an artificial wall, twice as high as the Great Wall of China, composed of urban buildings. Wherever this should appear across the meadow-view, the imagination would be checked abruptly, at short range. Natural objects were thus required to be interposed, which while excluding the buildings as much as possible from view, would leave an uncertainty as to the occupation of the space beyond, and establish a horizon line, composed, as much as possible, of verdure.

It was, then, first of all, required that such parts of the site as were available and necessary to the purpose should be assigned to the occupation of elements which would compose a wood-side, screening incongruous objects without the Park as much as possible from the view of observers within it.

Secondly, of the remaining ground, it was required to assign as much as was available to the occupation of elements which would compose tranquil, open, pastoral scenes.

Thirdly, it was required to assign all of the yet remaining

166

ground to elements which would tend to form passages of scenery contrasting in depth of obscurity and picturesque character of detail with the softness and simplicity of the open landscape.

By far the most extensive and important of the constructed accommodations of the Central Park are those for convenience of locomotion. How to obtain simply the required amount of room for this purpose, without making this class of its constructions everywhere disagreeably conspicuous, harshly disruptive of all relations of composition between natural landscape elements on their opposite borders, and without the absolute destruction of many valuable topographical features, was the most difficult problem of this design.

Observations of... [traffic difficulties] both in our own streets and in European parks, led to the planning of a system of independent ways; 1st for carriages; 2d, for horsemen wishing to gallop; 3d, for footmen; and 4th, for common street traffic requiring to cross the Park. By this means it was made possible, even for the most timid and nervous, to go on foot to any district of the Park designed to be visited, without crossing a line of wheels on the same level, and consequently, without occasion for anxiety or hesitation.

Incidentally, the system provided, in its arched ways, substantial shelters scattered through the Park, which would be rarely seen above the general plane of the landscape, and which would be made as inconspicuous as possible, but to be readily found when required in sudden showers.

Without taking the present occasion to argue the point, we may simply refer to another incidental advantage of the system which, so far as we have observed, has not been publicly recognized, but which, we are confident, may be justly claimed to exist, in the fact that to the visitor, carried by occasional defiles from one field of landscape to another, in which a wholly different series of details is presented, the extent of the Park is practically much greater than it would otherwise be.

167

Robert Lowell (1917-1977), a major American poet of this century, was born in Boston but lived on and off in New York for many years.

CENTRAL PARK

Scaling small rocks, exhaling smog,
gasping at game-scents like a dog,
now light as pollen, now as white
and winded as a grounded kite —
I watched the lovers occupy
every inch of earth and sky:
one figure of geometry,
multiplied to infinity,
straps down, and sunning openly . . .
each precious, public, pubic tangle
an equilateral triangle,
lost in the park, half covered by
the shade of some low stone or tree.
The stain of fear and poverty
spread through each trapped anatomy,
and darkened every mole of dust.
All wished to leave this drying crust,
borne on the delicate wings of lust
like bees, and cast their fertile drop
into the overwhelming cup.

Drugged and humbled by the smell
of zoo-straw mixed with animal,
the lion prowled his slummy cell,
serving his life-term in jail —
glaring, grinding, on his heel,
with tingling step and testicle . . .
Behind a dripping rock, I found
a one-day kitten on the ground —
deprived, weak, ignorant and blind,
squeaking, tubular, left behind —
dying with its deserter's rich
Welfare lying out of reach:
milk cartons, kidney heaped to spoil,
two plates sheathed with silver foil.

Shadows had stained the afternoon;
high in an elm, a snagged balloon
wooed the attraction of the moon.
Scurrying from the mouth of night,
a single, fluttery, paper kite
grazed Cleopatra's Needle, and sailed
where the light of the sun had failed.
Then night, the night – the jungle hour,
the rich in his slit-windowed tower . . .
Old Pharaohs starving in your foxholes,
with painted banquets on the walls,
fists knotted in your captives' hair,
tyrants with little food to spare –
all your embalming left you mortal,
glazed, black, and hideously eternal,
all your plunder and gold leaf
only served to draw the thief . . .

We beg delinquents for our life.
Behind each bush, perhaps a knife;
each landscaped crag, each flowering shrub,
hides a policeman with a club.

CHAPTER 9

THE FIRE KING

The Fire-king reigns supreme in this devoted city; what with alterations, pulling down and burning up, the city in the aggregate is rebuilt, I should think, about once in seven years.

The Great Fire of 1836 was one of the most devastating in the history of New York. Philip Hone witnessed the damage.

How shall I record the events of last night, or how attempt to describe the most awful calamity which has ever visited these United States? The greatest loss by fire that has ever been known, with the exception perhaps of the conflagration of Moscow, and that was an incidental concomitant of war. I am fatigued in body, disturbed in mind, and my fancy filled with images of horror which my pen is inadequate to describe. Nearly one-half of the first ward is in ashes, five hundred to seven hundred stores, which with their contents are valued at $20,000,000 to $40,000,000, are now lying in an indistinguishable mass of ruins. There is not, perhaps, in the world the same space of ground covered by so great an amount of real and personal property as the scene of this dreadful conflagration. The fire broke out at nine o'clock last evening. I was writing in the library when the alarm was given, and went immediately down. The night was intensely cold, which was one cause of the unprecedented progress of the flames, for the water froze in the hydrants, and the engines and their hose could not be worked without great difficulty. The firemen, too, had been on duty all last night, and were almost incapable of performing their usual services. The fire originated in the store of Comstock & Adams, in Merchant street, – a narrow, crooked street, filled with high stores lately erected and occupied by dry-goods and hardware merchants, which led from Hanover to Pearl street. When I arrived at the spot the scene exceeded all description; the progress of the flames, like flashes of lightning, communicated in every direction, and a few minutes sufficed to level the lofty edifices on every side. It crossed the block to Pearl street. I perceived that the store of my son was in danger, and made the best of my way, by Front street around the old Slip, to the spot. We succeeded in getting out the stock of valuable dry goods, but they were put in the square, and in the course of the night our labours were rendered unavailing, for the fire reached and destroyed them, with a great part of all which were saved from the neighbouring stores; this part of Pearl street consisted of dry-goods stores, with stocks of immense value, of which little or nothing was saved. At this period the flames were unmanageable, and the crowd, including the firemen, appeared to look on with the apathy of despair, and the destruction continued until it reached Coenties Slip, in that direction, and Wall street down to the river, including all South street and Water street; while to the west, Exchange street, including all Post's stores, Lord's beautiful row, William street, Beaver and Stone streets, were destroyed. The splendid edifice erected a few years ago by the liberality of the merchants, known as the Merchants' Exchange, and one of the ornaments of the city, took fire in the rear, and is now a heap of ruins. The façade and magnificent marble columns fronting on Wall street are all that remain of this noble building, and resemble the ruins of an ancient temple rather than the new and beautiful resort of the merchants. When the dome of this edifice fell in, the sight was awfully grand; in its fall it demolished the statue of Hamilton, executed by Ball Hughes, which was erected in the rotunda only eight months ago, by the public spirit of the merchants. . .

The buildings covered an area of a quarter of a mile square, closely built up with fine stores of four and five stories in height, filled with merchandise, all of which lie in a mass of burning, smoking ruins, rendering the streets indistinguishable.

The Triangle Shirt Waist Company fire of the early twentieth century took many lives and in raising the issue of safety at work in such a devastating manner gave a great boost to trade union organisation in the garment industry. Sholem Asch (1880-1957) incorporated the incident into his novel, East River, *first published in Yiddish in 1946.*

TRIANGLE FIRE

Mary had been working at Greenspan's shop for about two months. She and Sarah Lifschitz had become close friends. One day, as the two girls sat together eating lunch, Sarah said:

'Listen to this, Mary. The Triangle Waist Company on

Washington Place is looking for girls to work on blouses. It's easy work, one of the girls who works there told me, because this season's styles are simple, not much fancy stuff. It's not a union shop, but even if you're a union member you can get in – you just don't have to tell them. The pay's wonderful, ten or twelve dollars a week, if you work from half-past seven in the morning to six. With overtime some of the girls make fourteen dollars a week, even though they don't pay extra rates for overtime. It's a big shop, and the working conditions are pretty good. I'm going to try to get a job there; I wouldn't mind earning more money; they need it at home. What do you say? Do you want to come with me?'

'Twelve dollars a week!' Mary could hardly believe it. 'And fourteen with overtime! Sure I'll go with you. I'm sick of this place, with all the smells of that darned restaurant. And I can't stand working with all those old men. I'd like to work among a lot of girls in a real shop for a change, even though it would take longer to get all the way down there. I get up early, anyway. I have to make breakfast for my father – my grandma hasn't been feeling well lately and my mother's supposed to stay in bed as much as she can. I could use a few extra dollars. The kids at home are in rags; my mother can't patch Jimmy's pants any more. I'd like to earn some extra money and get some new clothes for the kids as a surprise for Easter.'

A few days later both girls went over to the Triangle firm on Washington Place to ask about jobs. When they satisfied the foreman that they were experienced hands and didn't belong to the union, he took them on.

That evening Mary came home radiant. At last she would be working in a real shop. Besides, she would be earning at least six dollars a week more than she was getting at Greenspan's; with some overtime she might even make as much as fourteen dollars a week.

The Triangle firm was housed in a modern building, practically a skyscraper, situated on the edge of the enormous open square in the heart of the city. The factory took up several floors of the building. The offices, showrooms, and cutting rooms were on the lower floors. On the ninth floor about two hundred and thirty girls and a few men worked at sewing machines. Other hands worked on the eighth floor. The tenth floor housed the finishers, cleaners, and examiners. Besides a large number of men, cutters and pressers, Triangle employed more than seven hundred girls.

Entrance and exit to the ninth floor were furnished by two doors, one opposite the other. One of them, the one giving on the stairway on the Washington Square side, was always kept locked. The other door opened on the corridor and elevator leading to Greene Street. This door was constantly guard by a watchman who looked the girls over each time they left the shop. His beady eyes were like exploring, impudent fingers, making sure that a girl didn't have a blouse or a stray piece of material concealed under her dress or coat. Nor did he hesitate to paw them for a more thorough inspection. There was no other way for the girls to enter or leave the shop except through the door guarded by the watchman.

March twenty-fifth fell on a Saturday. Through the wide windows overlooking Washington Place the afternoon sky was snow-laden and gloomy. The ninth floor bustled with activity. Rows of girls sat at the sewing machines, the electric bulbs gleaming over their bowed heads. The work was going on at full speed; all the girls were hurrying to get through with the day's work so as to get home as early as possible. Although Saturday was a full working day, the girls were permitted to leave an hour earlier if the day's quota was disposed of. Saturday was payday, another inducement to hurry; everyone had plans for the evening, to go visiting, to go shopping, to go to the movies or to a dance.

Mary and Sarah sat at adjoining machines. As they worked they chatted of their evening plans. The electricity-driven leather belts of the machines clattered so noisily they were barely able to hear one another.

Sarah was in an elated mood. This week she had managed to earn, with overtime, all of fourteen dollars, an enormous sum. Besides, she was going to a dance in the evening; Jack Klein, who worked in the factory, had invited her. Her problem was what to wear, the new evening dress she had bought with her increased earnings at Triangle, or her black skirt and waist; the waist was a Triangle number; she might even have worked on it herself.

'Gee, Sarah,' Mary commented, 'I love those new waists with the ribbon at the collar that we're making now. But I guess it's really a question of how interested you are in Jack. Do you want to look gorgeous – or just attractive?'

'Well, naturally, a girl wants to look gorgeous when a fellow

175

takes her out to a dance for the first time,' Sarah replied.

'In that case you better wear your evening dress. A girl looks more – more important in an evening dress. That's what the fellows like.'

As they talked above the whirr of the machines a sudden quiet fell on the shop; even the machines sounded subdued. Something seemed to be happening at the far end of the room. Sarah stood up to see what was going on. Mary scrambled up beside her. They could see nothing.

'What is it?' Mary asked in sudden alarm.

'I don't know,' Sarah answered.

All at once they saw puffs of thick smoke coming up between the cracks of the floor boards near the door leading to the elevator. Forked flames of fire followed the smoke. All the fright in the world broke out in a chorus of hysterical screams.

'Fire! Fire! Fire!'

Panic swept through the room. There was the noise of running feet, the clatter of chairs and stools being thrown over. The two girls began to run with the rest.

The running mob pushed them toward the exit door on the Greene Street side. It was near the door leading to the elevator that the flames were licking through the planks of the floor. They remembered that no stairway descended from the corridor. The elevator was the only exit. They would be trapped in the corridor by the flames. The smoke and fire coming through the floor near the door terrified them. The crowd veered and dashed to the other side of the loft, where the door led to the stairway that went down to Washington Place. Mary and Sarah, holding each other by the hand, ran with the rest.

They stumbled over chairs and upended stools. They were blocked by hysterical girls who were too terrified to move. Sarah and Mary tried to drag some of them along with them. Here and there tongues of fire were coming up through the floor. Around the sewing machines the heaps of remnants of material and trimmings, silks, linings, padded cotton, the oil-soaked rags which the girls used to clean the machines after oiling them, blazed into flame. The oil-soaked rags were the first to catch fire, setting alight the piles of cuttings and feeding the flames from one machine to the next. The grease-covered machines themselves began to blaze together with piles of material on them. The fire grew in volume by the minute. It spread like a stream overflowing its banks. The waves of living flame licked at the skirts of the fleeing, screaming, trapped girls.

Barely had they escaped through the corridor of flame between the rows of machines when they were blocked by a wall of smoke which rose up from the large stacks of finished blouses. With the smoke came a suffocating odour. The smoke arose to the ceiling, where it hung like a cloud. They began to suffocate, gagging and choking. Her eyes blinded and her throat gasping, Sarah dragged Mary along. The door, when they reached it, was blocked with a mass of bodies. Hair loosed, clothing torn, the mob pulled and tore at each other in panicked attempts to get to the door. From the packed mass of bodies came a high-pitched keening, an hysterical yammering.

Those nearest the door were jammed against it, beating at it with their fists, tearing at it with their fingers, clawing at it with their nails. Some, in an ecstasy of terror, beat against it with their heads. The door did not budge.

The press around the door grew thicker. Sarah and Mary, midway in the mob, were held immovable and helpless in the tightly pressed crush of girls' bodies.

Some of the cooler heads among them tried to shout out advice to those nearest the door. Their shouts were lost in the hysterical shrieks of the terrified girls. Someone, more resourceful, managed to pass the metal head of a sewing machine over the struggling mob to the girls at the door. One of them began to beat the door frantically with the heavy metal head. The door did not yield.

The press of bodies was now an immovable mass. Sarah and Mary saw themselves hopelessly hemmed in. Sarah kept her senses. Unless they got out of the packed crowd around the door they were lost. She could see the tongues of flame coming closer and closer. With an energy born of desperation she grabbed Mary by the arm and began to drag her after her. With heads, shoulders, feet, and arms they managed to force their way through the mass of bodies and away from the door. Biting, scratching, tearing and clawing at arms, bodies, and legs, Sarah, half crawling, pulled Mary along after her, until they reached the outer edge of the crush.

Desperately Sarah looked around. Half of the floor was in flames, and the flames were coming toward them. The space near the windows which overlooked Washington Place was still untouched. In front of the windows frantic girls were weaving, clutching at the window sills, desperately trying to find some way of escape.

Near one of the windows the flames were coming closer. Here only a few girls were gathered. If there was any escape it would have to be through this window, the thought flashed through Sarah's mind. They would have to get through it before the flames reached it. She began to drag Mary toward the window. Mary showed no resistance. She was only half conscious. She let the other do what she willed.

The window was nailed down. It resisted all Sarah's efforts to open it. There was a small, jagged break in the pane, stained with blood about the edges; others had tried to shatter the glass. Sarah banged her clenched fist against the glass again and again and made the opening larger.

When the opening was big enough she put her head through.

On the street below she could see crowds of people. She could see firemen holding safety nets to catch the girls who dropped from the openings in other windows. From the crowd came frantic shouts. The wails of the girls answered them. The firemen made unavailing attempts to raise their too-short ladders to the upper floors. One girl after another dropped from the windows. Sarah looked to see if there was a ledge below the window which she might be able to reach with her toes. Outside the eighth floor window there was a small iron balcony, it might be possible to reach that, and from there to the balcony outside the seventh floor window, and so on down to safety.

She turned to Mary. 'Quick, crawl through to the window ledge!'

'I'm afraid. . . .'

'Quick! Come on! Here, through the broken glass.'

'I can't! I can't! What will I hold on to?'

'I'll hold your arms. Try to get your toes on the iron balcony down there. Look, the other girls are doing it.'

'You go first, Sarah.'

'No, I'm stronger than you. I'll be able to hold on to you. You're too weak to hold on to me. I'll come after you. Go ahead!'

The flames came closer. Urged on by Sarah and driven by the terrifying spectacle of the approaching tongues of flame, Mary scrambled onto the sill, and, with her back to the street, managed to get her legs through the hole in the window, holding on frantically to Sarah's shoulders. She gashed her knee on the jagged edges of the glass but never felt the pain. Holding tightly to Sarah, she groped for some projecting ledge to support her. Except for the balconies outside the line of windows below her, the wall fell sheer. But the balcony was too far down; she couldn't reach it. Sarah, holding Mary firmly by the arms, reached out of the window as far as she dared, trying to lower her as close as possible to the balcony. It was still too far to be reached.

Yells came up to Mary's ears from the street, but she could not understand what they were shouting. Only one thought possessed her, how to get a toehold on the iron balcony below. She still gripped Sarah's arms in an iron clutch. Sarah managed to shift her hold so as to grab Mary by both hands, thus lowering her body farther down. Mary strained to reach the balcony; still it was no use. Sarah strained even farther out of the window; she was now halfway out of the jagged opening. The sharp edges of the broken glass cut into her arms and chest. As Mary strained with her feet to find a hold, the jagged edges cut deeper and deeper in Sarah's flesh. She felt the raw edges going into her, but she felt no pain. There was only the one overwhelming urge – to lower Mary closer to the balcony. She strained farther out. Suddenly she felt a fierce wave of heat licking at her legs. The anguish was so intense, the instinct for self-preservation so compelling, that all thoughs of Mary disappeared from her mind. She couldn't withdraw her body into the room to face the enemy that was attacking her. But she knew what the enemy was. The flames were licking at her stockings. In another moment her dress would be on fire.

'Mamma!' she screamed hysterically. Her body went farther out through the window. The broken edges of the jagged glass tore at her flesh.

With the tips of her toes Mary could feel the balcony under her feet. The faint hint of safety only served to heighten her terror. Through the mist of consciousness left to her Sarah saw that Mary could now find a footing. 'Just a little more. Just a little more,' she thought. She could feel herself moving farther forward. She could feel the flames licking up her shoes, climbing her legs. Then she could feel nothing. If only she could lean out a little more, Mary would reach the balcony. She dare not let go of Mary's hands. She was no longer herself. She no longer existed. She had become a part of Mary. She was only an instrument to help her reach the balcony. . . . Now she could reach it. Sarah threw the upper half of her body violently forward. Mary felt below her feet the firm surface of the balcony. Her hands, suddenly released, clutched at the bare sides of the building. Above her, out of the shattered window, a flaming body fell, like a living torch, down to the street below.

Mary knew that flaming torch. She opened her mouth to shriek Sarah's name. In her pain and terror no sound came from her lips. Now the single thought of escape obsessed her. From the window outside of which she stood, a wave of blasting heat came to her from the roaring flames inside.

She threw a terrified glance to the street below. It was so far away that it seemed to her that it must be a distant, unattainable world. The area immediately below her was an empty expanse. The crowds had been herded away by lines of police; there were only the firemen and fire-fighting apparatus. She could see safety nets held out, spread by groups of firemen. She could see bodies falling from the walls of the building with hair and clothing aflame. She could hear voices calling to her; she did not know what they were shouting. She looked around her at the other windows of the building. She could see girls crawling through the windows on hands and knees, trying frantically to hold on to the bare walls. Others seemed to be hanging in mid-air, their falling bodies caught by projecting cornices.

The second that she remained crouched on the balcony seemed like an eternity. Angry flames were shooting out through the window, licking at her. She was alone now; there was no Sarah holding on to her hands. Her consciousness and resourcefulness began to function; she would have to depend on her own initiative now. Driven more by fear of the flames that licked at her from the window than by any considered design, she held on to the iron rail of the balcony and let her body down. Her feet swung in the air; she hadn't looked first to see whether she could reach the landing below. She was afraid to let go of the rail. Her feet sought for a foothold; they found none; the wall was smooth and unbroken. Again and again her toes sought out a niche in the wall, but they found only a sheer surface. Her hands were getting weak, she would have to let go the iron rail; it was hot from the flames which were shooting farther and farther through the window. The palms of her hands burned. She could feel her fingers relaxing. She would let herself go, like the others, to fall into the safety net – or to crash onto the sidewalk.

180

She couldn't summon up the courage to let go. But she knew if she didn't let go herself, her fingers would slip from the rail and she would fall onto the sidewalk. She must jump. She must try to jump to the nets spread below. Her lips kept murmuring 'Jesus, Christ, Jesus, Mary.' She closed her eyes for a second. She saw before her the carved wooden figure of Jesus to which she prayed in the Italian church. She knelt before it and prayed her familiar prayer. 'Sweet Jesus, save me.' As her lips murmured the words her fingers let go their clutch on the iron balcony rail and her body fell.

She did not fall to the ground. Her dress caught on the iron bar of a sign extending outside the third floor window. In the second that she remained suspended, strong arms reached out of the window and pulled her in.

For three weeks Mary was kept at the hospital. By the end of that time her gashed knee had healed. Also her shattered nerves.

More than one hundred and fifty girls had lost their lives in the fire. They were buried at mass funerals; the Jewish girls in Jewish cemeteries, the Christian girls in Christian cemeteries. The survivors soon began to search for work in other factories. The wave of excitement and anger that swept through the city and all through the country didn't last very long. A commission was appointed to investigate fire hazards in the state's garment factories. Some bills were introduced into the Assembly. There were heated debates; some measures were adopted, others were defeated. When it was all over, everything in the needle industries remained the same.

The McCarthy family had become accustomed to Mary's contributions to the household; now they found it impossible to manage on the reduced scale. Patrick McCarthy renewed his old, endless arguments. Although most of the victims were Jewish girls, only a few Gentile girls having been killed, McCarthy blamed the fire and everything about it on the Jews. He swore he would not allow Mary to go back to work, but he soon began to drown his troubles in drink – with the help of the rent money to which Mary had so substantially contributed in the weeks past. After she had been out of the hospital for about two weeks, the McCarthy larder was so empty that Mary had to go out looking for a job.

She found work in a factory whose owner assured her it was

fireproof. McCarthy made a show protesting, but, like the rest of the family, he knew well enough what Mary's earnings meant. Since she had been working he had been able to go more often to the rent money in the bowl in the cupboard with less pangs of conscience.

'Fire or no fire,' Grandma McCarthy said, 'the world has to go on about its business. Coal miners go back to the pit after a mine disaster.'

They all had to agree with her.

One vivid vision remained in Mary's memory: Sarah's terrified eyes staring from below her flaming hair.

In The American Scene, *Henry James described one of the distinctive features of the New York City landscape – the fire-escapes.*

FIRE ESCAPES

There it was, there it is, and when I think of the dark, foul, stifling Ghettos of other remembered cities, I shall think by the same stroke of the city of redemption, and evoke in particular the rich Rutgers Street perspective – rich, so peculiarly, for the eye, in that complexity of fire-escapes with which each house-front bristles and which gives the whole vista so modernized and appointed a look. Omnipresent in the "poor" regions, this neat applied machinery has, for the stranger, a common side with the electric light and the telephone, suggests the distance achieved from the old Jerusalem. (These frontal iron ladders and platforms, by the way, so numerous throughout New York, strike more New York notes that can be parenthetically named – and among them perhaps most sharply the note of the ease with which, in the terrible town, on opportunity, "architecture" goes by the board; but the appearance to which they often most conduce is that of the most spaciously organized cage for the nimbler class of animals in some great zoological garden. This general analogy is irresistible – it seems to offer, in each district, a little world of bars and perches and swings for human squirrels and monkeys. The very name of architecture perishes, for the fire-escapes look like abashed afterthoughts, staircases and communications forgotten in the construction; but the inhabitants lead, like the squirrels and monkeys, all the merrier life.)

CHAPTER 10

CHANGE

From The American Scene, *by Henry James.*

NEW LANDMARKS CRUSHING THE OLD

If it had been the final function of the Bay to make one feel one's age, so, assuredly, the mouth of Wall Street proclaimed it, for one's private ear, distinctly enough; the breath of existence being taken, wherever one turned, as that of youth on the run and with the prize of the race in sight, and the new landmarks crushing the old quite as violent children stamp on snails and caterpillars.

One of Stephen Crane's New York City Sketches.

A MOURNFUL OLD BUILDING

A mournful old building stood between two that were tall and straight and proud. In a way, it was a sad thing; symbolizing a decrepit old man whose lean shoulders are jostled by sturdy youth. The old building seemed to glance timidly upward at its two neighbors, pleading for comradeship, and at times it assumed an important air derived from its environment, and said to those who viewed from the side-walks: 'we three – we three buildings.'

It stood there awaiting the inevitable time of downfall, when progress to the music of tumbling walls and chimneys would come marching up the avenues. Already, from the roof one could see a host advancing, an army of enormous buildings, coming with an invincible front that extended across the city, trampling under their feet the bones of the dead, rising tall and supremely proud on the crushed memories, the annihilated hopes of generations gone. At sunset time, each threw a tremendous shadow, a gesture of menace out over the low plain of the little buildings huddling afar down.

Once this mournful old structure had been proud. It had stood with its feet unconcernedly on the grave of a past ambition and no doubt patronized the little buildings on either side.

Robert Moses played a major role in transforming the face of modern New York. Having created Jones and Orchard Beaches, the West Side Highway, the Belt Parkway, the Triborough Bridge, the 1939 World's Fair site, and many other highways, bridges, and parks, Moses turned to the Bronx in the 1950's. Marshal Berman, who witnessed the upheaval caused by the construction of the Cross-Bronx Expressway, describes it in his book, All That is Solid Melts in the Air.

CROSS BRONX EXPRESSWAY

But then, in the spring and fall of 1953, Moses began to loom over my life in a new way: he proclaimed that he was about to ram an immense expressway, unprecedented in scale, expense and difficulty of construction, through our neighborhood's heart. At first we couldn't believe it; it seemed to come from another world. First of all, hardly any of us owned cars: the neighborhood itself, and the subways leading downtown, defined the flow of our lives. Besides, even if the city needed the road – or was it the state that needed the road? (in Moses' operations, the location of power and authority was never clear, except for Moses himself) – they surely couldn't mean what the stories seemed to say: that the road would be blasted directly through a dozen solid, settled, densely populated neighborhoods like our own; that something like 60,000 working- and lower-middle-class people, mostly Jews, but with many Italians, Irish and Blacks thrown in, would be thrown out of their homes. The Jews of the Bronx were nonplussed: could a fellow-Jew really want to do this to us? (We had little idea of what kind of Jew he was, or of how much we were all an obstruction in his path.) And even if he did want to do it, we were sure it couldn't happen here, not in America. We were still basking in the afterglow of the New Deal: the government was *our* government, and it would come through to protect us in the end. And yet, before we knew it, steam shovels and bulldozers were there, and people were getting notice that they had better clear out fast. They looked numbly at the wreckers, at the disappearing streets, at each other, and they went. Moses was coming through, and no temporal or spiritual power could block his way.

For ten years, through the late 1950s and early 1960s, the center of the Bronx was pounded and blasted and smashed. My friends and I would stand on the parapet of the Grand Concourse, where 174th Street had been, and survey the work's

185

progress – the immense steam shovels and bulldozers and timber and steel beams, the hundreds of workers in their variously colored hard hats, the giant cranes reaching far above the Bronx's tallest roofs, the dynamite blasts and tremors, the wild, jagged crags of rock newly torn, the vistas of devastation stretching for miles to the east and west as far as the eye could see – and marvel to see our ordinary nice neighborhood transformed into sublime, spectacular ruins.

In college, when I discovered Piranesi, I felt instantly at home. Or I would return from the Columbia library to the construction site and feel myself in the midst of the last act of Goethe's *Faust*. (You had to hand it to Moses: his works gave you ideas.) Only there was no humanistic triumph here to offset the destruction. Indeed, when the construction was done, the real ruin of the Bronx had just begun. Miles of streets alongside the road were choked with dust and fumes and deafening noise – most strikingly, the roar of trucks of a size and power that the Bronx had never seen, hauling heavy cargoes through the city, bound for Long Island or New England, for New Jersey and all points south, all through the day and night. Apartment houses that had been settled and stable for twenty years emptied out, often virtually overnight; large and impoverished black and Hispanic families, fleeing even worse slums, were moved in wholesale, often under the auspices of the Welfare Department, which even paid inflated rents, spreading panic and accelerating flight. At the same time, the construction had destroyed many commercial blocks, cut others off from most of their customers and left the storekeepers not only close to bankruptcy but, in their enforced isolation, increasingly vulnerable to crime. The borough's great open market, along Bathgate Avenue, still flourishing in the late 1950s, was decimated; a year after the road came through, what was left went up in smoke. Thus depopulated, economically depleted, emotionally shattered – as bad as the physical damage had been the inner wounds were worse – the Bronx was ripe for all the dreaded spirals of urban blight.

Moses seemed to glory in the devastation. When he was asked, shortly after the Cross-Bronx road's completion, if urban expressways like this didn't pose special human problems, he replied impatiently that 'there's very little hardship in the thing. There's a little discomfort and even that is exaggerated.' Compared with his earlier, rural and suburban highways, the

186

only difference here was that 'There are more houses in the
way. . . more people in the way – that's all.' He boasted that
'When you operate in an overbuilt metropolis, you have to hack
your way with a meat ax.'

*James Merrill was born in New York City in 1926. His many collections of
poems have established him as a major contemporary poet. This poem is from*
Water Street *(1962).*

An Urban Convalescence

Out for a walk, after a week in bed,
I find them tearing up part of my block
And, chilled through, dazed and lonely, join the dozen
In meek attitudes, watching a huge crane
Fumble luxuriously in the filth of years.
Her jaws dribble rubble. An old man
Laughs and curses in her brain,
Bringing to mind the close of *The White Goddess.*

As usual in New York, everything is torn down
Before you have had time to care for it.
Head bowed, at the shrine of noise, let me try to recall
What building stood here. Was there a building at all?
I have lived on this same street for a decade.

Wait. Yes. Vaguely a presence rises
Some five floors high, of shabby stone
—Or am I confusing it with another one
In another part of town, or of the world?—
And over its lintel into focus vaguely
Misted with blood (my eyes are shut)
A single garland sways, stone fruit, stone leaves,
Roots down, even into the poor soil of my seeing.
When did the garland become part of me?
I ask myself, amused almost,
Then shiver once from head to toe,

Transfixed by a particular cheap engraving of garlands
Bought for a few francs long ago,
All calligraphic tendril and cross-hatched rondure,
Ten years ago, and crumpled up to stanch
Boughs dripping, whose white gestures filled a cab,
And thought of neither then nor since.
Also, to clasp them, the small, red-nailed hand
Of no one I can place. Wait. No. Her name, her features
Lie toppled underneath that year's fashions.
The words she must have spoken, setting her face
To fluttering like a veil, I cannot hear now,
Let alone understand.

So that I am already on the stair,
As it were, of where I lived,
When the whole structure shudders at my tread
And soundlessly collapses, filling
The air with motes of stone.
Onto the still erect building next door
Are pressed levels and hues—
Pocked rose, streaked greens, brown whites.
Who drained the pousse-café?
Wires and pipes, snapped off at the roots, quiver.

Well, that is what life does. I stare
A moment longer, so. And presently
The massive volume of the world
Closes again.

Upon that book I swear
To abide by what it teaches:
Gospels of ugliness and waste,
Of towering voids, of soiled gusts,
Of a shrieking to be faced
Full into, eyes astream with cold—

With cold?
All right then. With self-knowledge.

188

Indoors at last, the pages of *Time* are apt
To open, and the illustrated mayor of New York,
Given a glimpse of how and where I work,
To note yet one more house that can be scrapped.

Unwillingly I picture
My walls weathering in the general view.
It is not even as though the new
Buildings did very much for architecture.

Suppose they did. The sickness of our time requires
That these as well be blasted in their prime.
You would think the simple fact of having lasted
Threatened our cities like mysterious fires.

There are certain phrases which to use in a poem
Is like rubbing silver with quicksilver. Bright
But facile, the glamour deadens overnight.
For instance, how 'the sickness of our time'

Enhances, then debases, what I feel.
At my desk I swallow in a glass of water
No longer cordial, scarcely wet, a pill
They had told me not to take until much later.
With the result that back into my imagination
The city glides, like cities seen from the air,
Mere smoke and sparkle to the passenger
Having in mind another destination

Which now is not that honey-slow descent
Of the Champs-Elysées, her hand in his,
But the dull need to make some kind of house
Out of the life lived, out of the love spent.

Isaac Bashevis Singer, born in Poland in 1904, emigrated to New York in 1935, when he began writing in Yiddish for the Jewish Daily Forward. He is the author of many novels and stories and winner of the 1978 Nobel Prize for literature.

SAM PALKA AND DAVID VISHKOVER

Sam Palka sat on the sofa – stocky, a tuft of white hair on each side of his bald head, his face red, with bushy brows and bloodshot eyes that changed from pale blue to green to yellow. A cigar stuck out between his lips. His belly protruded like that of a woman in late pregnancy. He wore a navy-blue jacket, green pants, brown shoes, a shirt with purple stripes, and a silk tie on which was painted the head of a lion. Sam Palka himself looked to me like a lion which by some magic had turned into a rich man in New York, a Maecenas to Yiddish writers, a supporter of the Yiddish theater, president of an old-age home in the Bronx, the treasurer of a society that supported orphans in Israel.

Talking to me, Sam Palka shouted as though I were deaf. He lifted a thick manuscript from the coffee table and yelled, 'Over a thousand pages, huh! And this is not one-hundredth part of what I could have written. But fix it up the way it is.'

'I will do what I can.'

'Money doesn't matter. Even if I should live a thousand years, I have enough. I will pay you three thousand dollars for the editing, and when the book comes out and they write about it in the papers I will give you – what do they call it? – a bonus. But make it tasty. I can't read the books writers bring me – three or four lines of a novel and you have to fight to stay awake. In my day a book grabbed you. You began to read a novel and couldn't put it down, because you wanted to know what happened. Dieneson, Spector, Seifert! And there were thoughts that took you who knows where. They contained history, too. Samson and Delilah, Jephthah's daughter, Bar Kochba. They hit the spot. Today you read half a book and you still don't know what it's about. These scribblers write of love, but they know as much of love as I know of what's going on on the moon. How should they know? They sit all day long and half the night in the Café Royal and argue about how great they are. They have sour milk and ink in their veins, not blood. I haven't forgotten Yiddish. The man I dictated this book to tried to correct me all the time; he didn't like

190

my Polish Yiddish. But he didn't bother me. I would dictate an episode and he would ask, 'How can that be. It's not realistic.' He came from Ishishok, some godforsaken village, and to him whatever he hadn't experienced didn't exist – a bookworm, an idiot.

'Now, I want you to know that even though I dictated over one thousand pages I had to leave out the main thing. I could not describe it because the heroine is alive and she reads. She does one thing in her life – she reads. She has heard of all today's writers. Wherever a new book can be found, she gets it and reads it from cover to cover. My life wouldn't be worth living if I were to publish the truth and she should learn about it. What I am going to tell you can be written only after my death. But who is there to do it? You are still a young man, you know your way around, and when I kick the bucket I want you to add this story to the book. Without it the whole thing isn't worth a damn. I will provide for your additional work in my will.

'Where should I begin? I was born in a pious home. My parents were old-fashioned Jews, but even when I was still a cheder boy I heard about love. Does one have to look far for it? It's right in the Torah. Jacob loved Rachel, and when Laban, the cheat, substituted Leah in the dark night Jacob labored another seven years. Well, and what about King David and King Solomon with the Queen of Sheba and all that stuff? Book peddlers used to come to our village and they brought storybooks – two pennies to buy a book, one penny to borrow it. I was a poor boy, but whenever I could get hold of a penny I spent it on reading. When I came to America and I earned three dollars a week, I spent my last cent on books or on tickets for the Yiddish theater. In those times actors were still actors and not sticks of wood. When they appeared on stage the boards burned under their feet. I saw all of them! Adler, Mme. Liptzin, Schildkraut, Kessler, Tomashevsky – every one of them. Well, and the playwrights of those times – Goldfaden, Jacob Gordin, Lateiner! Each word had to do with love, and you could have kissed each one. When you read my book you will see that I had no luck in my marriage. I fell for a rotten woman – a bitter piece, a bitch. How she ruined my days and how she set my children against me is all there. As long as I was young and poor I worked in a sweatshop, and then I took to peddling. I had no time for love. I lived in a dark alcove and I couldn't afford to buy clothes. We worked then fourteen hours a day, and when it was busy even eighteen. When it became slack we had barely a crust to eat. If your stomach is empty you forget about love.

'I built my first bungalow quite a number of years after I married, and I soon became so successful it was as though Elijah had blessed me. One day I had nothing and the next money poured in from all sides. But I still worked hard, perhaps even harder than ever. No matter how successful a man is, he can slip in no time from the top of the heap to the very bottom. You have to be on the watch every minute. As long as I had a job or carried a pack on my shoulders and peddled, at least I rested on the Sabbath. With prosperity, my Sabbaths too were gone. My wife got wind that I had a spare dollar and began to tear pieces off me. We moved from the Lower East Side and took an apartment uptown. The children came one after the other and there were doctors, private schools, and the devil knows what else. My wife – Bessie was her name – bedecked herself with so much jewelry you could hardly see her. She came from petty and mean people, and when these get the smell of money they lose their heads. I was in my late thirties, and I still had not tasted real love. If I had ever loved my wife it was only from Monday to Tuesday. We quarreled constantly, and she threatened me with jail and judges. She kept reminding me that in America a lady is something so special you have to bow to her as though she were an idol. She carried on until I couldn't look at her any more. When I heard her voice I felt like vomiting. She indulged in all sorts of trickery, but she still expected me to be a husband to her. Impossible! We no longer shared a bedroom. By this time I had an office, and secretly I got a little apartment in one of my buildings. I'm sorry to admit it, but if you hate a wife you're bound to care less for the children. After Bessie, that fishwife, realized we would never be close again, she began to look for others. She did it so crudely men were afraid to start anything with her. She snatched at their sleeves like Potiphar's wife. I know what you want to ask me – why didn't I get a divorce. First of all, in those times to get a divorce you had to jump through hoops, knocking on the doors of the courts and so on. Today you fly to Reno and in six weeks you are as free as a bird. Secondly, she would have set a bunch of shysters on me and they would have fleeced me of my last penny. Besides, one gets a divorce when one is in love with someone else. If no one is waiting for you, why look for more headaches? I had partners in the business, and even though they had good wives they kept company with loose women. Today these women have become fancy call girls, but a whore is a whore. They all did it — the manufacturers, the jobbers, anyone who could pay. For them it was a game. But if these prostitutes were all you had, you realized your misfortune. It happened more than once that I just looked at one of these sluts and lost my appetite. I would give her a few dollars and run away like a yeshiva boy. I would go to a movie and for hours watch the gangsters shooting one another. So the years passed, and I thought that I would never learn what love was. Do you want to hear more?'

'Yes, of course.'

'This alone would make a book. When you write it, you will know how to embellish it.'

'Why embellish? As you tell it it is good enough.'

'Well, writers like to embellish.'

'When I was about forty-two or forty-three I was really rich. Once the money starts to flow, you can't stop it. I bought houses and lots and made huge profits. I bought stocks and they rose overnight. Taxes were nothing in those days. I owned a limousine and wrote checks for all kinds of charities. Now women swarmed around me like bees around honey. I got more love in a week than I could make use of in a year. But I am not a man who fools himself. I knew what they wanted was my money, not me. As they kissed me and tried to make me believe I was the great lover, they talked about what they would get out of it: trips to Florida, to Europe; mink coats; diamonds. It was all bluff. You lie in bed with them and they don't let you forget that what you really are is a sugar daddy. I wished I could meet a woman who did not know about my money or an heiress so rich that in comparison I would seem poor. But where and when? I began to think that true love was not for me. How do they say it in Poland? Sausage is not for dogs.

'Suddenly a miracle happened. I acquired an old house on Blake Avenue in Brownsville. Today Brownsville is full of Negroes and Puerto Ricans; then it was the land of Israel. You couldn't find a Gentile to save your life. I wanted to put up a new building, but first I had to get rid of the tenants. Often these things went easily, but this time some of them balked. I didn't believe in going to court; I preferred to settle with them myself. I had a free Sunday and decided to go and see what could be done. My car happened to be in the garage, so I took the subway. After all, I wasn't born a Rockefeller.

'At the house I knocked on a door, but in Brownsville they didn't know the meaning of that. I pushed the latch, the door opened, and I saw a room that looked exactly like one in the old country. If I hadn't known that I was in Brownsville, I would have thought that I was in Konskowola: whitewashed walls, a board floor, a broken-down sofa with the stuffing sticking out. Even the smells were from Konskowola – fried onions, chicory, moldy bread. On the sofa sat a girl as beautiful as Queen Esther. One difference. Esther was supposed to be greenish and this girl was white, with blue eyes and golden hair – a beauty. She was dressed like a greenhorn who had just arrived: a long skirt and shoes with buttons. And what was she doing? Reading a storybook: *Sheindele with the Blue Lips.* I had read it years before on the other side. I though I was dreaming and I pinched myself, but it was no dream.

'I wanted to tell her that I was the landlord and had come to make her move out. But some power stopped me. I began to play a role as if I were an actor in the theater. She asked me who I was and I said I was a salesman of sewing machines. I could get one for her cheap. She said, 'What do I need a sewing machine for? When I want to sew something, I use my own ten fingers.' She spoke a familiar Yiddish.

'I could sit with you until tomorrow and not tell half of it, but I will make it short. She had been in this country only two years. Her father had been a Talmud teacher in Poland. He was brought to this land of gold by an uncle. Three days after the father and daughter left Ellis Island, the uncle died. Her father became a beadle for some little rabbi here. I asked her how old she was and she said twenty-six. 'How does it happen,' I asked her, 'that such a beautiful girl is unmarried?' She answered, 'They offered me many matches but I refused to marry through a matchmaker. I have to be in love.' What she said was not silly; she was like a child and her talk was also like that of a little girl. She was not retarded – just naïve. She had lived for twenty-four years in a tiny village in the hinterland –'Wysoka. Her mother died when she was still young. Each word she uttered was the pure truth. She could as much lie as I could be the wife of a rabbi. I asked her name and she said, 'Channah Basha.' Why drag it out? I fell in love with her – head over heels. I couldn't tear myself from her. I was afraid she would make me go, but she asked, 'Aren't you hungry?' 'Yes, I am hungry,' I said and I thought, For you! She said, 'I cooked burned-flour grits and I have a full pot of it.' I hadn't heard the words 'burned-flour grits' for goodness knows how long and, believe me, no aria sung by an opera singer could have sounded sweeter.

'Soon we were seated at a broken-down table, eating the burned-flour grits like an old couple. I told her that I too read storybooks. I could see that she had a whole pile of them, all brought over from the old country: *The Story of the Three Brothers, The Tale of Two Butchers, The Adventures of the Pious Reb Zadock and the Twelve Robbers*. She asked me, 'Do you earn a living by selling sewing machines?' I said, 'I manage to scratch together a few dollars.' She asked, 'Do you have a wife and children?' I told her about my wife and poured out my bitter heart to her. Channah Basha listened and she grew pale. 'Why do you hold on to such a shrew?' I said, 'Here in America when you divorce a wife you have to pay alimony. If not you go to jail. The alimony amounts to more than a man earns. This is the justice in the land of Columbus.' She said, 'God waits long but He punishes severely. She will soon come to a bad end.' She cursed my wife. She said, 'How do you live if she takes away your last bite?' I said, 'I still have enough for a piece of bread.' She said, 'Come to me. I often cook more than I need for my father and myself. I am always alone because my father comes home late, and with you it will be cozy.' It was the first time that someone showed compassion for me and wanted to give instead of take. We ate the grits with fresh bread from the bakery and we washed it down with watery tea while we babbled about the Three Brothers, of whom the first took upon himself the good deed of ransoming innocent prisoners, the second of helping poor orphans to marry, and third of honoring the Sabbath. Then I told her a story about a young man who found a golden hair and traveled all over the world in search of the woman from whose head it had fallen. He found her on the island of Madagascar and she was the queen herself. Channah Basha listened eagerly to every word.

'Why go on? There grew up a great love between us. I saw to it that the house remained untouched. I visited her each week, and some weeks I took the Canarsie line to Brownsville two or three times. Whenever I went there, I wore a shabby suit and an old hat. I brought her presents of the kind that a sewing-machine salesman might bring: a pound of farmer cheese, a basket of fruit, a box of tea. The neighbors knew me and they wanted to buy sewing machines on the installment plan. I soon realized that if I sold them such bargains all of Brownsville would run after me, and I told Channah Basha that I had changed to the insurance business. I have forgotten the main thing: I called myself by another name – David Vishkover. It wasn't invented; I had a cousin of that name.

'For some time I managed to avoid her father, the beadle. As for Channah Basha, she fell in love with me with such passion that no words can describe it. One day I was a stranger and four weeks later her whole life hung on me. She knitted sweaters for me and cooked for me every dish I like. Whenever I tried to give her a few dollars she gave the money back and I had to beg her to accept it. I was a virtual millionaire, but on Blake Avenue I became a poor insurance agent, a starving schlemiel whose wife bled him of his last penny. I know what you want to ask; yes, Channah Basha and I became like husband and wife. She was a pure virgin. How a girl like that could be talked into an affair is a story in itself. I know a little Jewish law, and I persuaded her that according to the Torah a man is permitted to have two wives. As far as she was concerned, since she was unmarried she was not committing adultery. If I had told her to stand on her head, she would have done that too.

'As long as Channah Basha's father did not learn what was going on, everything went smoothly. We lived like two pigeons. But how long can such an affair remain a secret? When he found out that a married man was visiting his daughter and she had accepted him like a bridegroom, all hell broke loose. I assured him that the moment my vixen of a wife divorced me I would stand under the wedding canopy with his daughter.

'Just as Channah Basha was beautiful, her father was ugly, sick, a broken shard. He warned me that I would be excommunicated. As time went on he grew more violent; he even hinted that he might have me thrown into prison. I was frightened, all right. One shouldn't say it, but luck was on my side. He became mortally sick. He had bad kidneys and God knows what else. I sent him to doctors, took him to the hospital, paid for nurses, and I pretended that he was getting all this care for nothing. He lingered a few months and then he died. I erected a tombstone for

196

him that cost fifteen hundred dollars and I made his daughter believe that it came from the *landsleit* of Wysoka. One lie leads to another. How is it written in the Talmud?'

'One sin drags another after it,' I said.

'Right.

'After her father's death, Channah Basha became even more childish than before. She mourned him as I never saw a daughter mourn her father. She hired a man to recite the Kaddish for him. She lighted candles in the synagogue. Every second week she visited his grave. I told her that my business was going well and I tried to give her more money. But no matter how little it was, she insisted it was too much. All she needed, she said, was a loaf of bread, a few potatoes, and once in a while a pound of tripe. Years passed and she still wore her same shabby dresses from the old country. I wanted to give her an apartment on Ocean Avenue and furnish it. She refused to move. She kept on dusting and polishing her old junk. She read the Yiddish papers, and once she found my picture there. I had become the president of an old-age home and it was written up. She said, 'See here, that Sam Palka looks just like you. Is he a relative or something?' I said, 'I wish he was a relative. In my family we are all paupers.' If I had told her then that I was Sam Palka, our love would have been finished. She needed a poor man to look after, not a rich one to pamper her. Every time I left her to go home she offered me a bag of food so that I wouldn't starve on my wife's rations. Funny, isn't it?

'The years passed and I scarcely knew where they went. One day I had dark hair and it seemed overnight that I turned gray. Channah Basha too was no longer a spring chicken. But her thoughts stayed those of a child. The house on Blake Avenue became so ramshackle I worried that the walls might cave in. I had to bribe the inspectors not to condemn it. The storybooks that Channah Basha brought from Wysoka had finally fallen apart, and she now read the books of the Yiddish writers in America. There was no lack of that merchandise in my house! Every time I went to Brownsville I brought her a stack, and she admired them all no matter how bad they were. She loved everyone except my wife. On her she poured sulphur and fire. She never tired of hearing about the troubles Bessie made for me, and I had plenty to tell. She had gotten herself a gigolo, a faker, and she traveled all over Europe with him. My children gave me no joy, either. My son didn't even graduate from high school. I have three daughters and none of them married happily. Their mother planted hatred of me in them. I was good for only one thing – to write checks. Still, I had a great happiness: Channah Basha. She was always the same. In all those years she learned only a few words of English. Most of the Jewish tenants had moved out of the house and Puerto Ricans had moved in. Only two old women – widows – stayed, and Channah Basha watched over them. One had cataracts and later became blind. The other one had dropsy. Channah Basha took care of them like the best nurse.

'Would you believe it? In all this time Channah Basha never visited Manhattan. The subway terrified her with its din and noise. There was a Yiddish theater on Hopkinson Avenue, and once in a while I took her there. Sometimes they showed a Yiddish movie. There were moments when I thought I ought to put an end to this false game I was playing. Why shouldn't she enjoy my riches? In the summer I wanted to rent a cottage in the Catskills for her. I offered her a trip with me to California. But she wouldn't hear of it. Air conditioning did not exist then, and I wanted to buy her a fan. She refused it. She had a deathly fear of machines. She wouldn't allow me to install a telephone. The one thing she accepted was a radio; it took her a long time to learn how to turn on the Yiddish stations. This is Channah Basha – so will she be until her last day.

'My dear friend, I promised to make it short and I will keep my word. Bessie died. She had a quarrel with her gigolo – the pimp – and she went alone to Hong Kong. What she was looking for there I will never know. One day she collapsed in a restaurant and died. It was 1937. In all the years I had been coming to Channah Basha, we promised ourselves that if something happened to Bessie we would get married. But somehow I postponed telling her. There could be no thought of living with Channah Basha in the ruins of Blake Avenue. It was just as impossible to take her to my ten-room apartment on Park Avenue. My neighbors were all snooty rich. I had a Negro maid and an Irish housekeeper. I went to parties and I gave parties. No one spoke a word of Yiddish in my crowd. How could I bring Channah Basha into this Gentile-like world? With whom would she be able to talk? Besides, to find out that I had been lying to her all these years might be a shock that would tear our love apart like a spider web. I began to plan to go with her to Palestine, maybe to settle somewhere in Jerusalem or at Rachel's grave, but Hitler was already baring his teeth. At a time like that it was good to be in America, not wandering around in faraway countries.

'I put things off from day to day, from month to month. Why deny it – I wasn't completely faithful to her during all those years. As long as I didn't have true love I spat on frivolous women, but now that I had a true love it suited me to play around with others too. When women know that a man is alone they offer themselves by the dozen. I became a real Don Juan. I frequented nightclubs and restaurants where you meet the big shots. My name was even mentioned in the gossip columns. But these phony loves were enjoyable only because in Brownsville on Blake Avenue a real love waited. Who said it? One ounce of truth has more weight than ten tons of lies. I figured one way, then another, and meanwhile the war broke out. There was no place for us to flee to any more – unless, perhaps, Mexico or South America. But what would we two do there?

'My dear man, nothing has changed up to today, except that I have become an old man and Channah Basha is in her fifties. But you should see her; her hair is still gold and her face is that of a young girl. It is said that this comes from a pure conscience. Now that there was war and she heard how the Jews were tortured in Europe, she began to cry; she went on crying for years. She fasted and recited prayers, like the God-fearing matrons in my village. Some organization advertised that they mailed packages to Russia, and every cent that I gave her Channah Basha sent there. She was so upset that she forgot I was a poor insurance agent and she took large sums of money from me I was supposed to have been saving for my old age. If she hadn't been Channah Basha she would have recognized that something was wrong. But suspicion was not in her nature. She hardly knew the value of money – especially when it was in checks. I knew that the shrewd people in charge of those packages swindled her right and left, but I also knew that if even one dollar out of a hundred served its purpose the deed was good. Besides, if I had told Channah Basha that people with beards and sidelocks stole money from refugees, she could have suffered a heart attack. Finally, I gave her so much that I had to tell her I was connected with a relief organization and they provided me with funds. She questioned nothing. Later, when Palestine became a Jewish state and the troubles with the

199

Arabs began, she again tried to help. Believe it or not, I am still getting money from all those nonexistent committees.'

Sam Palka winked and laughed. He puffed once on his extinguished cigar and threw it in the ashtray. He lit another and said, 'You may call me a charlatan, but I have never been able to tell her the truth. She loved David Vishkover, the poor man, the victim of a false wife, not Sam Palka, the landlord, the millionaire, the woman chaser, the gambler. Everthing had to stay the same. I still visit her on Blake Avenue. It has become almost completely black. It makes no difference to Channah Basha. 'Here I have lived,' she says, 'and here I want to die.' I come to her in the morning, spend the day with her – we take a walk and go to bed right after supper. I'm known there. The blacks and the Puerto Ricans say, 'Hi, Mr. Vishkover.' We still eat burned-flour grits, noodles with beans, kasha with milk, and we talk about the old country as though we had stepped off the ship just yesterday. It's no longer a game. To her, Bessie is still alive, making me miserable. She thinks that I sustain myself on a small annuity from the insurance company and my Social Security. The buttons keep falling off the jacket and pants I wear, and Channah Basha continues to sew on others. She begs me to bring her my shirts; she wants to wash them. She darns my socks. A pair of my pajamas that are twenty years old hang in her bathroom. Every time I come, I have to report about Bessie. Is she still so wicked? Haven't the years softened her? I tell her that age doesn't change character – once bad, always bad. Channah Basha asked me to buy a plot in the cemetery of the Wysoka *landsleit* so that when we die we can lie side by side. I did so, even though another plot awaits for me next to Bessie's grave. I will have to die twice. When I die, Channah Basha is going to be surprised by my legacy to her. I have made her the beneficiary of an insurance policy for fifty thousand dollars. The house on Blake Avenue will also be hers. But what will she do with it? There comes a day when money is useless. We are both on diets. She now cooks with vegetable oil instead of butter. I am afraid to eat a piece of babka – cholesterol.

'One day I was sitting with Channah Basha and we were talking about olden days – how they used to bake matzo, send gifts on Purim, decorate the windowpanes for Shevuot – and suddenly she asked, 'What is the matter with your wife? Will her end never come?' I answered, 'Weeds are hardy.' Channah Basha said, 'I would still like to be your wife before God and the people, even if only for one year.'

'When I heard these words I was beside myself. I wanted to cry out, 'Channah Basha, my darling, no one stands in our way any more. Come with me to City Hall and we will get the license.' But this meant killing David Vishkover. Don't laugh – he is a real person to me. I have lived with him so long that he is closer to me than Sam Palka. Who is Sam Palka? An old lecher who has made a fortune and doesn't know what to do with it. David Vishkover is a man like my father, peace be with him. Well – and what would happen to Channah Basha if she should hear the truth? Instead of becoming Sam Palka's wife, she would become David Vishkover's widow.'

Translated by the author and Dorothea Straus

CHAPTER 11

BUT WHO'D WANT
TO LIVE THERE?

The inconveniences and unpleasantnesses of New York are legendary. E. B. White examined some of them in Here is New York.

IMPLAUSIBLE

. . . It is a miracle that New York works at all. The whole thing is implausible. Every time the residents brush their teeth, millions of gallons of water must be drawn from the Catskills and the hills of Westchester. When a young man in Manhattan writes a letter to his girl in Brooklyn, the love message gets blown to her through a pneumatic tube – *pfft* – just like that. The subterranean system of telephone cables, power lines, steam pipes, gas mains and sewer pipes is reason enough to abandon the island to the gods and the weevils. Every time an incision is made in the pavement, the noisy surgeons expose ganglia that are tangled beyond belief. By rights New York should have destroyed itself long ago, from panic or fire or rioting or failure of some vital supply line in its circulatory system or from some deep labyrinthine short circuit. Long ago the city should have experienced an insoluble traffic snarl at some impossible botteneck. It should have perished of hunger when food lines failed for a few days. It should have been wiped out by a plague starting in its slums or carried in by ships' rats. It should have been overwhelmed by the sea that licks at it on every side. The workers in its myriad cells should have succumbed to nerves, from the fearful pall of smoke-fog that drifts over every few days from Jersey, blotting out all light at noon and leaving the high offices suspended, men groping and depressed, and the sense of world's end. It should have been touched in the head by the August heat and gone off its rocker.

Mass hysteria is a terrible force, yet New Yorkers seem always to escape it by some tiny margin: they sit in stalled subways with claustrophobia, they extricate themselves from panic situations by some lucky wisecrack, they meet confusion and congestion with patience and grit – a sort of perpetual muddling through. Every facility is inadequate – the hospitals and schools and playgrounds are overcrowded, the express highways are feverish, the unimproved highways and bridges are bottlenecks; there is not enough air and not enough light, and there is usually either too much heat or too little. But the city makes up for its hazards and its deficiencies by supplying its citizens with massive doses of a supplementary vitamin – the sense of belonging to something

204

unique, cosmopolitan, mighty and unparalleled.

To an outlander a stay in New York can be and often is a series of small embarrassments and discomforts and disappointments: not understanding the waiter, not being able to distinguish between a sucker joint and a friendly saloon, riding the wrong subway, being slapped down by a bus driver for asking an innocent question, enduring sleepless nights when the street noises fill the bedroom. Tourists make for New York, particularly in summertime – they swarm all over the Statue of Liberty (where many a resident of the town has never set foot), they invade the Automat, visit radio studios, St. Patrick's Cathedral, and they window shop. Mostly they have a pretty good time. But sometimes in New York you run across the disillusioned – a young couple who are obviously visitors, newlyweds perhaps, for whom the bright dream has vanished. The place has been too much for them: they sit languishing in a cheap restaurant over a speechless meal.

The oft-quoted thumbnail sketch of New York is, of course: 'It's a wonderful place, but I'd hate to live there.'

From The American Scene, *by Henry James.*

LAOCOON

Free existence and good manners, in New York, are too much brought down to a bare rigour of marginal relation to the endless electric coil, the monstrous chain that winds round the general neck and body, the general middle and legs, very much as the boa-constrictor winds round the group of the Laocoon. It struck me that when these folds are tightened in the terrible stricture of the snow-smothered months of the year, the New York predicament leaves far behind the anguish represented in the Vatican figures.

Will Rogers (1879-1935) the great American humorist from the West, cast a jaundiced eye on Big City life.

INNOCENT BYSTANDERS

Hardly a day goes by, you know, that some innocent bystander ain't shot in New York City. All you got to do is be innocent and stand by and they're gonna shoot you. The other day, there was four innocent people shot in one day – four innocent people – in New York City. Amazing. It's kind of hard to *find* four innocent people in New York.

Tom Wolfe, born in Virginia in 1931, is the author of The Electric Kool-Aid Acid Test, The Kandy Kolored Flake Streamline Baby, *and many other books, including* In Our Time *from which this is taken.*

SOHO

Oh, to be young and come to New York and move into your first loft and look at the world with eyes that light up even the rotting fire-escape railings, even the buckling pressed-tin squares on the ceiling, even the sheet-metal shower stall with its belly dents and rusting seams, the soot granules embedded like blackheads in the dry rot of the window frames, the basin with the copper-green dripping-spigot stains in the cracks at the bottom, the door with its crowbar-notch history of twenty-five years of break-ins, the canvas-bottom chairs that cut off the circulation in the sural arteries of the leg, the indomitable roach that appears every morning in silhouette on the cord of the hot plate, the doomed yucca straining for light on the windowsill, the two cats nobody ever housebroke, the garbage trucks with the grinder whine, the leather freaks and health-shoe geeks, the punkers with chopped hair and Korean warm-up jackets, the herds of Uptown Boutique bohemians who arrive every weekend by radio-call cab, the bag ladies who sit on the standpipes swabbing the lesions on their ankles – oh, to be young and in New York and to have eyes that light up all things with the sweetest and most golden glow!

Lewis Mumford was born in Flushing, Long Island in 1895. In his many books and essays he examined the history of urban development and of New York in particular. For many years he wrote the architectural criticism column in the New Yorker, Sky Line, *from which the following is an excerpt, written in 1956.*

Is New York Expendable?

The frantic effort to crowd the central district of Manhattan with enough tall office buildings to make traffic a permanent tangle is rapidly approaching complete success. Already, after ten in the morning, a reasonably healthy pedestrian can get across town faster than the most skillful taxi-driver. All this may persuade someone in authority to suggest turning the midtown district into a vast pedestrian mall, closed to private vehicles during the day, as some of the narrow streets in the financial district are now. Unfortunately, the load of pedestrians has likewise become so heavy, not merely at the lunch hour or during Christmas shopping but during most of the day, that the walker is frequently slowed down to the exhausting creep of the car or the bus. One would think that this situation might cause some serious thought among the bankers and investors and business enterprisers who have been fostering this congestion, admittedly with the sanction of the municipality's zoning laws. Their lack of concern for the end product has been explained to me by one of the most successful of our urban space men. " 'Money,' " he said, giving the word the sort of halo a Roman might attach to his tutelary deity, 'is not interested in looking further ahead than the next five years.' If this truly represents the prevailing mood, the people who are so ebulliently strangling the economic life of New York and canceling out, one by one, every sound reason for living here must consider that New York is expendable.

Allen Ginsberg was born in Paterson, New Jersey in 1926. His first major work, Howl, *was published in 1956 and he has remained a leading poetic, cultural, and political influence ever since. In between his many travels to all parts of the world Ginsberg has resided on the Lower East Side of New York. The poem overleaf was published in* Mind Breaths *(1977).*

Tonite I walked out of my red apartment door on East tenth
street's dusk—

Walked out my home ten years, walked out in my honking
neighborhood

Tonite at seven walked out past garbage cans chained to concrete
anchors

Walked under black painted fire escapes, giant castiron plate
covering a hole in ground

—Crossed the street, traffic lite red, thirteen bus roaring by
liquor store,

past corner pharmacy iron grated, past Coca Cola & My-Lai
poster fading scraped on brick

Past Chinese Laundry wood door'd, & broken cement stoop steps
For Rent hall painted green & purple Puerto Rican style

Along E. 10th's glass splattered pavement, kid blacks & Spanish
oiled hair adolescents' crowded house fronts—

Ah, tonite I walked out on my block NY City under humid
summer sky Halloween,

thinking what happened Timothy Leary joining brain police for a
season?

thinking what's all this Weathermen, secrecy & selfrighteousness
beyond reason – F.B.I. plots?

Walked past a taxicab controlling the bottle strewn curb—

past young fellows with their umbrella handles & canes leaning
against ravaged Buick

—and as I looked at the crowd of kids on the stoop – a boy
stepped up, put his arm around my neck

tenderly I thought for a moment, squeezed harder, his umbrella
handle against my skull,

and his friends took my arm, a young brown companion tripped
his foot 'gainst my ankle—

as I went down shouting Om Ah Hūṁ to gangs of lovers on the
stoop watching

slowly appreciating, why this is a raid, these strangers mean
strange business

with what – my pockets, bald head, broken-healed-bone leg, my
softshoes, my heart—

Have they knives? Om Ah Hūṁ – Have they sharp metal wood
to shove in eye ear ass? Om Ah Hūṁ

& slowly reclined on the pavement, struggling to keep my woolen
bag of poetry address calendar & Leary-lawyer notes hung
from my shoulder

dragged in my neat orlon shirt over the crossbar of a broken metal
door

dragged slowly onto the fire-soiled floor an abandoned store,
laundry candy counter 1929—

now a mess of papers & pillows & plastic covers cracked cock-
roach-corpsed ground—

my wallet back pocket passed over the iron foot step guard

and fell out, stole by God Muggers' lost fingers, Strange—
my bank money for a week

old broken wallet – and dreary plastic contents – Ammex card
& Manf. Hanover Trust Credit too – business card from
Mr. Spears British Home Minister Drug Squad – my draft
card – membership ACLU & Naropa Institute Instructor's
identification

Om Ah Hūṁ I continued chanting Om Ah Hūṁ

Putting my palm on the neck of an 18 year old boy fingering my
back pocket crying 'Where's the money'

'Oh Ah Hūṁ there isn't any'

My card Chief Boo-Hoo Neo American Church New Jersey &
Lower East Side

Om Ah Hūṁ – what not forgotten crowded wallet – Mobil
Credit, Shell? old lovers addresses on cardboard pieces,
booksellers calling cards—

– 'Shut up or we'll murder you' – 'Om Ah Hūṁ take it easy'

Lying on the floor shall I shout more loud? – the metal door
closed on blackness

one boy felt my broken healed ankle, looking for hundred dollar
bills behind my stocking weren't even there – a third boy
untied my Seiko Hong Kong watch rough from right wrist
leaving a clasp-prick skin tiny bruise

'Shut up and we'll get out of here' – and so they left,

as I rose from the cardboard mattress thinking Om Ah Hūṁ
didn't stop em enough,

the tone of voice too loud – my shoulder bad with 10,000 dollars
full of poetry left on the broken floor—

Nov 2, 1974

Went out the door dim eyed, bent down & picked up my glasses
　　from step edge I placed them while dragged in the store –
　　looked out—
Whole street a bombed-out face, building rows' eyes & teeth
　　missing
burned apartments half the long block, gutted cellars, hallways'
　　charred beams
hanging over trash plaster mounded entrances, couches &
　　bedsprings rusty after sunset
Nobody home, but scattered stoopfuls of scared kids frozen in
　　black hair
chatted giggling at house doors in black shoes, families cooked
　　For Rent some six story houses mid the street's wreckage
Nextdoor Bodega, a phone, the police? 'I just got mugged' I said
to man's face under fluorescent grocery light tin ceiling—
puffy, eyes blank & watery, sickness of beer kidney and language
　　tongue
thick lips stunned as my own eyes, poor drunken Uncle minding
　　the store!
O hopeless city of idiots empty staring afraid, red beam top'd car
　　at street curb arrived—
'Hey maybe my wallet's still on the ground got a flashlight?'
Back into the burnt-doored cave, & the policeman's grey
　　flashlight broken no eyebeam—
'My partner all he wants is sit in the car never gets out Hey Joe
　　bring your flashlight –'
a tiny throway beam, dim as a match in the criminal dark
'No I can't see anything here'. . . 'Fill out this form'
Neighborhood street crowd behind a car 'We didn't see nothing'
Stoop young girls, kids laughing 'Listen man last time I messed
　　with them see this –'
rolled up his skinny arm shirt, a white knife scar on his brown
　　shoulder
'Besides we help you the cops come don't know anybody we all
　　get arrested
go to jail I never help no more mind my business everytime'
'Agh!' upstreet think 'Gee I don't know anybody here ten years
　　lived half block crost Avenue C
and who knows who?' – passing empty apartments, old lady with
　　frayed paper bags
sitting in the tin-boarded doorframe of a dead house.

December 10, 1974

Fran Liebowitz is a contemporary New York observer, satirist, and survivor.

DIARY OF A NEW YORK APARTMENT HUNTER

Friday: Awakened at the crack of dawn by a messenger bearing this coming Sunday's *New York Times* Real Estate section. First six apartments gone already. Spent a good fifteen minutes dividing the number of *New York Times* editors into the probable number of people looking for two-bedroom apartments. Spent additional half-hour wondering how anyone who has a paper to get out every day could possibly have time to keep up eleven hundred friendships. Realized this theory not plausible and decided instead that the typesetters all live in co-ops with wood-burning fireplaces. Wondered briefly why listings always specify *wood-burning* fireplaces. Decided that considering the prices they're asking, it's probably just a warning device for those who might otherwise figure what the hell, and just burn money.

Called V.F. and inquired politely whether anyone in his extremely desirable building had died during the night. Reply in the negative, I just don't get it. It's quite a large building and no one in it has died for months. In my tiny little building they're dropping like flies. Made a note to investigate the possibility that high ceilings and decorative moldings prolong life. Momentarily chilled by the thought that someone who lives in a worse building than mine is waiting for *me* to die. Cheered immeasurably by realization that a) nobody lives in a worse building than mine and b) particularly those who are waiting for me to die.

Saturday: Uptown to look at co-op in venerable midtown building. Met real estate broker in lobby. A Caucasian version of Tokyo Rose. She immediately launched into a description of all the *respectably* employed people who were waiting in line for this apartment. Showed me living room first. Large, airy, terrific view of well-known discount drugstore. Two bedrooms, sure enough. Kitchen, sort of. When I asked why the present occupant had seen fit to cut three five-foot arches out of the inside wall of the master bedroom, she muttered something about cross ventilation. When I pointed out that there were no windows on the opposite wall, she ostentatiously extracted a sheaf of papers from her briefcase and studied them closely. Presumably these contained the names of all the Supreme Court Justices who were waiting for

211

this apartment. Nevertheless I pressed on and asked her what one might do with three five-foot high arches in one's bedroom wall. She suggested stained glass.I suggested pews in the living room and services every Sunday. She showed me a room she referred to as the master bath. I asked her where the slaves bathed. She rustled her papers ominously and showed me the living room again. I looked disgruntled. She brightened and showed me something called a fun bathroom. It had been covered in fabric from floor to ceiling by someone who obviously was not afraid to mix patterns. I informed her unceremoniously that I never again wanted to be shown a fun bathroom. I don't want to have fun in the bathroom; I just want to bathe my slaves.

She showed me the living room again. Either she just couldn't get enough of that discount drugstore or she was trying to trick me into thinking there were three living rooms. Impudently I asked here where one ate, seeing as I had not been shown a dining room and the kitchen was approximately the size of a brandy snifter.

'Well,' she said, 'some people use the second bedroom as a dining room.' I replied that I needed the second bedroom to write in. This was a mistake because it reminded her of all the ambassadors to the U.N. on her list of prospective tenants.

'Well,' she said, 'the master bedroom is rather large.'

'Listen,' I said, 'I already eat on my bed. In a one-room, rent-controlled slum apartment, I'll eat on the bed. In an ornately priced, high-maintenance co-op, I want to eat at a table. Call me silly, call me foolish, but that's the kind of girl I am.' She escorted me out of the apartment and left me standing in the lobby as she hurried off – anxious, no doubt to call Cardinal Cooke and tell him okay, the apartment was his.

Sunday: Spent the entire day recovering from a telephone call with a real estate broker, who, in response to my having expressed displeasure at having been shown an apartment in which the closest thing to a closet had been the living room, said, 'Well, Fran, what do you expect for $1,400 a month?' He hung up before I could tell him that actually, to tell you the truth, for $1,400 a month I expected the Winter Palace – furnished. Not to mention fully staffed.

Monday: Looked this morning at the top floor of a building which I have privately christened Uncle Tom's Brownstone. One end of the floor sloped sufficiently for me to be able to straighten up and ask why the refrigerator was in the living room. I was promptly put in my place by the owner, who looked me straight in the eye and said, 'Because it doesn't fit in the kitchen.'

'True,' I conceded, taking a closer look, 'that is a problem. I'll tell you what, though, and this may not have occurred to you, but that kitchen does fit in the refrigerator. Why don't you try it?'

I left before he could act on my suggestion and repaired to a phone booth. Mortality rate in V.F.'s building still amazingly low.

Called about apartment listed in today's paper. Was told fixture fee $100,000. Replied that unless Rembrandt had doodled on the walls, $100,000 wasn't a fixture fee; it was war reparations.

Tuesday: Let desparation get the best of me and went to see an apartment described as 'interesting'. 'Interesting' generally means that it has a skylight, no elevator and they'll throw in the glassine envelopes for free. This one was even more interesting than usual because, the broker informed me, Jack Kerouac had once lived here. Someone's pulling your leg, I told him; Jack Kerouac's still living here.

Wednesday: Ran into a casual acquaintance on Seventh Avenue. Turns out he too is looking for a two-bedroom apartment. We compared notes.

'Did you see the one with the refrigerator in the living room?' he asked.

'Yes, indeed,' I said.

'Well,' he said, 'today I looked at a dentist's office in the East Fifties.'

'A dentist's office,' I said. 'Was the chair still there?'

'No,' he replied, 'but there was a sink in every room.' It sounded like a deal for someone. I tried to think if I knew of any abortionists looking for a two-bedroom apartment. None sprang to mind.

Called real-estate broker and inquired as to price of newly advertised co-op. Amount in substantial six figures. 'What about financing?' I asked.

'Financing?' She shuddered audibly. 'This is an all-cash building.'

I told her that to me an all-cash building is what you put on Boardwalk or Park Place. She suggested that I look farther uptown. I replied that if I looked any farther uptown I'd have to take karate lessons. She thought that sounded like a good idea.

Thursday: Was shown co-op apartment of recently deceased actor. By now so seasoned that I didn't bat an eye at the sink in the master bedroom. Assumed that either he was a dentist on the side or that it didn't fit in the bathroom. Second assumption proved correct. Couldn't understand why, though; you'd think that there not being a shower in there would have left plenty of room for a sink. Real-estate broker pointed out recent improvements: tangerine-colored kitchen appliances; bronze-mirrored fireplace; a fun living room. Told the broker that what with the asking price, the maintenance and the cost of unimproving, I couldn't afford to live there and still wear shoes on a regular basis.

Called V.F. again. First the good news: a woman in his building died. Then the bad news: she decided not to move.

Pedro Pietri was born in Puerto Rico in 1944. He lives, works, and writes in New York.

3170 BROADWAY

we took the elevator to our eyes
we got off at the wrong floor
we knocked on the wrong door
we enter without moving an inch
we hear the apartment bleeding
we jump out of the window of our mind
we wake up inside mail boxes
we are attacked by airmail stamps
we hide inside our back pockets
we swallow obsolete calendars
we discover snow in our sweat
we get bored with so much darkness

the radio that was not on
was playing loud enough

to be heard from the 1st floor
to the 21st floor & the roof
but all the tenants had turned
on their television sets
and stereo record players
at full blast from the 1st day
they moved into the projects
making hearing impossible

in a matter of seconds
our father which art in the backseat
of a lincoln continental limousine
known in some circles as Mister Clean
will give the housing authority
the middle finger sign
and all the tenants will find
themselves on the 21st floor
and the only way you will be able
to see the streets again
will be by jumping out the window

isolation is the name of the game
you do not know
your next door neighbors name
your next door neighbor
does not know your name
you have been living on
the same floor since this
so-called promisedland opened
the only way you get to know each other
is after one or the other dies

everybody has a headache
in these human file cabinets
known as the housing projects

when the night comes
those who were not mugged
were stuck in the elevator
for a couple of hours
others fell down the stairs

chasing their minds
to bring it back to jesus
the bookie is the only one
who loves the projects

you go to sleep on the 17th floor
you wake up on the 13th floor
you walk down to the 7th floor
to borrow aspirins from somebody
who borrowed them on the 15th floor
from somebody who found them
on the 20th floor after somebody
on the 8th floor lost them
the night they lost everything
playing cards on the 2nd floor

muggers and junkies and pushers
succeed in life in the projects
the housing police cannot stop them
because the housing police
does not exist everyday of the week
they only come around once
every other ten weeks to tell you
not to stand in the lobby
of the building you have been living
and dying in for the past fifteen years

when the elevators
are finally fixed
they only function properly
for a couple of minutes
before the buttons
start hallucinating again
and you find yourself moving
up & down & sidewards
when the elevator stops

you get off on the same floor
you got on
like you have to get high
on something else

if you want to get
to the floor you came down from

somedays the sun comes out
& the tenants say to each other
'nice day' & nothing else
the only other time they talk
to each other is to find out
what number came out somebody
is always attending a funeral
in the projects death brings
the tenants closer to each other
until whoever died is buried

the pope
will never go near
the projects
regardless of
how many tenants
are members
of his fan club
the housing authority
employees will
not be caught dead
in the projects
after the sun
that never came out
goes down and
the deadly
weapon wind
blows backwards

from the 1st floor
to the 21st floor
everybody is saving money
to move to a better neighborhood
because the buildings
look worse than the buildings
they moved you out from
the promisedland
has become the garbage can

Woody Allen (1935-) in his book Side Effects, *reminisces on places and people.*

BROOKLYN

Tree-lined streets. The Bridge. Churches and cemeteries everywhere. And candy stores. A small boy helps a bearded old man across the street and says, 'Good Sabbath.' The old man smiles and empties his pipe on the boy's head. The child runs crying into his house. . . Stifling heat and humidity descend on the borough. Residents bring folding chairs out onto the street after dinner to sit and talk. Suddenly it begins to snow. Confusion sets in. A vender wends his way down the street selling hot pretzels. He is set upon by dogs and chased up a tree. Unfortunately for him, there are more dogs at the top of the tree.

'Benny! Benny!' A mother is calling her son. Benny is sixteen but already has a police record. When he is twenty-six, he will go to the electric chair. At thirty-six, he will be hanged. At fifty, he will own his own dry-cleaning store. Now his mother serves breakfast, and because the family is too poor to afford fresh rolls he spreads marmalade on the News.

CHAPTER 12

DEMOCRACY

From Manhattan Transfer, *by John Dos Passos.*

SOAPBOX

A man is shouting from a soapbox at Second Avenue and Houston in front of the Cosmopolitan Cafè: '. . . these fellers, men. . . wageslaves like I was. . . are sittin on your chest. . . they're takin the food outen your mouths. Where's all the pretty girls I used to see walkin up and down the bullevard? Look for em in the uptown cabarets. . . . They squeeze us dry friends. . . feller workers, slaves I'd oughter say. . . they take our work and our ideers and our women. . . . They build their Plaza Hotels and their millionaire's clubs and their million dollar theayters and their battleships and what do they leave us? . . . They leave us shopsickness an the rickets and a lot of dirty streets full of garbage cans. . . . You look pale you fellers. . . . You need blood. . . . Why dont you get some blood in your veins? . . . Back in Russia the poor people. . . not so much poorer'n we are. . . believe in wampires, things come suck your blood at night. . . . That's what Capitalism is, a wampire that suck your blood. . . day. . . and. . . night.'

It is beginning to snow. The flakes are giltedged where they pass the streetlamp. Through the plate glass the Cosmopolitan Cafè full of blue and green opal rifts of smoke looks like a muddy aquarium; faces blob whitely round the tables like illassorted fishes. Umbrellas begin to bob in clusters up the snowmottled street. The orator turns up his collar and walks briskly east along Houston, holding the muddy soapbox away from his trousers.

From the Diary *of Philip Hone, 1834.*

ELECTIONS, 1834

Tuesday, April 8. – The election for mayor and charter officers commenced this day with a degree of spirit and zeal in both parties never before witnessed. This is the first election for mayor by the people since the new law, and has acquired immense importance, since it is considered a test of the approval or disapproval of the people of New York of the arbitrary and unconstitutional measures of the President and his advisers, and as it will influence the politics of the State in the more important elections next fall. The number of votes will be very great (probably thirty-five thousand); the Whig party, whose candidate for mayor is Mr. Verplanck, are active, zealous, and confident of success. A great meeting was held yesterday at four o'clock, at the Exchange, at which Benjamin Strong presided, and John W. Leavitt and Edmund Penfold were secretaries. The meeting was addressed by John A. Stevens, George W. Bruen, James G. King, Charles H. Russell, and Chandler Starr, and several resolutions were passed, one of which recommends to the merchants and traders to omit their usual attendance at the Exchange, and to close their stores and places of business at noon on each of the three days of the election, in order to devote their undivided attention to the great business of reform at the polls. This last suggestion has been in part observed; many stores are closed to-day, and several have notices on the doors that the inmates are gone to the polls to vote for Verplanck. A very large meeting was also held last evening of adopted citizens at Masonic Hall to approve the course of Dr. MacNeven in joining our party. After the meeting adjourned they went to his house and cheered him, and he addressed them, wishing the party success. They came also before my door and gave me some hearty huzzas, but I was unfortunately absent, having gone to the theatre with my girls and Miss Kane. My wife was alarmed at the row, as I had a visit of another kind a few evenings since from a party of the retainers of Tammany Hall, and she was not able in her fright to disting-uish between the shouts of enemies and the cheers of friends.

Thursday, April 10. – Last day of the election; dreadful riots between the Irish and the Americans have again disturbed the public peace. The Mayor arrived with a strong body of watchmen, but they were attacked and overcome, and many of the watchmen are severely wounded. Eight of them were carried to the hospital where I went to visit them. The Mayor has ordered out Colonel Sanford's regiment and a troop of horse, and proper measures have been taken to preserve order, but we apprehend a dreadful night. This outrage has been instigated by a few men in the sixth ward, – George D. Strong, Abraham LeRoy, Dr. Rhinelander, Preserved Fish, and a few like him. Let them answer for it.

Friday, April 11. – Such an excitement! So wonderful is the result of this election that all New York has been kept in a state of alarm; immense crowds have been collected at Masonic and

Tammany Halls, but the greatest concourse was in front of the Exchange. The street was a dense mass of people. Partial returns were coming in every few minutes, and so close has been the vote that the Whigs at the Exchange and the small party for Jackson in front of the office of the 'Standard' opposite shouted alternately as the news was favourable to one or the other; and up to the last moment the result was doubtful, when, at the close of the canvass, the majority for Mr. Lawrence, the Jackson candidate, out of the immense number of votes – thirty-five thousand one hundred and forty-one – was found to be one hundred and seventy-nine. There is no doubt, however, that we have elected a majority of aldermen and assistants. The Common Council is reformed, and we shall succeed in the great fall election. It is a signal triumph of good principles over violence, illegal voting, party discipline, and the influence of office-holders.

April 12. – The following gentlemen dined with us, all Whigs, amd most of them active men in the last contest; it was a feast of triumph for the result of the election, and we drank success to the cause in the best wine I had to give them: Francis Granger, John Greig, Bryant P. Tilden, of Boston, who has just arrived from Canton, Sydney Brooks, William H. Aspinwall, Simeon Draper, Jr., Charles King, Charles H. Hammond, Isaac S. Hone, Charles H. Russell, and James Monroe.

April 15. – This was the day of the great *fête* at Castle Garden to celebrate the triumph gained by the Whig party in the late charter election in this city, and it went off gloriously. Tens of thousands of freemen, full of zeal and patriotism, filled the area of the castle; every inch of ground was occupied. Tables were spread in a double row within the outer circumference; three pipes of wine and forty barrels of beer were placed in the centre under an awning, and served out during the repast. Many speeches were made, regular and volunteer toasts were drunk, and the beautiful little frigate 'Constitution,' which has borne so conspicuous a station in the late struggle, was placed upon the top of the building which forms the entrance to the garden, from which she fired a salute during the *fête*. All was enthusiasm, and the shouts from time to time rent the air. But on a signal given the immense concourse broke up in good order, and no excess or rioting marred the pleasure of the day. Six or eight thousand men formed a procession, and marched off the Battery, preceded by a band of music.

*In the first half of the nineteenth century companies of 'volunteer fireman'
served the politicians as vote-gatherers and occasionally as outright political
mobs. Herbert Asbury described some of their activities in his book* The
Gangs of New York, *published in 1928.*

VOLUNTEER FIREMEN

Little knowledge of the activities of most of the early Bowery
gangs has survived, but the lore of the street is rich in tales of the
Bowery Boys and the prowess of their mighty leaders. Sometimes
this gang was called Bowery B'hoys, which is sufficient indication
of its racial origin. It was probably the most celebrated gang in
the history of the United States, but before the eminent Chuck
Conners appeared in the late eighties and transformed the type
into a bar fly and a tramp, the Bowery Boy was not a loafer except
on Sundays and holidays. Nor was he a criminal, except on
occasion, until the period of the Civil War. He was apt to earn his
living as a butcher or apprentice mechanic, or as a bouncer in a
Bowery saloon or dance cellar. But he was almost always a
volunteer fireman, and therein lay much of the strength of the
gang, for in the early days before the Civil War the firemen, most
of them strong adherents of Tammany Hall, had much to say
about the conduct of the city's government. Many of the most
eminent politicians belonged to the fire brigade, and there was
much rivalry between the companies, which gave their engines
such names as White Ghost, Black Joke, Shad Belly, Dry Bones,
Red Rover, Hay Wagon, Big Six, Yaller Gal, Bean Soup, Old
Junk, and Old Maid. Such famous New York political leaders as
Cornelius W. Lawrence, Zophar Mills, Samuel Willetts, William
M. Wood, John J. Gorman and William M. Tweed were
volunteer firemen. In still earlier days even George Washington
was an ardent chaser after the fire engines, and for a short time
during his residence in the metropolis was head of the New York
department. Before the formation of a paid fire fighting force one
of the great events of the year was the Fireman's Parade, and
great crowds lined the sidewalks and cheered the red-shirted,
beaver-hatted brawlers as they pulled their engines over the
cobble-stones, while before them marched a brass band blaring
away at *Solid Men to the Front*, a rousing tune which was a favorite
for many years.

But the rivalry between the fire companies whose membership

223

included men of substance was friendly if strenuous, while the Bowery Boy loved his fire engine almost as much as he did his girl, and considered both himself and his company disgraced if his apparatus was beaten to a conflagration. And the acme of humiliation was to roll to a fire and find that all of the fire plugs had been captured by other companies. To prevent this the Bowery Boy resorted to typically direct methods. When the fire alarm sounded he simply grabbed an empty barrel from a grocery store and hurried with it to the fire plug nearest the burning building. There he turned the barrel over the plug and sat on it, and defended it valorously against the assaults of rival firemen until his own engine arrived. If he succeeded he was a hero and his company had won a notable victory. Frequently the fight for fire plugs was so fierce that the Bowery Boys had no time to extinguish the flames.

The state and city elections of 1894 produced a number of upsets. The former Governor of New York State, David Bennett Hill, was defeated in his attempt to recapture the State House by Republican Levi Morton. The Republican ticket of William Strong, for Mayor, and John Goff, for city recorder, defeated the Tammany Hall ticket lead by 'Hughie' Grant and backed by Boss Richard Croker. Stephen Crane put together this sketch of the election, which first appeared in the New York Press, *from remarks overheard in the street.*

ELECTION NIGHT, 1894

'Hully chee! Everything's dumped!'

'S'cuse me, g'l'men, fer bein' s'noisy, but, fact is, I'm Repu'lican! What? Yessir! Morton by seventy-fi' thousan'. Yessir! I'm goin' holler thish time 'til I bust m' throat – tha's what I am.'

'Can you tell me, please, if the returns indicate that Goff has a chance?'
'Who? Goff? Well, I guess! He's running like a race-horse. He's dead in it.'

'That's all right. Wait 'til later. Then, you'll see. Morton never

224

had a show. Hill will swamp him.'

'Oh, hurry up with your old slide. Put on another. Good thing – push it along. Ah, there we are. 'Morton's – plurality – over – Hill – is – estimated – at – 10,135.' Say, look at that, would you? Don't talk to me about the unterrified Democracy. The unterrified Democracy can be dog goned. There's more run than fight in them this trip. Hey, hurry up, Willie, give us another one. It's a good thing, but push it along.'

'Say, that magic lantern man is a big fakir. Lookatim pushin' ads in on us. Hey, take that out, will yeh? You ain't no bill-poster are yeh?'

'Strong has got a cinch. He wins in a walk. Ah there, Hughie, ah there.'

'Well, I guess not. If Hill wins this time, he's got to have iceboats on his feet. He ain't got a little chance.'

'Down in Fourteenth street,
'Hear that mournful sound;
'All the Indians are a-weeping,
'Davie's in the cold, cold ground.'

'If Tammany wins this time, we might as well all quit the town and go to Camden. If we don't beat 'em now, we're a lot of duffers and we're only fit to stuff mattresses with.'

'Say, hear'em yell 'Goff.' Popular? I guess yes.'
'He won't, hey? You just wait, me boy. If Hill can't carry this State at any time in any year, I'll make you a present of the Brooklyn bridge, and paint it a deep purple with gold stripes, all by myself.'

'Goff! Goff! John – W – Goff!
'Goff! Goff! John – W – Goff!'

'Voorhis and Taintor! They're the only two. The rest –'
'Well, this is what comes from monkeyin' with the people. You think you've got 'em all under a board when, first thing you know, they come out and belt you in the neck.'

'Oh, everything's conceded. Yes, they admit the whole thing. They didn't get a taste. It's a walk-over.'

'Hully chee!
'Who are we?
'The men who did up Tammanee!'

'I've only seen two Tammany Democrats to-night. There's another. That makes three.'

'Oh, my, what a surprise! Little David Bennett Hill is now going down the back-stairs in his stocking-feet.'

'Who said Tammany couldn't be thrown down? Grady did. Ah there, Grady.'

'There never was a minute
'Little Goffie wasn't in it.'

'I'd like to see Dickie Croker now and ask him how he knew when to get in and out of the wet. I tell you what it is – there's no use saying anything about Dickie's eyesight.'

'Don't be too sure, sonny. I tell you, Dave Hill is a foxey man, and you better wait until it's a dead sure thing before you holler. I've seen a good deal of this sort of thing. In 1884 –'

'Strong's got a regular pie.'

'Ta-ra-ra-ra-boom-de-aye,
'Hughie Grant has had his day,
'Safely now at home he'll stay,
'Ta-ra-ra-boom-de-aye.'

'Now, I'll tell you just one thing – if this don't prove to politicians that a man has got to be always on the level if he wants to hold his snap. Why, they're about as thick-headed a gang as there is on the face of the earth. The man who is always on the level is the man who gets there in the end. If you ain't on the level, you get a swift, hard throw-down sooner or later – dead sure.'

'Hurray for Goff!'

" 'Eternal vigilance is the price of liberty.' That's what it is.
The people lost their liberty because they went to sleep. Then all
of a sudden they wake up and slug around and surprise all of the
men who thought they were in a trance. They ought to have done
it long ago. And now they are awake, they don't want to do a
thing but sit up night and day and lay for robbers. This waking
up every ten or twelves years gives me a pain."

'There never was a doubt of it. No, sir. It was playing a sure
thing from start to finish. I tell you, when the avalanche starts,
you want to climb a hill near by and put all your money on the
avalanche.'

'I'm a Tammany Hall man, but I put my vote on John W. Goff.
I did. What? Hill. Well, any man would tumble if a brick steeple
fell on him.'

'Parkhurst was his Jonah.'

'Who's all right? Strong! Hurrah for Strong!'

'Say, lookut d' blokie flashin' er patent-medicine ad. on d'
canvas. He's a Dimmy-crat. Who won't be 'lected? Goff? I bet
'che he will. Soitently! Say, Jimmie, gimme change for a nick! Ah,
I bet'che Goff'll leave 'm at 'd post. Say, who 'er yez fer, anyhow?
Ah, he'll git it in d'troat. Goff'll smother 'im.'

'By bolly, I bed you Morton is elected by a hundret thousand
votes. Suah! I am a Republican effery leetle minnet. I am so
excited my hand shake.'

'Oh, what a cinch they thought they had. Say, those fellers
thought they had New York locked in a box. And they got left,
didn't they?'

'Good-bye, Hughie! Good-bye, Hughie!
'Good-bye, Hughie, you'll have to leave us now.'

'Well, they monkeyed with the band wagon and they got

slumped. Good job. Very surprising way the American people have of throttling a man just when he thinks he's got 'em dead under his thumb.'

'It was easy, after all, wasn't it? Truth is, New York has been held down by a great big, wire-edged bluff. Tammany said she couldn't be beaten, and everybody believed it.'

'What? Git out! Entire Republican ticket, cit and State? Well, for the love of Mike! Holy smoke, ain't we in it!'

'Is they any Democrats left?'

'Where's all the Tammany men?'

'Somebody tell Hill where he's at.'

'Tammany's in the soup.'

'Oh, what a roast!'

'Hully chee! Everyt'ing's dumped!'

Jimmy Walker (1881-1946) was born and reared in New York. Backed by Tammany Hall he was elected Mayor of the City in 1925 and re-elected in 1929. He was forced to resign after allegations of corruption in 1932. Just as much of a celebrity of the time was the author of this sketch, journalist Walter Winchell, who as a columnist for the New York Daily Mirror *and national radio broadcaster was often said to be more interested in making the news than reporting it.*

JIMMY WALKER

James J. Walker ('Jimmy' to those who liked him and didn't) was the living spirit of the terrific 1920's. . . way back to when we saps believed a rising stock market was taking us nearer to heaven on earth; when everybody thought the lottery had more prizes than tickets. When flaming youth and lights of Broadway were the vogue – and the torch of the Statue of Liberty was a forgotten, burned-out electric bulb – Jimmy Walker led the parade. He was more than a product of that age. He was the expression of it. To pussyfoot around and say Jimmy was below the conscience of the American people is sheer, unadulterated bunk.

In the 1920's the American people were hell-bent for prosperity and riches. And they wanted a politician who was hell-bent only for reelection. . . in short, a guy who would go along with the times – a man who would respect the national rush to get rich, who would accept greed, avarice and the lust for quick gain as a legitimate expression of the will of the people.

As a politician, Walker knew what the people wanted. And as a mayor, he gave it to them.

Once Walker entered a nightclub and was jostled by a small-town big shot who didn't recognize him. Walker bowed, then smiled, but the big shot would have none of it. 'Do you know who you are talking to?' he asked Jimmy very belligerently.

'No,' said Jimmy, 'but take my chair and I'll go and find out for you.'

One of the best exchanges occurred when La Guardia opposed Mayor Walker's raise in salary from twenty-five to forty thousand dollars. La Guardia said forty thousand a year was too much. 'Think how much it would cost,' said the never-punctual Jimmy, 'if I worked full time!'

Mr. Walker, a handsome hunk of he-man had been parted (for decades) from Mrs. Walker, a devout Catholic. It cost him the goodwill of the Church – and of Governor Al Smith, also a devout man. Jimmy fell in love with former show girl Betty Compton. Their courtship was Topic A in Manhattan and elsewhere.

Fiorello La Guardia, the Fusion candidate for mayor of New York, was running to dispossess 'Mr. New York.' La Guardia's team heard about Jimmy and Betty and breathlessly reported the scandilly to 'The Little Flower.' 'Fahevvensakes!' exclaimed respectable La Guardia, 'don't let that get into the papers – it'll get Walker another hundred thousand votes!'

Jimmy shrugged off the criticism by the Church, the Governor, and Catholics in high and low places. One night at the Stork Club, he told me: 'I make my private life pretty public. I don't sneak in and out of restaurants, nightclubs, the Central Park Casino [his pet spot], the fights at Madison Square Garden, or the opening nights at the Broadway theaters. I take Betty with me everywhere – always where the lights are brightest. Right down front at ringside in Madison Square Garden or in Row A at the plays! The whole audience sees me and Betty. I have nothing to hide. I'm in love.

The newspapers published pix of their hand-holding almost daily. When editorialists and others condemned Walker for the romance – and the way he flaunted it – he went into the New York history books with this oft-quoted crack: 'I'll match my private life with any man's!'

Nobody ever risked it.

When Walker ran for reelection the last time, he did so under great pressure from Tammany Hall, every New York Democrat's Svengali. He didn't want to run.

Tammany chiefs insisted that the party couldn't win unless he did. He finally persuaded and told them he would run – providing he didn't have to make any speeches.

In the final week of that campaign they told Walker that unless he was willing to get out and do some campaigning, the ticket would flop. Angry as he was, Jimmy obliged his bosses and during the last week made several glib speeches daily.

The traditional last Democratic rally in the mayoralty election was always held at the Savoy Ballroom in Negro-populated Harlem. At that event Jimmy ('Mr. Unpunctual') arrived at the Savoy about an hour tardy – after making about a dozen speeches in the five boroughs of Greater New York.

By this time Our Hero was pretty squiffed but – with a little assistance from aides – he made the podium and delivered what I have always considered to be the shortest and sockiest political speech in the history of American politics.

'Ladies and Gentlemen. . . [the usual Walker pause]. . . and I mean Ladies and Gentlemen. . . [lusty hand clapping]. . . while I was driving up to this last big and most important rally of my campaign, a man on one side was telling me about all the things I did for the Negro while I was in the State Assembly. A fellow on the other side of me was telling me of all the things I did for the Negro while I was mayor of the City of New York.

'Well, I'll tell you the truth. In all my political life I never did anything for the Negro!. . . [big Walker pause – with consternation on all sides]. . . I never did anything for the Catholics either; I never did anything for the Jews or Italians or the Germans – because, Ladies and Gentlemen, I don't know the difference! Good night.'

Melech Ravitch, born in Eastern Europe in 1893, emigrated to the New World at the beginning of the century. On his way to Ellis Island, where new immigrants disembarked, he passed the Statue of Liberty. Years later, he composed this poem about its meaning and promise.

In the New York Statue of Liberty

I am a man of blood, flesh and bone.
My soul is love, laughter and tears.
And you? Woman, hollow, steel giant
With the torch in your right hand high,
You are a golem-woman, with a tinny skin
Taut over a steel skeleton.
Your tin lips have never kissed bread.
Yor iron ribs have never cradled a man in bed.
And. . . I love you with young love, flaming and tender.
Thirty years of my youth and manhood I yearned,
For your first glance pined.

I am a poet and a wanderer and a Jew.
The steps to my soul are trembling strophes of my verse.
And to yours – which is only one of millions of heads –
To your head and thought, hundreds of stairs of iron.
Empty is your soul: winter – cold, summer – hot, as in any edifice
    of tin.

And yet this is so enormous and so wonderful
In your soul, with hundreds of others on stairs to wander and tire
And sing in oneself a glowing, warmly human love song
To you! That in your veins of wire and of steel
Flow electric lights, instead of living blood
While you are golem only, monument of Liberty, symbol. . .
And while you are golem, symbol, Liberty's monument,
I'm writing this song in love and youthful excitement. My hand
    trembles,
Sparkle the eyes, burns the blood.
Believe me, lady, when I pressed my lips to your tin walls
And to the walls of your proud neck and – hidden – secretly kissed
    them,
That no one should see and say maybe, a poet insane perhaps.
This was the love of purest spirit,

Like a love song – this pitifully sincere song;
While never did I so love,
Never, any woman so
As the Liberty that to you once and for all
Was granted the right the symbol to be.

Your torch is directed
To New York, but your light burns
To all the ends of the world.
One blesses and one curses you,
One honors and another hates,
One is earnest, another frivolous.
And I have purely love and faith
For curse and hatred are wind, sawdust.

Oh, is it true, you woman, you freedom, you're today a fallen
    woman,
And perhaps – perhaps because of that is my love for you so
    tender and so deep.
In your tin belly, you tin symbol,
Are you pregnant with the new savior of the worlds.
They may laugh at you, they may curse you –
You, only you, will bear him in light and in faith.
On your hands will you him – your son –
Like the torch above, raise high over all mankind.

And laugh will he who now weeps.
And weep he who curses.
Now.
'United.
Led by a child.
Liberty, beloved, yours, only yours, only your son
Will be the savior of the world.
A son of the spirit of all in love with you!

Oh, also shall the breath of this love song, in love to you
    conceived,
Be then a part of the spirit that impregnated you.

CHAPTER 13

RIOTS &
REBELLIONS

The Battle of New York in 1776 was a resounding triumph for the British, who continued to occupy the city for the duration of the Revolutionary War. Among the many political leaders serving in Washington's first disastrous campaign was the young Aaron Burr, later to become Senator for New York State, founder of Tammany Hall, and Vice-President, before his duel with Alexander Hamilton, another New Yorker prominent in the formation of the Republic, finished his political career. In his historical novel Burr, *published in 1973, Gore Vidal, born at West Point, New York, in 1925, recreated the conspiracies and confusion in Washington's camp before the British invasion of the City – through the eyes of the young Aaron Burr.*

THE BATTLE OF NEW YORK

Soon after I arrived a soldier named Hickey had been hanged for treason, to the delight of 20,000 New Yorkers. I was not present at the execution but I did read with amusement Washington's statement to the troops. According to our commander, the English-born Hickey has gone-over to the British not for money but because *he was a life-long prey to lewd women!* It was a sermon worthy of my grandfather. Incidentally, the private soldiers disliked Washington as much as he disdained them. On the other hand, the young officers (with at least one exception) adored their commander, and it is the young officer not the private soldier who eventually decides what is history.

I have never known New York so gay – despite the British fleet which materialized in the harbour June 29. The Battery was regularly subjected to bombardments that did no damage. The girls, however, enjoyed squealing with excitement and rushing for protection to our strong arms.

On July 3, the British army under General Howe disembarked on Staten Island, a Tory stronghold. Although our position was perilous, everyone had confidence in Washington. A confidence that was to evaporate when presently he contrived to lose both Long Island and New York City.

As I have already noted, Washington had had very little experience of actual war before 1776. Years before he had been involved in a few disastrous skirmishes with the French and their Indian allies on the Ohio. His first fame was the result of a despatch he sent to the Virginia governor in which he referred to the sound of the bullets that whistled past his head as 'charming'. Strange word. Strange young man.

In my view had Gates or Lee been placed in command of the army the war would have ended at least three years sooner. Each was brilliant. Each understood the enemy (Lee, in fact, knew personally the British commanders). Each won true victories in the field against the British, something Washington was never able to do. But though Washington could not defeat the enemy in battle, he had a fine talent for defeating rival generals in the Congress. At the end he alone was at the pinnacle, as he intended from the beginning.

Washington did have a most unexpected *penchant* for espionage. Our intelligence was almost always better than that of the British. Unfortunately Washington's judgment sometimes disallowed facts. For instance, despite every possible warning, he never believed that the British would attack New York Island when and where they did. Yet he must be given credit for tenacity. Although the war dragged on year after year due to his eerie incompetence, I suspect that the kind of victory he did achieve could only have been the work of a man who combined resolute courage with a total absence of imagination.

I fear that I did not properly appreciate being an aide to Washington. I did not enjoy copying out letters asking Congress for money that was seldom forthcoming: the American soldier was as mercenary as any Hessian. No money, no battle. Nor did I much enjoy listening to the worshipful talk of the other aides who flattered Washington monstrously, to his obvious pleasure. I, on the other hand, was prone to question his judgment although I had been advised by everyone that independence of mind was not a quality he demanded of subordinates. We were happy to be rid of one another.

I was to have a better time of it with my good, old General Israel Putnam whose headquarters I joined in July 1776 at the corner of the Battery and the Broad Way. A former tavern-keeper, Putnam had the amiability of that class as well as a good if crude intelligence. His only fault was a tendency to repeat himself. Whenever the enemy drew close, he would invariably instruct the men not to shoot 'till you see the whites of their eyes'! Having made the line famous at Bunker Hill, he tended to plagiarize himself, to the amusement of everyone except those officers who thought the firing ought to begin long *before* the whites became apparent to some of our myopic riflemen.

On July 9, I took the salute at General Putnam's side in the

Bowling Green. Then at the request of the Continental Congress, our adjutant read aloud to the troops a document newly received from Philadelphia.

I confess to not having listened to a word of the Declaration of Independence. At the time I barely knew the name of the author of this sublime document. I do remember hearing someone comment that since Mr. Jefferson had seen fit to pledge so eloquently our lives to the cause of independence, he might at least join us in the army. But wise Tom preferred the safety of Virginia and the excitement of local politics to the discomforts and dangers of war. . .

. . . By the end of August 1776, General Howe had assembled on Staten Island some 34,000 men. It was his intention to seize New York City, take command of the Hudson and split the colonies in two. May I say, what he intended to do, he proceeded easily to do.

Immediately after the arrival of the British, I was sent by Putnam to every one of our outposts from the Brooklyn Heights to the Haarlem Heights. I had never seen men less prepared for a battle with anyone, much less with fresh modern European troops. Junior though I was to the great commanders, I took seriously my task which was to assess our situation as accurately as I could. My gloomy written report to General Putman was sent on to the commanding general.

Two days later I encountered His Excellency on the Battery. A sulphurous New York August day. Tempers were short. Sweat mixed with the chalk the General used to powder his hair trickled down cheeks fiery from heat and bad temper. His mood was not improved by the sight of the British fleet making complicated manoeuvres just opposite us, cannon beautifully polished, white sails pretty beneath a leaden sky.

'What, Sir, do you think the result will be should the enemy begin an assault?' I was taken by surprise: Washington seldom asked such questions of senior officers; never of junior officers.

'Why, Sir, we shall be routed,' I said with stupid honesty.

'Never!' The 'never' was from a permanent member of the chorus of worshippers that was to follow Washington throughout the Revolution. . . nay, throughout his long life, even to the grave! No man was ever so much praised and fortified by those about him.

I continued. 'It is my belief, Sir, that the wisest course would be the one you have so far pursued with such success since Cambridge.' Yes, I was a courtier, too.

'What, Sir, do you think that to be?' Our suspicious warlord suspected even then that I was not entirely in thrall to his legend which, quite mysteriously, continued to grow from month to month no matter when he won or lost or, as was more usual, did nothing.

'To imitate Fabius Cunctator. To avoid meeting head-on a superior enemy. To draw him away from his supplies. To draw him deeper and deeper into the continent where the advantage is ours not his. Sir, I would abandon New York City today. Give General Howe the sea-coast. He will take it anyway. But by withdrawing now, we keep intact the army, such as it is. . .'

I had gone too far. One of the aides reprimanded me. 'The best troops of the colonies are here, Major Burr. The best commanders. . .'

'You under-estimate us, Major.' Washington was unexpectedly mild. With a lace handkerchief, he mopped his chalk-streaked face; the pits from the small pox were particularly deep about the mouth.

'You have asked for my report, Sir.'

'Yes.' Washington turned his back to the port and gazed at the sooty old fort that used to dominate what was still a small Dutch town with rose brick houses and slender church-spires. But then John Astor was still a butcher boy in Waldorf, Germany.

'We shall defend the city.' Washington's mistakes were always proclaimed with the sort of finality that made one feel any criticism was to deface a tablet newly brought down from Sinai.

'Sir, I would burn the city to the ground tomorrow and withdraw into Jersey.'

'Thank you, Major. My compliments to General Putnam. Good day, Sir.'

In defence of Washington, I must note that at the time very few of us knew much about the powerful secret forces at work upon him. There is evidence that he would have liked to destroy the city but was stopped by the local merchants (to a man pro-British) and by the Congress at Philadelphia which, eventually, *ordered* him under no circumstances to fire the city. Yet it was his decision – and no one else's – to confront the enemy with all his forces at Brooklyn in Long Island. This was to be Washington's first set battle; it was very nearly the last. Even today's hagiographers admit his sole responsibility for the disaster.

Right off, Washington split into two parts an army which,

entire, was not capable at that time of stopping a British brigade. Then he chose personally to respond to a dazzling series of British and Hessian feints: in a matter of hours, he was out-manned and out-generalled.

Thrown back to his main line of defence, the Brooklyn Heights, Washington was faced with the loss of his entire army if he remained on Long Island or humiliating defeat if he chose to give up the Heights and withdraw to New York Island. He chose humiliation.

On the unseasonably cold and foggy night of August 29, I stood in a water-melon patch near the slip of the Brooklyn ferry and watched the evacuation of the army. All night boats went back and forth between New York and Brooklyn. Low dark shapes appearing and disappearing into a strange soft fog. The only sounds the soft moans of the wounded, the whispered commands of officers, the jangle of General Washington's bridle as he presided over the *débâcle* he had devised for us.

On September 15, 1776, the British fleet appeared at Kip's Bay about four miles north of the Battery. As usual, we were surprised. A powerful bombardment began at 11:00 a.m. Then the British and Hessians disembarked. Our troops promptly fled, despite the presence of Washington himself who shrieked at his own men like a man demented, broke his stick over a brigadier's head, cut a sergeant with his sword – to no avail. Raging and weeping, he was dragged away to the sound of British bugles mocking him with the fox-hunter's 'View, halloo! Fox on the run!'

Washington retreated up the island to the Morris mansion on the Haarlem Heights (now the home of Colonel and Mrs. Aaron Burr *ci devant Jumel*) which was to be his headquarters for the rest of September. This must have been the lowest point of his career; worse, in some ways, than the winter at Valley Forge.

I sit now in what was his office, as I amend these notes, and think of him more than half a century ago, scribbling those long, ungrammatical, disingenuous letters to the Congress, trying to explain how he managed at such a cost to lose Long Island and New York City.

During this period I saw General Washington only once at the Morris mansion. It was September 22, and I had accompanied General Putnam to a meeting of the senior officers. There was a good deal to talk about. The previous night almost a third of New City had gone up in flames.

238

'Someone has done us a good turn.' Washington stood at the foot of the stairs with his plump favourite young Colonel Knox. Before General Putnam could say anthing, Washington turned to me and I received for the first and only time his bleak dark-toothed smile. 'I would not, Sir, have put it past you to have done this thing.'

'Only at your order, Your Excellency.'

General Putman and Colonel Knox had no idea what we were talking about.

Conscription was introduced by the Federal Government in 1863. The Civil War was relatively unpopular in New York and the bias of the draft laws towards the rich further undermined their acceptability to the populace. For three bloody days in July, 1863, New York City was torn by the worst civil disturbances in its history, quelled in the end only by the arrival of Federal troops from Pennsylvania. In Black Manhattan, *James Weldon Johnson describes the riots and their effect on New York's black community.*

DRAFT RIOTS, 1863

Conscription was nowhere popular, but in New York City it was met with open hostility and violence. For four days in July 1863 the Draft Riots raged and the city was in the hands of a mob against which the police were powerless. After demolishing draft headquarters the mob proceeded to wreak vengeance upon Negroes wherever found. They were chased and beaten and killed – hanged to trees and lamp posts. Thousands fled the city, hiding themselves "on the outskirts of the city, in the swamps and woods back of Bergen, New Jersey, at Weeksville, and in the barns and outhouses of the farmers of Long Island and Morrisania"; and hundreds sought refuge in the police stations. A historian of the time gives this description:

The sight of one in the streets would call forth a halloo as when a fox breaks cover, and away would dash a crowd of men in pursuit. . . . At one time there lay at the corner of 27th Street and Seventh Avenue the dead body of a Negro, stripped nearly naked, and around it a collection of Irishmen dancing or shouting like wild Indians. . . . The hunt for these poor creatures became so fearful, and the impossibility to protect them in their scattered localities so apparent, that they were received into

239

the police stations. But this soon proved inadequate and they were taken to the arsenal where they could be protected against the mob. Here the poor creatures were gathered by hundreds and slept on the floor and were regularly fed by the authorities.

The Colored Orphan Asylum occupied a block on Fifth Avenue between Forty-third and Forty-fourth streets. More than two hundred children were housed there in a wooden building four stories high. The insatiate mob marched against this institution. The superintendent and matrons, who had been watching through hours of terror, hastily led the inmates out by the rear as the mob entered through the front. In a few moments the building was in flames. The children, at first quartered in the police stations, were finally gathered up, and, with a strong guard of police at the front and rear and a detachment of soldiers on either side, they toddled down to the foot of East Thirty-fifth Street and were taken aboard ferryboats to Blackwell's Island, where they were given a refuge. In the Draft Riots more than a thousand persons were killed and wounded, and something like a million dollars' worth of property was destroyed.

The reaction from the Draft Riots was a flood of kindly feeling towards the Negro and of indignation against the mob. Within a few months a regiment of Negro troops, raised and equipped by the Union League Club, marched down to Broadway on their way to the front escorted by leading citizens and cheered by thousands that lined the sidewalks.

Albert Halper was born in Chicago in 1904. He came to New York as a young man where he worked in a number of laboring jobs, which provided source material for his novels of the thirties. In this short story he describes one of the great taxi strikes which hit the city in that decade.

SCAB!

I pulled out of the Big Garage on West Fifty-fourth Street early in the morning, because I thought the pickets wouldn't be on the job yet. But they were. At the door, Mrs. Steur, the wife of the fleet manager, checked me out, holding the big book in her hand. I spoke my number so low she didn't hear me at first. She stuck her head into the cab.

'1544,' I said again.

'Listen,' she told me, 'don't let them scare you, fella, the police are behind us, they can't do anything to you,' and she gave me a big smile as I zoomed out of the garage.

Mrs. Steur is big and getting stout and knows how to give the boys a big smile. Since this strike has been going on she has done a lot of smiling, especially when we roll out of the garage in the morning, but she isn't fooling any of us. She wears a fur coat that must have cost her five hundred dollars if it cost her a nickel, and every time I look at it I think of my own wife and two kids and I get mad around the mouth. Goddam her anyway. Last week, just before the strike started, she used to give us dirty looks every time she checked us out in the morning, and her dirty looks said: 'You bums are lousy drivers, you don't know how to hack, all you do is to warm your fannies in our nice comfortable cabs while Jake and me worry over the intake.' But now she calls us sonny and fella and all that baloney.

I zoomed out of the Big Garage in third and saw the pickets strung all along the street with signs on their backs. But luck was with me. The green light was showing up the block so I hit the bus up to forty-five miles an hour and none of them jumped on my running-board to argue with me. I've been working for the Steurs for over two years now and every hack-man in the garage knows I'm a square-shooter, and they can't figure out why I'm driving with the strike going on. Only a few know about the hole I'm in and about the wife's operation – But what the hell, I'm not telling everybody about my troubles, everybody's got plenty of their own these days, so I don't say anything to anybody.

I whizzed up the block as fast as I could hit it up. There were two cops on motorcycles resting at the corner and though I was going way over the speed limit they didn't stop me but waved their hands and smiled. I smiled back, but it was not the same kind of smile they gave to me. My smile said, 'To hell with you, beefsteaks!'

Two blocks down, three of the boys started running towards my cab, so I had to cut west on Fifty-second. This is a bad street with some deep holes in it, but I shook them off. Then I cut east again and headed toward Fifth Avenue, praying for a fare. It was already half-past seven in the morning and the city was waking up. As I sent the car along I could see pieces of fog floating up the street. I like to drive early in the morning. There is something about cruising in an empty cab with the fog coming up the street which gets me. I don't know what it is. Sometimes I can almost smell it. A lot of times, if business has been good the day before, that is, if I make over three dollars, I will coast about in the East Sixties and Seventies for a good half hour just to get that feeling on a foggy morning. In the East Sixties and Seventies there is not even a dog in sight at 7 a.m. and most of the houses are boarded up because the rich people that own them spend their time mostly down in Florida or in Europe, so it's nice and still and quiet there early in the morning.

But I was out for business today, so I didn't stall around. I picked up a fare on Eighth Avenue and carried him to Fifth and Fifty-ninth. The fare was one of those tall rich guys around fifty who like to bend forward and act chummy with the driver, just to show you he's a regular fella. I know those kind. They tip dimes and always expect you to say thank-you twice.

'Do you mind if I turn the radio off?' he asks me, leaning forward.

I felt like telling him he could throw it out the window for all I cared. When I hear that goddam sad music early in the morning I keep on thinking about the wife and how the doctors bungled the job and it gets me nuts sometimes. Why did they have to put radios in cabs for anyway?

'How is the strike going?' the man asks me next.

'I guess it's going,' I mumbled back.

He kind of laughed soft-like and said the men didn't have a chance. With my left arm I reached around and turned the radio on again, real loud, because I started feeling down at the mouth again. It was those exercises this time: "One-two, bend from the waist, three-four, take a deep breath." You know those kind of daily dozen business they have on the air in the morning.

I was glad when the fare stepped out. But he sure surprised me. I mean he gave me fifteen cents. I picked up another load and took her to Grand Central. She wore a classy shiny brown fur coat and looked to be the bucks. Just before she got out she says to me, 'You men are having trouble with your employers, aren't you?' I said yes. Then she gave me a quarter tip. 'Well, I hope you win out,' she said, in a kind of nice tone. 'I like to see you men put up a fight.'

I sat in the cab burning up after she was gone. Did she say that to me on purpose, just to get my goat? Didn't she know I was a scab?

Then I hears some one hollering at me and when I looked back I saw a big guy in a cap running toward me. I wasn't taking any chances, so I started roaring up the block away from him. When I looked back again he was still hollering and waving at me, and then I saw him step into another cab. He wasn't out to slug me after all. He was a fare. I got my nerve back, turned around in the middle of the block, and played the line on Lexington Avenue. There were only three cabs in line. In half a minute all of us got fares.

Luck was with me all morning. I mean that every single fare I carried wasn't near Times Square or downtown. It was mostly East Side business with swell tips. By eleven o'clock I took in almost seven dollars. This is swell business even in a snow storm.

But after noon the trouble started. I was passing Thirty-fourth Street and Seventh Avenue when another cab cruises up to me and the driver calls out, 'They're burning and wrecking cabs downtown, don't go below Fourteenth Street.'

So I turned one fare down. I told the man I'd take him as far as Eighteenth Street where he could get a subway, but he looked at me disgusted and called another cab. I wasn't taking any chances. What would happen to Ethel and the kids if I got put away in the hospital? Goddam the whole business anyway! Why can't it be worked out somehow that we men could get paid a decent wage so that we wouldn't have to go out on strike and have the papers say nasty and untrue things about us? Why can't — Goddammit, I forgot. I'm a scab! I'm a —

'Hey, you!' yelled a blonde dame. 'Can you take me to Twelfth Street?'

'Sure,' I hollered back, sore at myself. 'I'll take you any-wheres.'

'What a man!' she sings out and steps high, wide, and handsome into the cab and when she gets inside she lights a cigarette and starts humming a song. I had a feeling right away she was good for a two-bit tip. 'Play, taxi, play!' she sings out and turned on the radio. It was one of those damn sad songs again which I can't stand right after noon and I started thinking of Ethel and the doctors, but I didn't tell the fare to turn it off. She was painted up like hell, but I saw right away she was a good sport.

At Sixteenth Street they stopped me. There must have been

over fifty of them. There were three cops, but the cops couldn't do anything.

'Come on, lady, get out,' the drivers hollered.

The fare told them to go to hell. I had to hand it to her.

'Come on, get out, or we'll knock you out!'

'You and who else?' she hollers at them.

'Turn that damn radio off!' they yelled at me.

I turned it off. Then two of them hopped on the running-board and I had to kill the engine. They bunched all around me. The cops tried to get to me, but the boys kept shoving them away. They shoved in a kind of good natured way, but they meant business. It was a kind of shoving that told the cops that all they had to do was to just start to get fresh and the boys would have flattened them. Then one of the boys who jumped onto the running-board poked his head inside, and I saw it was Goldstein.

'It's Tom Davlin,' he said, and he started talking to the others to let me alone.

'To hell with that!' the others told him. 'Let's drag him out if he doesn't turn around and shoot back to the garage right away. Let's drag him out!'

But Goldstein kept on arguing. Goldie is one of the few fellows in the Big Garage who knows what a hole I'm in. I heard him whispering something and I felt cheap as hell sitting there, but they wouldn't listen to him. 'Drag him out!' they said again. I sat there wringing wet. 'Drag him out!' they hollered, and I thought they were going to give it to me for sure, and I wouldn't have put up a battle, because I knew just how they felt. But just then three patrol cars came up with their sirens screaming and the cops piled out. They started swinging their clubs and cleared a way for my cab. I shot the car into second and tore like hell down the street.

'What was that pal of yours whispering to the others?' the fare asked me when we were a block away. 'Have you fellas got a magic pass-word?'

'I don't know nothing,' I said.

'Oh, so that's the way you feel about it,' she said, then turned on the radio again. 'Play, taxi, play!' she sang out, and Christ, what a nice long beautiful throat that woman had! She was singing happy over something and couldn't keep it down. She must have gotten a good hunk of cash from her daddy or something, I figured to myself.

'Hey, you,' she called to me from the back seat, 'hey, you, do you know what?'

'What?' I says, not turning around.

'I'm going to have a baby,' she sings out to me, 'and I feel so goddamned happy.'

Then I knew she was tight. Any girl like that who feels happy over a kid must be either tight or crazy. I figured she was nutty.

She gave me the address and I stopped in front of a doctor's place.

'Here, sweetheart,' she says and gives me two one-dollar bills. 'Keep the change, handsome,' and then she goes up to the door and rings the doctor's bell. A girl dressed like a nurse opens it. Then the door closed again.

What a tip! A dollar and twenty cents! I took time out and went into a coffee pot on Bank Street for some grub. There were two or three guys at the counter looking funny at me, so my meal was spoiled. I got up and paid and walked out. Goddammit, I'm a scab! I said to myself.

I shot the car into third and cruised east. When I hit Fourth Avenue I heard a lot of yelling and hollering. I got off at University Place and let the motor run. Then I hoofed it to Fourth.

There was a mob there, almost three hundred drivers. They were burning three taxi-cabs, while a big crowd of people were watching on the sidewalks. The cops couldn't do anything. They hit a few of the boys, but the boys socked them back. I saw them stepping on one policeman. They got him down and started tearing his overcoat to pieces. You ought to have seen their faces when they were doing that! the cop reached for his gun, but they stepped on his hand. They were yelling and screaming at him all the time. I got into the crowd and started helping them. A cop came for me, but I cracked him one. Then I got a sweet blow behind the ear and the next thing I knew I was laying on the street. Two of the boys helped me up and I sat on the curb for a while with my head in my hands. I was half-unconscious but I could smell burnt rubber, burnt paint, and the stink of gasoline. And all the while the crowd was yelling crazy.

I got up again, but by this time the cops on horseback came up. They started hitting the boys right and left. It was terrible. One fellow's ear was hanging by a piece of flesh and he kept holding his hand to his ear trying to put it back. The cops went for him

245

and cracked him another one. There were a few women, and nice looking ones, standing on the curb who started screaming at the cops to let the poor boy alone. One of them even came over to the horses and started to argue.

Then the fire engines came. They tried to put out the flames. They lay hoses from Tenth and Eleventh Street, but by the time the water was turned on the cabs weren't worth a dime. Then the gang started toward Union Square. I started with them, then suddenly remembered I had my bus parked up the street, I started thinking of Ethel and the kids again. Goddammit anyway!

I walked back to the cab and shot it west. I picked up a fare and took her uptown to Forty-fourth Street. She tipped me twenty cents. My pockets were heavy with silver so I got out and went into a restaurant and had it changed to paper money. The cashier looked funny at me. I felt so lousy that I didn't count my money twice and maybe he gypped me out of a quarter or so, because I remember –

Then I heard yelling on Seventh Avenue. I ran out and started the bus in a hurry. I didn't stop until I got to the Sixties. I cruised up and down those side streets until I got my nerve back. It started raining a little. A fare hailed me, but I didn't stop because I didn't have a good grip on myself yet. But in another minute I got another, this time for Ninety-second Street.

When I dropped that fare the rain stopped for a while. I was good and hungry again, because I had only taken a few bites out of my sandwich in that coffee pot on Bank Street, so I went into a place on Ninety-third, but first I put my hat in the cab.

But when I came in, some truck drivers at the counter recognized that I was a hack-man anyway. You can always tell one if you know them. We all have clothes shiny around the seat, and that shininess is a special cab driver's gloss. I can't just describe it, but the gloss gives us away. I can be walking down the street with the missus and if I see a fellow walking ahead of me with that gloss on his rear-end, I can turn to the wife and say, 'Two to one that guy is a hacker.' Ethel knows that I am not the betting kind, but she gets sore at me sometimes. 'Can't you forget your lousy business even when you're not working?' she asks me. This gets me sore sometimes, but I know she hasn't been herself since the operation. So I just keep quiet.

Anyway, when I sat down and ordered a bowl of soup I saw the truck drivers giving me the once-over. Then one of them started talking louder. 'I bet he's a scab,' he said. I turned around with murder in my eye. 'Goddam you, what if I am?' I hollered at him and I was so worked up that I started spilling all about my wife and the kids and the deep hole I'm in. The cook came out from the kitchen and looked at me. By the time I was through I was almost screaming. The guy who had called me a scab didn't know what to say and sat there looking at the counter.

'All right, all right,' he says kind of quiet and he wanted to let the matter drop.

'All right hell!' I screamed at him and got up and went out.

The cook hollered at me to pay the check, but I told him to come outside and I'd beat hell out of him, and he didn't make a move when I told him that.

I got into the bus and had to cruise around for a good fifteen minutes to cool off. I was so hopping mad I felt like speeding the car up to sixty miles an hour and driving square into a building.

But when a fare hailed me, I calmed down. I started to think of Ethel and the kids and I realized I couldn't act like a damn fool.

So I picked up the fare and cooled off. It started to rain again. When I dropped the fare, I got another right away. I kept uptown. Business was heavy and I was on the jump all the time.

I worked straight through until eight o'clock, then I bought a newspaper to see how the strike was coming on. The headlines said the strike was still dead-locked. There was a lot of stuff written about what the fleet owners said about company unions, but we all know what those company unions are. The boys were still putting up a fight. I parked my bus in a side street and read the piece to the last line. When I read about the fights and the riots and the burning of the cabs I felt so thrilled I wanted to sing and scream with happiness. Then all of a sudden I remembered I wasn't in it, and the feeling flopped inside of me.

A half hour later when I pulled into the Big Garage, Mrs. Steur let out a big sigh of relief. 'Oh thank God,' she said, 'I thought they burned your cab.'

Then she saw the dented fenders and the broken windows and her face fell. She started cursing the strikers to beat the band. I never heard her swear like that before. Then she told me to check in and go home and get a good night's rest and report for duty in the morning. When she saw the meter reading she complimented me, but she was still swearing at the drivers.

I got home an hour later, tired as a dog. The first thing when I

247

closed the door, Ethel asked me how much I made. I put eleven dollars on the table. It was the most I had ever made in a single day's hacking. She looked at my face and didn't say anything. I started to tell her I was through until the strike was over, when I heard Sonny start to bawl in the bedroom. Then I kept my mouth shut.

When we sat down to eat Ethel got me to talk. I told her how I had seen the burning cabs, how they had stopped me, and how Goldie and the cops had saved me from getting slugged. I didn't tell her how I got out and socked a cop and then got flattened out. Women sometimes can't see things a man's way.

'You'd think they'd let a man work in peace,' she said finally, and then I got sore as hell. I started to holler. I couldn't help myself. I told her how I had gone to the coffee pots and couldn't eat because I was looked at in a funny way, I told her how I felt about it, and I said something about the fog drifting up the street and the East Sixties and the Seventies where the houses were boarded up with rich people spending the winter down in Florida or over in Europe, and the first thing I knew I was standing up and screaming at her across the table.

The kids started bawling in the bedroom. Ethel hollered at me, but I couldn't stop.

'Goddam it to hell,' I screamed, 'I'm through! I'm not the only guy driving a hack with a wife and kids on his hands. I'm through, I tell you. How do you suppose I feel at the wheel of my cab making money with my buddies out on strike? I tell you I'm through. I'm not reporting in the morning, nor the day after. I don't care if we starve. I'm going tearing through the streets with the other drivers because that's where I belong. I'm going to help them burn and wreck every goddam cab in sight!'

And then I told Ethel something I promised myself I would never tell to anybody.

I told her about how just before I started back to the garage I parked in a side street and took out my tire-wrench and bashed in the fenders of my cab and then broke every goddamned window with my own hands, I screamed that out to her. She asked me why I had done it, and I didn't know what to answer.

Then I hollered out, louder than ever: 'A man's got to keep some of his self-respect, don't he? What do you take me for, a scab?'

Ralph Ellison, born in Oklahoma in 1914, came to New York in the thirties. His classic novel, Invisible Man, *published in 1952, draws a detailed picture of the politics and people of Harlem in the depression. Its climax is a violent, turbulent riot, into which the anonymous narrator finds himself unwittingly drawn.*

HARLEM UPRISING

One Hundred and Twenty-fifth Street came quickly. I stumbled off, hearing the bus pull away as I faced the water. There was a light breeze, but now with the motion gone the heat returned, clinging. Far ahead in the dark I saw the monumental bridge, ropes of lights across the dark river; and close, high above the shoreline, the Palisades, their revolutionary agony lost in riotous lights of roller coasters. 'The Time Is Now. . .' the sign across the river began, but with history stomping upon me with hobnailed boots, I thought with a laugh, why worry about time? I crossed the street to the drinking fountain, feeling the water cooling, going down, then dampened a handkerchief and swabbed my face, eyes. The water flashed, gurgled, sprayed. I pressed forward my face, feeling wet cool, hearing the infant joy of fountains. Then heard the other sound. It was not the river nor the curving cars that flashed through the dark, but pitched like a distant crowd or a swift river at flood tide.

I moved forward, found the steps and started down. Below the bridge lay the hard stone river of the street, and for a second I looked at the waves of cobblestones as though I expected water, as though the fountain above had drawn from them. Still I would enter and go across to Harlem. Below the steps the trolley rails gleamed steely. I hurried, the sound drawing closer, myriad-voiced, humming, enfolding me, numbing the air, as I started beneath the ramp. It came, a twitter, a coo, a subdued roar that seemed trying to tell me something, give me some message. I stopped, looking around me; the girders marched off rhythmically into the dark, over the cobblestones the red light shone. Then I was beneath the bridge and it was as though they had been waiting for me and no one but me – dedicated and set aside for me – for an eternity. And I looked above towards the sound, my mind forming an image of wings, as something struck my face and streaked, and I could smell the foul air now, and see the encrusted barrage, feeling it streak my jacket and raising my brief case

249

above my head and running, hearing it splattering around, falling like rain. I ran the gauntlet, thinking, even the birds; even the pigeons and the sparrows and the goddam gulls! I ran blindly, boiling with outrage and despair and harsh laughter. Running from the birds to what, I didn't know. I ran. Why was I here at all?

I ran through the night, ran within myself. Ran.

When I reached Morningside the shooting sounded like a distant celebration of the Fourth of July, and I hurried forward. At St. Nicholas the street lights were out. A thunderous sound arose and I saw four men running towards me pushing something that jarred the walk. It was a safe.

'Say,' I began.

'Get the hell out of the way!'

I leaped aside, into the street, and there was a sudden and brilliant suspension of time, like the interval between the last axe stroke and the felling of a tall tree, in which there had been a loud noise followed by a loud silence. Then I was aware of figures crouching in doorways and along the kerb; then time burst and I was down in the street, conscious but unable to rise, struggling against the street and seeing the flashes as the guns went off back at the corner of the avenue, aware to my left of the men still speeding the rumbling safe along the walk as back up the street, behind me, two policemen, almost invisible in black shirts, thrust flaming pistols before them. One of the safe-rollers pitched forward, and farther away, past the corner, a bullet struck an auto tyre, the released air shrieking like a huge animal in agony. I rolled, flopping around, willing myself to crawl closer to the kerb but unable, feeling a sudden wet warmth upon my face and seeing the safe shooting wildly into the intersection and the men rounding the corner into the dark, pounding, gone; gone now, as the skittering safe bounded off at a tangent, shot into the intersection and lodged in the third rail and sent up a curtain of sparks that lit up the block like a blue dream; a dream I was dreaming and through which I could see the cops braced as on a target range, feet forward, free arms akimbo, firing with deliberate aim.

'Get hold of Emergency!' one of them called, and I saw them turn and disappear where the full glint of trolley rails faded off into the dark.

Suddenly the block leaped alive. Men who seemed to rise up

out of the sidewalks were rushing into the store fronts above me, their voices rising excitedly. And now the blood was in my face and I could move, getting to my knees as someone out of the crowd was helping me to stand.

'You hurt, daddy?'

'Some – I don't know –' I couldn't quite see them.

'Damn! He's got a hole in his head!' a voice said.

A light flashed in my face, came close. I felt a hard hand upon my skull and moved away.

'Hell, it's just a nick,' a voice said. 'One of them forty-fives hit your little finger you got to go down!'

'Well, this one over here is gone down for the last time,' someone called from the walk. 'They got him clean.'

I wiped my face, my head ringing. Something was missing.

'Thanks,' I said, peering into their dim, blue-tinted features. I looked at the dead man. He lay face forward, the crowd working around him. I realized suddenly that it might have been me huddled there, feeling too that I had seen him there before, in the bright light of noon, long ago. . . how long? Knew his name, I thought, and suddenly my knees flowed forward. I sat there, my fist gripped the brief case bruising against the street, my head slumped forward. They were going around me.

'Get off my foot, man,' I heard. 'Quit shoving. There's plenty for everybody.'

There was something I had to do and I knew that my forgetfulness wasn't real, as one knows that the forgotten details of certain dreams are not truly forgotten but evaded. I knew, and in my mind I was trying to reach through the grey veil that now seemed to hang behind my eyes as opaquely as the blue curtain that screened the street beyond the safe. The dizziness left and I managed to stand, holding on to my brief case, pressing a handkerchief to my head. Up the street there sounded the crashing of huge sheets of glass and through the blue mysteriousness of the dark the walks shimmered like shattered mirrors. All the street's signs were dead, all the day sounds had lost their stable meaning. Somewhere a burglar alarm went off, a meaningless blangy sound, followed by the joyful shout of looters.

'Come on,' someone called nearby.

'Let's go, buddy,' the man who had helped me said. He took my arm, a thin man who carried a large cloth bag slung over his shoulder.

251

'The shape you in wouldn't do to leave you round here,' he said. 'You act like you drunk.'

'Go where?' I said.

'Where? Hell, man. Everywhere. We git to moving, no telling where we might go – Hey, Dupre!' he called.

'Say, man – Goddam! Don't be calling my name so loud,' a voice answered. 'Here, I am over here, gitting me some work shirts.'

'Git some for me, Du,' he said.

'All right, but don't think I'm your papa,' the answer came.

I looked at the thin man, feeling a surge of friendship. He didn't know me, his help was disinterested. . .

'Hey, Du,' he called, 'we go'n do it?'

'Hell yes, soon as I git me these shirts.'

The crowd was working in and out of the stores like ants around spilled sugar. From time to time there came the crash of glass, shots; fire trucks in distant streets.

'How you feel?' the man said.

'Still fuzzy,' I said, 'and weak.'

'Le's see if it's stopped bleeding. Yeah, you'll be all right.'

I saw him vaguely though his voice came clear.

'Sure,' I said.

'Man, you lucky you ain't dead. These sonsabitches is really shooting now,' he said. 'Over on Lenox they was aiming up in the air. If I could find me a rifle, I'd show 'em! Here, take you a drink of this good Scotch,' he said, taking a quart bottle from a hip pocket. 'I got me a whole case stashed what I got from a liquor store over there. Over there all you got to do is breathe, and you drunk, man. Drunk! Hundred proof bonded whisky flowing all in the gutters.'

I took a drink, shuddering as the whisky went down but thankful for the shock it gave me. There was a bursting, tearing movement of people around me, dark figures in a blue glow.

'Look at them take it away,' he said, looking into the dark action of the crowd. 'Me, I'm tired. Was you over on Lenox?'

'No,' I said, seeing a woman moving slowly past with a row of about a dozen dressed chickens suspended by their necks from the handle of a new straw broom. . .

'Hell, you ought to see it, man. Everything is tore up. By now the womens is picking it clean. I saw one ole woman with a whole side of a cow on her back. Man, she was 'bout bent bowlegged trying to make it home – Here come Dupre now,' he said, breaking off.

I saw a little hard man come out of the crowd carrying several boxes. He wore three hats upon his head, and several pairs of suspenders flopped about his shoulders, and now as he came towards us. I saw that he wore a pair of gleaming new rubber hip boots. His pockets bulged and over his shoulder he carried a cloth sack that swung heavily behind him.

'Damn, Dupre,' my friend said, pointing to his head, 'you got one of them for me? What kind is they?'

Dupre stopped and looked at him. 'With all them hats in there and I'm going to come out with anything but a *Dobbs*? Man, are you *mad*? All them new, pretty-coloured *Dobbs*? Come on, let's get going before the cops git back. Damn, look at that thing blaze!'

I looked towards the curtain of blue fire, through which vague figures toiled. Dupre called out and several men left the crowd and joined us in the street. We moved off, my friend (Scofield, the others called him) leading me along. My head throbbed, still bled.

'Looks like you got some loot too,' he said, pointing to my brief case.

'Not much,' I said, thinking, loot? *Loot?* . . .

'Fill it up, man. Don't you be bashful. You wait till we tackle one of these pawnshops. That Du's got him a cotton-picking sack fulla stuff. *He* could go into business.'

'Well, I'll be damn,' a man on the other side of me said. 'I *thought* that was a cotton sack. Where'd he get that thing?'

'He brought it with him when he come North,' Scofield said. 'Du swears that when he goes back he'll have it full of ten-dollar bills. Hell, after tonight he'll need him a warehouse for all the stuff he's got. You fill that brief case, buddy. Get yourself something!

'No,' I said, 'I've got enough in it already.' And now I remembered very clearly where I'd started out for but could not leave them.

'Maybe you right,' Scofield said. 'How I know, you might have it full of diamonds or something. A man oughtn't to be greedy. Though it's time something like this happened.'

We moved along. Should I leave, get on to the district? Where were they, at the birthday celebration?

'How did all this get started?' I said.

Scofield seemed surprised. 'Damn if I know, man. A cop shot a woman or something.'

Another man moved close to us as somewhere a piece of heavy steel rang down.

'Hell, that wasn't what started it,' he said. 'It was that fellow, what's his name. . . ?'

'Who?' I said. 'What's his name?'

'That young guy!'

'You know, everybody's mad about it. . .'

Clifton, I thought. It's for Clifton. A night for Clifton.

'Aw man, don't tell me,' Scofield said. 'Didn't I see it with my own eyes? About eight o'clock down on Lenox and 123rd this paddy slapped a kid for grabbing a Baby Ruth and the kid's mama took it up and then the paddy slapped her and that's when hell broke loose.'

'You were there?' I said.

'Same's I'm here. Some fellow said the kid made the paddy mad by grabbing a candy named after a white woman.'

'Damn if that's the way I heard it,' another man said. 'When I come up they said a white woman set it off by trying to take a black gal's man.'

'Damn *who* started it,' Dupre said. 'All I want is for it to last a while.'

'It was a white gal, all right, but that wasn't the way it was. She was drunk —' another voice said.

But it couldn't have been Sybil, I thought; it had already started.

'You wahn know who started it?' a man holding a pair of binoculars called from the window of a pawnshop. 'You wahn really to know?'

'Sure,' I said.

'Well, you don't need to go no further. It was started by that great leader, Ras the Destroyer!'

'That monkey-chaser?' someone said.

'Listen, bahstard!'

'Don't nobody know how it started,' Dupre said.

'Somebody has to know,' I said.

Scofield held his whisky towards me. I refused it.

'Hell, man, it just exploded. These is dog days,' he said.

'*Dog* days?'

'Sho, this hot weather.'

'I tell you they mad over what happen to that young fellow, what's-his-name. . .'

We were passing a building now and I heard a voice calling frantically, 'Coloured store! Coloured store!'

'Then put a sign, mother-fouler,' a voice said. 'You probably rotten as the others.'

'Listen at the bastard. For one time in his life he's glad to be coloured,' Scofield said.

'Coloured store,' the voice went on automatically.

'Hey! You sho you ain't got some white blood?'

'No, *sir!*' the voice said.

'Should I bust him, man?'

'For what? He ain't got a damn thing. Let the mother-fouler alone.'

A few doors away we came to a hardware store. 'This is the first stop, men,' Dupre said.

'What happens now?' I said.

'Who you?' he said, cocking his thrice-hatted head.

'Nobody, just one of the boys —' I began.

'You sho you ain't somebody I know?'

'I'm pretty sure,' I said.

'He's all right, Du,' said Scofield. 'Them cops shot him.'

Dupre looked at me and kicked something – a pound of butter, sending it smearing across the hot street. 'We fixing to do something what needs to be done,' he said. 'First we gets a flashlight for everybody. . . And let's have some organization, y'all. Don't everybody be running over everybody else. Come on!'

'Come on in, buddy,' Scofield said.

I felt no need to lead or leave them; was glad to follow; was gripped by a need to see where and to what they would lead. And all the time the thought that I should go to the district was with me. We went inside the store, into the dark glinting with metal. They moved carefully, and I could hear them searching, sweeping objects to the floor. The cash register rang.

'Here some flashlights over here,' someone called.

'How many?' Dupre said.

'Plenty, man.'

'Okay, pass out one to everybody. They got batteries?'

'Naw, but there's plenty them too, 'bout a dozen boxes.'

'Okay, give me one with batteries so I can find the buckets. Then every man get him a light.'

255

'Here some buckets over here,' Scofield said.

'Then all we got to find is where he keeps the oil.'

'Oil?' I said.

'*Coal* oil, man. And hey, y'all,' he called, 'don't nobody be smoking in here.'

I stood beside Scofield listening to the noise as he took a stack of zinc buckets and passed them out. Now the store leaped alive with flashing lights and flickering shadows.

'Keep them lights down on the floor,' Dupre called. 'No use letting folks see who we are. Now when you get your buckets line up and let me fill 'em.'

'Listen to ole Du lay it down – he's a bitch, ain't he, buddy? He always liked to lead things. And always leading me into trouble.'

'What are we getting ready to do?' I said.

'You'll see,' Dupre said. 'Hey, you over there. Come on from behind that counter and take this bucket. Don't you see ain't nothing in that cash register, that if it was I'd have it myself?'

Suddenly the banging of buckets ceased. We moved into the back room. By the light of a flash I could see a row of fuel drums mounted on racks. Dupre stood before them in his new hip boots and filled each bucket with oil. We moved in slow order. Our buckets filled, we filed out into the street. I stood there in the dark feeling a rising excitement as their voices played around me. What was the meaning of it all? What should I think of it, *do* about it?

'With this stuff,' Dupre said, 'we better walk in the middle of the street. It's just down around the corner.'

Then as we moved off a group of boys ran among us and the men started using their lights, revealing darting figures in blonde wigs, the tails of their stolen dress coats flying. Behind them in hot pursuit came a gang armed with dummy rifles taken from an Army & Navy Store. I laughed with the other, thinking: A holy holiday for Clifton.

'Put out them lights!' Dupre commanded.

Behind us came the sound of screams, laughter; ahead the footfalls of the running boys, distant fire trucks, shooting, and in the quiet intervals, the steady filtering of shattered glass. I could smell the kerosene as it sloshed from the buckets and slapped against the street.

Suddenly Scofield grabbed my arm. 'Good God, look-a-yonder!'

256

And I saw a crowd of men running up pulling a Borden's milk wagon, on top of which, surrounded by a row of railroad flares, a huge woman in a gingham pinafore sat drinking beer from a barrel which sat before her. The men would run furiously a few paces and stop, resting between the shafts, run a few paces and rest, shouting and laughing and drinking from a jug, as she on top threw back her head and shouted passionately in a full-throated voice of blues singer's timbre:

'If it hadn't been for the referee,
Joe Louis woulda killed
Jim Jeffrie
Free beer!'

– sloshing the dipper of beer around.

We stepped aside, amazed, as she bowed graciously from side to side like a tipsy fat lady in a circus parade, the dipper like a gravy spoon in her enormous hand. Then she laughed and drank deeply while reaching over nonchalantly with her free hand to send quart after quart of milk crashing into the street. And all the time the men running with the wagon over the debris. Around me there were shouts of laughter and disapproval.

'Somebody better stop them fools,' Scofield said in outrage. 'That's what I call taking things too far. Goddam, how the hell they going to get her down from there after she gits fulla beer? Somebody answer me that. How they going to get her down? 'Round here throwing away all that good milk!'

The big woman left me unnerved. Milk and beer – I felt sad, watching the wagon careen dangerously as they went around a corner. We went on, avoiding the broken bottles as now the spilling kerosene splashed into the pale spilt milk. How much has happened? Why was I torn? We moved around a corner. My head still ached.

Scofield touched my arm. 'Here we is,' he said.

We had come to a huge tenement building.

'Where are we?' I said.

'This is the place where most of us live,' he said. 'Come on.'

So that was it, the meaning of the kerosene. I couldn't believe it, couldn't believe they had the nerve. All the windows seemed empty. They'd blacked it out themselves. I saw now only by flash or flame.

'Where will you live?' I said, looking up, up.

'You call *this* living?' Scofield said. 'It's the only way to git rid of it, man. . . '

I looked for hesitation in their vague forms. They stood looking at the building rising above us, the liquid dark of the oil simmering dully in the stray flecks of light that struck their pails, bent forward, their shoulders bowed. None said 'no', by word or stance. And in the dark windows and on the roofs above I could now discern the forms of women and children.

Dupre moved towards the building.

'Now look ahere, y'all,' he said, his triple-hatted head showing grotesquely atop the stoop. 'I wants all the women and chillun and the old and the sick folks brought out. And when you takes your buckets up the stairs I wants you to go clean to the top. I mean the *top*! And when you git there I want you to start using your flashlights in every room to make sure nobody gits left behind, then when you git 'em out start splashing coal oil. Then when you git it splashed I'm going to holler, and when I holler three times I want you to light them matches and git. After that it's every tub on its own black bottom!'

It didn't occur to me to interfere, or to question. . . They had a plan. Already I could see the women and children coming down the steps. A child was crying. And suddenly everyone paused, turning, looking off into the dark. Somewhere nearby an incongruous sound shook the dark, an air hammer pounding like a machine gun. They paused with the sensitivity of grazing deer, then returned to their work, the women and children once more moving.

'That's right, y'all. You ladies move on up the street to the folks you going to stay with,' Dupre said. 'And keep holt them kids!'

Someone pounded my back and I swung around, seeing a woman push past me and climb up to catch Dupre's arm, their two figures seeming to blend as her voice arose, thin, vibrant and desperate.

'Please, Dupre,' she said, '*please*. You know my time's almost here. . . you *know* it is. If you do it now, where am I going to go?'

Dupre pulled away and rose to a higher step. He looked down at her, shaking his thrice-hatted head. 'Now git on out the way, Lottie,' he said patiently. 'Why you have to start this now? We done been all over it and you know I ain't go'n change. And lissen here, the resta y'all,' he said, reaching into the top of his hip boot and producing a nickel-plated revolver and waving it around, 'don't think they's going to be any *mind*-changing either. And I don't aim for no arguments neither.'

'You goddam right, Dupre. We wid you!'

'My kid died from the t-bees in that deathtrap, but I bet a man ain't no more go'n be *born* in there,' he said. 'So now, Lottie, you go on up the street and let us mens git going.'

She stood back, crying. I looked at her, in house shoes, her breasts turgid, her belly heavy and high. In the crowd, women's hands took her away, her large liquid eyes turned for a second towards the man in the rubber boots.

What type of man is he, what would Jack say of him? Jack. *Jack*? And where was he in this?

'Let's go, buddy,' Scofield said, nudging me. I followed him, filled with a sense of Jack's outrageous unreality. We went in, up the stairs, flashing our lights. Ahead I saw Dupre moving. He was a type of man nothing in my life had taught me to see, to understand, or respect, a man outside the scheme till now. We entered rooms littered with the signs of swift emptying. It was hot, close.

'This here's my own apartment,' Scofield said. 'And ain't the bedbugs going to get a surprise!'

We slopped the kerosene about, upon an old mattress, along the floor; then moved into the hall, using the flashlights. From all through the building came the sounds of footsteps, of splashing oil, the occasional prayerful protest of some old one being forced to leave. The men worked in silence now, like moles deep in the earth. Time seemed to hold. No one laughed. Then from below came Dupre's voice.

'Okay, mens. We got everybody out. Now starting with the top floor I want you to start striking matches. Be careful and don't set yourself on fire. . .'

There was still some kerosene left in Scofield's bucket and I saw him pick up a rag and drop it in; then came the sputtering of a match and I saw the room leap to flame. The heat flared up and I backed away. He stood there silhouetted against the red flare, looking into the flames, shouting.

'Goddam you rotten sonsabitches. You didn't think I'd do it but there it is. You wouldn't fix it up. Now see how you like it.'

'Let's go,' I said.

Below us, men shot downstairs five and six steps at a time,

moving in the weird light of flash and flame in long, dream-bounds. On each floor as I passed, smoke and flame arose. And now I was seized with a fierce sense of exaltation. They've done it, I thought. They organized it and carried it through alone; the decision their own and their own action. Capable of their own action. . .

There came a thunder of footfalls above me, someone calling, 'Keep going man, it's hell upstairs. Somebody done opened the door to the roof and them flames is leaping.'

'Come on,' Scofield said.

I moved, feeling something slip and was half-way down the next flight before realizing that my brief case was gone. For a second I hesitated, but I'd had it too long to leave it now.

'Come on, buddy,' Scofield called, 'we caint be fooling around.'

'In a second,' I said.

Men were shooting past. I bent over, holding on to the handrail and shouldered my way back up the stairs, using my flash along each step, back slowly, finding it, an oily footstep embedded with crushed pieces of plaster showing upon its leather side; getting it now and turning to bound down again. The oil won't come off easily, I thought with a pang. But this was it, what I had known was coming around the dark corner of my mind, had known and tried to tell the committee and which they had ignored. I plunged down, shaking with fierce excitement.

At the landing I saw a bucket half full of kerosene and seized it, flinging it impulsively into a burning room. A huge puff of smoke-fringed flame filled the doorway, licking outward towards me. I ran, choking and coughing as I plunged. They did it themselves, I thought, holding my breath – planned it, organized it, applied the flame.

I burst into the air and the exploding sounds of the night. . .

CHAPTER 14

HEARTLESS NEW YORK

Walt Whitman, a great defender of New York City, nonetheless felt obliged to give this advice to tourists in 1856.

ADVICE TO TOURISTS

Don't go wandering about the streets or parks unnecessarily in the evening. The degrading confession and warning is necessary, that New York is one of the most crime-haunted and dangerous cities in Christendom. There are hundreds – thousands – of infernal rascals among our floating population; street boys, grown up into rowdies, and the brutal scum of vile city ignorance and filth; shoulder-hitters and thieves, expelled, some of them, from distant San Francisco, vomited back among us to practice their criminal occupations, who will sneak up behind you, or pretend drunkenness and run against you, or inquire the way, or the hour, and snatch your watch, or take you unawares, like Brooks, knock you on the head, and rob you before you can even cry out. If you have evening errands, go circumspectly through respectable streets. If you are lost, ask a direction at a respectable store, or from the blue-coated and starred policeman, whom you will probably discern every square or two.

Here is an anonymous account from 1874 of the waterfront neighborhood now redeveloped as the South Street Seaport.

WATER STREET

The neighborhood of Water Street is about the most notorious in the metropolis for deeds of violence, flagrant vice, and scenes of debauchery. It abounds in lodging-houses for sailors, liquor-stores of the lowest class without number, dance-houses and concert saloons (at the very thought of which poor Decency hides her eyes in agony), and various other low places of amusement. Brothels of the worst description swarm in all directions; the wretched, half-drunken, shameless inmates being permitted by the police to flaunt their sin and finery and ply their hateful trade openly by day or night, without let or hinderance. The mixture and recklessness of vice, the unblushing effrontery with which it is carried on, the barefaced employment of loose women to entrap sailors, and the apparent carelessness or interestedness of the authorities in not suppressing these resorts, is a standing disgrace to the city of New York. The infamous proprietors of these dance and sailors' lodging-houses seem to consider that a staff of prostitutes is a necessary part of their stock in trade; a stock, if any thing, more remunerative than the sale of their villainous whisky.

At night the quarrels, fights, and noisy disturbances, make the darkness hideous, and are of such frequency that none can hope for a night's rest until they have been inured by habit to the ways and doings of this terrestrial pandemonium. Fights and desparate encounters among intoxicated men and women occur night after night and are looked upon as a regular part of the twenty-four hours' programme. Sailors, canalmen, dockmen, and landsmen, are continually fighting about the women who are *attachées* to these establishments, and it is only too common to see the most desparate encounters between the women themselves, who become perfect demons under such circumstances, and to see the lookers-on encourage the combatants instead of separating them. These wretched creatures have arrived at such a pass that they are actually compelled to madden themselves with drink in order to become sufficiently immoral and disgusting. The use of deadly weapons, too, is so common that murder provokes no sentiment of horror among the denizens of Water Street, but only excites in them a morbid curiosity to see the murderer as he is hurried off to jail by the police – if they know him, to shake him by the hand, and, if possible, to catch a glimpse of the murdered man.

And, if they have homes, what are they? The men, too often confirmed drunkards, and consequently continually out of work and unable to support their families honestly; the women – oh, horrible thought! earning the wages of sin with the consent of their husbands; the children literally brought up in the gutter; clothes, furniture, bedding, all gone to the pawnshop; the whole family huddled together at night on a dirty husk or straw mattress, or on the bare boards in one ill-built, badly-ventilated, and filthy room, where any pretense at decency is impossible. What is the inevitable result? The men and women only care for their daily allowance of rum, no matter how obtained; the boys are all thieves at ten years of age; at fourteen, the girls are all prostitutes.

The Irish were the first major immigrant group to make their mark in New York. In the wake of the famine of 1848 their numbers in America rapidly increased. Often employed as casual laborers, exploited by employers, landlords, and politicians, their life in those early days was difficult by any standards. John Maguire, an Irish journalist and politician (he sat as an Irish Independant for Cork in the House of Commons), visited America in 1866 to survey the conditions of his fellow countrymen in the New World. In his book, The Irish in America, *he recounts this tale of the plight of two new immigrants.*

COMPATRIOTS

The law also attempted to regulate the charges in boarding-houses, and protect the luggage of the emigrant from the clutches of the proprietors of these establishments; but it appeared only to render the lot of the emigrant one of still greater hardship; for what could no longer be legally retained was illegally made away with. In their Report for 1848, the Commissioners refer to the new system adopted in these houses:–'Of late, robberies of luggage from emigrant boarding-houses have become of frequent occurrence, so as to have excited the suspicion that in some instances the keepers of the houses are not altogether free from participation in the robbery. If the tavern keeper has reason to apprehend that the lodger will not be able to pay his bill, and knowing that the law prohibits his retaining the luggage, he may think it proper to secure his claim without law.'

I must confess to being immensely amused at hearing from one who had passed through the ordeal how he had been dealt with in the fine old time of unrestricted plunder, when the emigrant was left to his fate – that fate assuming the substantial form of the runner and the boarding-house keeper. My informant was a great, broad-shouldered, red-haired Irishman, over six feet 'in his stocking vamps,' and who, I may add, on the best authority, bore himself gallantly in the late war, under the banner of the Union. He was but a very young lad when, in 1848, he came to New York, with a companion of his own age, 'to better his fortune,' as many a good Irishman had endeavoured to do before him. He possessed, besides splendid health and a capacity for hard work, a box of tools, a bundle of clothes, and a few pounds in gold – not a bad outfit for a good-tempered young Irishman, with a red head, broad shoulders, grand appetite, and fast rising to the six feet.

The moment he landed his luggage was pounced upon by two runners, one seizing the box of tools, the other confiscating the clothes. The future American citizen assured his obliging friends that he was quite capable of carrying his own luggage; but no, they should relieve him – the stranger, and guest of the Republic – of that trouble. Each was in the interest of a different boarding-house, and each insisted that the young Irishman with the red head should go with him – a proposition that, to any but a New York runner, would seem, if not altogether impossible, at least most difficult of accomplishment. Not being able to oblige both the gentlemen, he could only oblige one; and as the tools were more valuable than the clothes, he followed in the path of the gentleman who had secured that portion of the 'plunder.' He remembers that the two gentlemen wore very pronounced green neckties, and spoke with a richness of accent that denoted special if not conscientious cultivation; and on his arrival at the boarding-house, he was cheered with the announcement that its proprietor was from 'the ould counthry, and loved every sod of it, God bless it!' In a manner truly paternal the host warned the two lads against the danger of the streets; and so darkly did he paint the horrors, and villanies, and murders of all kinds, that were sure to rain down upon their innocent heads, that the poor boys were frightened into a rigid seclusion from the world outside, and occupied their time as best they could, not forgetting 'the eating and the drinking' which the house afforded. The young Irishman with the red head imparted to the host the fact of his having a friend in Canal Street – 'wherever Canal Street was;' and that the friend had been some six years in New York, and knew the place well, and was to procure employment for him as soon as they met; and he concluded by asking how he could get to Canal Street. 'Canal Street! – is it Canal Street? – why then what a mortal pity, and the stage to go just an hour before you entered this very door! My, my! that's unfortunate; isn't it? Well, no matter, there'll be another in two days' time, or three at farthest, and I'll be sure to see you sent there all right – depend your life on me when I say it,' said the jovial kindly host. For full forty-eight hours the two lads, who were as innocent as a brace of young goslings, endured the irksome monotony of the boarding-house, even though that abode of hospitality was cheered by the presence of its jovial host, who loved every sod of the 'ould counthry;' but human nature cannot endure beyond a certain limit – and the two lads resolved, in sheer desperation, to break bounds at any hazard. They roamed through the streets for some time, without any special ill befalling them. Meeting a policeman, the young fellow with the red head suggested to his companion the possibility of the official knowing something about Canal Street; and as his companion had nothing to urge against it, they approached that functionary, and boldly propounded the question to him – where Canal Street was, and how it could be reached? 'Why, then, my man,' replied the policeman, who also happened to be a compatriot, 'if you only follow your nose for the space of twenty minutes in that direction, you'll come to Canal Street, and no mistake about it; you'll see the name on the corner, in big letters, if you can read – as I suppose you can, for you look to be two decent boys.' Canal Street in twenty minutes! Here indeed was a pleasant surprise for the young fellows, who had been told to wait for the stage, which, according to the veracious host, 'was due in about another day.' Of course they did follow their respective noses until they actually reached Canal Street, found the number of the house in which their friend resided, and discovered the friend himself, to whom they recounted their brief adventures in New York. Thanks to the smartness of their acclimated friend, they recovered their effects, but not before they disbursed to the jovial host, who 'loved every sod of the ould counthry, God bless it!' more than would have enabled them to fare sumptuously at the Astor. And as the great strapping fellow – who had since seen many a brave man die with his face to the foe – told the tale of his first introduction to the Empire City, he actually looked sheepish at its recollection, and then laughed heartily at a simplicity which had long since become, with him, a weakness of the past.

From Manhattan Transfer, *by John Dos Passos.*

A NEWCOMER IN NEW YORK

With a long slow stride, limping a little from his blistered feet, Bud walked down Broadway, past empty lots where tin cans glittered among grass and sumach bushes and ragweed, between ranks of billboards and Bull Durham signs, past shanties and abandoned squatters' shacks, past gulches heaped with wheel-scarred rubbishpiles where dumpcarts were dumping ashes and clinkers, past knobs of gray outcrop where steamdrills continually tapped and nibbled, past excavations out of which wagons full of rock and clay toiled up plank roads to the street, until he was walking on new sidewalks along a row of yellow brick apartment houses, looking in the windows of grocery stores, Chinese laundries, lunchrooms, flower and vegetable shops, tailors', delicatessens. Passing under a scaffolding in front of a new building, he caught the eye of an old man who sat on the edge of the sidewalk trimming oil lamps. Bud stood beside him, hitching up his pants; cleared his throat:

'Say mister you couldnt tell a feller where a good place was to look for a job?'

'Aint no good place to look for a job, young feller. . . There's jobs all right. . . I'll be sixty-five years old in a month and four days an I've worked sence I was five I reckon, an I aint found a good job yet.'

'Anything that's a job'll do me.'

'Got a union card?'

'I aint got nothin.'

'Cant git no job in the buildin trades without a union card,' said the old man. He rubbed the gray bristles of his chin with the back of his hand and leaned over the lamps again. Bud stood staring into the dustreeking girder forest of the new building until he found the eyes of a man in a derby hat fixed on him through the window of the watchman's shelter. He shuffled his feet uneasily and walked on. If I could git more into the center of things. . .

At the next corner a crowd was collecting round a high-slung white automobile. Clouds of steam poured out of its rear end. A policeman was holding up a small boy by the armpits. From the car a redfaced man with white walrus whiskers was talking angrily.

'I tell you officer he threw a stone. . . . This sort of thing has got to stop. For an officer to countenance hoodlums and rowdies. . . .'

A woman with her hair done up in a tight bunch on top of her head was screaming, shaking her fist at the man in the car, 'Officer he near run me down he did, he near run me down.'

Bud edged up next to a young man in a butcher's apron who had a baseball cap on backwards.

'Wassa matter?'

'Hell I dunno. . . One o them automoebile riots I guess. Aint you read the paper? I dont blame em do you? What right have those golblamed automoebiles got racin round the city knockin down wimen an children?'

'Gosh do they do that?'

'Sure they do.'

'Say. . . er. . . kin you tell me about where's a good place to find out about gettin a job?' The butcherboy threw back head and laughed.

'Kerist I thought you was goin to ask for a handout. . . I guess you aint a Newyorker. . . I'll tell you what to do. You keep right on down Broadway till you get to City Hall. . . '

'Is that kinder the center of things?'

'Sure it is. . . An then you go upstairs and ask the Mayor. . . Tell me there are some seats on the board of aldermen. . . '

'Like hell they are,' growled Bud and walked away fast.

Thomas Wolfe (1900-1938) was born in Asheville, North Carolina. He arrived in New York City in 1924 and lived there off and on for the rest of his life. His first novel, Look Homeward, Angel, *was published in 1929. This story is from the collection,* From Death to Morning, *published in 1935.*

ONLY THE DEAD KNOW BROOKLYN

Dere's no guy living' dat knows Brooklyn t'roo an' t'roo, because it'd take a guy a lifetime just to find his way aroun' duh ———— town.

So like I say, I'm waitin' for my train t' come when I sees dis big guy standin' deh–dis is duh foist I eveh see of him. Well, he's lookin' wild, y'know, an' I can see dat he's had plenty, but still he's holdin' it; he talks good an' is walkin' straight enough. So den, dis big guy steps up to a little guy dat's standin' deh, an' says, 'How d'yuh get t' Eighteent' Avenoo an' Sixty sevent' Street?' he says.

'Jesus! Yuh got me, chief,' duh little guy says to him. 'I ain't been heah long myself. Where is duh place?' he says. 'Out in duh Flatbush section somewhere?'

'Nah,' duh big guy says. 'It's out in Bensonhoist. But I was never deh befoeh. How d'yuh get deh?'

'Jesus,' duh little guy says, scratchin' his head, y'know – yuh could see duh little guy didn't know his way about – 'yuh got me, chief. I neveh hoid of it. Do any of youse guys know where it is?' he says to me.

'Sure,' I says. 'It's out in Bensonhoist. Yuh take duh Fourt' Avenoo express, get off at Fifty-nint' Street, change to a Sea Beach local deh, get off at Eighteent' Avenoo an' Sixty-toid, an' den walk down foeh blocks. Dat's all yuh got to do,' I says.

'G'wan!' some wise guy dat I neveh seen befoeh pipes up. 'Whatcha talkin' about?' he says – oh, he was wise, y'know. 'Duh guy is crazy! I tell yuh what yuh do,' he says to duh big guy. 'Yuh change to duh West End line at Toity-sixt',' he tells him. 'Get off at Noo Utrecht an' Sixteent' Avenoo,' he says. 'Walk two blocks oveh, foeh blocks up,' he says, 'an' you'll be right deh.' Oh, a *wise* guy, y'know.

'Oh, yeah?' I says. 'Who told *you* so much?' He got me sore because he was so wise about it. 'How long you been livin' heah?' I says.

'All my life,' he says. 'I was bawn in Williamsboig,' he says. 'An' I can tell you t'ings about dis town you neveh hoid of,' he says.

'Yeah?' I says.

'Yeah,' he says.

'Well, den, you can tell me t'ings about dis town dat nobody else has eveh hoid of, either. Maybe you make it all up yoehself at night,' I says, 'befoeh you go to sleep – like cuttin' out papeh dolls, or somp'n.'

'Oh, yeah?' he says. 'You're pretty wise, ain't yuh?'

'Oh, I don't know,' I says. 'Duh boids ain't usin' my head for Lincoln's statue yet,' I says. 'But I'm wise enough to know a phony when I see one.'

'Yeah?' he says. 'A wise guy, huh? Well, you're so wise dat some one's goin' t'bust yuh one right on duh snoot some day,' he says. 'Dat's how wise *you* are.'

Well, my train was comin', or I'da smacked him den and dere, but when I seen duh train was coming', all I said was, 'All right, mugg! I'm sorry I can't stay to take keh of you, but I'll be seein' yuh sometime, I hope, out in duh cemetery.' So den I says to duh big guy, who'd been standin' deh all duh time, 'You come wit me,' I says. So when we gets onto duh train I says to him, 'Where yuh goin' out in Bensonhoist?' I says. 'What numbeh are yuh lookin for?' I says. *You* know – I t'ought if he told me duh address I might be able to help him out.

'Oh,' he says, 'I'm not lookin' for no one. I don't know no one out deh.'

'Then watcha goin' out deh for?' I says.

'Oh,' duh guy says, 'I'm just goin' out to see duh place,' he says. 'I like duh sound of duh name – Bensonhoist, y'know – so I t'ought I'd go out an' have a look at it.'

'Whatcha tryin' t'hand me?' I says. 'Whatcha tryin' t'do – kid me?' *You* know, I t'ought duh guy was bein' wise wit' me.

'No,' he says, 'I'm tellin' yuh duh troot. I like to go out an' take a look at these places wit nice names like dat. I like to go out an' look at all kinds of places,' he says.

'How'd yuh know deh was such a place,' I says, 'if yuh neveh been deh befoeh?'

'Oh,' he says, 'I got a map.'

'A *map?*' I says.

'Sure,' he says, 'I got a map dat tells me about all dese places. I take it wit me every time I come out heah,' he says.

And Jesus! Wit dat, he pulls it out of his pocket, an' so help me, but he's *got* it – he's tellin' duh troot – a big map of duh whole —— place with all duh different pahts mahked out. You know – Canarsie an' East Noo Yawk an' Flatbush, Bensonhoist, Sout' Brooklyn, duh Heights, Bay Ridge, Greenpernt – duh whole goddam layout, he's got it right deh on duh map.

'You been to any of dose places?' I says.

'Sure,' he says, 'I been to most of 'em. I was down in Red Hook just last night,' he says.

'Jesus! Red Hook!' I says. 'Watcha do down deh?'

'Oh' he says, 'nuttin' much. I just walked aroun'. I went into a coupla places an' had a drink,' he says, 'but most of the time I just walked aroun'.'

'Just walked aroun'?' I says.

'Sure,' he says, 'just lookin' at t'ings, y'know.'

'Where'd yuh go?' I asts him.

'Oh,' he says, 'I don't know duh name of duh place, but I could find it on my map,' he says. 'One time I was walkin' across some big fields where deh ain't no houses,' he says, 'but I could see ships oveh deh all lighted up. Dey was loadin'. So I walks across

270

duh fields,' he says, 'to where duh ships are.'

'Sure,' I says, 'I know where you was. You was down to duh Erie Basin.'

'Yeah,' he says, 'I guess dat was it. Dey had some of dose big elevators an' cranes an' dey was loadin' ships, an' I could see some ships in dry dock all lighted up, so I walks across duh fields to where dey are,' he says.

'Den what did yuh do?' I says.

'Oh,' he says, 'nuttin' much. I came on back across duh fields after a while an' went into a coupla places an' had a drink.'

'Didn't nuttin' happen while yuh was in dere?' I says.

'No,' he says. 'Nuttin' much. A coupla guys was drunk in one of duh places an' started a fight, but dey bounced 'em out,' he says, 'an' den one of duh guys stahted to come back again, but duh bartender gets his baseball bat out from under duh counteh, so duh guy goes on.'

'Jesus!' I said. 'Red Hook!'

'Sure,' he says. 'Dat's where it was, all right.'

'Well, you keep outa deh,' I says. 'You stay away from deh.'

'Why?' he says. 'What's wrong wit it?'

'Oh,' I says, 'it's a good place to stay away from, dat's all. It's a good place to keep out of.'

'Why?' he says. 'Why is it?'

Jesus! Whatcha gonna do wit a guy as dumb as dat? I saw it wasn't no use to try to tell him nuttin', he wouldn't know what I was talkin' about, so I just says to him, 'Oh, nuttin'. Yuh might get lost down deh, dat's all.'

'Lost?' he says. 'No, I wouldn't get lost. I got a map,' he says. A map! Red Hook! Jesus!

So den duh guy begins to ast me all kinds of nutty questions: how big was Brooklyn an' could I find my way aroun' in it, an' how long would it take a guy to know duh place.

'Listen!' I says. 'You get dat idea outa yoeh head right now,' I says. 'You ain't neveh gonna get to know Brooklyn,' I says. 'Not in a hundred yeahs. I been livin' heah all my life,' I says, 'an' I don't even know all deh is to know about it, so how do you expect to know duh town,' I says, 'when you don't even live heah?'

'Yes,' he says, 'but I got a map to help me find my way about.'

'Map or no map,' I says, 'yuh ain't gonna get to know Brooklyn wit no map,' I says.

'Can you swim?' he says, just like dat. Jesus! By dat time,

y'know, I begun to see dat duh guy was some kind of nut. He'd had plenty to drink, of course, but had dat crazy look in his eye I didn't like. 'Can you swim?' he says.

'Sure,' I says. 'Can't you?'

'No,' he says. 'Not more'n a stroke or two. I neveh loined good.'

'Well, it's easy,' I says. 'All yuh need is a little confidence. Duh way I loined, me older bruddeh pitched me off duh dock one day when I was eight yeahs old, cloes an' all. 'You'll swim,' he says. 'You'll swim all right – or drown.' An', believe me, I *swam!* When yuh know yuh got to, you'll do it. Duh only t'ing yuh need is confidence. An' once you've loined,' I says, 'you've got nuttin' else to worry about. You'll neveh forget it. It's somp'n dat stays wit yuh as long as yuh live.'

'Can yuh swim good?' he says.

'Like a fish,' I tells him. 'I'm a regulah fish in duh wateh,' I says. 'I loined to swim right off duh docks wit all duh oddeh kids,' I says.

'What would you do if yuh saw a man drownin'?' duh guy says.

'Do? Why, I'd jump in an' pull him out,' I says. 'Dat's what I'd do.'

'Did yuh eveh see a man drown?' he says.

'Sure,' I says. 'I see two guys – bot' times at Coney Island. Dey got out too far, an' neider one could swim. Dey drowned befoeh anyone could get to 'em.'

'What becomes of people after dey've drowned out heah?' he says.

'Drowned out where?' I says.

'Out heah in Brooklyn.'

'I don't know whatcha mean,' I says, 'Neveh hoid of no one drownin' heah in Brooklyn, unless you mean a swimmin' pool. Yuh can't drown in Brooklyn,' I says. 'Yuh gotta drown somewhere else – in duh ocean, where dere's wateh.'

'Drownin',' duh guy says, lookin' at his map. 'Drownin'.' Jesus! I could see by den he was some kind of nut, he had dat crazy expression in his eyes when he looked at you, an' I didn't know what he might do. So we was comin' to a station, an' it wasn't my stop, but I got off anyway, an' waited for duh next train.

'Well, so long chief,' I says. 'Take it easy, now.'

'Drownin',' duh guy says, lookin' at his map. 'Drownin'.'

Jesus! I've t'ought about dat guy a t'ousand times since den an' wondered what eveh happened to 'm goin' out to look at Bensonhoist because he liked duh name! Walkin' aroun' t'roo Red Hook by himself at night an' lookin' at his map! How many people did I see get drowned out heah in Brooklyn! How long would it take a guy wit a good map to know all deh was to know about Brooklyn!

Jesus! What a nut *he* was! I wondeh what eveh happened to 'im, anyway! I wondeh if someone knocked him on duh head, or if he's still wanderin' aroun' in duh subway in duh middle of duh night wit his little map! Duh poor guy! Say, I've got to laugh, at dat, when I t'ink about him! Maybe he's found out by now dat he'll neveh live long enough to know duh whole of Brooklyn. It'd take a guy a lifetime to know Brooklyn t'roo an' t'roo. An' even den, you wouldn't know it all.

The poet e. e. cummings (1894-1962) was born in Massachusetts but lived most of his adult life in Greenwich Village. He developed an idiosyncratic style which could be highly effective in capturing the rhythms and diction of the language of the streets, as in this untitled poem.

> buncha hardboil guys from duh A.C. fulla
> hooch kiddin eachudder bout duh clap an
> talkin big how dey could kill
> sixereight cops – "I sidesteps im an draws
> back huly jeezus" – an – "my
> speciality is takin fellers' goils away
> frum dem" – "somebody hung uh gun on
> Marcus" – "duh Swede rolls down tree flights an Sam
> begins boxin im on duh
> koib" – you
> know
> alotta sweet bull like dat
>   . . . suddenly
> i feels so lonely fer duh good ole days we
> spent in '18 kickin duh guts outa dem
> doity frogeaters an humpin duh
> swell janes on
> duh boollevares an wid tears

streamin down my face i hauls
out uh flask an offers it tuh duh whole gang accrost
duh table – "fellers
have some
on
me" – dey was petrified.

De room swung roun an crawled up into
itself
an awful big light squoits down my spine like
i was dead er sumpn:next i

knows me(er
somebody is sittin in uh green
field watchin four crows drop into
sunset,playin uh busted harmonica

The novelist James Baldwin, though born in Harlem in 1924, spent much of his life abroad. In Another Country *(1962) he describes the feelings of a Black New Yorker on his return to the City after an absence of several years.*

A NATIVE RETURNS

New York seemed very strange indeed. It might, almost, for strange barbarity of manner and custom, for the sense of danger and horror barely sleeping beneath the rough, gregarious surface, have been some impenetrably exotic city of the East. So superbly was it in the present that it seemed to have nothing to do with the passage of time: time might have dismissed it as thoroughly as it had dismissed Carthage and Pompeii. It seemed to have no sense whatever of the exigencies of human life; if was so familiar and so public that it became, at last, the most despairingly private of cities. One was continually being jostled, yet longed, at the same time, for the sense of others, for a human touch; and if one was never – it was the general complaint – left alone in New York, one had, still, to fight very hard in order not to perish of loneliness. This fight, carried on in so many different ways, created the strange climate of the city. The girls along Fifth Avenue wore their bright clothes like semaphores, trying helplessly to bring to the male attention the news of their mysterious trouble. The men could not read this message. They strode purposefully along, wearing little anonymous hats, or bareheaded, with youthfully parted hair, or crew cuts, accoutred with attaché cases, rushing, on the evidence, to the smoking cars of trains. In this haven, they opened up their newspapers and caught up on the day's bad news. Or they were to be found, as five o'clock fell, in discreetly dim, anonymously appointed bars, uneasy, in brittle, uneasy, female company, pouring down joyless martinis.

This note of despair, of buried despair, was insistently, constantly struck. It stalked all the New York avenues, roamed all the New York streets; was as present in Sutton Place, where the director of Eric's play lived and the great often gathered, as it was in Greenwich Village, where he had rented an apartment and been appalled to see what time had done to people he had once known well. He could not escape the feeling that a kind of plague was raging, though it was officially and publicly and privately denied. Even the young seemed blighted – seemed most blighted of all. The boys in their blue jeans ran together, scarcely daring to trust one another, but united, like their elders, in a boyish distrust of the girls. Their very walk, a kind of anti-erotic, knee-action lope, was a parody of locomotion and of manhood. They seemed to be shrinking away from any contact with their flamboyantly and paradoxically outlined private parts. They seemed – but could it be true? and how had it happened? to be at home with, accustomed to, brutality and indifference, and to be terrified of human affection. In some strange way they did not seem to feel that they were worthy of it.

Kathy Acker, contemporary writer and New Yorker, author of Blood and Guts in High School, *imagined this scene in front of the once-trendy Mudd Club, in her short story* New York City in 1979.

IN FRONT OF THE MUDD CLUB

Two rich couples drop out of a limousine. The women are wearing outfits the poor people who were in ten years ago wore ten years ago. The men are just neutral. All the poor people who're making this club fashionable so the rich want to hang out here, even though the poor still never make a buck off the rich pleasure, are sitting on cars, watching the rich people walk up to the club.

Some creeps around the club's entrance. An open-shirted skinny guy who say's he's just an artist is choosing who he'll let into the club. Since it's 3:30 a.m. there aren't many creeps. The artist won't let the rich hippies into the club.

—Look at that car.

—Jesus. It's those rich hippies' car.

—Let's take it.

—That's the chauffeur over there.

—Let's kidnap him.

—Let's knock him over the head with a bottle.

—I don't want no terrorism. I wanna go for a ride.

—That's right. We've got nothing to do with terrorism. We'll just explain we want to borrow the car for an hour.

—Maybe he'll lend us the car if we explain we're terrorists-in-training. We want to use that car to try out terrorist tricks.

After 45 minutes the rich people climb back into their limousine and their chauffeur drives them away.

A girl who has gobs of brown hair like the foam on a cappuccino in Little Italy, black patent leather S&M heels, two unfashionable tits stuffed into a pale green corset, and extremely fashionable black fake leather tights heaves her large self off a car top. She's holding an empty bottle.

Diego senses there's going to be trouble. He gets off his car top. Is walking slowly towards the girl.

The bottle keeps waving. Finally the girl finds some courage heaves the bottle at the skinny entrance artist.

The girl and the artist battle it out up the street. Some of the people who are sitting on cars separate them. We see the girl throw herself back on a car top. Her tits are bouncing so hard she must want our attention and she's getting insecure, maybe violent, cause she isn't getting enough. Better give us a better show. She sticks her middle finger into the air as far as she can. She writhes around on top of the car. Her movements are so spasmatic she must be nuts.

A yellow taxi cab is slowly making its way to the club. On one side of this taxi cab's the club entrance. The other side is the girl writ(h)ing away on the black car. Three girls who are pretending to be transvestites are lifting themselves out of the cab elegantly around the big girl's body. The first body is encased into a translucent white girdle. A series of diagonal panels leads directly to her cunt. The other two dresses are tight and white. They are wriggling their way toward the club. The big girl, whom the taxi driver refused to let in his cab, wriggling because she's been rejected but not wriggling as much, is bumping into them. They're tottering away from her because she has syphilis.

It's four o'clock a.m. It's still too hot. Wet heat's squeezing this city. The air's mist. The liquid's that seeping out of human flesh pores is gonna harden into a smooth shiny shell so we're going to become reptiles.

No one wants to move anymore. No one wants to be in a body. Physical possessions can go to hell even in this night.

Now the big girl is unsuccessfully trying to climb through a private white car's window now she's running hips hooking even faster into an alleyway taxi whose driver is locking his doors and windows against her. She's offering him a blow-job. Now an ugly boy with a huge safety pin stuck through his upper lip, walking up and down the street, is shooting at us with his watergun.

The dyke sitting next to me is saying earlier in the evening she pulled at this safety pin.

Grandmaster Flash and the Furious Five had a hit in 1982 with their soul rap The Message.

THE MESSAGE

Don't push me
Cause I'm close to the edge
I'm trying not
To lose my head

It's like a jungle sometimes
It makes me wonder
How I keep from going under

Broken glass everywhere
People pissing on the stair
You know they just don't care

277

I can't take the smell
Can't take the noise
Got no money to move on
Guess I got no choice

Rats in the front room
Roaches in the back
Junky in the alleyway
With a baseball bat
I tried to get away
Couldn't get far
Cause the man from Prudential
Reposessed my car

Don't push me
Cause I'm close to the edge
I'm trying not
To lose my head

It's like a jungle sometimes
It makes me wonder
How I keep from going under. . .

My son said daddy I don't want to go to school
The teacher's a jerk
He must think I'm a fool
And all the kids smoke reefer
I think it'd be cheaper
If I just got a job
Learned to be a street sweeper

I dance to the beat
Shuffle my feet
Wear a shirt and tie
Run with the creeps
Cause it's all about money
Ain't a damn thing funny
And you got to have a con
In this land of milk and honey. . .

CHAPTER 15

CHARACTERS

Journalist, sports writer, chronicler of Broadway low-life and master of the old New York street argot, Damon Runyon (1884-1946) wrote this story for Cosmopolitan Magazine *in 1929. It was later filmed twice by Frank Capra, once as* Lady for a Day, *and once again as* Pocketful of Miracles.

MADAME LA GIMP

One night I am passing the corner of Fiftieth Street and Broadway, and what do I see but Dave the Dude standing in a doorway talking to a busted-down old Spanish doll by the name of Madame La Gimp. Or rather Madame La Gimp is talking to Dave the Dude, and what is more he is listening to her, because I can hear him say yes, yes, as he always does when he is really listening to anybody, which is very seldom.

Now this is a most surprising sight to me, because Madame La Gimp is not such an old doll as anybody will wish to listen to especially Dave the Dude. In fact, she is nothing but an old haybag, and generally somewhat ginned up. For fifteen years, or maybe sixteen, I see Madame La Gimp up and down Broadway, or sliding through the Forties, sometimes selling newspapers, and sometimes selling flowers, and in all these years I seldom see her but what she seems to have about half a heat on from drinking gin.

Of course nobody ever takes the newspapers she sells, even after they buy them off of her, because they are generally yesterday's papers, and sometimes last week's, and nobody ever wants her flowers, even after they pay her for them because they are flowers such as she gets off an undertaker over in Tenth Avenue, and they are very tired flowers, indeed.

Personally, I consider Madame La Gimp nothing but an old pest, but kind-hearted guys like Dave the Dude always stake her to a few pieces of silver when she comes shuffling along putting on the moan about her tough luck. She walks with a gimp in one leg, which is why she is called Madame La Gimp, and years ago I hear somebody say Madame La Gimp is once a Spanish dancer, and a big shot on Broadway, but that she meets up with an accident which puts her out of the dancing dodge, and that a busted romance makes her become a ginhead.

I remember somebody telling me once that Madame La Gimp is quite a beauty in her day, and has her own servants and all this and that, but I always hear the same thing about every bum on Broadway, male and female, including some I know are bums, in spades, right from taw, so I do not pay any attention to these stories.

Still, I am willing to allow that maybe Madame La Gimp is once a fair looker, at that, and the chances are has a fair shape, because once or twice I see her when she is not ginned up, and has her hair combed, and she is not so bad-looking, although even then if you put her in a claiming race I do not think there is any danger of anybody claiming her out of it.

Mostly she is wearing raggedy clothes, and busted shoes, and her gray hair is generally hanging down her face, and when I say she is maybe fifty years old I am giving her plenty the best of it. Although she is Spanish, Madame La Gimp talks good English, and in fact she can cuss in English as good as anybody I ever hear, barring Dave the Dude.

Well, anyway, when Dave the Dude sees me as he is listening to Madame La Gimp, he motions me to wait, so I wait until she finally gets through gabbing to him and goes gimping away. Then Dave the Dude comes over to me looking much worried.

'This is quite a situation,' Dave says. 'The old doll is in a tough spot. It seems that she once has a baby which she calls by the name of Eulalie, being it is a girl baby, and she ships this baby off to her sister in a little town in Spain to raise up, because Madame La Gimp figures a baby is not apt to get much raising-up off of her as long as she is on Broadway. Well, this baby is on her way here. In fact,' Dave says, 'she will land next Saturday and here it is Wednesday already.'

'Where is the baby's papa?' I ask Dave the Dude.

'Well,' Dave says, 'I do not ask Madame La Gimp this, because I do not consider it a fair question. A guy who goes around this town asking where babies' papas are, or even who they are, is apt to get the name of being nosey. Anyway, this has nothing whatever to do with the proposition, which is that Madame La Gimp's baby, Eulalie, is arriving here.'

'Now,' Dave says, 'it seems that Madame La Gimp's baby, being now eighteen years old, is engaged to marry the son of a very proud old Spanish nobleman who lives in this little town in Spain, and it also seems that the very proud old Spanish nobleman, and his ever-loving wife, and the son, and Madame La Gimp's sister, are all with the baby. They are making a tour of the whole world, and will stop over here a couple of days just to see Madame La Gimp.'

'It is commencing to sound to me like a movie such as a guy is apt to see at a midnight show,' I say.

'Wait a minute,' Dave says, getting impatient. 'You are too gabby to suit me. Now it seems that the proud old Spanish nobleman does not wish his son to marry any lob, and one reason he is coming here is to look over Madame La Gimp, and see that she is okay. He thinks that Madame La Gimp's baby's own papa is dead, and that Madame La Gimp is now married to one of the richest and most aristocratic guys in America.'

'How does the proud old Spanish nobleman get such an idea as this?' I ask. 'It is a sure thing he never sees Madame La Gimp, or even a photograph of her as she is at present.'

'I will tell you how,' Dave the Dude says. 'It seems Madame La Gimp gives her baby the idea that such is the case in her letters to her. It seems Madame La Gimp does a little scrubbing business around a swell apartment hotel in Park Avenue that is called the Marberry, and she cops stationery there and writes her baby in Spain on this stationery saying this is where she lives, and how rich and aristocratic her husband is. And what is more, Madame La Gimp has letters from her baby sent to her in care of the hotel and gets them out of the employees' mail.'

'Why,' I say, 'Madame La Gimp is nothing but an old fraud to deceive people in this manner, especially a proud old Spanish nobleman. And,' I say, 'this proud old Spanish nobleman must be something of a chump to believe a mother will keep away from her baby all these years, especially if the mother has plenty of dough, although of course I do not know just how smart a proud old Spanish nobleman can be.'

'Well,' Dave says, 'Madame La Gimp tells me the thing that makes the biggest hit of all with the proud old Spanish nobleman is that she keeps her baby in Spain all these years because she wishes her raised up a true Spanish baby in every respect until she is old enough to know what time it is. But I judge the proud old Spanish nobleman is none too bright, at that,' Dave says, 'because Madame La Gimp tells me he always lives in this little town which does not even have running water in the bathrooms.'

'But what I am getting at is this,' Dave says. 'We must have Madame La Gimp in a swell apartment in the Marberry with a rich and aristocratic guy for a husband by the time her baby gets here, because if the proud old Spanish nobleman finds out Madame La Gimp is nothing but a bum, it is a hundred to one he will cancel his son's engagement to Madame La Gimp's baby and break a lot of people's hearts, including his son's.

'Madame La Gimp tells me her baby is daffy about the young guy, and he is daffy about her, and there are enough broken hearts in this town as it is. I know how I will get the apartment, so you go and bring me Judge Henry G. Blake for a rich and aristocratic husband, or anyway for a husband.'

Well I know Dave the Dude to do many a daffy thing but never a thing as daffy as this. But I know there is no use arguing with him when he gets an idea, because if you argue with Dave the Dude too much he is apt to reach over and lay his Sunday punch on your snoot, and no argument is worth a punch on the snoot, especially from Dave the Dude.

So I go out looking for Judge Henry G. Blake to be Madame La Gimp's husband,. although I am not so sure Judge Henry G. Blake will care to be anybody's husband, and especially Madame La Gimp's after he gets a load of her, for Judge Henry G. Blake is kind of a classy old guy.

To look at Judge Henry G. Blake, with his gray hair, and his nose glasses, and his stomach, you will think he is very important people, indeed. Of course Judge Henry G. Blake is not a judge, and never is a judge, but they call him Judge because he looks like a judge, and talks slow, and puts in many long words, which very few people understand.

They tell me Judge Blake once has plenty of dough, and is quite a guy in Wall Street, and a high shot along Broadway, but he misses a few guesses at the market, and winds up without much dough, as guys generally do who miss guesses at the market. What Judge Henry G. Blake does for a living at this time nobody knows, because he does nothing much whatever, and yet he seems to be a producer in a small way at all times.

Now and then he makes a trip across the ocean with such as Little Manuel, and other guys who ride the tubs, and sits in with them on games of bridge, and one thing and another, when they need him. Very often when he is riding the tubs, Little Manuel runs into some guy he cannot cheat, so he has to call in Judge Henry G. Blake to outplay the guy on the level, although of course Little Manuel will much rather get a guy's dough by cheating him than by outplaying him on the level. Why this is, I do not know, but this is the way Little Manuel is.

Anyway, you cannot say Judge Henry G. Blake is a bum, especially as he wears good clothes, with a wing collar, and a derby hat, and most people consider him a very nice old man. Personally I never catch the judge out of line on any proposition whatever, and he always says hello to me, very pleasant.

It takes me several hours to find Judge Henry G. Blake, but finally I locate him in Derle's billiard room playing a game of pool with a guy from Providence, Rhode Island. It seems the judge is playing the guy from Providence for five cents a ball, and the judge is about thirteen balls behind when I step into the joint, because naturally at five cents a ball the judge wishes the guy from Providence to win, so as to encourage him to play for maybe twenty-five cents a ball, the judge being very cute this way.

Well, when I step in I see the judge miss a shot anybody can make blindfolded, but as soon as I give him the office I wish to speak to him, the judge hauls off and belts in every ball on the table, bingity-bing, the last shot being a bank that will make Al de Oro stop and think, because when it comes to pool, the old judge is just naturally a curly wolf.

Afterwards he tells me he is very sorry I make him hurry up this way, because of course after the last shot he is never going to get the guy from Providence to play him pool even for fun, and the judge tells me the guy sizes up as a right good thing, at that.

Now Judge Henry G. Blake is not so excited when I tell him what Dave the Dude wishes to see him about, but naturally he is willing to do anything for Dave, because he knows that guys who are not willing to do things for Dave the Dude often have bad luck. The judge tells me that he is afraid he will not make much of a husband because he tries it before several times on his own hook and is always a bust, but as long as this time it is not to be anything serious, he will tackle it. Anyway, Judge Henry G. Blake says, being aristocratic will come natural to him.

Well, when Dave the Dude starts out on any proposition, he is a wonder for fast working. The first thing he does is to turn Madame La Gimp over to Miss Billy Perry, who is now Dave's ever-loving wife which he takes out of tap-dancing in Miss Missouri Martin's Sixteen Hundred Club, and Miss Billy Perry calls in Miss Missouri Martin to help.

This is water on Miss Missouri Martin's wheel, because if there is anything she loves it is to stick her nose in other people's business, no matter what it is, but she is quite a help at that, although at first they have a tough time keeping her from telling Waldo Winchester, the scribe, about the whole cat-hop, so he will put a story in the *Morning Item* about it, with Miss Missouri Martin's name in it. Miss Missouri Martin does not believe in ever overlooking any publicity bets on the layout.

Anyway, it seems that between them Miss Billy Perry and Miss Missouri Martin get Madame La Gimp dolled up in a lot of new clothes, and run her through one of these beauty joints until she comes out very much changed, indeed. Afterwards I hear Miss Billy Perry and Miss Missouri Martin have quite a few words, because Miss Missouri Martin wishes to paint Madame La Gimp's hair the same color as her own, which is a high yellow, and buy her the same kind of dresses which Miss Missouri Martin wears by herself, and Miss Missouri Martin gets much insulted when Miss Billy Perry says no, they are trying to dress Madame La Gimp to look like a lady.

They tell me Miss Missouri Martin thinks of putting the slug on Miss Billy Perry for this crack, but happens to remember just in time that Miss Billy Perry is now Dave the Dude's ever-loving wife, and that nobody in this town can put the slug on Dave's ever-loving wife, except maybe Dave himself.

Now the next thing anybody knows, Madame La Gimp is in a swell eight- or nine-room apartment in the Marberry, and the way this comes about is as follows: It seems that one of Dave the Dude's most important champagne customers is a guy by the name of Rodney B. Emerson, who owns the apartment, but who is at his summer home in Newport, with his family, or anyway with his ever-loving wife.

This Rodney B. Emerson is quite a guy along Broadway, and a great hand for spending dough and looking for laughs, and he is very popular with the mob. Furthermore, he is obligated to Dave the Dude, because Dave sells him good champagne when most guys are trying to hand him the old phonus bolonus, and naturally Rodney B. Emerson appreciates this kind treatment.

He is a short, fat guy, with a round, red face, and a big laugh, and the kind of guy Dave the Dude can call up at his home in Newport and explain the situation ask for the loan of the apartment, which Dave does.

Well, it seems Rodney B. Emerson gets a big bang out of the

idea, and he says to Dave the Dude like this:

'You not only can have the apartment, Dave, but I will come over and help you out. It will save a lot of explaining around the Marberry if I am there.'

So he hops right over from Newport, and joins in with Dave the Dude, and I wish to say Rodney B. Emerson will always be kindly remembered by one and all for his cooperation, and nobody will ever again try to hand him the phonus bolonus when he is buying champagne, even if he is not buying it off of Dave the Dude.

Well, it is coming on Saturday and the boat from Spain is due, so Dave the Dude hires a big town car, and puts his own driver, Wop Sam, on it, as he does not wish any strange driver tipping off anybody that it is a hired car. Miss Missouri Martin is anxious to go to the boat with Madame La Gimp, and take her jazz band, the Hi Hi Boys, from her Sixteen Hundred Club with her to make it a real welcome, but nobody thinks much of this idea. Only Madame La Gimp and her husband, Judge Henry G. Blake, and Miss Billy Perry go, though the judge holds out for some time for Little Manuel, because Judge Blake says he wishes somebody around to tip him off in case there are any bad cracks made about him as a husband in Spanish and Little Manuel is very Spanish.

The morning they go to meet the boat is the first time Judge Henry G. Blake gets a load of his ever-loving wife, Madame La Gimp, and by this time Miss Billy Perry and Miss Missouri Martin give Madame La Gimp such a going-over that she is by no means the worst looker in the world. In fact, she looks first-rate, especially as she is off gin and says she is off it for good.

Judge Henry G. Blake is really quite surprised by her looks as he figures all along she will turn out to be a crow. In fact, Judge Blake hurls a couple of shots into himself to nerve himself for the ordeal, as he explains it, before he appears to go to the boat. Between these shots, and the nice clothes, and the good cleaning-up Miss Billy Perry and Miss Missouri Martin gave Madame La Gimp, she is really a pleasant sight to the judge.

They tell me the meeting at the dock between Madame La Gimp and her baby is very affecting indeed, and when the proud old Spanish nobleman and his wife, and their son, and Madame La Gimp's sister, all go into action, too, there are enough tears around there to float all the battleships we once sink for Spain. Even Miss Billy Perry and Judge Henry G. Blake do some first-class crying, although the chances are the judge is worked up to the crying more by the shots he takes for his courage than by the meeting.

Still, I hear the old judge does himself proud, what with kissing Madame La Gimp's baby plenty, and duking the proud old Spanish nobleman, and his wife, and son, and giving Madame La Gimp's sister a good strong hug that squeezes her tongue out.

It turns out that the proud old Spanish nobleman has white sideburns, and is entitled Conde de Something, so his ever-loving wife is the Condesa, and the son is a very nice-looking quiet young guy any way you take him, who blushes every time anybody looks at him. As for Madame La Gimp's baby, she is as pretty as they come, and many guys are sorry they do not get Judge Henry G. Blake's job as stepfather, because he is able to take a kiss at Madame La Gimp's baby on what seems to be very small excuse. I never see a nicer-looking young couple, and anybody can see they are very fond of each other, indeed.

Madame La Gimp's sister is not such a doll as I will wish to have sawed off on me, and is up in the paints as regards to age, but she is also very quiet. None of the bunch talk any English, so Miss Billy Perry and Judge Henry G. Blake are pretty much outsiders on the way uptown. Anyway, the judge takes the wind as soon as they reach the Marberry, because the judge is now getting a little tired of being a husband. He says he has to take a trip out to Pittsburgh to buy four or five coal mines, but will be back the next day.

Well, it seems to me that everything is going perfect so far, and that it is good judgment to let lay as it is, but nothing will do Dave the Dude but to have a reception the following night. I advise Dave the Dude against this idea, because I am afraid something will happen to spoil the whole cat-hop, but he will not listen to me, especially as Rodney B. Emerson is now in town and is a strong booster for the party, as he wishes to drink some of the good champagne he has planted in his apartment.

Furthermore, Miss Billy Perry and Miss Missouri Martin are very indignant at me when they hear about my advice, as it seems they both buy new dresses out of Dave the Dude's bank roll when they are dressing up Madame La Gimp, and they wish to spring these dresses somewhere where they can be seen. So the party is on.

I get to the Marberry around nine o'clock and who opens the door of Madame La Gimp's apartment for me but Moosh, the door man from Miss Missouri Martin's Sixteen Hundred Club. Furthermore, he is in his Sixteen Hundred Club uniform, except he has a clean shave. I wish Moosh a hello, and he never raps to me but only bows and takes my hat.

The next guy I see is Rodney B. Emerson in evening clothes, and the minute he sees me he yells out, 'Mister O. O. McIntyre.' Well, of course I am not Mister O. O. McIntyre, and never put myself away as Mister O. O. McIntyre, and futhermore there is no resemblance whatever between Mister O. O. McIntyre and me, because I am a fairly good-looking guy, and I start to give Rodney B. Emerson an argument, when he whispers to me like this:

'Listen,' he whispers, 'we must have big names at this affair, so as to impress these people. The chances are they read the newspapers back there in Spain, and we must let them meet the folks they read about, so they will see Madame La Gimp is a real big shot to get such names to a party.'

Then he takes me by the arm and leads me to a group of people in a corner of the room, which is about the size of the Grand Central waiting room.

'Mister O. O. McIntyre, the big writer!' Rodney B. Emerson says, and the next thing I know I am shaking hands with Mr. and Mrs. Conde, and their son, and with Madame La Gimp and her baby, and Madame La Gimp's sister, and finally with Judge Henry G. Blake, who has on a swallowtail coat, and does not give me much of a tumble. I figure the chances are Judge Henry G. Blake is getting a swelled head already, not to tumble up a guy who helps him get his job, but even at that I wish to say the old judge looks immense in his swallowtail coat, bowing and giving one and all the old castor oil smile.

Madame La Gimp is in a low-neck black dress and is wearing a lot of Miss Missouri Martin's diamonds, such as rings and bracelets, which Miss Missouri Martin insists on hanging on her, although I hear afterwards that Miss Missouri Martin has Johnny Brannigan, the plain clothes copper, watching these diamonds. I wonder at the time why Johnny is there but figure it is because he is a friend of Dave the Dude's. Miss Missouri Martin is no sucker, even if she is kind-hearted.

Anybody looking at Madame La Gimp will bet you all the coffee in Java that she never lives in a cellar over in Tenth Avenue, and drinks plenty of gin in her day. She has her gray hair piled up high on her head, with a big Spanish comb in it, and she reminds me of a picture I see somewhere, but I do not remember just where. And her baby, Eulalie, in a white dress is about as pretty a little doll as you will wish to see, and nobody can blame Judge Henry G. Blake for copping a kiss off her now and then.

Well, pretty soon I hear Rodney B. Emerson bawling, 'Mister Willie K. Vanderbilt,' and in comes nobody but Big Nig, and Rodney B. Emerson leads him over to the group and introduces him.

Little Manuel is standing alongside Judge Henry G. Blake, and he explains in Spanish to Mr. and Mrs. Conde and the others that "Willie K. Vanderbilt" is a very large millionaire, and Mr. and Mrs. Conde seem much interested, anyway, though naturally Madame La Gimp and Judge Henry G. Blake are jerry to Big Nig, while Madame La Gimp's baby and the young guy are interested in nobody but each other.

Then I hear, "Mister Al Jolson," and in comes nobody but Tony Bertazzola, from the Chicken Club, who looks about as much like Al as I do like O. O. McIntyre, which is not at all. Next comes the "Very Reverend John Roach Straton," who seems to be Skeets Bolivar to me, then "the Honorable Mayor James J. Walker," and who is it but Good Time Charley Bernstein.

"Mister Otto H. Kahn" turns out to be Rochester Red, and "Mister Heywood Broun" is Nick the Greek, who asks me privately who Heywood Broun is, and gets very sore at Rodney B. Emerson when I describe Heywood Broun to him.

Finally there is quite a commotion at the door and Rodney B. Emerson announces, "Mister Herbert Bayard Swope" in an extra loud voice which makes everybody look around, but it is nobody but the Pale Face Kid. He gets me to one side, too, and wishes to know who Herbert Bayard Swope is, and when I explain to him, the Pale Face Kid gets so swelled up he will not speak to Death House Donegan, who is only "Mister William Muldoon."

Well, it seems to me they getting too strong when they announce "Vice-President of the United States, the Honorable Charles Curtis," and in pops Guinea Mike, and I say as much to Dave the Dude, who is running around every which way looking after things, but he only says, 'Well, if you do not know it is Guinea Mike, will you know it is not Vice-President Curtis?'

But it seems to me all this is most disrespectful to our leading citizens, especially when Rodney B. Emerson calls, "The

Honorable Police Commissioner, Mister Grover A. Whalen," and in pops Wild William Wilkins, who is a very hot man at this time, being wanted in several spots for different raps. Dave the Dude takes personal charge of Wild William and removes a rod from his pants pocket, because none of the guests are supposed to come rodded up, this being strictly a social matter.

I watch Mrs. and Mrs. Conde, and I do not see that these names are making any impression on them, and I afterwards find out that they never get any newspapers in their town in Spain except a little local bladder which only prints the home news. In fact, Mr. and Mrs. Conde seem somewhat bored, although Mr. Conde cheers up no little and looks interested when a lot of dolls drift in. They are mainly dolls from Miss Missouri Martin's Sixteen Hundred Club, and the Hot Box, but Rodney B. Emerson introduces them as "Sophie Tucker," and "Theda Bara," and "Jeanne Eagels," and "Helen Morgan" and "Aunt Jemima," and one thing and another.

Well, pretty soon in comes Miss Missouri Martin's jazz band, the Hi Hi Boys, and the party commences getting up steam, especially when Dave the Dude gets Rodney B. Emerson to breaking out the old grape. By and by there is dancing going on, and a good time is being had by one and all, including Mr. and Mrs. Conde. In fact, after Mr. Conde gets a couple of jolts of the old grape, he turns out to be a pretty nice old skate, even if nobody can understand what he is talking about.

As for Judge Henry G. Blake, he is full of speed, indeed. By this time anybody can see that the judge is commencing to believe that all this is on the level and that he is really entertaining celebrities in his own home. You put a quart of good grape inside the old judge and he will believe anything. He soon dances himself plumb out of wind, and then I notice he is hanging around Madame La Gimp a lot.

Along about midnight, Dave the Dude has to go out into the kitchen and settle a battle there over a crap game, but otherwise everything is peaceful. It seems that "Herbert Bayard Swope," "Vice-President Curtis" and "Grover Whalen" get a little game going, when "the Reverend John Roach Straton" steps up and cleans them in four passes, but it seems they soon discover that "the Reverend John Roach Straton" is using tops on them, which are very dishonest dice, and so they put the slug on "the Reverend John Roach Straton' and Dave the Dude has to split them out.

By and by I figure on taking the wind, and I look for Mr. and Mrs. Conde to tell them good night, but Mr. Conde and Miss Missouri Martin are still dancing, and Miss Missouri Martin is pouring conversation into Mr. Conde's ear by the bucketful, and while Mr. Conde does not savvy a word she says, this makes no difference to Miss Missouri Martin. Let Miss Missouri Martin do all the talking, and she does not care a whoop if anybody understands her.

Mrs. Conde is over in a corner with "Herbert Bayard Swope," or the Pale Face Kid, who is trying to find out from her by using hog Latin and signs on her if there is any chance for a good twenty-one dealer in Spain, and of course Mrs. Conde is not able to make heads or tails of what he means, so I hunt up Madame La Gimp.

She is sitting in a darkish corner off by herself and I really do not see Judge Henry G. Blake leaning over her until I am almost on top of them, so I cannot help hearing what the judge is saying.

'I am wondering for two days,' he says, 'if by any chance you remember me. Do you know who I am?'

'I remember you,' Madame La Gimp says. 'I remember you – oh, so very well, Henry. How can I forget you? But I have no idea you recognize me after all these years.'

'Twenty of them now,' Judge Henry G. Blake says. 'You are beautiful then. You are still beautiful.'

Well, I can see the old grape is working first-class on Judge Henry G. Blake to make such remarks as this, although at that, in the half light, with the smile on her face, Madame La Gimp is not so bad. Still, give me them carrying a little less weight for age.

'Well, it is all your fault,' Judge Henry G. Blake says. 'You go and marry that chile con carne guy, and look what happens!'

I can see there is no sense in me horning in on Madame La Gimp and Judge Henry G. Blake while they are cutting up old touches in this manner, so I think I will just say good-by to the young people and let it go at that, but while I am looking for Madame La Gimp's baby, and her guy, I run into Dave the Dude.

'You will not find them here,' Dave says. 'By this time they are being married over at Saint Malachy's with my ever-loving wife and Big Nig standing up with them. We get the license for them yesterday afternoon. Can you imagine a couple of young saps wishing to wait until they go plumb around the world before getting married?'

Well, of course this elopement creates much excitement for a few minutes, but by Monday Mr. and Mrs. Conde and the young folks and Madame La Gimp's sister take a train for California to keep on going around the world, leaving us nothing to talk about but old Judge Henry G. Blake and Madame La Gimp getting themselves married too, and going to Detroit where Judge Henry G. Blake claims he has a brother in the plumbing business who will give him a job, although personally I think Judge Henry G. Blake figures to do a little booting on his own hook in and out of Canada. It is not like Judge Henry G. Blake to tie himself up to the plumbing business.

So there is nothing more to the story, except that Dave the Dude is around a few days later with a big sheet of paper in his duke and very, very indignant.

'If every single article listed here is not kicked back to the owners of the different joints in the Marberry that they are taken from by next Tuesday night, I will bust a lot of noses around this town,' Dave says. 'I am greatly mortified by such happenings at my social affairs, and everything must be returned at once. Especially,' Dave says, 'the baby grand piano that is removed from Apartment 9-D.'

Though writer Truman Capote (1924-1984) was born and bred a Southerner he always had a sharp eye and ear for the vagaries of New York life.

MARY SANCHEZ

SCENE: *A rainy April morning, 1979. I am walking along Second Avenue in New York City, carrying an oilcloth shopping satchel bulging with house-cleaning materials that belong to Mary Sanchez, who is beside me trying to keep an umbrella above the pair of us, which is not difficult as she is much taller than I am, a six-footer.*

Mary Sanchez is a professional cleaning woman who works by the hour, at five dollars an hour, six days a week. She works approximately nine hours a day, and visits on the average twenty-four different domiciles between Monday and Saturday: generally her customers require her services just once a week.

Mary is fifty-seven years old, a native of a small South Carolina town who has "lived North" the past forty years. Her husband, a Puerto Rican, died last summer. She has a married daughter who lives in San Diego, and three sons, one of whom is a dentist, one who is serving a ten-year sentence for armed robbery, a third who is "just gone, God knows where. He called me last Christmas, he sounded far away. I asked where are you, Pete, but he wouldn't say, so I told him his daddy was dead, and he said good, said that was the best Christmas present I could've given him, so I hung up the phone, slam, and I hope he never calls again. Spitting on Dad's grave that way. Well, sure, Pedro was never good to the kids. Or me. Just boozed and rolled dice. Ran around with bad women. They found him dead on a bench in Central Park. Had a mostly empty bottle of Jack Daniel's in a paper sack propped between his legs; never drank nothing but the best, that man. Still, Pete was way out of line, saying he was glad his father was dead. He owed him the gift of life, didn't he? And I owed Pedro something too. If it wasn't for him, I'd still be an ignorant Baptist, lost to the Lord. But when I got married, I married in the Catholic church, and the Catholic church brought a shine to my life that has never gone out, and never will, not even when I die. I raised my children in the Faith; two of them turned out fine, and I give the church credit for that more than me."

Mary Sanchez is muscular, but she has a pale round smooth pleasant face with a tiny upturned nose and a beauty mole high on her left cheek. She dislikes the term "black," racially applied. "I'm not black. I'm brown. A light-brown colored woman. And I'll tell you something else. I don't know many other colored people that like being called blacks. Maybe some of the young people. And those radicals. But not folks my age, or even half as old. Even people who really are black, they don't like it. What's wrong with Negroes? I'm a Negro, and a Catholic, and proud to say it."

I've known Mary Sanchez since 1968, and she has worked for me, periodically, all these years. She is conscientious, and takes far more than a casual interest in her clients, many of whom she has scarcely met, or not met at all, for many of them are unmarried working men and women who are not at home when she arrives to clean their apartments; she communicates with them, and they with her, via notes: "Mary, please water the geraniums and feed the cat. Hope this finds you well. Gloria Scotto."

Once I suggested to her that I would like to follow her around during the course of a day's work, and she said well, she didn't see anything wrong with that, and in fact, would enjoy the company: "This can be kind of lonely

293

work sometimes."

Which is how we happen to be walking along together on this showery April morning. We're off to her first job: a Mr. Andrew Trask, who lives on East Seventy-third Street.

TC: What the hell have you got in this sack?

MARY: Here, give it to me. I can't have you cursing.

TC: No. Sorry. But it's heavy.

MARY: Maybe it's the iron.

TC: You iron their clothes? You never iron any of mine.

MARY: Some of these people just have no equipment. That's why I have to carry so much. I leave notes: get this, get that. But they forget. Seems like all my people are bound up in their troubles. Like this Mr. Trask, where we're going. I've had him seven, eight months, and I've never seen him yet. But he drinks too much, and his wife left him on account of it, and he owes bills everywhere, and if ever I answered his phone, it's somebody trying to collect. Only now they've turned off his phone.

(We arrive at the address, and she produces from a shoulder-satchel a massive metal ring jangling with dozens of keys. The building is a four-storey brownstone with a midget elevator.)

TC *(after entering and glancing around the Trask establishment – one fair-sized room with greenish arsenic-colored walls, a kitchenette, and a bathroom with a broken, constantly flowing toilet)*: Hmm. I see what you mean. This guy has problems.

MARY *(opening a closet crammed and clammy with sweat-sour laundry)*: Not a clean sheet in the house! And look at that bed! Mayonnaise! Chocolate! Crumbs, crumbs, chewing gum, cigarette butts. Lipstick! What kind of woman would subject herself to a bed like that? I haven't been able to change the sheets for weeks. Months.

(She turns on several lamps with awry shades; and while she labors to organize the surrounding disorder, I take more careful note of the premises. Really, it looks as though a burglar had been plundering there, one who had left some drawers of a bureau open, others closed. There's a leather-framed photograph on the bureau of a stocky swarthy macho man and a blond hoity-toity Junior League woman and three tow-headed grinning snaggle-toothed

294

suntanned boys, the eldest about fourteen. There is another unframed picture stuck in a blurry mirror: another blonde, but definitely not Junior League – perhaps a pickup from Maxwell's Plum; I imagine it is her lipstick on the bed sheets. A copy of the December issue of True Detective *magazine is lying on the floor, and in the bathroom, stacked by the ceaselessly churning toilet, stands a pile of girlie literature –* Penthouse, Hustler, Oui; *otherwise, there seems to be a total absence of cultural possessions. But there are hundreds of empty vodka bottles everywhere – the miniature kind served by airlines.)*

TC: Why do you suppose he drinks only these miniatures?

MARY: Maybe he can't afford nothing bigger. Just buys what he can. He has a good job, if he can hold on to it, but I guess his family keeps him broke.

TC: What does he do?

MARY: Airplanes.

TC: That explains it. He gets these little bottles free.

MARY: Yeah? How come? He's not a steward. He's a pilot.

TC: Oh, my God.

(A telephone rings, a subdued noise, for the instrument is submerged under a rumpled blanket. Scowling, her hands soapy with dishwater, Mary unearths it with the finesse of an archeologist.)

MARY: He must have got connected again. Hello? *(Silence)* Hello?

A WOMAN'S VOICE: Who *is* this?

MARY: This is Mr. Trask's residence.

A WOMAN'S VOICE: Mr. Trask's *residence? (Laughter; then, hoity-toity)* To whom am I speaking?

MARY: This is Mr. Trask's maid.

A WOMAN'S VOICE: So Mr. Trask has a maid, has he? Well, that's more than *Mrs.* Trask has. Will Mr. Trask's maid please tell Mr. Trask that Mrs. Trask would like to speak to him?

MARY: He's not home.

MRS. TRASK: Don't give me that. Put him on.

MARY: I'm sorry, Mrs. Trask. I guess he's out flying.

MRS. TRASK: *(bitter mirth):* Out flying? He's always flying, dear. Always.

MARY: What I mean is, he's at work.

MRS. TRASK: Tell him to call me at my sister's in New Jersey. Call the instant he comes in, if he knows what's good for him.

MARY: Yes, ma'am. I'll leave that message. *(She hangs up)* Mean woman. No wonder he's in the condition he's in. And now he's out of a job. I wonder if he left me my money. Uh-huh. That's it. On top of the fridge.

(Amazingly, an hour or so afterward she has managed to somewhat camouflage the chaos and has the room looking not altogether shipshape but reasonably respectable. With a pencil, she scribbles a note and props it against the bureau mirror: "Dear Mr. Trask yr. wive want you fone her at her sistar place sinsirly Mary Sanchez." Then she sighs and perches on the edge of the bed and from her satchel takes out a small tin box containing an assortment of roaches; selecting one, she fits it into a roach-holder and lights up, dragging deeply, holding the smoke down in her lungs and closing her eyes. She offers me a toke.)

TC: Thanks. It's too early.

MARY: It's never too early. Anyway, you ought to try this stuff. *Mucho cojones.* I get it from a customer, a real fine Catholic lady; she's married to a fellow from Peru. His family sends it to them. Sends it right through the mail. I never use it so's to get high. Just enough to lift the uglies a little. That heaviness. *(She sucks on the roach until it all but burns her lips)* Andrew Trask. Poor scared devil. He could end up like Pedro. Dead on a park bench, nobody caring. Not that I didn't care none for that man. Lately, I find myself remembering the good times with Pedro, and I guess that's what happens to most people if ever they've once loved somebody and lose them; the bad slips away, and you linger on the nice things about them, what made you like them in the first place. Pedro, the young man I fell in love with, he was a beautiful dancer, oh he could tango, oh he could rumba, he taught me to dance and danced me off my feet. We were regulars at the old Savoy Ballroom. He was clean, neat – even when the drink got to him his fingernails were always trimmed and polished. And he could cook up a storm. That's how he made a living, as a short-order cook. I said he never did anything good for the children; well, he fixed their lunch-boxes to take to school. All kinds of sandwiches wrapped in wax paper. Ham, peanut butter and jelly, egg salad, tuna fish, and fruit, apples, bananas, pears, and a

296

thermos filled with warm milk mixed with honey. It hurts now to think of him there in the park, and how I didn't cry when the police came to tell me about it; how I never did cry. I ought to have. I owed him that. I owed him a sock in the jaw, too.

I'm going to leave the lights on for Mr. Trask. No sense letting him come home to a dark room.

(When we emerged from the brownstone the rain had stopped, but the sky was sloppy and a wind had risen that whipped trash along the gutters and caused passers-by to clutch their hats. Our destination was four blocks away, a modest but modern apartment house with a uniformed doorman, the address of Miss Edith Shaw, a young woman in her mid-twenties who was on the editorial staff of a magazine. "Some kind of news magazine. She must have a thousand books. But she doesn't look like no bookworm. She's a very healthy kind of girl, and she has lots of boyfriends. Too many – just can't seem to stay very long with one fellow. We got to be close because. . . Well, one time I came to her place and she was sick as a cat. She'd come from having a baby murdered. Normally I don't hold with that; it's against my beliefs. And I said why didn't you marry this man? The truth was, she didn't know who to marry; she didn't know who dad was. And anyway, the last thing she wanted was a husband or a baby.")

MARY: *(surveying the scene from the opened front door of Miss Shaw's two-room apartment)*: Nothing much to do here. A little dusting. She takes good care of it herself. Look at all those books. Ceiling to floor, nothing but library.

(Except for the burdened bookshelves, the apartment was attractively spare, Scandinavianly white and gleaming. There was one antique: an old roll-top desk with a typewriter on it; a sheet of paper was rolled into the machine; and I glanced at what was written on it:

> "Zsa Zsa Gabor is
> 305 years old
> I know
> Because I counted
> Her Rings"

And triple-spaced below that, was typed:

> "Sylvia Plath, I hate you
> And your damn daddy.
> I'm glad, do you hear,
> Glad *you stuck your head*
> In a gas-hot oven!"*

TC: Is Miss Shaw a poet?

MARY: She's always writing something. I don't know what it is. Stuff I see, sounds like she's on dope to me. Come here, I want to show you something.

(She leads me into the bathroom, a surprisingly large and sparkling chamber. She opens a cabinet door and points at an object on a shelf: a pink plastic vibrator molded in the shape of an average-sized penis.)

Know what that is?

TC: Don't you?

MARY: I'm the one asking.

TC: It's a dildo vibrator.

MARY: I know what a vibrator is. But I never saw one like that. It says "Made in Japan."

TC: Ah, well. The Oriental mind.

MARY: Heathens. She's sure got some lovely perfumes. If you like perfume. Me, I only put a little vanilla behind my ears.

In his book The Americans, *Italian author Luigi Barzini describes an encounter with an American Mafia Don.*

DON TURI

Don Turi lived in a decayed section of Brooklyn in a house surrounded by an iron fence. The house was old, but the fence was new. Don Turi was a kindly old gentleman, fat but still fast on his feet like an old house cat. He had watchful and alert black eyes, younger than his face; wore a woollen peaked cap indoors and a travel rug over his shoulders to protect himself from colds. He received me in a room whose walls were practically papered with framed photographs from the old country. There were peasant brides and grooms galore, some of the girls in their ancient costumes; young men in the last war's military uniforms, and some in *carabinieri* dress uniform holding the regulation Napoleonic hat with plume (known technically as *la lucerna,* or oil lamp) under an arched arm. *Carabinieri* and bandits have always been recruited among the same people in Italy. There were also many priests, nuns, monks, and one bishop smiling benignly at me.

Don Turi sat on an American straight-backed armchair, with a silent and attentive young man sitting behind him, his oldest son. Oldest sons are always present at their Sicilian fathers' more important interviews and never speak, because their job is more or less that of what is now known as a tape recorder. They must listen and remember, in case something happens to the old man, but they cannot be played back by third parties. Don Turi spoke his obscure dialect, slowly and with royal dignity. He seemed to use the *pluralis majestatis* like the Pope, but, in fact, when he said "we," he literally meant many men, the *amici* and *gli amici degli amici*. This is, more or less, what I think he said:

"Mike told me what you have done for him. It shows you have generous sentiments and are a gallant young man one can rely on. This is very rare among North Italians, Americans, and other foreigners. We thank you. We're in your debt. We never forget our debts. You know that. We never forget wrongs done to us, either. Someday you may need our help, Don Luigi, even when I am no longer here." (Mike and his son murmured, "As late as possible, with the help of God," as automatically as the faithful answered " . . . *qui tollit peccata mundi*" when the priest said "*Agnus Dei. . . .*") "That day," Don Turi continued, "you can count on us, provided, of course, your request agrees with the laws of honor. Not today, however, the way you suggest. Mike says you want to defend the Sicilians' name from defamation, explain to the American public what laws we obey, and how we help each other like brothers in this strange, difficult, and hostile country." (That, of course, was the explanation I had given Mike.) "It is a noble wish. We commend you. But I'm afraid the moment is not opportune. We're at war. We Sicilians in America must think of ourselves like the Jews in Egypt before the Exodus. Everybody around us is our enemy and our oppressor. We have to be very prudent. Prudence, the Church teaches us, is one of the cardinal virtues. We showed our trust in you when we agreed to receive you in our house. But we cannot go further. Whatever you might write will be either accurate or wrong. If accurate, you will not be able to produce proof when it is denied and you will be accused by some of betraying us. Something unpleasant might happen to you. If it was wrong or exaggerated, it certainly would not have been worth your while to come and see me. Whether accurate or inaccurate, what you might write will be misunderstood anyway. Nobody understands (or wants to understand) us. You'll be bothered by the police, who are dull, ignorant, corrupt, and brutal people, mostly Irish. They will never leave you alone in order to get my name and my address, which they already have anyway. Yours is a dangerous errand, believe me, you yourself do not realize how dangerous. For your own sake it is my duty to discourage you, as I would discourage a grandson of mine. Some other time, perhaps, but not now." He gave me a glass of sweet wine with a biscuit, then shook my hand, and dismissed me, walking me ceremoniously to the iron garden gate. That was the end of that.

David Jackson, fiction writer and historian, was a friend of W. H. Auden for over twenty years. Here he recalls Auden's apartment in New York.

W. H. AUDEN

1973 In Auden's New York apartment on St. Mark's Place, shared for nearly two decades with Chester. I've arrived for supper before taking Chester on to a New Year's Eve party in Harlem. The possible dangers lurking in Harlem preoccupy Wystan: 'My dear, does Jimmy [Merrill] know you're going up there?' I try to distract him by describing the elaborate flat of the musician, David Fontaine, where we've gone to other parties, met people like Mae Barnes and Arthur Mitchell, but see that he is still leery and agree to call my host: 'David, uh, I'm driving up there with Chester and Tom Victor, uh, is there a place to park near you?' A pause while David cleverly takes in my question, then: 'Oh, yes, I'm sure you can squeeze your little car in among those Cadillacs outside.' Chester remarks, 'I might have known, just another Uptown party!'

Meanwhile, one looks around. No self-respecting Welfare Recipient would spend a night in this flat. A sad scene of sagging bookshelves, sprung-seat overstuffed chairs, a dusty and scarred "cozy-corner" and everywhere litter, piles of paper and magazines, this morning's crusted dish of egg. I go to the toilet – not looking long into the kitchen – and switch on the light, they've *flocked* the walls! Then these move, a vertical nation of cockroaches shifting about uneasily. One of Chester's lesser dinners is set down on the dining room table. This, covered in glass, has a great crumb-filled crack running through it. We chat. 'Wystan, aren't you sad to be leaving New York?' Between spoonfuls he thinks; at last he answers – the tone, is it the poet's, the lover's fond oblivion to the work of time? There is a touch of a sigh. 'Yes, yes, particularly now that we've fixed the place up.'

Truman Capote's exquisite novella of war-time life in the City, Breakfast at Tiffany's *(1958), produced one fictional character who has become a touchstone for New York eccentrics.*

HOLLY GOLIGHTLY

'It's like Tiffany's,' she said. 'Not that I give a hoot about jewellery. Diamonds, yes. But it's tacky to wear diamonds before you're forty; and even that's risky. They only look right on the really old girls. Maria Ouspenskaya. Wrinkles and bones, white hair and diamonds: I can't wait. But that's not why I'm mad about Tiffany's. Listen. You know those days when you've got the mean reds?'

'Same as the blues?'

'No,' she said slowly. 'No, the blues are because you're getting fat or maybe it's been raining too long. You're sad, that's all. But the mean reds are horrible. You're afraid and you sweat like hell, but you don't know what you're afraid of. Except something bad is going to happen, only you don't know what it is. You've had that feeling?'

'Quite often. Some people call it *angst*.'

'All right. *Angst*. But what do you do about it?

'Well, a drink helps.'

'I've tried that. I've tried aspirin, too. Rusty thinks I should smoke marijuana, and I did for a while, but it only makes me giggle. What I've found does the most good is just to get into a taxi and go to Tiffany's. It calms me down right away, the quietness and the proud look of it; nothing very bad could happen to you there, not with those kind men in their nice suits, and that lovely smell of silver and alligator wallets. If I could find a real-life place that made me feel like Tiffany's, then I'd buy some furniture and give the cat a name.'

301

CHAPTER 16

ACTS OF
CREATION

Creative people get inspiration from their immediate environment, and New York has the most immediate environment in the world.

Joseph Papp

All Johnny wants to do is make music. He wants to keep everyone and everything who takes him away from his music off him. Since he can't afford human contact, he can't afford desire. Therefore he hangs around with rich zombies who never have anything to do with feelings. This is a typical New York artist attitude.

Kathy Acker

In New York I first loved, and I first wrote of the things I saw with a fierce joy of creation – and knew at last that I could write. There I got the first perceptions of the life of my time. The city and its people were an open book to me; everything had its story, dramatic and full of ironic tragedy and terrible humor. There I first saw that reality transcended all the fine poetic inventions of fastidiousness and medievalism. I was never happy or well long away from New York.

John Reed

The theatre was not only a place of entertainment for New Yorkers in the first half of the nineteenth century but also a forum in which were fought out all kinds of ideological and ethnic differences. As Philip Hone records in his Diary, *these differences not infrequently led to violence.*

THEATRE RIOTS, 1831

Thursday, Oct. 13. – Mr. Anderson, who came out lately from England, was announced this evening at the Park Theatre, for his first appearance in America, in the character of Henry Bertram in the opera of "Guy Mannering." The house was filled by persons who had prepared to assist in or witness the riot which was expected. He is said to have behaved ill on the passage and abused the Yankees, and a quarrel with the mate was settled after his arrival by the latter giving him a flogging, the effects of which has prevented him from appearing until now.

Saturday, Oct. 15. – Mr. Anderson was announced again for this evening in the part of Henry Bertram. The house was filled very early to suffocation. When I went in the whole interior was a solid mass of men. Not a single female present, except two or three in the upper tier. The first part of the opera was listened to, and when Mrs. Sharpe appeared she was received with the most marked approbation, intended, no doubt, as the *amende honorable* for the share which she was compelled to receive of the ill-treatment intended for Mr. Anderson on Thursday. At the commencement of the second act, previously to the time when he should have appeared, Simpson came forward and attempted to read his apology. This was the signal for the commencement of the riot, and from that time the disturbance continued during the whole night. Apples, eggs, and other missiles were showered upon the stage, and although Barry announced that the unhappy wight was withdrawn who had committed the unatonable offence which called down the vengeance of the sovereigns, and that the play would be changed, they would not be pacified. They went to the theatre for a row, and they would not be disappointed. The only interval of order was during the time that little Burke was brought forward and played on his violin in the overture to "Guy Mannering," at the unanimous call of the house. The street in front of the theatre was filled by the mob, the lamps were broken, and the interior of the theatre sustained considerable injury, notwithstanding a strong force of watchmen and constables in attendance.

Monday, Oct. 17. – The disgraceful riots of Thursday and Saturday nights were continued on a more extensive scale last night. During the whole of yesterday the sanctity of the day was violated by the collection of groups of idlers in front of the theatre, and soon after dark the numbers had increased in a manner which caused serious alarm to the neighbourhood. Cries, shouts, and huzzas marked the commencement of the attack, and about nine o'clock I was disturbed by the noise of the crash of broken windows and the battering of the front doors. This continued half an hour without the interference of the municipal authorities. I then went out to find the Mayor. He was not at home, and could not be found. I then went around to the scene of action, when I found that the whole of this outrage was committed by about twenty boys, who were instigated and encouraged by the mob, and every crash of broken glass was followed by their shouts. At this time Hays came up with a pretty strong body of watchmen, and order was for a time restored. Several men and boys were carried to the watch-house, of whom nearly the whole were discharged in a short time, and several at my solicitation. The mob in front of the theatre continued, but no more injury was done to the building. Indeed, there was not much left to be done, unless the mob could have forced an entrance, when the scene would have been dreadful. The American and tricoloured flags were exhibited from the upper windows to appease the populace, which served to allay the tumult; but the noise continued all night, and I doubt if any person in the neighbourhood of the park had what is called a *good night's rest.*

To-day the front of the theatre is covered with transparencies of patriotic subjects, – flags and eagles in abundance, – which appears to have propitiated the mob. I went into the house. Burke is playing, and things go on tolerably quietly. The crowd in front is tremendously great, but orderly, and there is a large body of watchmen, with the Mayor in person, so that there is reason to hope that this foolish affair has come to an end.

THEATRE RIOTS, 1834

July 10. – Our city last evening was the scene of disgraceful riots. The first was at the Bowery Theatre. An actor by the name of Farren, whose benefit it was, had made himself obnoxious by some ill-natured reflections upon the country, which called down the vengeance of the mob, who seemed determined to deserve the bad name which he had given to them. An hour after the performance commenced the mob broke open the doors, took possession of every part of the house, committed every species of outrage, hissed and pelted poor Hamblin, not regarding the talisman which he relied upon, the American flag, which he waved over his head. This they disregarded, because the hand which held it was that of an Englishman, and they would listen to

306

nobody but "American Forrest." He assured them that the object of their rage, Mr. Farren, had made a hasty exit, and the mob retired to enact a more disgraceful scene in another quarter.

After the First World War a number of young people found their way to the streets of New York with high hopes of establishing themselves as writers or artists in the great city. Malcolm Cowley, in Exile's Return, *recalls their struggles.*

THE LONG FURLOUGH

After college and the war, most of us drifted to Manhattan, to the crooked streets south of Fourteenth, where you could rent a furnished hall-bedroom for two or three dollars weekly or the top floor of a rickety house for thirty dollars a month. We came to the Village without any intention of becoming Villagers. We came because living was cheap, because friends of ours had come already (and written us letters full of enchantment), because it seemed that New York was the only city where a young writer could be published. There were some who stayed in Europe after the war and others who carried their college diplomas straight to Paris: they had money. But the rest of us belonged to the proletariat of the arts and we lived in Greenwich Village where everyone else was poor.

"There were," I wrote some years ago, "two schools among us: those who painted the floors black (they were the last of the aesthetes) and those who did not paint the floors. Our college textbooks and the complete works of Jules Laforgue gathered dust on the mantelpiece among a litter of unemptied ashtrays. The streets outside were those of Glenn Coleman's early paintings: low red-brick early nineteenth-century houses, crazy doorways, sidewalks covered with black snow and, in the foreground, an old woman bending under a sack of rags."

The black snow melted: February blustered into March. It was as if the war had never been fought, or had been fought by others. We were about to continue the work begun in high school, of training ourselves as writers, choosing masters to imitate, deciding what we wanted to say and persuading magazines to let us say it. We should have to earn money, think about getting jobs:

307

the war was over. But besides the memories we scarcely mentioned, it had left us with a vast unconcern for the future and an enormous appetite for pleasure. We were like soldiers with a few more days to spend in Blighty: every moment was borrowed from death. It didn't matter that we were penniless: we danced to old squeaky victrola records – *You called me Baby Doll a year ago; Hello Central, Give Me No Man's Land* – we had our first love affairs, we stopped in the midst of arguments to laugh at jokes as broad and pointless as the ocean, we were continually drunk with high spirits, transported by the miracle of no longer wearing a uniform. As we walked down Greenwich Avenue we stopped to enjoy the smell of hot bread outside of Cushman's bakery. In the spring morning it seemed that every ash barrel was green-wreathed with spinach.

It was April now, and the long furlough continued. . . You woke at ten o'clock between soiled sheets in a borrowed apartment; the sun dripped over the edges of the green windowshade. On the dresser was a half-dollar borrowed the night before from the last guest to go downstairs singing: even at wartime prices it was enough to buy breakfast for two – eggs, butter, a loaf of bread, a grapefruit. When the second pot of coffee was emptied a visitor would come, then another; you would borrow fifty-five cents for the cheapest bottle of sherry. Somebody would suggest a ride across the bay to Staten Island. Dinner provided itself, and there was always a program for the evening. On Fridays there were dances in Webster Hall attended by terrible uptown people who came to watch the Villagers at their revels and buy them drinks in return for being insulted; on Saturdays everybody gathered at Luke O'Connor's saloon, the Working Girls' Home; on Sunday nights there were poker games played for imaginary stakes and interrupted from moment to moment by gossip, jokes, plans; everything in those days was an excuse for talking. There were always parties, and if they lasted into the morning they might end in a "community sleep": the mattresses were pulled off the beds and laid side by side on the floor, then double blankets were unfolded and stretched length-wise across them, so that a dozen people could sleep there in discomfort, provided nobody snored. One night, having fallen asleep, you gave a snore so tremendous that you wakened to its echo, and listened to your companions drowsily cursing the snorer, and for good measure cursed him yourself. But always, before going to bed, you borrowed fifty cents for breakfast. Eight hours' foresight was sufficient. Always, after the coffee pot was drained, a visitor would come with money enough for a bottle of sherry.

But it couldn't go on forever. Some drizzly morning late in April you woke up to find yourself married (and your wife perhaps, suffering from a dry cough that threatened consumption). If there had been checks from home, there would be no more of them. Or else it happened after a siege of influenza, which that year had curious effects: it left you weak in body, clear in mind, revolted by humanity and yourself. Tottering from the hospital, you sat in the back room of a saloon and, from the whitewood table sour with spilled beer, surveyed your blank prospects. You had been living on borrowed money, on borrowed time, in a borrowed apartment: in three months you had exhausted both your credit and your capacity to beg. There was no army now to clothe and feed you like a kind-hateful parent. No matter where the next meal came from, you would pay for it yourself.

In the following weeks you didn't exactly starve; ways could be found of earning a few dollars. Once a week you went round to the editorial offices of the *Dial,* which was then appearing every two weeks in a format something like that of the *Nation.* One of the editors was a friend of your wife's and he would give you half a dozen bad novels to review in fifty or a hundred words apiece. When the reviews were published you would be paid a dollar for each of them, but that mightn't be for weeks or months, and meanwhile you had to eat. So you would carry the books to a bench in Union Square and page through them hastily, making notes – in two or three hours you would be finished with the whole armful and then you would take them to a secondhand bookstore on Fourth Avenue, where the proprietor paid a flat rate of thirty-five cents for each review copy; you thought it was more than the novels were worth. With exactly $2.10 in your pocket you would buy bread and butter and lamb chops and Bull Durham for cigarettes and order a bag of coal; then at home you would broil the lamb chops over the grate because the landlady had neglected to pay her gas bill, just as you had neglected to pay the rent. You were all good friends and she would be invited to share in the feast. Next morning you would write the reviews, then start on the search for a few dollars more.

You began to feel that one meal day was all that anyone needed and you wondered why anyone bothered to eat more. Late on a June day you were sitting in Sheridan Square trying to write a poem. 'Move along, young fella,' said the cop, and the poem was forgotten. Walking southward with the Woolworth Building visible in the distance you imagined a revolution in New York. Revolution was in the air that summer; the general strike had failed in Seattle, but a steel strike was being prepared, and a coal strike, and the railroad men were demanding government ownership – that was all right, but you imagined another kind of revolt, one that would start with a dance through the streets and barrels of cider opened at every corner, and beside each barrel a back-country ham fresh from the oven; the juice squirted out of it when you carved the first slice. Then – but only after you had finished the last of the ham and drained a pitcher of cider and stuffed your mouth with apple pie – then you would set about hanging policemen from the lamp posts, or better still from the crossties of the Elevated, and beside each policeman would be hanged a Methodist preacher, and beside each preacher a pansy poet. Editors would be poisoned with printer's ink: they would die horribly, vomiting ink on white paper. You hated editors, pansipoetical poets, policemen, preachers, you hated city streets. . . and suddenly the street went black. You hadn't even time to feel faint. The pavement rose and hit you between the eyes.

Nobody came to help, nobody even noticed that you had fallen. You scrambled to your feet, limped into a lunch wagon and spent your last dime for a roll and a cup of coffee. The revolution was postponed (on account of I was hungry, sergeant, honest I was too hungry) and the war was ended (listen, sojer, you're out of that man's army now, you're going back behind the plow, you gotta get rich, you son of a bitch). The war was over now and your long furlough was over. It was time to get a job.

Trumpet-player Max Kaminsky recalled the great Billie Holiday in his book Jazz Band.

BILLIE HOLIDAY

Like most of the other clubs on Fifty-second Street, the Famous

Door was on the street floor of a brownstone house and upstairs on the first floor there was a big foyer with built-in leather seats lining the walls, and beyond that were the bathrooms. After playing the first set the first night, I went upstairs to the washroom. A stately young colored girl in a white evening dress sitting alone in a corner of the deserted foyer threw me a half-timid, half-scornful look when I appeared in the doorway.

'What are you doing here all alone?' I asked her, surprised.

When she told me her name was Billie Holiday and that she was working there, too, singing with the Teddy Wilson trio, I remembered that I had seen her up in Harlem a few years before, singing and waiting on tables at the Alhambra Grill, where we used to go to hear Bobby Henderson's fine piano. The fact that I had heard her uptown made us good friends because she was a colored girl downtown in the white section and she felt good knowing I knew about Harlem, and when I heard her sing again I knew why I had remembered her name. She really sang in those days. Her voice *was* the blues, but she could make you feel so happy, too. In her peak years, between 1935 and 1941, her stunning sense of phrasing and tempo were still completely unself-conscious and the unaffected sweet-sadness of her voice could make you ring with joy as well as sorrow. A large, fleshy, but beautifully boned woman with a satin-smooth beige skin, she always possessed an air of hauteur, not only in her manner but in the arch of her brow, the poise of her head, and the dignity of her carriage, but her haughtiness hid a shyness so vast that she spoke in practically a whisper. When she talked to musicians, the subject was usually her mother, to whom she was devoted. There was nothing wild about her in those days; there was nothing showing then but the terrible, proud shyness; and even in her most turbulent, tortured days later on, she was always basically what she had been then – an uncompromising, devastatingly honest kind of girl, and always, in the deepest sense, a lady. Her sobriquet, Lady Day, suited her exactly. Whatever led her to self-destruction was also there: a bitterness – not simply the bitterness of her color or life, but the bitterness that often seems to go with singular talent and that drives a Eugene O'Neill, or a Bix Beiderbecke, or a John Barrymore or a Charlie Parker to destroy himself with drink and drugs and excess. If Bix Beiderbecke had been a Negro they would all have seized on that as the underlying cause of his drinking himself to death.

311

As a singer Billie had few physical mannerisms. She held her arms in the position of a runner ready to sprint, scarcely moving them except occasionally to snap her fingers in a lazy, leisurely movement. Like Bix, all the hotness and intensity and concentration were inside so that she rode a song with the languid grace of a native boy riding a surfboard. Billie had the gift of expressing the perfect mood of a song, happy or sad, rollicking or blue. The basis of her phrasing was the beat, and she didn't distort the melody, but the stress and accent and meaning she gave the words just somehow made the song larger than lifesize. I've always felt that the whole new form sprang complete in her mind with the first note she sang of any song. The art of improvising lies in the sense of structure, in the ability to build a new story out of the bricks and mortar of the original song. Most so-called or would-be jazzmen can play a thousand ad-lib notes and not say a thing; not rearrange or conceive of them so that they tell a new story, with a beginning, middle, and end. Billie was a master architect.

The poet Frank O'Hara (1926-1966) was a curator at the Museum of Modern Art and an influential figure in the New York art scene. Here he recalls the moment he learned of the death of Billie Holiday, known to admirers as "Lady Day".

THE DAY LADY DIED

It is 12:20 in New York a Friday
Three days after Bastille day, yes
it is 1959 and I go to get a shoeshine
because I will get off the 4:19 in Easthampton
at 7:15 and then go straight to dinner
and I don't know the people who will feed me

I walk up the muggy street beginning to sun
and have a hamburger and a malted and buy
an ugly NEW WORLD WRITING to see what the poets
in Ghana are doing these days
                                    I go on to the bank
and Miss Stillwagon (first name Linda I once heard)
doesn't even look up my balance for once in her life
and in the GOLDEN GRIFFIN I get a little Verlaine

312

for Patsy with drawings by Bonnard although I do
think of Hesiod, trans. Richmond Lattimore or
Brendan Behan's new play or *Le Balcon* or *Les Nègres*
of Genet, but I don't, I stick with Verlaine
after practically going to sleep with quandariness

and for Mike I just stroll into the PARK LANE
Liquor Store and ask for a bottle of Strega and
then I go back where I came from to 6th Avenue
and the tobacconist in the Ziegfeld Theatre and
casually ask for a carton of Gauloises and a carton
of Picayunes, and a NEW YORK POST with her face on it

and I am sweating a lot by now and thinking of
leaning on the john door in the 5 SPOT
while she whispered a song along the keyboard
to Mal Waldron and everyone and I stopped breathing

(1959)

*When that monument to capitalism, Rockefeller Center, was nearing
completion in the early thirties the owners looked for a major world artist to
paint a mural in the lobby. Strange that they should have chosen Mexican
artist Diego Rivera (1886-1957), an avowed Marxist and revolutionary. In*
Portrait of America, *Rivera recounted the ensuing controversy, which
culminated in the destruction of the painting because the artist had insisted
on including a portrait of Lenin.*

THE BATTLE OF ROCKEFELLER CENTER

I received a definite offer to paint three panels in the lobby of the
RCA Building in Rockefeller Center. Matisse and Picasso, I was
informed, were to be offered the two lateral corridors in which
each was to paint five panels. I was very doubtful that these two
painters would accept, and said so to the architect of the building
who was negotiating with me; nevertheless, the possible company
of these painters (which was certainly good company), and above
all the large, well-proportioned, and well-lighted wall that was
offered me, decided me to accept. Even the theme was not bad,

313

although it had been worded in very pretentious terms by the general staff of the management: "Man at the Crossroads Looking with Uncertainty but with Hope and High Vision to the Choosing of a Course Leading to a New and Better Future.". . .

. . . As I had expected, the painters first proposed refused the commission. Matisse objected that neither the building nor the size of the wall was suited to his intimate style; while Picasso would not even receive Raymond Hood, the architect, nor Mr. Todd, of the contractors, to discuss the project with them. Since they were unable to secure the work of these two good painters, the management thereupon engaged José María Sert and Frank Brangwyn.

. . .The owners of the building were perfectly familiar with my personality as artist and man and with my ideas and revolutionary history. There was absolutely nothing that might have led them to expect from me anything but my honest opinions honestly expressed. Certainly I gave them no reason to expect a capitulation. Moreover, I carried my care in dealing with them to the point of submitting a written outline (after having prepared the sketch which contained all the elements of the final composition) in detailed explanation of the esthetic and ideological intentions that the painting would express. There was not in advance, nor could there have been, the slightest doubt as to what I proposed to paint and how I proposed to paint it.

. . . The attack was at first veiled, and couched in the courteous language of diplomacy. But when the painter failed to give ground before the conciliatory offers of these patrons of the arts; when, before the power of the richest people in the country, the colors of the painting did not pale or a single form disappear; then these all-powerful lords sent their trusted employees, the executors of their peremptory orders, to deal drastically with the situation.

I preserve a beautiful memory of this "Battle of Rockefeller Center." A mysterious warlike atmosphere made itself felt from the very morning of the day that hostilities broke out. The private police patrolling the Center had already been reinforced during the preceding week, and on that day their number was again doubled. Towards eleven o'clock in the morning, the commander-in-chief of the building and his subordinate generals of personnel issued orders to the uniformed porters and detectives on duty to deploy their men and to begin occupying the important strategic positions on the front line and flanks and even behind the little working shack erected on the mezzanine floor which was the headquarters of the defending cohorts. The siege was laid in strict accordance with the best military practice. The lieutenants ordered their forces not to allow their line to be flanked nor to permit entrance to the beleaguered fort to anyone besides the painter and his assistants (five men and two women!) who constituted the total strength of the army to be subdued and driven from its positions. And all this to prevent the imminent collapse of the existing social order! I wish I could have been equally optimistic!

Several days before, orders had been given out not to allow camera men to enter. They were now made even more stringent, and there was no doubt that the owners would under any circumstances try to prevent the publication of any reproduction of the fresco. Fortunately, Miss Lucienne Bloch, one of my assistants, was adroit enough to take a series of ten details, as well as one complete view, with a tiny Leica camera under the very noses of the enemy's spies, who were so efficient that they failed to notice it!

Throughout the day our movements were closely watched. At dinner time, when our forces were reduced to a minimum – only I, my Japanese assistant, Hideo Noda, my Bulgarian assistant, Stephen Dimitroff, and the Swiss-American, Lucienne Bloch, were on duty – the assault took place. Before opening fire, and simultaneously with the final maneuvers which occupied the strategic posts and reinforced those already occupied, there presented himself, in all the splendor of his power and glory, and in keeping with the best gentlemanly traditions of His Majesty's Army, the great capitalist plenipotentiary, Field-Marshal of the contractors, Mr. Robertson, of Todd, Robertson and Todd, surrounded by his staff. Protected by a triple line of men in uniform and civilian clothes, Mr. Robertson invited me down from the scaffold to parley discreetly in the interior of the working shack and to deliver the ultimatum along with the final check. I was ordered to stop work.

In the meantime, a platoon of sappers, who had been hidden in ambush, charged upon the scaffold, replaced it expertly with smaller ones previously prepared and held ready, and then began to raise into position the large frames of stretched canvas with which they covered the wall. The entrance to the building was closed off with a thick heavy curtain (was it also bullet-proof?),

315

while the streets surrounding the Center were patrolled by mounted policemen and the upper air was filled with the roar of airplanes flying round the skyscraper menaced by the portrait of Lenin. . .

Before I left the building an hour later, the carpenters had already covered the mural, as though they feared that the entire city, with its banks and stock exchanges, its great buildings and millionaire residences, would be destroyed utterly by the mere presence of an image of Vladimir Ilyitch. . .

The proletariat reacted rapidly. Half an hour after we had evacuated the fort, a demonstration composed of the most belligerent section of the city's workers arrived before the scene of battle. At once the mounted police made a show of their heroic and incomparable prowess, charging upon the demonstrators and injuring the back of a seven-year-old girl with a brutal blow of a club. Thus was won the glorious victory of Capital against the portrait of Lenin in the Battle of Rockefeller Center. . .

In the last years of his life comedian Lenny Bruce ran into repeated trouble with the law over the alleged "obscenity" of his act. Even in sophisticated New York, Bruce's home town, the harassment by police, judges, and reporters was constant.

NEW YORK TRIAL

New York, I'd been playing New York, concerts and night-club engagements, for eight years, but in 1964, I got busted for obscenity at the Café Au Go Go. I continued performing and got busted there again that same week.

Then I got pleurisy. My lung was filled with fluid. I couldn't breathe. I went to a doctor, but he wouldn't see me because he didn't want "to get involved." I finally did get a doctor – who, coincidentally, was a fan – and I ended up in a hospital, on the receiving end of a five-hour operation.

When *Newsweek* called up a friend of mine to find out how I was, he told them the surgeon cut all that *filth* out of my system, too.

The trial in New York was postponed while I recuperated in Los Angeles.

When I returned to New York, it turned out that the police didn't have complete tapes of the shows I was arrested for, so they actually had a guy in court *imitating my act* – a License Department Inspector who was formerly a CIA Agent in Vietnam – and in his courtroom impersonation of me, he was saying things that I had never said in my *life*, on stage or off.

Witnesses for the prosecution included *New York Daily News* columnist Robert Sylvester, Marya Mannes from *The Reporter*, John Fischer, editor of *Harper's* magazine, and a minister.

Witnesses for the defense included Jules Feiffer, Nat Hentoff, Dorothy Kilgallen and *two* ministers.

"Sitting in on Lenny Bruce's current New York "obscenity" trial," Stephanie Gervis Harrington wrote in the *Village Voice*, "one gets the feeling of being present at an historical event – the birth of the courtroom of the absurd. Of course, if you sit through it long enough, you gradually adjust to the fact that eight grown men are actually spending weeks of their time and an unreckoned amount of the taxpayers' money in deliberation – passionate deliberation on the prosecutor's good days – over whether another grown man should be able to use four-letter words in public without going to jail."

The ludicrousness of it all was inadvertently summed up by my attorney, Ephraim London, when he asked a witness who had been at my performance at the Café Au Go Go: 'Did you see Mr. Crotch touch his Bruce?'

On reporting the incident, *The Realist* predicted, "Henceforth and forevermore, we shall have had at that precise moment a meaningful new synonym added to our language." And the magazine's editorial proceeded to demonstrate its use:

"Mommy, look, there's a man sitting over there with his bruce hanging out."

"Beverly Schmidlap is a real bruceteaser, y'know?"

"Kiss my bruce, baby."

And a cartoon by Ed Fisher had a judge saying, 'Before I pass sentence on you, Lenny Bruce, is there anything you wish to say – anything printable, that is?'

Meanwhile, back in real life, a three-judge Criminal Court, in a 2–1 split vote, sentenced me to three four-month terms in the workhouse, to be served concurrently. But the State Supreme Court has granted me a certificate of reasonable doubt and – at this writing – the case is on appeal.

317

What does it mean for a man to be found obscene in New York? This is the most sophisticated city in the country. This is where they play Genet's *The Balcony*. If anyone is the first person to be found obscene in New York, he must feel utterly depraved.

I was so sure I could reach those judges if they'd just let me tell them what I try to do. It was like I was on trial for rape and there I was crying, 'But, Judge, I can't rape anybody, I haven't got the wherewithal,' but nobody was listening, and my lawyers were saying, 'Don't worry, Lenny, you got a right to rape anyone you please, we'll beat 'em in the appellate court.'

The *New York Journal* pleaded guilty to not publishing the lower court's statement, with an explanation: "The majority opinion, of necessity, cited in detail the language used by Bruce in his night-club act, and also described gestures and routines which the majority found to be obscene and indecent. The *Law Journal* decided against publication, even edited, on the grounds that deletions would destroy the opinion, and without the deletions publication was impossible within the *Law Journal* standards."

Among the examples of my "obscene references" that the court had quoted in its opinion, the very first was this: 'Eleanor Roosevelt and her display of "tits." '

Now, in the course of my research I obtained the legislative history from Albany of the statute under which I had been arrested, and I discovered back in 1931 there was added to that statute an amendment which *excludes from arrest* stagehands, spectators, musicians and *actors*. The amendment was finally signed into law by Governor Roosevelt. The court refused to be influenced by this information.

Well, I believe that ignoring the mandate of Franklin D. Roosevelt is a great deal more offensive than saying that Eleanor had lovely nay-nays.

In the fifties the New York School of Abstract Expressionist painters, including Jackson Pollock, Barnett Newman, Robert Motherwell, Franz Kline, Mark Rothko, and others, was fêted throughout Europe and America. It seemed the center of gravity of the art world had shifted from Paris to New York. The center of that center was the Cedar Tavern in Greenwich Village. Andy Warhol remembered it in his book POPism.

318

The world of the Abstract Expressionists was very macho. The painters who used to hang around the Cedar bar on University Place were all hard-driving two-fisted types who'd grab each other and say things like 'I'll knock your fucking teeth out' and 'I'll steal your girl.' In a way Jackson Pollock had to die the way he did, crashing his car up, and even Barnett Newman, who was so elegant, always in a suit and monocle, was tough enough to get into politics when he made a kind of symbolic run for mayor of New York in the thirties. The toughness was part of a tradition, it went with their agonized, anguished art. They were always exploding and having fist fights about their work and their love lives. This went on all through the fifties when I was just new in town, doing whatever jobs I could get in advertising and spending my nights at home drawing to meet deadlines or going out with a few friends.

I often asked Larry Rivers, after we got to be friends, what it had really been like down there then. Larry's painting style was unique – it wasn't Abstract Expressionist and it wasn't Pop, it fell into the period in between. But his personality was very Pop – he rode around on a motorcycle and he had a sense of humor about himself as well as everybody else. I used to see him mostly at parties. I remember a very crowded opening at the Janis Gallery where we stood wedged in a corner at right angles to each other and I got Larry talking about the Cedar. I'd heard that when he was about to go on "The $64,000 Question" on TV, he passed the word around that if he won, you could find him at the Cedar bar, and if he lost, he'd head straight for the Five-Spot, where he played jazz saxophone. He did win – $49,000 – and he went straight to the Cedar and bought drinks for around three hundred people.

I asked Larry about Jackson Pollock. 'Pollock? Socially, he was a real jerk,' Larry said. 'Very unpleasant to be around. Very stupid. He was always at the Cedar on Tuesdays – that was the day he came into town to see his analyst – and he always got completely drunk, and he made a point of behaving badly to everyone. I knew him a little from the Hamptons. I used to play saxophone in the taverns out there and he'd drop in occasionally. He was the kind of drunk who'd insist you play "I Can't Give You Anything but Love, Baby" or some other songs the

319

musicians thought were way beneath them, so you'd have to see if you could play it in some way that you wouldn't be putting yourself down *too* much. . . He was a star painter all right, but that's no reason to pretend he was a pleasant person. Some people at the Cedar took him very seriously; they would announce what he was doing every single second – "There's Jackson!" or "Jackson just went to the john!"

'I'll tell you what kind of guy he was. He would go over to a black person and say, 'How do you like your skin color?' or he'd ask a homosexual, 'Sucked any cocks lately?' He'd walk over to me and make shooting-up gestures on his arm because he knew I was playing around with heroin then. And he could be really babyish, too. I remember he once went over to Milton Resnick and said, 'You de Kooning imitator!' and Resnick said, 'Step outside.' Really.' Larry laughed. 'You have to have known these people to believe the things they'd fight over.' I could tell from Larry's smile that he still had a lot of affection for that whole scene.

'What about the other painters?' I asked him. 'Well,' he said, 'Franz Kline would certainly be at the Cedar every night. He was one of those people who always got there before you did and was still there after you left. While he was talking to you, he had this way of turning to someone else as you were leaving, and you got the feeling of automatic continuity – sort of, 'So long. . . So this guy comes over to me and . . .' and while you may have flinched at his indiscriminate friendliness, he did have the virtue of smiling and wanting to talk all the time. There were always great discussions going on, and there was always some guy pulling out his poem and reading it to you. It was a very heavy scene.' Larry sighed. 'You wouldn't have liked it at all, Andy.'

He was right. It was exactly the kind of atmosphere I'd pay to get out of. But it was fascinating to hear about, especially from Larry.

The crowd at the opening had thinned to the point where we could move out of our corner. 'You didn't go to the Cedar "to see the stars," though,' Larry added. 'Oh, sure, you may have liked being in their aura, but what you came back for night after night was to see your friends . . . Frank O'Hara, Kenneth Koch, John Ashbery. . .'

The art world sure was different in those days. I tried to imagine myself in a bar striding over to, say, Roy Lichtenstein and asking him to "step outside" because I'd heard he'd insulted my soup cans. I mean, how corny. I was glad those slug-it-out routines had been retired – they weren't my style, let alone my capability.

Larry had mentioned that Pollock came in from the country every Tuesday. That was part of the big out-of-the-city-and-into-the-country trend that the Abstract Expressionist painters had started in the late fifties when they were beginning to make money and could afford country places. Right in the middle of the twentieth century, artists were still following the tradition of wanting to get out there alone in the woods and do their stuff. Even Larry had moved to Southampton in '53 – and stayed out there for five years. The tradition was really ingrained. But the sixties changed all that back again – from country to city.

The early sixties saw Jazz artists such as John Coltrane and Ornette Coleman breaking new musical ground. Leroi Jones/Imamu Amiri Baraka watched the great players come into town and was overwhelmed by the new sounds they were making.

COLTRANE AND OTHERS

I still went to the Cedar and bellied up to the bar, but now I was much more into the jazz clubs that were opening and some coffeehouses and lofts that were playing "the new thing." The Five Spot was the center for us. When Thelonious Monk came in for his historic eighteen-week stay, with John Coltrane, I was there almost every night. I was there from the beginning listening to Trane try to get around on Monk's weird charts, and gradually Trane got hold to those "heads" and began to get inside Monk's music. Trane had just come from playing with the classic Miles Davis group that featured Cannonball, Philly Joe Jones, Paul Chambers, and Red Garland. The Club Bohemia was where I'd heard them "max out" and make their greatest music. And that was a slick nightclub, albeit in the Village. But the Five Spot was on the East Side, on the Bowery. C.T., Cecil Taylor, had really inaugurated the playing of the Music in the place. Before that it had been one of those typical grim Bowery bars, but some of the painters who had lofts on the Bowery and in the area began to come in and drink and they used to ask Joe and Iggy to bring in some music. So the completely unorthodox Cecil was one of the first to come in. By the time Monk and Trane got there, The Five Spot was the center of the jazz world!

In one sense our showing up on Cooper Square was right in tune with the whole movement of people East, away from the West Village with its high rents and older bohemians. Cooper Square was sort of the border line; when you crossed it, you were really on the Lower East Side, no shit. The Music itself, rapid motion during this period. Trane's leaving Miles and his graduate classes with T. Sphere Monk put him into a music so expressive and thrilling people all over tuned in to him. Miles' group was classic because it summed up what went before it as well as indicated what was to come. Miles' "perfection" was the interrelationship between the hard bop and the cool and in Miles, sassy and sly. So that on the one side the quiet little gurgles that we get as *fusion* also come out of Miles (all the leading fusionaires are Miles' alumni) as well as the new blast of life that Coltrane carried, thus giving us the Pharaoh Sanderses and Albert Aylers and the reaching searching cry for freedom and life that not only took the Music in a certain direction, but that direction was a reflection of where people themselves, particularly the African American people, were going. It is no coincidence that people always associate John Coltrane and Malcolm X, they are harbingers and reflectors of the same life development.

And so I, we, followed Trane. We watched him even as he stood staring from the Club Bohemia listening to Miles and going through some personal hells. We heard him blow then, long and strong, trying to find something, as Miles stood at the back of the stage and tugged at his ear, trying to figure out what the fuck Trane was doing. We could feel what he was doing. Amus Mor, the poet, in his long poem on Trane says Miles was cool, in the slick cocktail party of life, but Trane would come in "wrong," snatchin the sammiches off the plate.

The Five Spot gig with Monk was Trane coming into his own. After Monk, he'd play sometimes chorus after chorus, taking the music apart before our ears, splintering the chords and sounding each note, resounding it, playing it backwards and upside down trying to get to something else. And we heard our own search and travails, our own reaching for new definition. Trane was our flag.

Trane was leaping away from "the given," and the troops of

the mainstream were both shocked and sometimes scandalized, but Trane, because he had come up through the rank, had paid all the dues, from slicksteppin on the bars of South Philly, honking rhythm and blues, through big Maybelle and Diz on up to Miles and then Monk, could not be waved aside by anybody. Though some tried and for this they were confirming their ignorance.

But there were other, younger forces coming in at the time which spoke of other elements of the African American people. Ornette Coleman had come in, countrified, yet newer than new. He showed at The Five Spot, first with a yellow plastic alto saxopohone, with his band dressed in red Eisenhower jackets, talking about "Free." It was "a beboppier bebop," an atomic age bebop, but cut loose from regular chord changes. Rhythmically fresh, going past the church revivals and heavy African rhythm restoration that Sonny Rollins, Max Roach and the Messengers, Horace Silver had come out with, attempting to get us past the deadly cool of 50's "West Coast" jazz. Ornette went back to bop for his roots, his hip jagged rhythms, and said, 'Hey, forget the popular song, let's go for ourselves.' And you talking about being scandalized, some folks got downright violent. Cecil Taylor was on the scene first and his aerodynamic, million-fingered pianistics, which seemed connected to the European concert hall, made people gloss over the heavy line of Cecil's blue syncopation. The percussiveness of his piano was as traditional for black "ticklers" as you could get.

Plus, all of Ornette's band could play, they'd start and stop like it was *in medias res*, it seemed there was no beginning nor formal ending, yet they were always "together" – Don Cherry, like a brass pointillist, with his funny little pocket trumpets; Charlie Haden, the white bass player who got down on his instrument, strumming and picking it like a guitar, showing that he had heard Monk's great bassist, Wilbur Ware, and knew which way that ax chopped, but at the same time original and singing. And Billy Higgins, of the perpetual smile, cooking like you spose to, carrying the finally funky business forward. They all could play, and the cry of "Freedom" was not only musical but reflected what was going on in the marches and confrontations, on the streets and in the restaurants and department stores of the South.

The 60's had opened with the black movement stepping past the earlier civil rights phase. One key addition and change was that now the black students had come into the movement wholesale. So that from 1954 (after *Brown v. Bd. of Ed.*), when the people had forced an "all deliberate speed" out of the rulers, instead of the traditional "separate but equal," Martin Luther King and SCLC, black, Southern, big-city ministers, leading that struggle for democracy, were in center stage of the struggle. Then, in 1960, the student sit-ins began, and, on February 1, black students at Greensboro began a movement that brought hundreds of thousands of black students, and students of all nationalities, in the struggle for democracy. So that soon we could hear of SNCC, who, at first, were still hooked up with the middle-class ministers and their line of nonviolence, but that would change. But now, the cries of "Freedom" had been augmented, with "Freedom Now!"

So it was in the air, it was in the minds of the people, masses of people going up against the apartheid South. It was also coming out of people's horns, laid out in their music. People like Max Roach spoke eloquently for an older, hip generation. He said "Freedom Now," and Sonny Rollins had his "Freedom Suite." And nutty Charlie Mingus was hollering his hilarious "Fables of Faubus." I even got into a hassle with a bald-headed German clerk in a record store on 8th Street. I'd come in and asked for Jackie McLean's terrible side, "Let Freedom Ring," and the clerk wanted to give me a lecture about how "you people shouldn't confuse your sociology with music."

So there was a newness and a defiance, a demand for freedom, politically and creatively, it was all connected. I wrote an article that year, "The Jazz Avant-Garde," mentioning people like Cecil Ornette, and the others, plus Trane and the young wizard Eric Dolphy, the brilliant arranger and reed player Oliver Nelson, Earl Griffith, onetime Cecil Taylor vibist, and my neighbor Archie Shepp, who had come on the scene, also shaking it up.

I also wrote a piece for *Kulchur* called "Milneburg Joys, or Against Hipness As Such," taking on members of our various circles, the hippies (old usage) of the period who thought merely by initialing ideas which had currency in the circles, talking the prevailing talk, or walking the prevailing walk, that that was all there was to it. I was also reaching and searching, life had to be more than a mere camaraderie of smugness and elitist hedonism.

Ornette Coleman's "Free Jazz," the completely "free" improvisational record, with the cream of the new players, had

set the tone. It was as if the music was leading us. And older players like Trane and Rollins took up that challenge. Trane played
chordal music, but he got frantically chordal. The critics called it
"sheets of sound," many at a loss for words, like they'd been
when Bird had first appeared. *Downbeat* and *Metronome* had to re-
review all those old records, because they had put them all down
as fakery and they were classics of African American music, so
they tried to clean up behind them.

*Any visitor to New York will notice the graffiti-spattered subways and the
giant signatures of anonymous ghetto artists in unlikely places. Novelist
Norman Mailer met some of the graffiti greats and tried to discover what
made them tick. In this article he calls himself "A-I" (aesthetic
investigator) in the pseudonymous style of the graffiti writers.*

THE FAITH OF GRAFFITI

No, size doesn't come in packages, and the graffiti writers had
been all heights and all shapes, even all the ages from twelve to
twenty-four. They had written masterpieces in letters six feet high
on the side of walls and subway cars, and had scribbled furtive
little toys, which is to say small names without style, sometimes
just initials. There was panic in the act for you wrote with an eye
over your shoulder for oncoming authority. The Transit
Authority cops would beat you if they caught you, or drag you to
court, or both. The judge, donning the robes of Solomon, would
condemn the early prisoners to clean the cars and subway
stations of the names. HITLER 2 (reputed to be so innocent of
his predecessor that he only knew Hitler 1 had a very big rep!)
was caught, and passed on the word of his humiliation. Cleaning
the cars, he had been obliged to erase the work of others. All
proportions kept, it may in simple pain of heart have been not
altogether unequal to condemning Cézanne to wipe out the works
of Van Gogh.

So there was real fear of being caught. Pain and humiliation
were implacable dues, and not all graffiti artists showed equal
grace under such pressure. Some wrote like cowards, timidly,
furtively, jerkily. "Man," was the condemnation of the peers,
"you got a messed-up handwriting." Others laid one cool

flowering of paint upon another, and this was only after having passed through all the existential stations of the criminal act, even to first *inventing* the paint, which was of course the word for stealing the stuff from the stores. But then, an invention is the creation of something which did not exist before – like a working spray can in your hand. (Indeed, if Plato's Ideal exists, and the universe is first a set of forms, then what is any invention but a theft from the given universal Ideal?)

There was always an art in a criminal act – no crime could ever be as automatic as a production process – but graffiti writers were opposite to criminals since they were living through the stages of the crime in order to commit an artistic act – what a doubling of intensity when the artist not only steals the cans but tries them for the colors he wants, not only the marker and the color, but steal them in double amounts so you don't run out in the middle of a masterpiece. What a knowledge of cops' habits is called for when any Black or Puerto Rican adolescent with a big paper bag is bound to be examined by a Transit cop if he goes into the wrong station. So after his paint has been invented a writer has to decide by which subway entrance it is to be transported, and once his trip is completed back to the station which is the capital of his turf, he still has to find the nook where he can warehouse his goods for a few hours. To attempt to take the paint out of the station is to get caught. To try to bring it back to the station is worse. Six or seven kids entering a subway in Harlem, Washington Heights, or the South Bronx are going to be searched by Transit cops for cans. So they stash it, mill around the station for a time painting nothing, they are, after all, often in the subways – to the degree they are not chased, it is a natural clubhouse, virtually a country club for the sociability of it all – and when the cops are out of sight, and a train is coming in, they whip out their stash of paint from its hiding place, conceal it on their bodies, and in all the wrappings of oversize ragamuffin fatigues, get on the cars to ride to the end of the line where in some deserted midnight yard they will find their natural canvas which is of course that metal wall of a subway car ready to reverberate into all the egos on all the metal of New York, what an echo that New York metal will give into the slapped-silly senses of every child-psyche who grew up in New York, yes, metal as a surface on which to paint is even better than stone.

But it is hardly so quick or automatic as that. If they are to leave the station at the end of the line, there is foreign turf to traverse which guarantees no safe passage, and always the problem of finding your way into the yards.

In the A-train yard at 207th Street, the unofficial entrance was around a fence that projected out over a cliff and dropped into the water of the Harlem River. You went out one side of that fence on a narrow ledge, out over the water, and back the other side of the fence into the yards "where the wagons," writes Richard Goldstein, "are sitting like silent whales."

We may pick our behemoth – whales and dinosaurs, elephants folded in sleep. At night, the walls of cars sit there possessed of soul – you are not just writing your name but trafficking with the iron spirit of the vehicle now resting. What a presence. What a consecutive set of iron sleeping beasts down all the corrals of the yard, and the graffiti writers stealthy as the near-to-silent sound of their movements working up and down the line of cars, some darting in to squiggle a little toy of a name on twenty cars – their nerve has no larger surge – others embarking on their first or their hundred-and-first masterpiece, daring the full enterprise of an hour of living with this tension after all the other hours of waiting (once they had come into the yard) for the telepathic disturbance of their entrance to settle, waiting for the guards patrolling the lines of track to grow somnolent and descend into the early morning pall of the watchman. Sometimes the graffiti writers would set out from their own turf at dark, yet not begin to paint until two in the morning, hiding for hours in the surest corners of the yard or in and under the trains. What a quintessential marriage of cool and style to write your name in giant separate living letters, large as animals, lithe as snakes, mysterious as Arabic and Chinese curls of alphabet, and to do it in the heart of a winter night when the hands are frozen and only the heart is hot with fear. No wonder the best of the graffiti writers, those mountains of heavy masterpiece production, STAY HIGH, PHASE 2, STAR III, get the respect, they call it the glory, that they are known, famous and luminous as a rock star. It is their year. Nothing automatic about writing a masterpiece on a subway car. 'I was scared,' said Japan, 'all the time I did it.' And sitting in the station at 158th and St. Nicholas Avenue, watching the trains go by, talking between each wave of subway sound, he is tiny in size, his dark eyes as alert as any small and hungry animal who eats in a garden at night and does not know where the householder with his varmint gun may be waiting.

Now, as Japan speaks, his eyes never failing to miss the collection of names, hieroglyphs, symbols, stars, crowns, ribbons, masterpieces and toys on every passing car, there is a sadness in his mood. The city has mounted a massive campaign. There was a period in the middle when it looked as if graffiti would take over the world, when a movement that began as the expression of tropical peoples living in a monotonous iron-gray and dull brown brick environment, surrounded by asphalt, concrete, and clangor, had erupted to save the sensuous flesh of their inheritance from a macadamization of the psyche, save the blank city wall of their unfed brain by painting the wall over with the giant trees and petty plants of a tropical rain-forest. Like such a jungle, every plant, large and small, spoke to one another, lived in the profusion *and* harmony of a forest. No one wrote over another name, no one was obscene – for that would have smashed the harmony. A communion took place over the city in this plant growth of names until every institutional wall, fixed or moving, every modern new school which looked like a brand-new factory, every old slum warehouse, every standing billboard, every huckstering poster, and the halls of every high-rise low-rent housing projects which looked like a prison (and all did) were covered by a foliage of graffiti that grew seven or eight feet tall, even twelve feet high in those choice places worth the effort for one to stand on another, ah, if it had gone on, this entire city of blank architectural high-rise horrors would have been covered with paint. Graffiti writers might have become mountaineers with pitons for the ascent of high-rise high-cost swinger-single apartments in the East Sixties and Seventies. The look of New York, and then the world, might have been transformed, and the interlapping of names and colors, those wavelets of ego forever reverberating upon one another, could have risen like a flood to cover the monstrosities of abstract empty techno-architectural twentieth-century walls where no design ever pre-dominated over the most profitable (and ergo most monotonous) construction ratio implicit in a twenty-million-dollar bill.

The kids painted with less than this in view, no doubt. Sufficient in the graffiti-proliferating years of the early Seventies to paint the front door of every subway car they could find. The ecstasy of the roller coaster would dive down their chest if they were ever waiting in a station when a twelve-car train came

328

stampeding in and their name, HONDO, WILDCAT, SABU or LOLLIPOP, was on the *front!* Yes, the graffiti had not only the feel and all the super-powered whoosh and impact of all the bubble letters in all the mad comic strips, but the *zoom,* the *aghr,* and the *ahhr* of screeching rails, the fast motion of subways roaring into stations, the comic strips come to life. So it was probably not a movement designed to cover the world so much as the excrescence of an excrescence. Slum populations chilled on one side by the bleakness of modern design, and brain-cooked on the other by comic strips and TV ads with zooming letters, even brain-cooked by politicians whose ego is a virtue – I am here to help my nation – brained by the big beautiful numbers of the yard markers on football fields, by the whip of the capital letters in the names of the products, and gut-picked by the sound of rock and soul screaming up into the voodoo of the firmament with the shriek of the performer's insides coiling like neon letters in the blue satanic light, yes, all the excrescence of the highways and the fluorescent wonderlands of every Las Vegas sign frying through the Iowa and New Jersey night, all the stomach-tightening nitty-gritty of trying to learn how to spell was in the writing, every assault on the psyche as the trains came slamming in. Maybe it was no more than a movement which looked to take some of the excrescence left within and paint it out upon the world, no more than a species of collective therapy of grace exhibited under pressure in which they never dreamed of painting over the blank and empty modern world, but the authority of the city reacted as if the city itself might be in greater peril from graffiti than from drugs, and a war had gone on, more and more implacable on the side of the authority with every legal and psychological weedkiller on full employ until the graffiti of New York was defoliated, cicatrized, Vietnamized. Now, as A-I sat in the station with Jon Naar and Japan and they watched the trains go by, aesthetic blight was on the cars. Few masterpieces remained. The windows were gray and smeared. The cars looked dull red or tarnished aluminium – their recent coat of paint remover having also stripped all polish from the manufacturer's surface. New subway cars looked like old cars. Only the ghost-outline of former masterpieces still remained. The kids were broken. The movement seemed over. Even the paint could no longer be invented. Now the cans set out for display were empty, the misdemeanors were being upped to felony, the fines were severe, the mood was vindictive. Two hideous accidents had occurred. One boy had been killed beneath a subway car, and another had been close to fatally burned by an inflammable spray can catching a spark, yes, a horror was on the movement and transit patrols moved through the yards and plugged the entrances. The white monoliths of the high-rise were safe. And the subways were dingier than they had ever been. The impulse of the jungle to cover the walled tombs of technology had been broken. Was there a clue to graffiti in the opposite passion to look upon monotony and call it health? As A-I walked the streets with Jon Naar, they passed a sign: DON'T POLLUTE – KEEP THE CITY CLEAN. 'That sign,' the photographer murmured, 'is a form of pollution itself.'

Woody Allen (1935-) widely acknowledged to be among the masters of American cinema draws upon neurotic smart Jewish humour to create his witty and perceptive films on life in New York. These are the opening lines of his film Manhattan.

NEW YORK CITY

"Chapter One. He adored New York City, although to him, it was a metaphor for the decay of contemporary culture. How hard it was to exist in a society desensitized by drugs, loud music, television, crime, garbage." Too angry. I don't wanna be angry. "Chapter One. He was as . . . tough and romantic as the city he loved. Behind his black-rimmed glasses was the coiled sexual power of a jungle cat." I love this. "New York was his town. And it always would be."

CHAPTER 17

VISIONS

Washington Irving (1783-1859) was the first internationally famous New York writer. A world traveller, the author of such tales as Rip Van Winkle *and* The Legend of Sleepy Hollow, *Irving's first major work was an historical burlesque aimed at his fellow New Yorkers and published in 1809 under the name Diedrich Knickerbocker. In this excerpt from* A History of New York *Knickerbocker recounts the dream of Oloffe Van Cortlándt, "one of the first property speculators in these parts."*

OLOFFE VAN CORTLANDT'S DREAM

And the sage Oloffe dreamed a dream, – and lo, the good St. Nicholas came riding over the tops of the trees, in that self-same wagon wherein he brings his yearly presents to children, and he descended hard by where the heroes of Communipaw had made their late repast. And he lit his pipe by the fire, and sat himself down and smoked; and as he smoked, the smoke from his pipe ascended into the air and spread like a cloud overhead. And Oloffe bethought him, and he hastened and climbed up to the top of one of the tallest trees, and saw that the smoke spread over a great extent of country; and as he considered it more attentively, he fancied that the great volume of smoke assumed a variety of marvellous forms, where in dim obscurity he saw shadowed out palaces and domes and loft spires, all of which lasted but a moment, and then faded away, until the whole rolled off, and nothing but the green woods were left. And when St. Nicholas had smoked his pipe, he twisted it in his hatband, and laying his finger beside his nose, gave the astonished Van Kortlandt a very significant look; then mounting his wagon, he returned over the treetops and disappeared.

And Van Kortlandt awoke from his sleep greatly instructed; and he aroused his companions and related his dream, and interpreted it, that it was the will of St. Nicholas that they should settle down and build the city here; and that the smoke of the pipe was a type how vast would be the extent of the city, inasmuch as the volumes of its smoke would spread over a wide extent of country. And they all with one voice assented to this interpretation, excepting Mynheer Ten Broeck, who declared the meaning to be that it would be a city wherein a little fire would occasion a great smoke, or, in other words, a very vaporing little city; – both which interpretations have strangely come to pass!

The great object of their perilous expedition, therefore, being thus happily accomplished, the voyagers returned merrily to Communipaw – where they were received with great rejoicings. And here, calling a general meeting of all the wise men and the dignitaries of Pavonia, they related the whole history of their voyage, and of the dream of Oloffe Van Kortlandt. And the people lifted up their voices and blessed the good St. Nicholas; and from that time forth the sage Van Kortlandt was held in more honor than ever, for his great talent at dreaming, and was pronounced a most useful citizen and a right good man – when he was asleep.

Poet Vachel Lindsay (1879-1931) found glimpses of the divine in the ordinary details of American life.

A RHYME ABOUT AN
ELECTRICAL ADVERTISING SIGN

I look on the specious electrical light
Blatant, mechanical, crawling and white,
Wickedly red or malignantly green
Like the beads of a young Senegambian queen.
Showing, while millions of souls hurry on,
The virtues of collars, from sunset till dawn,
By dart or by tumble of whirl within whirl,
Starting new fads for the shame-weary girl,
By maggoty motions in sickening line
Proclaiming a hat or a soup or a wine,
While there far above the steep cliffs of the street
The stars sing a message elusive and sweet.

Now man cannot rest in his pleasure and toil
His clumsy contraptions of coil upon coil
Till the thing he invents, in its use and its range,
Leads on to the marvellous CHANGE BEYOND CHANGE.
Some day this old Broadway shall climb to the skies,
As a ribbon of cloud on a soul-wind shall rise,
And we shall be lifted, rejoicing by night,
Till we join with the planets who choir their delight.

The signs in the streets and the signs in the skies
Shall make a new Zodiac, guiding the wise,
And Broadway make one with that marvellous stair
That is climbed by the rainbow-clad spirits of prayer.

*Mani Leib (1883-1953), an immigrant from Eastern Europe, worked in the
sweat shops, and was one of the major Yiddish poets of all time.*

EAST BROADWAY

Of all rich streets, most dear to me
Is my shabby Jewish East Broadway.
Graying houses – two uneven rows:
Frail, restless and exhausted bodies:

The worry tinged with God's old fire –
It barely glows, yet it does not die.
And on the corners, seers and rebels
Who shout a nation's woe unto the sky.
And the poets. O rhapsodic brothers!
On the grime of each stone, you transmute
A nation's heart – finely –
Into the strains of a new hymnal.
Long after you, each stone will join
Your people in the prayer of your song.

Translated by Nathan Halper

*Andrew Holleran, short-story writer and chronicler of New York's gay
scene, tries in this essay to come to terms with the visionary delapidation of
New York.*

NOSTALGIA FOR THE MUD

New York, that accidental city, whose pleasures vanish sometimes without your ever having known they were there, had, from
October 3 to December 3 at the Whitney Museum, a piece of

334

environmental art by Michael McMillen called *Inner City:* a room-sized reconstruction of three entire blocks of a warehouse district in Los Angeles (it might well have been Manhattan). Large enough to walk around, and even, at one point, *through,* *Inner City* was complete with scaled-down neon signs, fire escapes, window shades, and even a squalid little poolroom with metal folding chairs strewn about, cues on the table, and a miniature ceiling fan rotating overhead. Like the rest of *Inner City* the poolroom was empty; but then, what city isn't empty, late at night in that part of town?

"It is only by directly experiencing the entire installation," states McMillen in the museum flyer, "that the position/concept of art as experience [may] be realized." But what *Inner City* actually amounts to, I think, is an extraordinary doll's house. (And a very evocative doll's house for anyone who has haunted such bleak, decaying blocks in reality. Consider: surely we would never have come to the purlieus of the Lower West Side but for the fact that they are the hunting grounds of other men looking for a certain style of sex. Who else knows this inner city? The poor, the recently arrived, the Hispanic.) How lovingly McMillen has recreated each detail of his urban doll's house: a hotel hallway, one-thousandth the size of its original, evokes precisely the erotic longing you feel walking home late at night in a run-down neighborhood, when physical loneliness corresponds exactly to psychic isolation, and you think – passing an abandoned truck, an empty lot screened by shrubbery or garbage under an open moon – wouldn't that be a wonderful place to make love? Just a few doors down from the tiny poolroom is a little bar, its door (no bigger than your thumb) half open; through the door come the sounds of the Village People singing "San Francisco," and the joyous hooting and screaming of (invisible) people within.

You stand back to gaze at the door, the darkness, the neon sign in the window. You say to yourself, "This is the door, the darkness, the music to which I have been drawn, irresistibly, so many winter nights; this the ruined neighborhood, the lonely street, the crumbling building (its shades drawn or half drawn); this the sordid, deserted, *poignant* place so many of us have wandered in for years. Look at it: a piece of art, life reconstructed to give you a feeling of distance from what embroils you."

'I was there last night,' muttered one of two friends at my side.

335

Women, children, and grandmothers stood beside us, exclaiming over the tiny chairs and cues in the poolroom. ("Harry, why don't you take this up? You need a hobby.") Then they moved on, around the corner, in the faint and lurid light. But we three remained rooted; there was no way we were going to leave the little doorway with the music pouring out. We waited (as we had waited so many nights when the Eagle had the best jukebox in town) to hear what song came next. And we looked at the other museum patrons, wondering if they understood, if they *felt* the peculiar magic of this place, its romantic significance. For this was the bar of the past ten years of our lives. It was Love Among the Ruins.

'Don't touch!' one mother commanded her daughter, slapping the child's wrist as she reached out to fondle a tiny fire escape. 'Look at the fan, Mom!' cried her son. And the Nuclear Family bent down to peer into a room where, in real life, young Chicanos or Puerto Ricans would surely cluster around the table, their transistor radio on a windowsill blarring salsa.

You imagine the empty streets of McMillen's papier-maché *Inner City* filled: outside the dark half-open door of this tiny bar should be a tiny man in chains; and ten feet (or, rather, half an inch) away, standing broken-hearted on the corner, another little man, wondering if the man in chains will follow him out of the bar. There should be miniature motorcycles, minute beards, and sweatshirts peeking out of little leather jackets, a minuscule cop car out of which miniature police with flashlights scramble to clear men out of the crevices where they are having sex with one another's miniature cocks; and a gang of tiny teenage boys waiting for a solitary man to walk by so they can beat him up.

There were no cops or thugs, no bare-chested man lounging in his doorway as you slowly walked past, wondering if he could really be that available; no one slowly masturbated in an upstairs window for all the world to see. But there was one advantage: late winter nights on West Street, passing the lit windows of otherwise deserted buildings, I often wonder what goes on inside and who could, who would, possibly live there; I needed only to peer through the tiny window of McMillen's Hotel Norton to see the poolroom, the bar. I was huge in relation to the cardboard-and-paint city blocks on the table before me, Gulliver among the Lilliputians, a Jolly Green Giant of a voyeur. I was free of the oppressive gloom I usually felt wandering the streets in real life.

But "San Francisco" is a long song; eventually we took our leave, without ever knowing what followed, and walked away from the Inner City.

'Why do gays love ruins?' I said to my friends when we emerged into the crisp autumn sunlight of a Sunday afternoon. 'The Lower West Side, the docks. Why do we love slums so much?'

'One can hardly suck cock on Madison Avenue, darling,' said the alumnus of the Mineshaft, curling his lip as we strolled down that very street: the *arrondissement* of gentility, so tasteful that coming uptown from his own street was truly traveling into another country. Nannies pushed strollers filled with fortunate heirs; adolescents in blazers, slacks, and Topsiders, young men in Rugby shirts passed by. 'If Westway is ever built,' continued my friend, 'and the shoreline made pretty by city planners – when the city is totally renovated, when gays have restored all the tenements, garden restaurants have sprouted on the Lower East Side, and the meatpacking district is given over entirely to boutiques and cardshops – then we'll build an island in New York Harbor composed entirely of rotting piers, blocks of collapsed walls, and litter-strewn lots. Ruins become decor, nostalgia for the mud. We all want to escape; you escaped to the city. Would you ever have ended up in the ruins had you not been gay?'

'If I weren't gay, I don't think I'd be in the city at all.'

'Especially on a day like this.'

We looked up at the hard blue sky, the brilliant autumn light, and rounded a corner to see the trees along Fifth Avenue already starting to change color.

'Soon New York will be occupied by no one but the rich and the perverted,' observed my friend, and at that moment we spotted a mutual friend who embodied both those traits standing in a worn leather jacket, faded, torn blue jeans, and scuffed engineer boots, hailing a cab.

'There's a perfect example,' I said. 'Why is there that strange axis between the extremely aesthetic' – the man getting into the cab possessed an encyclopedic knowledge of European culture and the history of ormolu – 'and the extremely sleazy?'

'God only knows,' sighed my other companion, whose neighborhood this was and who left it only to backpack in Vermont.

337

'Well,' said my first friend, 'ask yourself. Why could Brahms make love only in brothels? Why did Proust, the most sensitive and considerate of men, torture rats with pins? Why did he donate the furniture he inherited from his parents to a male brothel he frequented? What pleasure did he get from seeing a nude trolley-car conductor sitting on the sofa his grandmother had no doubt sat on to do needlepoint? Why did one of his characters, the lesbian daughter of a famous composer, spit on her father's photograph while making love? Why do we rush out to trick after talking to our mothers on the telephone? Why do we find graduate students from Princeton lying facedown in the Mineshaft?' – here he burst into laughter at some memory of the previous night. 'Why our desire to grovel, to wallow in the slime? Why the beauty of those neighborhoods? Why is there a truck without a chassis on the eighth floor of the baths so that people may do the curious thing of going to the baths to make love in a truck (or a jail cell, or a cheap hotel room)? Why the trucks at all? Why did Huck Finn flee Aunt Sally? Why does great politeness produce a strain that often can only be relieved by cruelty? Why did Marie Antoinette play shepherdess? Why do gays wear ripped clothing and congregate in ruins? Why do I feel a strange sense of freedom the moment I enter a decaying neighborhood? Why do I imagine, when I pass a tenement with a collapsed wall on Avenue B, giving a party there – or better yet, conjure up a slender fellow, half hidden by the rusted doorframe, inviting me into the rubble to make love, entirely in ruins?'

'I hate to say this,' said our third friend, 'but I don't know what you mean.'

'Pretentious prig!' we gasped.

And so we entered the sunny glade of Central Park and, watching children play with sailboats, forgot about these questions until later that evening. Just after sunset, we found ourselves drifting inevitably downtown to the very region whose simulacrum we had marveled at that afternoon. The shore, once lined with ships sailing for Le Havre and Cherbourg, was now (but for the new terminal at Forty-second Street) a series of rotting piers and empty lots from which isolated families fished; further south, behind the shattered windows of erstwhile shipping firms, moved silhouettes of men in search of another kind of nourishment. The warehouses, the bars, the cheap hotels pulled us into their shadows, into their peculiar mood. The detachment

338

afforded by art at the Whitney Museum was gone. The bar was life-sized now and stood on a cobblestone corner. We went through the door into its dark room to find a frieze of bearded faces regarding us like stone visages in the jungle: blank, cold, and waiting. Whatever their attraction, whatever their meaning, these ruins were real.

William Carlos Williams (1883-1963) was born in Rutherford, New Jersey, and spent most of his life practising there as a pediatrician. In his poetry he tried to capture distinctively American rhythms of speech and often dealt with equally distinctive American subjects. Watching New York City from the New Jersey shore, he considers the city, its power, and his own life.

THE FLOWER

A petal, colorless and without form
the oblong towers lie

beyond the low hill and northward the great
bridge stanchions,

small in the distance, have appeared,
pinkish and incomplete—

It is the city,
approaching over the river. Nothing

of it is mine, but visibly
for all that it is petal of a flower – my own.

It is a flower through which the wind
combs the whitened grass and a black dog

with yellow legs stands eating from a
garbage barrel. One petal goes eight blocks

past two churches and a brick school beyond
the edge of the park where under trees

leafless now, women having nothing else to do
sit in summer – to the small house

in which I happen to have been born. Or
a heap of dirt, if you care

to say it, frozen and sunstreaked in
the January sun, returning

Then they hand you – they who wish to God
you'd keep your fingers out of

their business – science or philosophy or
anything else they can find to throw off

to distract you. But Madame Lenine
is a benefactress when under her picture

in the papers she is quoted as saying:
Children should be especially protected

from religion. Another petal
reaches to San Diego, California where

a number of young men, New Yorkers most
of them, are kicking up the dust.

A flower, at its heart (the stamens, pistil,
etc.) is a naked woman, about 38, just

out of bed, worth looking at both for
her body and her mind and what she has seen

and done. She it was put me straight
about the city when I said, It

makes me ill to see them run up
a new bridge like that in a few months

and I can't find time even to get
a book written. They have the power,

that's all, she replied. That's what you all
want. If you can't get it, acknowledge

at least what it is. And they're not
going to give it to you. Quite right.

For years I've been tormented by
that miracle, the buildings all lit up –

unable to say anything much to the point
though it is the major sight

of this region. But foolish to rhapsodize over
strings of lights, the blaze of a power

in which I have not the least part.
Another petal reaches

into the past, to Puerto Rico
when my mother was a child bathing in a small

river and splashing water up on
the yucca leaves to see them roll back pearls.

The snow is hard on the pavements. This
is no more a romance than an allegory.

I plan one thing – that I could press
buttons to do the curing of or caring for

the sick that I do laboriously now by hand
for cash, to have the time

when I am fresh, in the morning, when
my mind is clear and burning – to write.

Crossing the Queensborough Bridge into Manhattan, F. Scott Fitzgerald's narrator in The Great Gatsby *is overcome with the limitless possibilities of life in the city.*

ON THE QUEENSBOROUGH BRIDGE

We passed Port Roosevelt, where there was a glimpse of red-belted ocean-going ships, and sped along a cobbled slum lined with the dark, undeserted saloons of the faded-gilt nineteen-hundreds. Then the valley of ashes opened out on both sides of us, and I had a glimpse of Mrs. Wilson straining at the garage pump with panting vitality as we went by.

With fenders spread like wings we scattered light through half Astoria – only half, for as we twisted among the pillars of the elevated I heard the familiar 'jug-jug-*spat!*' of a motorcycle, and a frantic policeman rode alongside.

'All right, old sport,' called Gatsby. We slowed down. Taking a white card from his wallet, he waved it before the man's eyes.

'Right you are,' agreed the policeman, tipping his cap 'Know you next time, Mr. Gatsby. Excuse *me!*'

'What was that?' I inquired. 'The picture of Oxford?'

'I was able to do the commissioner a favour once, and he sends me a Christmas card every year.'

Over the great bridge, with the sunlight through the girders making a constant flicker upon the moving cars, with the city rising up across the river in white heaps and sugar lumps all built with a wish out of non-olfactory money. The city seen from the Queensboro Bridge is always the city seen for the first time, in its first wild promise of all the mystery and the beauty in the world.

A dead man passed us in a hearse heaped with blooms, followed by two carriages with drawn blinds, and by more cheerful carriages for friends. The friends looked out at us with the tragic eyes and short upper lips of south-eastern Europe, and I was glad that the sight of Gatsby's splendid car was included in their sombre holiday. As we crossed Blackwell's Island a limousine passed us, driven by a white chauffeur, in which sat three modish negroes, two bucks and a girl. I laughed aloud as the yolks of their eyeballs rolled towards us in haughty rivalry.

'Anything can happen now that we've slid over this bridge,' I thought; 'anything at all. . . '

Even Gatsby could happen, without any particular wonder.

342

In this poem, the introduction to his sequence The Bridge *(1930), Hart Crane seeks out the metaphorical significance of the magnificent sweep of Brooklyn Bridge.*

To Brooklyn Bridge

How many dawns, chill from his rippling rest
The seagull's wings shall dip and pivot him,
Shedding white rings of tumult, building high
Over the chained bay waters Liberty –

Then, with inviolate curve, forsake our eyes
As apparitional as sails that cross
Some page of figures to be filed away;
– Till elevators drop us from our day. . .

I think of cinemas, panoramic sleights
With multitudes bent toward some flashing scene
Never disclosed, but hastened to again,
Foretold to other eyes on the same screen;

And Thee, across the harbor, silver-paced
As though the sun took step of thee, yet left
Some motion ever unspent in they stride,–
Implicitly they freedom staying thee!

Out of some subway scuttle, cell or loft
A bedlamite speeds to thy parapets,
Tilting there momently, shrill shirt ballooning,
A jest falls from the speechless caravan.

Down Wall, from girder into street noon leaks,
A rip-tooth of the sky's acetylene;
All afternoon the cloud-flown derricks turn. . .
Thy cables breathe the North Atlantic still.

And obscure as that heaven of the Jews,
Thy guerdon. . . Accolade thou dost bestow
Of anonymity time cannot raise:
Vibrant reprieve and pardon thou dost show.

343

O harp and altar, of the fury fused,
(How could mere toil align thy choiring strings!)
Terrific threshold of the prophet's pledge,
Prayer of pariah, and the lover's cry,–

Again the traffic lights that skim thy swift
Unfractioned idiom, immaculate sigh of stars,
Beading thy path – condense eternity:
And we have seen night lifted in thine arms.

Under thy shadow by the piers I waited;
Only in darkness is thy shadow clear.
The City's fiery parcels all undone,
Already snow submerges an iron year. . .

O Sleepless as the river under thee,
Vaulting the sea, the prairies' dreaming sod,
Unto us lowliest sometime sweep, descend
And of the curveship lend a myth to God.

Adrienne Rich, born in Baltimore in 1931, is a major American contemporary poet and feminist. Throughout much of the seventies she lived in New York City.

UPPER BROADWAY

The leafbud straggles forth
toward the frigid light of the airshaft   this is faith
this pale extension of a day
when looking up   you know   something is changing
winter has turned   though the wind is colder
Three streets away   a roof collapses   onto people
who thought they still had time   Time out of mind

I have written so many words
wanting to live inside you
to be of use to you

Now I must write for myself   for this blind
woman scratching the pavement   with her wand of thought
this slippered crone   inching on icy streets
reaching into wire trashbaskets   pulling out
what was thrown away   and infinitely precious

I look at my hands and see   they are still unfinished
I look at the vine and see the leafbud
inching towards life

I look at my face in the glass   and see
a halfborn woman

A poem from Planet News, *by Allen Ginsberg.*

WAKING IN NEW YORK

I

I place my hand before my beard with awe
and stare thru open-uncurtain window
        rooftop rose-blue sky thru
        which small dawn clouds ride
            rattle against the pane,
    lying on a thick carpet matter floor
        at last in repose on pillows my knees
        bent beneath brown himalayan blanket, soft –
fingers atremble to pen, cramp
        pressure diddling the page white
           San Francisco notebook –
And here am on the sixth floor cold
        March 5th Street old building plaster
        apartments in ruin, super he drunk
           with baritone radio AM nose-sex
Oh New York, oh Now our bird
        flying past glass window Chirp
      – our life together here
    smoke of tenement chimney pots dawn haze
        passing thru wind soar Sirs –

How shall we greet Thee this Springtime oh
                              Lords – ?
What gifts give ourselves, what police fear
                    stop searched in late streets
Rockerfeller Frisk No-Knock break down
                    my iron white-painted door?
Where shall I seek Law? in the State
                    in offices of telepath bureaucracy – ?
in my dis-ease, my trembling, my cry
                    – ecstatic song to myself
to my police my law my state my
                    many selfs –
Aye, Self is Law and State Police
        Kennedy struck down knew him Self
Oswald, Ruby ourselves
                    Till we know our desires Blest
                    with babe issue,
                              Resolve, accept
                    this self flesh we bear
                in underwear, Bathrobe, smoking cigarette
            up all night – brooding, solitary, set
                    alone, tremorous leg & arm –
                    approaching the joy of Alones
                    Racked by that, arm laid to rest,
                    head back wide-eyed

Morning, my song to Who listens, to
                    myself as I am
To my fellows in this shape that building
                    Brooklyn Bridge or Albany name –
                    Salute to the self-gods on
                              Pennsylvania Avenue!
May they have mercy on us all,
May be just men not murderers
        Nor the State murder more,
        That all beggars be fed, all
                    dying medicined, all loveless
                    Tomorrow be loved
                              well come & be balm.

3/16/64

346

On the roof cloudy sky fading sun rays
          electric torches atop –
auto horns – The towers
    with time-hands giant pointing
         late Dusk hour over
          clanky roofs
Tenement streets' brick sagging cornices
      baby white kite fluttering against giant
      insect face-gill Electric Mill
          smokestacked blue & fumes drift up
   Red messages, shining high floors,
      Empire State dotted with tiny windows
      lit, across the blocks
   of spire, steeple, golden topped utility
      building roofs – far like
      pyramids lit in jagged
         desert rocks –

The giant the giant city awake
      in the first warm breath of springtime
Waking voices, babble of Spanish
     street families, radio music
     floating under roofs, longhaired
        announcer sincerity squawking
           cigar voice
      Light zips up phallos stories
      beneath red antennae needling
       thru rooftop chimnies' smog
         black drift thru the blue air –

Bridges curtained by uplit apartment walls,
     one small tower with a light
   on its shoulder below the "moody, water-loving
              giants"
The giant stacks burn thick grey
     smoke, Chrysler is lit with green,
down Wall street islands of skyscraper
   black jagged in Sabbath quietness –

Oh fathers, how I am alone in this
                 vast human wilderness
Houses uplifted like hives off
                 the stone floor of the world –
the city too vast to know, too
                 myriad windowed to govern
                 from ancient halls –
"O edifice of gas!" – Sun shafts
     descend on the highest building's
          striped blocktop a red light
                 winks buses hiss & rush
                 grinding, green lights
                 of north bridges,
                     hum roar & Tarzan
                     squeal, whistle
                     swoops, hurrahs!

Is someone dying in all this stone building?
Child poking its black head out of the womb
                 like the pupil of an eye?
Am I not breathing here frightened
                     and amazed – ?
Where is my comfort, where's heart-ease,
          Where are tears of joy?
Where are the companions? in
                 deep homes in Stuyvesant Town
                 behind the yellow-window wall?
I fail, book fails, – a lassitude,
                 a fear – tho I'm alive
and gaze over the descending – No!
peer in the inky beauty of the roofs.

4/18/64

AUTHOR'S INDEX

GENERAL INDEX

352

354

356

ACKNOWLEDGMENTS

The compilers would like to thank all the people who advised them in selecting extracts for this book, particularly Paula Levey – their editor.

Grateful acknowledgment is made to the following for permission to reprint copyright material in this anthology:

Kathy Acker for 'In Front of the Mudd Club' from NEW YORK CITY IN 1979 by Kathy Acker.

Random House Inc for 'Brooklyn' from SIDE EFFECTS by Woody Allen. Copyright © 1980 by Woody Allen.

Random House Inc for 'New York City' from FOUR FILMS OF WOODY ALLEN by Woody Allen. Copyright © 1982 by Random House Inc.

Carroll & Graf Publishers Inc for 'Triangle Fire' from EAST RIVER by Sholem Asch. Copyright © 1983 by Sholem Asch.

The New York Times Company for 'Savage Sunsets' by Brooks Atkinson. Copyright © 1951 by the New York Times Company.

James Baldwin & Bernard Hassell for 'A Native Returns' from ANOTHER COUNTRY by James Baldwin. Copyright © 1962, 1963 by James Baldwin.

The Estate of Tallulah Bankhead for 'The Giants and Me' from TALLULAH by Tallulah Bankhead.

Linder AG of Zurich and Agenzia Letteraria Internazionale for 'Don Turi' from O AMERICA: *When You and I Were Young* by Luigi Barzini.

Saul Bellow and Weidenfeld & Nicolson Ltd for 'Mr Sammler Takes a Walk' from MR SAMMLER'S PLANET by Saul Bellow.

Simon & Schuster Inc for 'The Bronx Mural' and 'Cross Bronx Expressway' from ALL THAT IS SOLID MELTS IN THE AIR by Marshal Berman. Copyright © 1982 by Marshal Berman.

Warner Bros Inc for 'New York, New York' by Leonard Bernstein, lyrics by Adolph Green and Betty Conden. © 1945 (Renewed) Warner Bros Inc. All rights reserved.

Farrar, Straus & Giroux Inc for 'Invitation to Miss Marianne Moore' from ELIZABETH BISHOP: THE COMPLETE POEMS 1927-1979 by Elizabeth Bishop. Copyright 1949, renewed © 1976 by Elizabeth Bishop.

Random House Inc for 'Mary Sanchez' from MUSIC FOR CHAMELEONS by Truman Capote. Copyright © 1980 by Truman Capote.

Random House Inc for 'Holly Golightly' from BREAKFAST AT TIFFANY'S by Truman Capote. Copyright © 1958 by Truman Capote.

Miss D. E. Collins and A. P. Watt Ltd for 'A Meditation on Broadway' from WHAT I SAW IN AMERICA by G. K. Chesterton.

Viking Penguin Inc and Laurence Pollinger Ltd for 'The Long Furlough' and 'The Greenwich Village Idea' from EXILE'S RETURN by Malcolm Cowley.

Granada Publishing Ltd for the poem 'buncha hardboil guys from duh A. C. Fulla' from THE COMPLETE POEMS 1913-1962 by e. e. cummings.

Mrs John Dos Passos for 'Failure', 'Soapbox', 'Ebb and Flood' and 'A Newcomer in New York' from MANHATTAN TRANSFER by John Dos Passos.

Random House Inc for 'Harlem Uprising' from INVISIBLE MAN by Ralph Ellison. Copyright © 1947, 1948, 1952 by Ralph Ellison.

The Bodley Head Ltd for 'A Midwesterner in New York' and 'The Queensborough Bridge' from THE GREAT GATSBY by F. Scott Fitzgerald.

360

If, through inability to trace the present copyright owners, any copyright material is included for which permission has not specifically been sought, apologies are tendered in advance to proprietors and publishers concerned.

362